Shakespeare and the Materiality of Performance

Shakespeare and the Materiality of Performance

Erika T. Lin

palgrave
macmillan

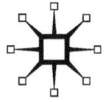

SHAKESPEARE AND THE MATERIALITY OF PERFORMANCE
copyright © Erika T. Lin, 2012.

Softcover reprint of the hardcover 1st edition 2012 978-1-137-00106-1

All rights reserved.

First published in 2012 by
PALGRAVE MACMILLAN®
in the United States—a division of St. Martin's Press LLC,
175 Fifth Avenue, New York, NY 10010.

Where this book is distributed in the UK, Europe and the rest of the world, this is by Palgrave Macmillan, a division of Macmillan Publishers Limited, registered in England, company number 785998, of Houndmills, Basingstoke, Hampshire RG21 6XS.

Palgrave Macmillan is the global academic imprint of the above companies and has companies and representatives throughout the world.

Palgrave® and Macmillan® are registered trademarks in the United States, the United Kingdom, Europe and other countries.

ISBN 978-1-349-43355-1   ISBN 978-1-137-00650-9 (eBook)
DOI 10.1057/9781137006509

Library of Congress Cataloging-in-Publication Data

Lin, Erika T., 1972–
   Shakespeare and the materiality of performance / Erika T. Lin.
      p. cm.
   Includes bibliographical references.

      1. Shakespeare, William, 1564–1616—Stage history—To 1625. 2. Shakespeare, William, 1564–1616—Stage history—England—London. 3. Theater audiences—England—London—History—16th century. 4. Theater audiences—England—London—History—17th century. 5. Theater and society—England—History—16th century. 6. Theater and society—England—History—17th century. I. Title.
PR3095.L56 2012
792.0942—dc23   2012011554

A catalogue record of the book is available from the British Library.

Design by Newgen Imaging Systems (P) Ltd., Chennai, India.

First edition: October 2012

10 9 8 7 6 5 4 3 2 1

In memoriam
Fouad Ahmad Siddiqi
1972–2010

Copyright Acknowledgments

Cover: Watercolor sketch of the Globe stage by C. Walter Hodges, 1946–47. By permission of the Folger Shakespeare Library.

An earlier version of chapter 1 appeared as Erika T. Lin, "Performance Practice and Theatrical Privilege: Rethinking Weimann's Concepts of *Locus* and *Platea*," *New Theatre Quarterly* 22, no. 3 (2006): 283–98. © Cambridge University Press. Reprinted with permission.

An earlier version of part of chapter 2 is reprinted by permission of Ashgate from Erika T. Lin, "Popular Worship and Visual Paradigms in *Love's Labor's Lost*," in *Religion and Drama in Early Modern England,* ed. Jane Hwang Degenhardt and Elizabeth Williamson (Farnham, UK: Ashgate, 2011), 89–113. Copyright © 2011.

An earlier version of a short excerpt from chapter 4 appeared as Erika T. Lin, "Recreating the Eye of the Beholder: Dancing and Spectacular Display in Early Modern English Theatre," in "Congress on Research in Dance 2010 Conference Proceedings: Embodying Power: Work over Time," ed. Karl Rogers, supplement, *Dance Research Journal* 43, no. S1 (2011): 10–19. © 2010, Erika T. Lin. Reprinted with permission.

A few paragraphs from chapter 5 were originally included in a separate essay, Erika T. Lin, "'Lord of thy presence': Bodies, Performance, and Audience Interpretation in Shakespeare's *King John*," in *Imagining the Audience in Early Modern Drama, 1558–1642,* ed. Jennifer A. Low and Nova Myhill (New York: Palgrave Macmillan, 2011), 113–33. Reproduced with permission of Palgrave Macmillan.

Contents

List of Figures	ix
Acknowledgments	xi
Note on Texts	xv

Part I Performance Effects

Introduction Materializing the Immaterial	3
1 Theorizing Theatrical Privilege: Rethinking Weimann's Concepts of *Locus* and *Platea*	23

Part II Theatrical Ways of Knowing

2 Staging Sight: Visual Paradigms and Perceptual Strategies in *Love's Labor's Lost*	41
3 Imaginary Forces: Allegory, Mimesis, and Audience Interpretation in *The Spanish Tragedy*	71

Part III Experiencing Embodied Spectacle

4 Dancing and Other Delights: Spectacle and Participation in *Doctor Faustus* and *Macbeth*	107
5 Artful Sport: Violence, Dismemberment, and Games in *Titus Andronicus, Cymbeline,* and *Doctor Faustus*	135
Notes	167
Bibliography	207
Index	227

Figures

0.1	Eyeballs. Helkiah Crooke, *Mikrokosmographia: A Description of the Body of Man* (1615)	4
1.1	Sketch of the view from the Lords' Rooms at the Globe (2012)	29
2.1	William Rogers, "A godly meditation day and night to be exercised" (ca. 1600)	48
2.2	Stage plans for Lucerne Passion Play (1583)	49
2.3	Detail of nineteenth-century additions to stage plans for Lucerne Passion Play (1583)	49
2.4	Draftsman drawing a nude (woodcut). Albrecht Dürer, *Vnderweysuug* [sic] *der Messung* (1538)	55
3.1	"The Palace of Sleep." Michel de Marolles, *Tableaux du temple des muses* (1655)	77
3.2	Title page from Thomas Kyd, *The Spanish Tragedie* (1615)	91
3.3	Frontispiece to John Bulwer, *Philocophus: or, The deafe and dumbe mans friend* (1648)	96
3.4	Seeing with the ears and hearing with the eyes. Detail from frontispiece to John Bulwer, *Philocophus: or, The deafe and dumbe mans friend* (1648)	97
4.1	Tumbling, rope-dancing, and other feats of activity. Johann Amos Comenius, *Orbis sensualium pictus* (1659; rep., 1685)	108
4.2	Printed text as spectacular feat. *Maroccus Extaticus. Or, Bankes bay horse in a Trance* (1595)	118
5.1	Dismembered heads on pikes above London Bridge. Detail from Claes Jansz. Visscher's view of London (1616)	140
5.2	Sarah Onsager as Lavinia and Jim Peck as Marcus in an Atlanta Shakespeare Company production of *Titus Andronicus* (1994)	146
5.3	Sarah Onsager as Lavinia and Stuart Culpepper as Titus in an Atlanta Shakespeare Company production of *Titus Andronicus* (1994)	147

Acknowledgments

A book is a performance whose meanings, like those of stage plays, are produced in the interstices between its many actors and audiences. The process of writing, though solitary, is also a communal experience, one in which readers are implicit participants who actively shape the performance. This book represents many years of individual labor, but it comes into being only through an entire community of scholars and friends. In naming what Shakespeare's contemporaries would call the "principal actors of the play," I present only a small token—an indexical signifier—of the myriad ways in which the very substance of this book is shot through with their contributions.

At the University of Pennsylvania, Phyllis Rackin was the best advisor possible, and Cary Mazer and Peter Stallybrass were also crucial in guiding this project in its earliest phases. I am grateful to them for their continued mentorship. Rebecca Bushnell, Margreta de Grazia, and the other faculty and graduate students in the Medieval-Renaissance group served as my first and most influential readers. I also owe a significant debt to Jim English, whose professional advice has been invaluable and who has always managed to dispense it with such sanity and good humor.

At the University of Louisville, I discovered a department whose collegiality is legendary. Susan Griffin was an exemplary chair, and I thank David Anderson, Matthew Biberman, Tom Byers, Karen Chandler, Aaron Jaffe, Karen Kopelson, Susan Ryan, Joanna Wolfe, and the rest of my colleagues for their wise counsel and friendship. Their support came at a critical stage of my career. A special word of thanks goes to Andrew Rabin, a dear friend and intellectual collaborator whose hilarious e-mails can scarcely make up for his office no longer being next door.

Since arriving at George Mason University, I have found myself blessed with yet another genial community. Denise Albanese, Devon Hodges, and Robert Matz have been the kind of senior colleagues that other junior faculty only dream of having. With her keen eye and unparalleled rigor, Denise offered incisive feedback that was pivotal for thinking through key issues in this project. Devon's strong departmental presence and deep knowledge of the university are enhanced by her personal wit and warmth. Robert's combination of energy, enthusiasm, and experience have made him not only a valued mentor but also an ideal chair. I am grateful as well to Deborah Kaplan for her sage advice, to Deb Shutika and Peggy Yocom for their guidance in folklore studies, to Beth Hoffman for her generous and extensive comments on my introduction, and to the entire faculty for their friendly welcome and ongoing support.

I have also benefited immensely from the stimulating questions and warm camaraderie of many other friends and colleagues, including Patsy Badir, Rob Barrett, Gina Bloom, Anston Bosman, Lara Bovilsky, Jane Degenhardt, Jean Feerick, Jen Higginbotham, Angela Ho, D. J. Hopkins, Jean Howard, Jonathan Hsy, Alex Huang, Jim Kearney, David Krasner, Eng-Beng Lim, Jennifer Low, Jack Lynch, Ellen MacKay, Paul Menzer, Nova Myhill, Elisa Oh, Lois Potter, Richard Preiss, Bruce Smith, Noël Sugimura, Henry Turner, Will West, Elizabeth Williamson, Susanne Wofford, and Mimi Yiu. Barbara Kirkpatrick and Joy Pohl were instrumental in my development as a scholar. Stephen Booth and Alan Nelson provided vital training and intellectual direction that have shaped my subsequent research. Robert Weimann and Bill Worthen offered interest and encouragement at key moments in the process. Kathleen Lynch and Owen Williams at the Folger Institute as well as the entire staff at the Folger Shakespeare Library have been amazing resources to have in the local area.

This project would not have been possible without significant institutional support, including research fellowships from the College of Arts and Sciences and the Senior Vice President for Research at the University of Louisville and from the College of Humanities and Social Sciences at George Mason University. Dan Traister and John Pollack at the University of Pennsylvania Libraries, Suzy Palmer and Mildred Franks at the University of Louisville Libraries, and Jen Stevens and Leah Richardson at the George Mason University Libraries were essential to the acquisition of materials for this project. I am grateful as well for the hard work of my graduate research assistants: Lucia Wolf, who helped with chapters 2 and 3, and Kaitlin Huggins, who stepped in briefly but critically at the final hour. My sincere thanks also to everyone at Palgrave Macmillan, especially my editors Samantha Hasey and Robyn Curtis, for their interest in this project and their efficiency at seeing it through to completion.

My family and friends know well how much I have needed them through the writing of this book. To my parents, Lucy and Kuang-hua Lin, who taught me to value scholarly inquiry, I owe my ability to think critically. That gift is the foundation for everything else, and it is a debt that can never be repaid. Monica Lin-Meyer is the best sister in the whole world—the kind of friend and confidante that makes other people wish they had a sibling like that, too. Alex Lin-Meyer is not just her husband but like a brother to me as well. My parents-in-law, Yael and Jerry Sears, have embraced me with open arms, and I thank Dan and Carissa Sears for welcoming me so warmly into the family. I am also blessed to have many friends who are like family, and words cannot express how much they mean to me: Sheila Avelin, Talia Ehrlich Dashow, Katherine Faulkner, Rachna Sizemore Heizer, Anna Ivy, Mark Rifkin, and Veronica Schanoes. Without them, this book would not exist. I am grateful as well to Jaryd Bern, Colleen Costello, Sandy Lee, and Doug Wilson, who were all there for me at crucial moments. Mónica Jutkowitz knows just how important she was to the completion of this project. My silly cats deserve a quick note, too, having sat on numerous drafts and insinuated their furry selves into every crevice of my keyboard. And finally, my partner, Tamara Sears, who is the most important of all and who has taught me many things about how to see and how to love—she is a part of me, and her way of looking at the world is woven together with mine. Her support, especially in the final phases of this process, made an enormous difference. This book bears her intellectual and emotional imprint through and through in profound and subtle ways.

There is one person whose contribution to this project is so extensive that my gratitude can know no proper bounds. Marissa Greenberg has read every single chapter in multiple versions from half-finished conference drafts onward. She has tirelessly and generously offered both expert feedback and moral support, often at the last minute, and she has demonstrated time and again her unique ability to articulate the thing in my head that I could not manage to say. Without her help, the writing process would be more arduous, the product impoverished, and the maker infinitely more lonely. As I always tell her, her name should no longer be a proper noun. Everybody should have a marissa; I'm lucky that I have the original one.

Note on Texts

Unless otherwise indicated, quotations from Shakespeare's plays are taken from Charlton Hinman, ed., *The First Folio of Shakespeare* (New York: Norton, 1968), with through line numbers (TLN) followed by act, scene, and line numbers from G. Blakemore Evans et al., eds., *The Riverside Shakespeare,* 2nd ed. (Boston: Houghton Mifflin, 1997). Excerpts from other early modern printed texts are drawn from electronic facsimiles of the originals in *Early English Books Online* (EEBO). In the case of plays, signature numbers from early modern texts are followed by act, scene, and line numbers from modern editions. Spelling and italics are retained exactly with the exception of the long *s,* which has been silently modernized, and tildes marking omitted letters, which have been lowered and italicized to accord with transcriptions of manuscript sources.

Part I

Performance Effects

Introduction

Materializing the Immaterial

In Shakespeare's *King Lear,* after Gloucester is viciously blinded by Regan and Cornwall, he is turned out of the house to wander comfortless and alone. Deceived by Lear's children and by his own bastard son, Edmund, he recognizes the full extent of their treachery only when his eyes are brutally destroyed. Gloucester cries out that he has no more need for mortal vision: "I haue no way, and therefore want no eyes: / I stumbled when I saw" (TLN 2199–200; 4.1.18–19). Bloody mutilation is here presented as potent reflection on the play's larger themes: it is only when Gloucester's eyes are ripped out that he can finally "see" the truth. Modern theatrical productions underscore this convergence of the literal and the figurative when they creatively stage the episode to avoid showing the blinding itself. Directors often present Gloucester bound to a chair that is then tipped back for the gruesome act. Just as the obliteration of physical vision ultimately enhances his perceptions, spectators who cannot literally view the violent action see its representation all the more clearly in their "mind's eye."

When *King Lear* was originally performed in Shakespeare's day, the theatrical strategies for presenting this scene were startlingly different. In the outdoor amphitheatres of early modern London, playgoers surrounded the stage on three—or sometimes even four—sides. Hiding the blinding by tipping back Gloucester's chair would have been difficult. Yet early modern evidence indicates no such attempts at theatrical subterfuge. English records of the technologies used for onstage blindings are scarce, but sources from the European Continent point to extremely graphic forms of stage violence. The contracts for the 1580 Modane Antichrist play, for example, describe how actors must "put out the eyes of the catholic with pointed skewers (*brochettes poignantes*), and to this end they shall make the necessary eyes and false faces or some alternative as skillfully as they can."[1] In the 1536 Bourges Acts of the Apostles, fake eyes were mounted on augers so that they emerged from the tools when Saint Matthew was blinded.[2] Such references underscore not so much the transcendent power of tragedy as the crude corporeality of vision. Eyes are treated as gross matter, akin to the fleshy substances described in anatomical treatises such as Helkiah Crooke's *Mikrokosmographia* (figure 0.1). In early modern stage performance, the figurative meanings of sight take a backseat to the gory physicality of eyeballs dripping with blood and spitted on sharp pokers.

Shakespeare's dialogue, too, curiously foregrounds the materiality of vision when it transforms metaphors of sight into bodily action. When interrogated as to why he sent the King to Dover, Gloucester defiantly declares, "Because I would not see thy cruell Nailes / Plucke out his poore old eyes" (TLN 2128–29; 3.7.56–57), and vows that "I shall see / The winged Vengeance ouertake such Children" (TLN 2137–38; 3.7.63–64). The word "see," which Gloucester uses figuratively, is made literal when Cornwall promptly responds by putting out one of his eyes: "See't shalt thou neuer. Fellowes hold yᵉ Chaire, / Vpon these eyes of thine, Ile set my foote" (TLN 2139–40; 3.7.65–66). The immediate trigger for Gloucester's mutilation is the word itself. This pattern continues when Cornwall's servant tries to end the torture and dies,

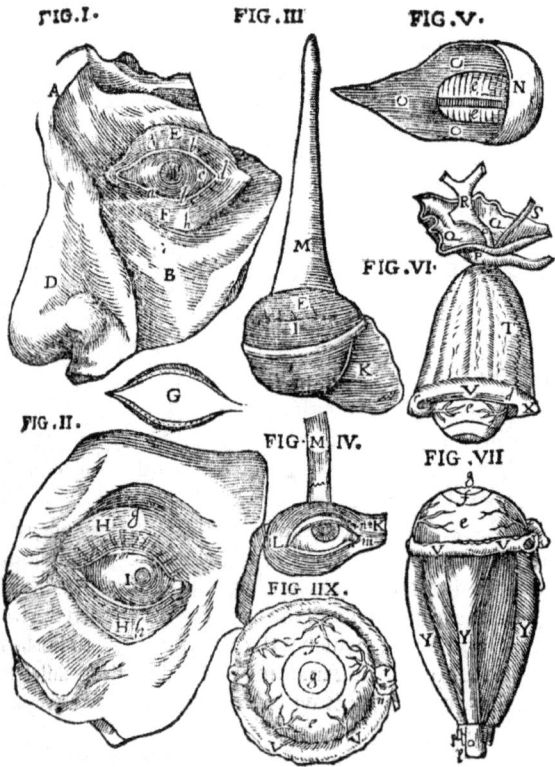

Figure 0.1 Eyeballs. Helkiah Crooke, *Mikrokosmographia: A Description of the Body of Man* (London, 1615), 539 [Zz6r]. Courtesy of the Horace Howard Furness Memorial (Shakespeare) Library, University of Pennsylvania.

saying, "Oh I am slaine: my Lord, you haue one eye left / To see some mischefe on him" (TLN 2156–57; 3.7.78–79). The word "see" here becomes the pretext for blinding the second eye: "Lest it see more, preuent it; Out vilde gelly: / Where is thy luster now?" (TLN 2158–59; 3.7.80–81). Unlike modern productions that try to conceal the violent act so as to enhance its tragic force, Shakespeare's dialogue consistently guides the spectator's gaze back to its horrifying specifics.

Rather than naturalizing the artificiality of the blinding, *King Lear* bizarrely foregrounds it by drawing attention to that which cannot be real: onstage mutilation. In doing so, it highlights theatre's special effects and flaunts the technical resources required for staging such a scene. In addition, the play does not simply perform the blinding; it also narrates the performance of the blinding. Having the bloody deed prompted by the immediately preceding dialogue, the episode constructs the act as curiously motivated not by character or theme but by the presentationality of rhetoric: the immediate pretext for the violence is the fact that a certain word is spoken at a certain moment onstage. The perfunctoriness of the local impetus for the blinding within the representational frame here complements the artificiality of the presentational action. Drawing attention to stage technologies, the play reminds spectators that what they see is *not* a blinding but a simulation of one.

Why would actors have gone to the trouble of offering such spectacular displays of violence only to undercut their believability? How did playgoers respond to such gruesome acts? What cultural resonances would blinding have had in early modern England, and how did they shape its onstage representation? When we read Shakespeare, it is easy to project our own modern theatrical practices and cultural meanings back onto an earlier era. When we consider his plays on their own terms, however, the answers to these kinds of questions are markedly different. Every time and place has its own particular style of performance and a set of unspoken assumptions taken for granted by players and spectators alike: a boy actor may play a female character, unbound hair may indicate madness, a trapdoor may represent hell, the color white may signify death. To those within a culture, this theatrical language is so obvious as to require no explanation; to those on the outside, it is ripe for misinterpretation. In our own theatres today, we do not need to be told explicitly that illuminated emergency exit signs are not part of the set, nor do we wonder at the dimming of house lights at the start of a show. We can well imagine how confusing such features might be for an early modern viewer magically transplanted to our own time—yet we easily forget just how foreign and opaque *their* theatrical standards might be to *us*.

This book reveals the unique and often surprising assumptions that governed theatrical performance for Shakespeare's original audience members. It analyzes the cultural attitudes and practices that conditioned typical ways of thinking and feeling, and it demonstrates how these familiar interpretive and experiential modes permeated the medium of performance. To uncover such intangible, yet crucial, aspects of early modern theatre, I survey a wide range of sixteenth- and seventeenth-century texts, from learned discussions of epistemology to popular accounts of violent sports, from religious treatises on visual perception to legal records of holiday festivity. Reading between the lines of these myriad forms of evidence, I reconstruct the underlying principles that framed the perception, interpretation, and phenomenological impact of early modern performance: the historically specific markers that distinguished meaningful theatrical signifiers from undifferentiated "background noise"; the interpretive paradigms that circumscribed audience understandings of mimesis; the affective responses generated by spectacle; and the dynamic interplay between theatre's representational strategies and presentational effects. My study moves beyond the cultural genesis of specific stage conventions to expose the fundamental assumptions that were constitutive of early modern theatrical literacy and that rendered performance intelligible. Any given individual may have deviated from these practices: actors could devise new styles of entertainment, and audience members could respond in a range of ways. Without detracting from the agency of individuals and their heterogeneous actions, however, this book aims to lay out the commonalities that tied them together, the shared habits of mind that circumscribed performance and the cultural logics that undergirded these collective understandings.

The Materiality of Performance

The paradigms that structured the production and reception of early modern performance grew out of a dynamic cultural field. Since the New Historicism of the mid-1980s, scholars have produced a significant body of work analyzing how plays both reflected broader cultural discourses and produced them. The same was true of the material practices through which these discourses were disseminated. As scholars of book history have shown, print was not merely the inert medium through which verbal content was conveyed but itself participated in the process of meaning-making. If these studies focus on "the materiality of the text," my project might rightly be called "the materiality of performance." Textual scholars have explored how printing and reading conventions actively constructed meaning rather than merely transmitting it; I demonstrate the ways in which cultural attitudes and practices were mediated through performance. Because performance is not a concrete object, however, it reveals aspects of materiality that we might miss in the case of printed texts. Performance's materiality cannot be reduced to the nuts and bolts of stagecraft that have long interested historians of early modern theatre: costumes and properties, playing spaces, technical resources, and repertory schedules.[3] Nor can its processes of production and reception be equated simply with sixteenth- and seventeenth-century acting and spectatorship.[4] Performance is, moreover, not the same as early modern theatre as a commercial entity, whose economic transactions constituted the institutional preconditions of performance but not performance itself.[5] All of these material objects and practices made possible the ephemeral experiences that took place in the theatre, but that experience is marked primarily by its *im*materiality.[6]

In order to understand the cultural implications of early modern theatrical performance, then, we must develop a more capacious sense of what materiality is and how it functions. In recent years, early modern scholars have been particularly interested in studying everyday objects, such as handkerchiefs, mirrors, furniture, clothing, jewelry, and tobacco.[7] This strand of criticism—variously dubbed "new materialism," "new antiquarianism," and "thing theory"—has departed from Marxist understandings of materiality to put the focus back on objects themselves. Rather than attending to how social relations are shaped by modes of production, distribution, and consumption, scholars working in this vein tend to favor thick descriptions of physical artifacts and their local circumstances.[8] Studies of book history draw more explicitly on Marxist notions of materiality in investigating the economic specifics of publication and reception, yet they share thing theory's preference for concrete, tangible forms. What counts as evidence in this strand of criticism are the material remains of ephemeral reading and writing practices: handwritten marginalia, archival documents, antique printing presses, even the composition of papers and inks. In both intellectual trends, scholarly energy has ultimately centered on objects, even when particular research projects have been devoted to the dynamics of production and circulation.

This narrowing of the definition of materiality to that which seems solid, physical, and concrete suggests the lure of a fixity that is specifically at odds with the fluidity of performance. Far from a physical object, performance is an action, an experience. It is more verb than noun, more sensation than thing. What, then, constitutes the materiality of performance? Judith Butler offers one compelling—and incredibly generative—answer to this question. She argues that matter becomes intelligible only through a process of reiterative citation, which actively produces the very terms for understanding that which it describes. Matter is thus inherently performative, a contingent stability that is constructed through repetition and exists in comprehensible form only within a discursive nexus that gives it meaning.[9] These citational acts tend to be naturalized and their material consequences effaced. In the case of performance, however, because we cannot lean on the physical artifact as a crutch, the semiotic and experiential processes through which meaning is produced come more readily into view. In this book, I take performance both as an object of study, located in the interstices between the tangible and the intangible, and as an epistemology, a way of knowing that bears within it transformative force. Its immateriality as the former is essential to its materiality as the latter: it is only because performance is *not* fixed that it can take one thing and turn it into something else. This process of transformation happens most overtly in theatre's semiotic function, as when a chair becomes a throne or a boy actor becomes a female character, and it is sometimes effected through speech acts, as when Rosalind in Shakespeare's *As You Like It* declares the bare platform stage to be the Forest of Arden. But speech is only one subset of the full range of theatre's signifying practices, which also includes bodily gestures, the use of space, iconography, nonverbal sounds, and a whole host of other material signifiers.[10]

When I speak of "the materiality of performance," then, I mean these sorts of theatrical conventions—but I also mean something more. To call theatre's signifying practices "conventions" presumes that the symbolic realm in which these practices exist is well-bounded, yet that semiotic system is likewise produced through a process of reiterative citation that may stabilize into a semblance of regularity but contains numerous gaps and fissures. For theatre to be legible as representation, it must cite cultural understandings that circumscribe what counts as semiotically viable. These understandings are constitutive of thought; they are that without which it is impossible for meaning to come into existence. By "the materiality of performance," then, I also mean these baseline assumptions and expectations, the codes of intelligibility imbricated in all aspects of social life. Foucault refers to these underlying cultural logics as the historical a priori, that which need never be spoken but which tacitly structures modes of comprehension. This historical a priori is nonmonolithic and never fully recoverable; moreover, it is always in the process of being constructed. My project might therefore be described as an archaeology of early modern performance, what Foucault calls the "never wholly achieved uncovering of the archive."[11]

This act of uncovering, though never complete, is also ultimately productive—and I use that word advisedly here. In analyzing the materiality of performance, I also analyze the process through which performance actively *produces* the historical a priori. Butler has pointed out that in Marx "[t]he materiality of objects...is constituted in and as transformative activity."[12] For Butler, "performativity" is this act of transformation; it brings matter into being in and through discourse. In Marxist theory, matter as such preexists culture, but "materiality" describes the social relations produced by physical conditions; discourse mystifies the uneven distribution of resources and labor. I am sympathetic to Marxist criticism in that I view the kind of transformative labor applied to physical objects by workers as of a different character entirely from the kind of transformative activity that Butler means when she speaks of matter being produced through a process of citation. However, what I find compelling about Butler's formulation is her central insight that, in rendering certain experiences intelligible, citational practices have social and physical consequences—material consequences. We might say at first glance that, as a representational practice, theatre takes on a second-order relationship to matter; the imaginative labor required to transform a chair into a throne is significantly less taxing than the labor, both physical and cognitive, of the carpenter who carves a throne out of oak. When we expand our view, however, to consider theatrical representation as itself inseparable from the broader social attitudes and practices that authorize its existence, we can see how enacting semiotic transformations onstage—say, chair to throne—might produce real material effects.

The material effects I trace in this book are not simply a consequence of theatre's function as representation, however, but also inhere in the presentational dimension of performance. In addition to the stories, characters, speeches, and themes mobilized within its fictional worlds, theatre also encompasses a range of nonmimetic performance practices that act upon playgoers. The material effects of these practices have been most fully explored in Marxist accounts of the political consequences of spectacle, an issue I discuss and complicate further in chapter 4. Yet nonverbal spectacle and other *pre*sentational effects also impact the way spectators experience theatre as a *re*presentational system. Interlocking puzzle pieces, representation and presentation are mutually constitutive citational practices that, taken together, impact the cultural attitudes and practices that give rise to the particular specificities of their relationship in the first place. Performance, then, "materializes" (in Butler's sense of the term) in two spheres at once: it cites particular cultural discourses related to specific semiotic transformations occurring within a play, *and* it cites affective and experiential dimensions of social life in its presentational effects. The dynamic interplay between these two sides of performance, between representation and presentation, further cites social logics underpinning theatrical performance as a whole. Performance is unique in that it itself is also the *act* of production; the medium *is* the process of transformation. This distinctive quality allows the study of performance to expand our view of materiality more generally: it reveals and exemplifies the ways presentationality informs *all* representational practices.

Theatrical performance is thus material in more than one sense. First, its signifiers are themselves material objects, such as chairs and bodies, rather than simply words (which, as we shall see in chapter 3, were understood in early modern England as also profoundly material). Second, performance as signifying practice "materializes" in Butler's sense: it is a transformative activity that turns onstage action into fictional representation in the manner of a speech act, though it is not limited to speech. Third, theatrical performance as a semiotic system is not a fixed, bounded set of conventions but is produced in dynamic relation to attitudes and practices outside the playhouse. Fourth, and most importantly, theatrical performance has real social and physical consequences. It differs from other representational practices in that it itself is also the presentational act of transformation and thus *by definition* produces material effects. We might conceive of these effects as the material "traces" of performance, but that would be to reify the object as the primary form of materiality and performance as its second cousin. I would argue, conversely, that, as the only material medium that is also simultaneously the act of becoming, performance opens up a whole range of questions about the materiality of other cultural practices. It highlights dynamics that are happening far beyond theatre, in cases where the empirical presence of physical artifacts might otherwise deflect attention away from the more intangible, yet still profoundly consequential, dimensions of materiality. To analyze the materiality of performance, then, is also to analyze the presentational process through which all materiality is (per)formed.

From Drama to Theatrical Event

Studying the materiality of performance thus poses some serious methodological challenges to conventional modes of scholarly inquiry. Indeed, the questions I ask are ultimately unanswerable by traditional evidentiary standards. Given that multiple and contradictory discourses can and will coexist simultaneously, how are we to choose dramatic examples that are representative of early modern English culture, a concept that itself cannot be defined because it is always in the process of being produced? And how many data points constitute a sampling broad enough for us to begin to theorize performance practices as a medium? There are no good answers to these questions, and my work is thus ultimately theoretical—and as with all theory, answers depend upon imaginative extrapolation. But these same objections necessarily characterize all scholarship: it is only because performance is explicitly defined as *im*material that analyzing its materiality exposes methodological difficulties obscured by the seeming solidity of other objects of study. Given that performance complicates and works against these epistemological paradigms, I have elected to be provocative rather than comprehensive in my choice of examples, to model a *way* of looking rather than to offer a seemingly conclusive set of evidence that imagines a closed system where none exists. To that end, I have limited my theatrical examples to a few brief snapshots from early modern plays instead of attempting a more comprehensive assessment of the dramatic canon. Although many of my examples are from Shakespeare and his more famous contemporaries, I choose them not because of their authorship but precisely because they are convenient: they are drawn from plays I expect my readers will know well. Likewise, although the same plays were sometimes performed in a variety of venues—not only in public and private theatres but also at court and on tour in the provinces—I constrain my geographical scope to London's public amphitheatres because these are the playing spaces most familiar to us today. This principle of selection underscores the fact that ultimately *any* example will do. The claims I make about particular theatrical episodes are, I contend, broadly applicable *across* early modern drama because my argument specifically concerns the medium itself. It is only because performance is not a physical object that the material conditions and practices that characterize and circumscribe it are seen as more amorphous and up for debate—and thus more in need of grounding through the seemingly concrete epistemological categories of evidence and scope.

I have applied a similar methodology in deciding which cultural factors to highlight in this book. Since theatre was ultimately informed by an endless number of discourses, I have chosen to concentrate on key issues that most tellingly reveal the contours and fissures of the medium of performance, even as I gesture toward the range and variety of these attitudes and practices. Because I treat theatre as popular entertainment, not high art, I have tended to pay particular attention to cultural practices that would have been shared by large sectors of the society. However, despite the care I have taken to provide a balanced view when drawing on anatomy texts, religious treatises, and other learned works, reliance on textual sources is unavoidable and will necessarily disadvantage popular beliefs and practices for which written evidence is scarce. To counteract this methodological difficulty, I have surveyed a wide cross section of early modern texts, and I have analyzed these sources not only for their surface content but also for what remains unsaid, for the unstated assumptions and attitudes that lie beneath the words. In addition, I incorporate some discussion of nontextual material, in particular visual artifacts and architecture, and I am especially attentive to the phenomenological dimensions of sight and sound. Because texts remain privileged sources of evidence for scholarly studies of earlier eras, popular performance can too easily disappear from view; drawing on texts from many different genres and reading between the lines are therefore essential components of this project.

In terms of temporal scope, although my book centers on the decades immediately before and after the turn of the seventeenth century, I am especially attentive to connections with prior performance traditions. The problematic tendency to imagine early modern theatre primarily as dramatic representation and, thus, to disregard its function as presentational spectacle derives in part from a peculiar critical myopia that relegates specific *types* of sixteenth-century British and European theatre to the "premodern"—morality drama and biblical cycle plays, for example—while elevating those with a more obvious classical heritage, such as the Tudor interludes, to the "early modern." Beneath such otherwise innocuous disciplinary practices and genre assignments lie implicit class distinctions: medieval drama is imagined as the Other, that which exhibits strange and vulgar behaviors and whose Catholic rituals prove not only religious alterity but also ignorant superstition; Shakespeare, by contrast, is thought of as the enlightened self—learned, secular, and inherently ennobling. My use of the term "early modern," then, should be construed not as an attempt to treat Shakespeare and his contemporaries as the venerable forefathers of modern drama but rather as dissatisfaction with the emphasis on social elitism implicit in the classical roots of the "Renaissance."[13]

The political implications of this study cannot be straightforwardly mapped onto designations of evidence and scope, however. As historians have noted, the construction of "popular" and "elite" as social categories can, in fact, be traced back to this period, when discursive distinctions between them were still quite permeable.[14] It is, therefore, worth underscoring Peter Burke's caution against homogenizing and romanticizing the popular: we should be careful, he reminds us, not to "equate the 'popular' with the 'radical,' ignoring evidence for popular conservatism."[15] If the theatrical practices I describe in this book seem politically progressive from our own post-Brechtian vantage point, it is important to historicize how we interpret these effects. Breaking the fourth wall, for instance, had very different valences in a culture whose assumptions about the nature of representation were markedly unlike those most prevalent in twentieth-century Europe and America. Moreover, as I demonstrate throughout this book, the kinds of affective experiences produced by early modern theatrical performance tended to construct playgoers as part of a communal whole, often reinscribing existing social hierarchies and belief systems rather than challenging them. This is not to say that moments of agency and subversion did not occur but instead to reframe the political implications of my work. In describing commonalities across diverse populations' ways of understanding and experiencing performance, I honor the deeply held beliefs, feelings, and practices that structured people's daily lives and that were refracted in, transformed by, and produced through the public theatre. Those attitudes were often founded on long-standing traditions and tended not to lead to unrest or revolution, but they were important to the people who possessed them. Writing this history is thus a particular kind of intervention, but my own political investments should not be confused with some sort of radicalism on the part of early modern plays or playgoers.

Nevertheless, my choice to focus on theatre as performance, not drama, does have distinct class valences. In analyzing the typical habits of mind that produced early modern theatre's signifying practices as well as the cultural consequences of embodied performance, my project shares certain affinities with recent work on "historical phenomenology," which attends to culturally specific experiences of bodily affect and perception,[16] and "historical formalism," which addresses the social and material implications of dramatic form and structure.[17] Where I differ from these approaches, however, is in my attention to the presentational dimensions of plays; in this, my project more closely resembles "material text studies," which considers the medium of print through which drama was circulated.[18] Yet in the case of Shakespeare and his fellow playwrights, the initial physical form was not the printed book. Plays were first performed and only later published, as numerous references on the title pages of playbooks attest. Moreover, the authority of these texts derived from the stage: the names of acting companies, playing venues, and even the feast days on which famous performances occurred featured more prominently on title pages than the names of the writers who penned the texts. Indeed, the number of people who encountered plays in the theatre was vastly greater than the number who could have read them in print. When Elizabeth I first came to the throne in 1558, only about 20 percent of men and 5 percent of women in England could sign their own names. By 1642, these numbers had risen to 30 percent and 10 percent respectively across the country and, in London, comprised about two-thirds of the total adult population.[19] It is true that counting signatures as an index of reading ability has its methodological drawbacks. Nevertheless, even assuming that these statistics are underestimates, it is clear that at least one out of every three people would have been unable to read plays in printed form.

Even the segment of the population that had achieved fluency with the written vernacular, however, was much more likely to have experienced plays on the stage than on the page. Though book publication as a whole increased during the sixteenth and seventeenth centuries, the number of dramatic titles printed each year was only a tiny fraction of this total. In 1530, there were only 214 different books published in all of England; by 1600, that number had increased slightly to 259; and by 1640, it had risen to 577.[20] In absolute terms, these numbers are quite small. Of the modest total number of books in print, only a handful were plays. As Peter Blayney describes, "In the two decades before the accession of James I, then, the average number of new plays published each year was 4.8. In the next two decades it was 5.75, and in the last two decades before the theaters were closed, exactly 8.0.... [P]rinted plays never accounted for a very significant fraction of the trade in English books."[21] Moreover, of those plays published, print runs were generally no more than 800 to 1,000 copies for first editions.[22] A good number of those books never sold but sat in booksellers' stalls gathering dust. The first print run of Shakespeare's *King Lear,* for example, was probably no more than 700 copies at most, and a portion of even that small quantity remained unsold over a decade later.[23] This situation was not uncommon, as Blayney attests: "Fewer than 21 percent of the plays published in the sixty years under discussion reached a second edition inside nine years. What that means is that no more than one play in five would have returned the publisher's initial investment inside five years. Not one in twenty would have paid for itself during its first year."[24]

When these publication figures are compared to the number of plays in performance, the difference is staggering. As W. R. Streitberger reminds us, "Between the time Shakespeare began his active career in the early 1590s and the closing of the theatres in 1642, there were about twenty professional companies that performed at one time or another in London."[25] Each of the playing companies produced approximately 35 plays a year, more than half of which were new.[26] Not only were there vastly more plays in the repertory than in print, the sheer numbers of people exposed to this medium were far greater than those who bought or read playbooks. Each new play had a run of roughly 8 to 12 performances distributed across four to six months.[27] Given that public theatres could typically hold as many as 2,500 to

3,000 spectators, with average attendance hovering around half capacity,[28] a single performance of a play in the theatre could reach more people than the entire print run of that play as a book.

As a rough comparison, then, let us imagine a hypothetical year in which five plays were published with print runs on the high side—say, 1,000 copies each for a total of 5,000 copies. And let us assume that one of these titles was a raging success and sold half its stock within the first year—a situation that Blayney tells us had less than a 1 in 20 chance, not 1 in 5—and the rest sold a good amount—say, a quarter of their stock. The total number of playbooks distributed to readers over the course of that year would be no more than 1,500. During that same year, let us estimate that only three acting companies were active in London, and for simplicity let us ignore performances in the provinces. Thirty-five plays at an average of ten performances per play and audiences of about 1,000 per performance comes out to 350,000. Andrew Gurr's own "conservative estimate" would almost double this figure: his total of almost 50 million visits for the period 1567 to 1642 puts the yearly average at 650,000.[29] But even sticking with my more modest number, for every individual who bought a play as a book, at least 233 spectators would have flocked to the theatre—or, to put it even more starkly, 99.6 percent of all unique interactions with a play occurred in theatrical performance. In an era before silent reading was the norm, books may well have been read aloud to other people once purchased. But even if we assume that each playbook was read to five other people, we are still looking at a ratio of 1 to 47; that is, 97.9 percent of all encounters with drama would have taken place in the theatre.[30] In terms of sheer exposure, the stage had far more influence than the page. Focusing on the tiny percentage of the population that actually read drama says less about early modern experiences and more about the primacy of the written word today.

Despite the vastly larger crowds that flocked to the theatre, it is true that the financial gains to be had in the nascent publishing industry were not insignificant. Lukas Erne has recently argued compellingly for dramatic authorship as a parallel business track for Shakespeare and other playwrights. Acting companies, he contends, could expand their theatrical audiences through print publication, so the two markets may well have complemented each other. He concludes that the concerns of print publication thus crucially shaped Shakespeare's plays as we know them today, since the only versions now extant were originally intended to be read as books.[31] Indeed, as Zachary Lesser has rightly pointed out, making a profit on plays was easier for publishers than it was for actors, who had to lay out money for expensive costumes, properties, and numerous other expenses. A playbook selling for 6 or 7d., Lesser notes, was "roughly equivalent to the cost of entrance to Blackfriars.... But while the cost to the consumer of an indoor stage play and a printed play are about the same, an utter disaster in the theatre... would be a fair success if the same number of people bought the play as saw it."[32] Money talks, Lesser argues: as book-buyers came to understand printed plays in the context of publishers' specialized lines, the "politics of publication" may have influenced "the text that early modern audiences heard in the theatre, turning it into the one that they bought in the bookshop and that we study today."[33] Shifting from the politics of production to the politics of reception, however, it becomes evident that the issue at stake is *scale*. If it takes the better part of a decade to turn a profit on a printed play, that won't help pay the rent today. Economically, the consumers one must please are those who will otherwise pelt the stage with debris.

Treating plays as books rather than as performances not only artificially inflates the impact of printed drama but also effaces the experiences of those lower in various social hierarchies. The price of a playbook would have been six times the cost of standing-room admission to the yard in a public playhouse. Not everyone had that much ready cash. For many members of society, an afternoon's entertainment at the outdoor amphitheatres was the more affordable option. Even for those more privileged, the public playhouses offered an indulgence that could be enjoyed with greater frequency than either books or Blackfriars, and reading ability varied widely among geographic locations, social classes, and genders. Studying the history of the book serves as a valuable corrective to treating plays as disembodied texts, floating free of the material conditions of their production, distribution, and reception, and it usefully complements work in historical formalism by attending to the medium of transmission. At the same time, treating theatre primarily as printed text skews our perception of the cultural landscape by ignoring over 99 percent of early modern encounters with plays. The history of the book offers an interesting window into the past, but, in the case of drama, it also necessarily privileges the history of the elite. In order to understand how everyone else experienced the plays of Shakespeare and his contemporaries, we must shift our frame of reference from drama to theatrical event.

The Boundaries of Theatrical Performance

How did early modern spectators conceptualize the theatrical event? To analyze performance as a material medium, we must first define what counted as theatrical performance. In her article, "What Was Performance?" Mary Thomas Crane usefully surveys the relevant early modern terminology to argue that performance was understood not as hollow, deceptive show but as potentially efficacious and transformative in the real world.[34] Here, I focus on a slightly different question: what exactly did audience members in Shakespeare's day think they were going to see or experience at the playhouse? By this, I do not mean how early modern theorists of theatre described it but rather the general expectations of everyday playgoers: what were their common understandings about the boundaries of performance?

The answer to this question lies not in the title of a play—the key determinant of a theatrical event today—but in the combination of seemingly disparate modes of entertainment, only some of which involved the representation of fictional characters and narratives. Turning to early modern texts, we find that John Rainolds's *Th'Overthrow of Stage-Playes* positions theatre as one among a range of dissolute "pleasures" and "vanities," as he condemns "apparell, gamening [sic], gadding to plaies, masking, dauncing, belliheare, shewes, or such like."[35] In a similar vein, Francis Lenton's *Characterismi* satirically describes the quintessential "yong Innes a Court Gentleman" whose "Recreations and loose expence of time, are his only studies (as Plaies, Dancing, Fencing, Tauerns, Tobacco, [sic]) and Dalliance."[36] These accounts of theatre as akin to other leisure pursuits gesture toward the range of entertainments on offer at playhouses. The letter to the reader prefacing Ben Jonson's *The Alchemist* laments that in theatres "the Concupiscence of Iigges, and Daunces so raigneth, as to runne away from Nature, and be afraid of her, is the onely point of art that tickles the *Spectators*."[37] A playbill from around 1630 likewise describes dancing and other spectacles as among the chief entertainments of English players on tour through Germany. The generically varied routines promised by the troupe's "right merry Clown, who will act every day fine Comedies, Tragedies, Pastorals, and Histories, intermixed with lovely and merry Interludes," were complemented by the stylistic hybridity on offer "to-day Wednesday the 21 April.... After the Comedy will be presented a fine Ballet and laughable Droll. The Lovers of such plays must make their appearance at the Fencing-house in the afternoon at 2 o'clock."[38] Intermingled with longer scripted scenarios were music, dance, and comic sketches—all deemed "plays" that might be presented at a "Fencing-house." Far from an ontologically distinct aesthetic mode, drama overlapped significantly with other recreations.

This slippage between theatre and entertainment more broadly defined becomes especially evident when we consider the early modern jig. Generically related to the "fine Ballet and laughable Droll" that followed the English comedy described in the previous playbill, the jig was a song and dance routine that sometimes involved a rudimentary plot dealing with adultery or other bawdy themes. It was regularly enacted at the public playhouses, but its precise bodily form is poorly understood. In his foundational study, *The Elizabethan Jig,* C. R. Baskervill carefully analyzed early modern uses of the term *jig* to reveal conceptual overlaps between stage jigs, songs and dialogues printed in broadside ballads, popular dances, and festive games.[39] Bruce Smith comes to a similar conclusion, noting that the term *jig* probably referred to "any number of devices: a one-person song like [that which]... concludes *Twelfth Night;* a song in dialogue like the printed broadside 'Frauncis new Iigge...'...; dancing without a dramatic scenario...; or dancing *with* a dramatic scenario."[40] William West takes this one step further, arguing that the jig was whatever "happened" or "was reminiscent of what happened at the end of the play" or was associated "with people...associated with jigging."[41] The difficulties involved in defining the jig as a form arise in part because this mode of entertainment made use of nonverbal, spectacular, and ephemeral elements—precisely those actions that did not lend themselves to setting down in print and which, we would do well not to forget, were also essential to dramatic narratives.

This flexibility in the early modern jig extended also to its multivalent and malleable relationship to theatrical representation. Just as the early modern staging of Gloucester's blinding in *King Lear* challenges modern conceptions of tragedy, the jig complicates typical assumptions about the emotional tenor and consistency of theatrical performance. Jigs took place after all kinds of plays, not just comedies. As the Swiss doctor Thomas Platter writes in his description of his 1599 visit to England,

> On September 21st after lunch, about two o'clock, I and my party crossed the water, and there in the house with the thatched roof witnessed an excellent performance of

the tragedy of the first Emperor Julius Caesar with a cast of some fifteen people; when the play was over, they danced very marvellously and gracefully together as is their wont, two dressed as men and two as women.[42]

Thomas Dekker's *Strange Horse-Race* likewise notes that jigs were performed after tragedies: "I haue often seene, after the finishing of some worthy Tragedy, or Catastrophe in the open Theaters, that the Sceane after the Epilogue hath beene more blacke (about a nasty bawdy Iigge) then the most horrid Sceane in the Play was."[43] Such generic incongruities do not seem to have troubled early modern spectators, who never remark on the inappropriateness of this juxtaposition. In fact, it is noteworthy that many playgoers appear to have *preferred* the jig to dramatic narratives. A 1612 "Order for suppressinge of Jigges att the ende of Playes," for instance, describes how

> Complaynte have beene made at this last Generall Sessions, that by reason of certayne lewde Jigges songes and daunces vsed and accustomed at the play-house called the Fortune in Gouldinglane, divers cutt-purses and other lewde and ill disposed persons in greate multitudes doe resorte thither at th'end of euerye playe, many tymes causinge tumultes and outrages.[44]

The fact that "great multitudes" went to the playhouses for what today might be considered merely ancillary entertainments suggests that drama constituted only one part of a larger performance event—and, in many cases, the plays of Shakespeare and his fellow playwrights were not even the primary show early modern spectators wanted to see.

Indeed, the fact that references from Shakespeare's day regularly refer to jigs coming "after" plays also sheds light on early modern conceptions of the theatrical event. For instance, James Shirley's *Changes* complains,

> Many Gentlemen
> Are not, as in the dayes of understanding,
> Now satisfied without a Iigge, which since
> They cannot, with their honour, call for, after
> The play, they looke to be serv'd up ith' middle.[45]

Shirley's comments are typical of the Caroline tendency to bemoan the decline of plays and the poor quality of playgoers, and his joke depends on understanding the jig as an after-show. Yet what is striking about his remarks and those of his contemporaries is that they never describe exactly *when* theatrical representation shifts to the modes of performance found in the jig. The obvious conclusion is that, although the two forms of entertainment were distinct, the difference between them had nothing to do with fidelity to a verisimilar frame. Plays, in other words, were internally inconsistent and bore a fluid relationship to other forms of entertainment. Whereas actors today often make their curtain calls in costume—and sometimes even in the costume that most epitomizes their character rather than the one they last wore during the play—the final image left with early modern spectators did not necessarily have anything to do with the scripted play at all. Yet there is no indication that early modern audiences found this unusual or jarring. Rather, the boundary between the play and the jig was permeable because both were understood as part of the larger performance event.

If jigs challenge our modern notions of the boundaries of the theatrical event, about what defines its outside perimeter, dances incorporated into dramatic narratives complicate how we imagine the internal edges distinguishing theatre's various parts. Directors often cut these episodes from modern productions of the plays; scholars, too, tend to view dances as gratuitous action, taking place while "in the meane time, some necessary Question of the Play be then to be considered" (*Hamlet*, TLN 1890–91; 3.2.42–43). The witches' dance in act 4, scene 1 of *Macbeth* is a case in point. Often treated as superfluous to the play proper, the episode is generally relegated to Thomas Middleton, whose textual authority fails to match that of Shakespeare. To make matters worse, the episode bears some relationship to similar dances in two other dramatic works: Ben Jonson's *Masque of Queens*, performed at Whitehall on February 2, 1609, and Middleton's *The Witch*, performed by the King's Men sometime between 1613 and 1616.[46] Spectacle, here the product of secondary authorship and dubious lineage, seems from a modern perspective to complicate the integrity of the play. Even scholars interested in theatre as embodied performance have difficulty with the episode. Alan Brissenden considers the narrative pretext for the witches' dance in *Macbeth* to be "a rather thin excuse."[47] John Russell Brown reads the moment as a "wordless show of evil," which "can seem entirely purposeless, except as an expression of triumph" since "it alone is without specific meaning."[48] The dance's failure to mobilize a convincing explanation within the representational narrative results in a kind of semiotic void, rendering the spectacle unintelligible in these accounts.[49]

Yet dancing—and singing—witches were, in fact, the norm on the early modern stage,[50] and their popularity led to the elaboration of such episodes during the course of the seventeenth century. In William Davenant's 1674 revision of *Macbeth*, the spectacular elements of the play were enhanced with flying machines for the witches. Pepys wrote in 1667 that, "though I have seen it often, yet is it one of the best plays for a stage, and variety of dancing and music, that ever I saw."[51] Interestingly, the witches' dances in these episodes were generically related to the jig. As musicologist Amanda Winkler notes, in Davenant's play, the witches' dance was "diatonic, triple meter, and major key" with "jig dance rhythms" similar to those of other late seventeenth-century stage witches: "[O]ne of the sources for Locke's dance, *Musicks Delight on the Cithren*, labels it 'A Jigg called Macbeth.'"[52] And records of eighteenth- and nineteenth-century performances of *Macbeth* indicate the ongoing centrality of the witches' dance.[53] Far from being "extra," it was an integral part of the performance event, offering onstage spectacle exciting for its own sake and connected to the musical form of the jig.

Such terpsichorean extravaganzas also appear to have been related to entertainments offered during intermissions—further complicating the boundaries of the performance event. Breaks between acts of plays were originally introduced in the indoor theatres for the purpose of trimming the lights and seem to have spread from the private to the public playhouses after 1607.[54] Such intervals were usually brief—no more than the equivalent of about thirty lines of verse[55]—and often involved music and dancing. Shakespeare and Fletcher's *The Two Noble Kinsmen* is an especially telling example of the fluidity between dramatic narratives and such entertainments. As with the witches' dance in *Macbeth,* this episode has often been treated as an unnecessary interpolation. John Forrest, for instance, describes it as "clearly an interruption to the main narrative of the play, and the whole conceit rather artificially grafted in."[56] In the quarto edition of the play is a peculiar stage direction scribbled in the margins of the page: "Knocke for Schoole. Enter The Dance."[57] Although *knock* typically referred to a sound related to a visitor's arrival, here the use of the term suggests a kind of conceptual slippage in the minds of theatrical personnel between the play proper and the music and dancing offered during intervals. Alan Dessen and Leslie Thomson point out that, "in the annotated quarto of *Two Merry Milkmaids* a bookkeeper wrote '*Knock Act*' (E2r) before the first *entr'acte* entertainment, probably as a reminder to call up the performers."[58] The stage direction in *The Two Noble Kinsmen,* they suggest, "may carry a similar meaning."[59] Playgoers were no strangers to such narrative incongruities. Indeed, as Edmund Gayton colorfully describes, they sometimes demanded that players

> act what the major part of the company had a mind to; sometimes *Tamerlane,* sometimes *Iugurth,* sometimes the Jew of *Malta,* and sometimes parts of all these, and at last, none of the three taking, they were forc'd to undresse and put off their Tragick habits, and conclude the day with the merry milk-maides. And unlesse this were done, and the popular humour satisfied, as sometimes it so fortun'd, that the Players were refractory; the Benches, the tiles, the laths, the stones, Oranges, Apples, Nuts, flew about most liberally.[60]

Gayton's comment about the popularity of *The Two Merry Milkmaids* is noteworthy, given the annotation regarding between-act entertainments in the quarto of the play. Such references suggest that, for early modern spectators, theatrical performance was defined less as representational coherence than as spectacular entertainment.

The fluidity of form that characterized theatrical performance also extended to its temporal boundaries, which were informed by the cyclical rhythms of the ritual year. As Roslyn Knutson notes, playing companies nearly always performed on certain holidays, which tended to draw larger-than-normal crowds. These feast days included, among others, "Easter Week, Whitsun Week, and the Nativity of John the Baptist," also known as Midsummer.[61] Although scholars of early modern drama have tended to focus on thematic and ideological issues related to depictions of calendar customs within plays, thinking about theatrical performance as a presentational form reveals numerous overlaps with popular festivity.[62] Take, for example, the dance of the courtiers dressed as shepherds in Shakespeare and Fletcher's *Henry VIII.* The burning of the Globe Theatre on Tuesday, June 29, 1613, allows us to fix this play's temporal coordinates with more precision than most. According to a letter from Henry Bluett to his uncle Richard Weekes, the fire occurred only shortly after the play had been introduced into the repertory:

> On tewsday last there was acted at the Globe a new play called all is triewe which had beene acted not passing 2 or 3 times before there came many people to see it in

somuch that ye howse was very full and as the play was almost ended the house was fired with shooting off a Chamber which was stopt with towe which was blown vp into the thetch of the house and so burnt downe to the ground.[63]

Roslyn Knutson has demonstrated that "[t]he first few performances of a new offering were often scheduled within a week of one another, but by the fourth show the performances were more widely spaced," with only one or two performances each month.[64] If, as Bluett's letter suggests, *Henry VIII* "had beene acted not passinge 2 or 3 times before" the Globe fire, it seems likely that the play's original debut was in May or early June of 1613.

The major holidays during the season between Easter and Midsummer—May Day, Whitsuntide, and the Feast of Corpus Christi—often involved the crowning of a "summer lord." Recent work associated with the *Records of Early English Drama* (REED) project has demonstrated the continuing popularity of Robin Hood gatherings, the election of mock kings and queens, and other forms of class inversion and role-playing at this time of year. It is frequently assumed that these activities were the legacy of dying "medieval" practices, but they actually continued to flourish long after the Protestant Reformation purged the liturgical calendar of the feast days of saints.[65] Although the traditional custom of "bringing in the May" (that is, the medieval practice of fetching greenery and making garlands to bedeck houses and churches—a practice that continued into the nineteenth century) led Sir James Frazer to view the summer lord as the legacy of pagan agricultural rites,[66] mock kings were also closely linked to role-playing games in the urban context. In his *Anatomie of Abuses*, the notorious antitheatricalist Philip Stubbes describes summer games as being organized by the "Graund-Captain (of all mischeefe) whome they innoble with the title of my Lord of Mis-rule."[67] Other accounts more frequently give this title to the leader of *winter* revels at universities, aristocratic households, and the Inns of Court. The overlapping terminology reveals a similarity of function between winter Lords of Misrule and the summer lords incorrectly imagined as rural.[68] The episode in *Henry VIII* in which the monarch and his courtiers dress as shepherds can be seen as part and parcel of this festive tradition. At a time of year when games involving class inversion were so popular, representing a king taking part in festive disguise foregrounds the role-playing in which the actors themselves engaged. Moreover, the courtiers' shepherd costumes resonated with the annual sheep-shearing festivals that took place in May and June.[69] Such instances expose the permeability of early modern dramatic representation to festive customs associated not with the temporalities of the fictional narrative but with the seasonality of its performance.

Moreover, because portraying dancing within the imaginary world of the play required actors to actually dance onstage, representation was also necessarily enactment. This phenomenological condition not only suggests overlaps between theatrical performance, festive practices, and spectacular entertainments (such as the jig and the witches' dance) but also exemplifies how the presentational dimension of performance might reshape the implications of dramatic narratives. Drawn from a purportedly historical event narrated in Holinshed's *Chronicles,* the scene from *Henry VIII* has been read as a kind of antimasque in which the aristocrats' seemingly subversive costumes ultimately function to consolidate and legitimate royal authority.[70] This interpretation, though certainly compelling, focuses primarily on the dramatic representation: as masked "disguisers," the nobles represent a festive dance taking place within the imaginary world of the play. The political valences of this moment become more complicated, however, when we consider its onstage presentation. Although the King and his followers are dressed as shepherds, they most likely performed a *courtly* dance onstage, as can be seen when Cardinal Wolsey remarks, "Your Grace / I feare, with dancing is a little heated," and the King responds, "I feare too much" (TLN 807–9; 1.4.99–101). Beyond offering oblique commentary on Henry's attraction to Anne, these remarks would be particularly appropriate after a fast courtly dance, such as a *coranto, galliard,* or *volta*.[71] Courtly dancing in early modern England was an essential form of aristocratic self-fashioning, a rarefied skill that required the tutelage of expensive instructors.[72] Skiles Howard has argued that courtly dancing onstage destabilized social hierarchies: when actors demonstrated their mastery of such exclusive skills, they revealed that aristocratic identities, like dance steps, could be learned and performed.[73] The scene from *Henry VIII* takes this dynamic one step further by integrating this potential subversiveness into the semiotics of theatre: by presenting a dance where the performers are dressed as shepherds yet are enacting a courtly dance, the scene highlights the fact that these dancers are not nobles but rather actors from lower social stations. The play here not only represents class cross-dressing within the fictional narrative but also draws attention to the presentational dynamics of theatrical performance—undermining the consolidation of royal authority and interpolating the play into the popular tradition of festive class inversion. Continuities between theatrical performance and seasonal customs in early modern England indicate more than simply the existence of overlapping and contemporaneous cultural practices; they suggest that generic distinctions between theatre and festivity are, for this period, very difficult to sustain.[74] For Shakespeare's playgoers, the boundaries of performance were extremely porous, encompassing a range of spectacular entertainments integrated in complex ways into social life.

* * *

What lay within the permeable and flexible boundaries of the theatrical event is the subject of my first chapter, "Theorizing Theatrical Privilege." If not all moments in plays are created equal, which ones would the medium of early modern performance itself have privileged? Revising Robert Weimann's influential concepts of *locus* and *platea,* this chapter argues that theatrical authority derived not from stage geography and actor-audience interactivity but from the dynamic interplay between representation and presentation. Through careful analysis of a range of scenes from Shakespeare's plays, I demonstrate that moments in plays that self-referentially highlighted their own semiotic strategies were precisely those privileged by performance in early modern England. Building on this discussion, each of the subsequent chapters focuses on a different kind of theatrically privileged episode in order to illuminate the cultural implications of the performance medium.

Part II, "Theatrical Ways of Knowing," examines the historically specific perceptual and interpretive practices through which playgoers made sense of what they saw onstage. Chapter 2, "Staging Sight," begins with a seemingly simple question: What counted as an intentional theatrical signifier? Using as my case study the sonnet-reading episode from Shakespeare's *Love's Labor's Lost,* I demonstrate how visual paradigms in early modern art, science, and religion shaped which stage actions were understood as visible within the dramatic representation. Because these habits of mind run counter to the perceptual logics upon which modern scholarly reconstructions of Shakespearean stagecraft depend, I argue that they have significant implications for how we conceptualize early modern theatrical blocking and dramatic asides. Chapter 3, "Imaginary Forces," builds on this discussion of perception to address the modes of interpretation required by the medium of performance. Rather than assuming that spectators valued verisimilitude and thus used their imaginations to make onstage action seem more real, I demonstrate how overlaps between allegorical and mimetic modes in early modern theatre complicated the act of decoding performance. Juxtaposing several scenes from Kyd's *The Spanish Tragedy* with early modern accounts of ghosts, demons, and false dreams, I articulate the challenges early modern spectators faced when they attempted to decipher visual information presented onstage, and I show how these interpretive difficulties were not merely thematized within the dramatic fiction but woven into the semiotics of the medium itself. Metatheatricality and plays-within-plays, I contend, thus served not as dramatic commentary on the interplay between illusion and reality; rather, they integrated early modern understandings of spectatorship's moral and epistemological stakes into the very medium of performance.

In Part III, "Experiencing Embodied Spectacle," I turn to the presentational impact of spectacular display. Chapter 4, "Dancing and Other Delights," begins by analyzing how feats of physical skill were understood in travel narratives, medical texts, and other extratheatrical discourses in addition to the playhouses. I argue that the language of pleasure and delight, often used to describe spectator responses, encoded within it contradictory notions of spectacle as both healthfully refreshing and dangerously seductive. I then turn to two specific examples—the dance of the devils in Marlowe's *Doctor Faustus* and that of the witches in Shakespeare's *Macbeth*—to show how watching spectacle did not dazzle audience members into passivity (as we might assume from our post-Brechtian, post-Benjaminian perspective) but interpellated them as active participants complicit in what they saw. Playgoers, I maintain, were thus imagined as actors long after the audience's central role in medieval religious drama had supposedly disappeared, a dynamic that contributed to theatre's continued viability as a communal social practice. With chapter 5, "Artful Sport," I move from bodily feats directly experienced by audiences to spectacles produced through the power of representation. Early modern plays repeatedly foregrounded the semiotic practices through which property heads and limbs came to stand in for human parts. I argue that this theatrical tendency produced not a pseudo-Brechtian alienation effect but a peculiar emphasis on the ontological status of the actor's body. Focusing in particular on Shakespeare's *Titus Andronicus* and *Cymbeline* as well as Marlowe's *Doctor Faustus,* I analyze the theatrical effects generated when the theatrical constraints of staging violence clashed with cultural discourses surrounding justice, martyrdom, and murder. Bodily fragmentation in the playhouses, I reveal, functioned as enactment of festive sport, akin to popular practices such as football and animal baiting. Extending beyond the dramatic narrative, theatrical dismemberment served as efficacious performance, reinscribing paradigms of social integration that lay at the heart of the violence of stake, scaffold, and sport.

The kinds of questions with which this book concludes take us back full circle to the issue of materiality with which I began. In representing the *un*presentable, that which could not literally be shown onstage, theatrical violence made material the very social formations out of which early modern theatre grew. It exemplifies how performance produced the attitudes, discourses, and institutional structures that rendered it intelligible as a semiotic system. The process through which theatre became culturally legible and the consequences of its performance dynamics were bound up with the historical particularities of early modern England. Yet the story I tell is ultimately not just about Shakespeare's theatre but about performance as a material medium. Foucault describes the system of implicit cultural rules that constitute the historical a priori as that which can only be seen from the outside: "[I]t is not possible," he says, "for us to describe our own archive, since it is from within these rules that we speak."[75] The cultural meanings and effects produced by performance may be more difficult to see in a contemporary context whose epistemological categories and generic forms permeate our everyday lives. Looking at early modern theatre, then, is one way of imaginatively exploring how performance might function in our own era. Performance as a material practice is historically specific; as a materializing force, however, it is not of an age but for all time.

Chapter 1

Theorizing Theatrical Privilege: Rethinking Weimann's Concepts of *Locus* and *Platea*

Not all moments in plays are created equal. Some scenes, characters, and actions imprint themselves indelibly on the minds of theatregoers, whereas others are quickly forgotten. The plays of Shakespeare and his contemporaries are often used as evidence for sixteenth- and seventeenth-century social attitudes and practices, yet interpreting these references without considering the varying impact of different moments in performance can skew our perceptions of the cultural landscape. Soliloquies affected spectators differently from dialogue; pronouncements made during battles scenes were less likely to have been heard than those during quieter interludes. Such concerns shaped the experiences of early modern audience members, yet drama has often been read in a "flat" way, as if its discursive practices were verbal utterances separate from the material conditions of performance. To understand the cultural implications and effects of early modern theatre, we must first theorize how the performance medium shaped the impact of different moments in plays.

This chapter maps the contours of the medium of performance by asking which elements might have been most privileged by early modern dramaturgy. It lays the groundwork for subsequent chapters by theorizing the relative weight accorded to different aspects of performance, aspects whose cultural valences I explore later in this book. I take as my starting point Robert Weimann's well-established but still enormously influential concepts of *locus* and *platea*. I suggest both the ways his formulation is useful and the ways it needs to be revised. Then, focusing, as Weimann does, primarily on Shakespeare's plays, I propose an alternative model for understanding the authority of performance in early modern drama. This analysis establishes the foundational principles through which early modern theatre produced its effects and outlines the kinds of privileged moments that will be investigated in greater detail in later chapters.

Weimann's Influence: Dramaturgical Authority and Stage Geography

In his theory first laid out in *Shakespeare and the Popular Tradition in the Theater*, Robert Weimann argues that the dramaturgy of Shakespeare's theatre derived from popular traditions of medieval stagecraft.[1] He identifies two key locations on the stage, each embodying a specific mode of performance and serving as a particular expression of social authority. The *locus* was "a scaffold, be it a *domus, sedes,* or throne," and was the playing area that was most distant from the audience.[2] Associated with it were "a rudimentary element of verisimilitude" and the representation of "fixed, symbolic locations."[3] By contrast, the *platea* was a "platform-like acting area" situated closest to the audience. On the *platea*, "the play world continue[d] to be frankly treated as a theatrical dimension of the real world," and this nonillusionistic mode of performance corresponded to "unlocalized" or "neutral" space.[4] Each of these locations was further associated with a particular place in the social hierarchy:

> As a rule, it was the more highly ranked persons who sat on the scaffolds: God the father, the "King" in *The Pride of Life*, Decius (enthroned as in the Fouquet miniature). Significantly, while some high-born members of the audience were also seated on these scaffolds, or at any rate on neighboring scaffolds, the ordinary public stood crowded below in the *champ*. This was the case in *The Castle of Perseverance*: the noble "syrys semly" sat at the sides of the scaffolds while the simple "wytis" were in the "pleyn place," that is, in the middle of the green or field. It was among these simple folk, or in front of them, that soldiers and serfs, the shouting messenger of "N-town," and of course the devil, grimacing "in the most oryble wyse" (465–66), played their parts.[5]

For Weimann, "[t]he proximity between actor and audience was not only a physical condition, it was at once the foundation and the expression of a specific artistic endeavor."[6] Servants, clowns, and other *platea* characters shared the low social rank of plebeian spectators. Their physical closeness to audience members simultaneously expressed these social affinities and promoted interactivity between playgoers and performers. Kings and other highborn figures in the *locus* were both physically and socially removed from that sphere. The physical distance and social exclusivity of the *locus* discouraged actor-audience exchanges and led to greater dramatic isolation. The elite, rhetorical knowledge of the *locus* was balanced by the *platea*'s assertion of the plebeian audience's "collective understanding of the world…rooted in the common experience and inherited traditions of the people," a "viable alternative" or "counterperspective" to the "main or state view of things."[7] What is particularly striking about Weimann's formulation is the way in which it inverts expectations about theatrical authority. Even though *locus* characters had high social status within the fictional world of the play, the interactivity of the *platea* meant that characters with little social authority were, in fact, more *theatrically* privileged.[8]

The widespread influence of Weimann's work can be seen in the now-commonplace assumptions that soliloquies were spoken in the downstage area of the platform and that clowns and Vice figures were popular because of their highly interactive engagement with the audience. A quick look at a number of critical conversations suggests the impact of Weimann's work on a variety of different fields.

Introductory texts geared toward undergraduates regularly draw on Weimann's concepts. For example, in *Theory/Theatre: An Introduction,* Mark Fortier notes that "upstage is mainly a place for authoritative pronouncements" whereas "the lip of the stage is a place for characters to become informal and intimate with the lower-class audience."[9] In *Shakespeare's Theatre,* Peter Thomson remarks that "[t]he distinction between downstage and upstage at the Globe defines the relationship of the actor and his audience.... Whilst King Lear remains regal, he will keep his distance, but the experience of the heath can carry him down to the edges and corners of the platform, where the Fool and Clown will always be at ease."[10] Weimann's work has also had an impact on theatre practitioners and performance critics. In his lengthy history of Shakespeare productions in Germany, Wilhelm Hortmann devotes an entire chapter to East German theatre during the 1960s and 1970s. He describes Weimann's *Shakespeare and the Popular Tradition in the Theater* as "[a]fter Brecht, the greatest single influence on Shakespeare stagings in East Germany at the time."[11] In analyzing the more recent 1997 Rylance/Olivier production of *Henry V* at the New Globe, Yu Jin Ko draws on Weimann's theories in order to explain the interplay of subversion and containment in modern performance.[12] Teachers, students, and those engaged in producing and critiquing contemporary theatre have all been affected by Weimann's work.

Literary scholars, especially those engaged in materialist and historicist criticism, have also been drawn to Weimann. Focusing less on his theories of theatre and more on his analysis of cultural authority, these critics foreground the *platea* as a space of resistance to established social hierarchies. In their introduction to *Staging the Renaissance,* David Scott Kastan and Peter Stallybrass stress that "[c]ultures should... be seen less as bounded wholes than as articulations of uneven temporalities and contradictory discursive practices." They cite Weimann's work as an example of this critical approach, noting that "[p]opular staging practices... regularly shift the action between an upstage *locus* and a downstage *plataea* [*sic*] and thus continually displace the dominant aristocratic ideology, submitting its postures and assumptions to the interrogation of clowns and commoners."[13] Anticipating Weimann's own emphasis in *Author's Pen and Actor's Voice,* Richard Helgerson connects these ideological concerns with issues of orality and literacy: the *platea,* he suggests, "belongs to the actor" and functions as "a space given over to unauthorized speech and action. In this respect the author's perspective was shared by the state.... The unitary voice of the author and the unitary voice of the state would gladly combine to exclude the clown's disruptive and discordant improvisation."[14] Jean Howard and Phyllis Rackin find the ideological implications of Weimann's work valuable for feminist interpretations of Shakespeare's plays. In their discussion of women's roles in *Richard III,* they note that "[e]nobled" female characters move "into the privileged *locus* of hegemonic representation," which simultaneously "subsumes them into the patriarchal project of that representation and distances them from the present theater audience."[15] For all of these historicist scholars, the *platea* embodies the subversive potential of popular performance. Because of Weimann's engagement with questions of authority, his work has been particularly useful to scholars concerned with the ideological implications of early modern drama. As Louis Montrose remarks, "Dialectical, historicist, and materialist work has become central to the study of Shakespeare in the United States and Britain since the publication of *Shakespeare and the Popular Tradition in the Theater;* and such work—including mine—has been enabled by the critical perspective announced and exemplified in Weimann's landmark book."[16]

A major strength of Weimann's work, then, is its ability to bring together performance concerns with literary criticism and cultural history.[17] Many scholars have explored the material and social contexts surrounding early modern theatre as a cultural institution.[18] Others have analyzed the plays of Shakespeare and his contemporaries from more theatrical or stage-centered perspectives.[19] However, while spectacle and "theatricality" have been examined in relation to ideology, the gap between historicist literary criticism and theatre history is still marked where studies of early modern drama are concerned. As W. B. Worthen notes, "actual stage performance" is frequently omitted from New Historicist projects that aim to situate drama "within the discourses of cultural life": "Whether by design or by default, literary criticism of the drama tends to assign the textualities of performance to the subjective caprice of the actor's freedom."[20] Performance criticism, in turn, suffers from its own unique blind spots. Stage-centered scholarship on early modern drama has traditionally imagined performance as "a way to recover meanings intrinsic to the text,"[21] and reconstructions of early modern stagecraft are often intended to illuminate literary "themes." Moreover, few historians of early modern theatre regularly incorporate the theoretical insights and challenges to positivist historiography that have been such central tenets of the field ever since the advent of poststructuralism and subsequent dominance of New Historicism.

Weimann's work very usefully bridges the gap between historicist literary criticism and studies by performance-oriented critics and theatre historians. In his initial discussion of *locus* and *platea* in *Shakespeare and the Popular Tradition in the Theater,* Weimann combined "literary" close reading techniques with historical inquiry in order to explore the different linguistic registers constituting early English dramaturgy. His more recent book complicates his earlier emphasis on the verbal aspects of plays and draws more extensively on poststructuralist theory and historicist methodologies.[22] Such an integrated approach has important implications for current and future interdisciplinary scholarship. Most historicist scholars focus primarily on the verbal aspects of plays at the expense of more evanescent aspects of theatre. Attention, therefore, often centers on the fictional worlds represented within plays, rather than on the strategies through which those worlds are created. Limiting investigations in this way emphasizes elite, verbal ways of knowing the world while effacing less textually oriented forms of cultural production. The resulting research may inadvertently reproduce class hierarchies even when intended to critique them. Moreover, ignoring the impact of performance on the transmission of cultural discourses can lead to fundamental misinterpretations of their original effects. Scholars who examine, say, early modern travel and empire, useful and necessary topics of investigation, might focus on plays that depict foreigners or racialized subjects. However, statements by a *locus* character about empire would have had a different impact on early modern playgoers from statements on the same subject by a *platea* figure. Focusing on the nonverbal aspects of plays and on the relationship between actors and audience members allows us to take into account not only what occurs within the fictional story but also the means by which that representation was effected. Weimann's methodology points the way to such fruitful avenues for interdisciplinary collaboration between stage-centered and historicist criticism.

So far I have focused primarily on the value of Weimann's work. I would like to turn now to one of its more problematic aspects. Although Weimann himself has repeatedly emphasized the "fluidity" of early modern dramaturgy and its capacity to "sustain...both illusionistic and nonillusionistic effects" at the same time,[23] scholars who appropriate the concepts of *locus* and *platea* sometimes apply distinctions of stage geography too literally. This critical tendency is especially apparent when Weimann's work is cited only in passing. In such cases, the upstage-downstage dichotomy is often presented as central to the definition of *locus* and *platea*.[24] Even studies more deeply engaged with Weimann's work tend to reduce his theory to a rather binary schematic. Michael Mooney, for instance, in his "well-focused study,"[25] applies Weimann's "complex idea of *Figurenposition* (or 'figural positioning')" to Shakespeare's tragedies.[26] Although Mooney admits that "a character *did not* have to move, literally, in order to create a shift in *Figurenposition*," his investment in "the 'traditional interplay' between a downstage place (or *platea*) and an upstage location (or *locus*)"[27] means that the spatial component of Weimann's formulation still figures very prominently throughout his work.

This tendency to foreground Weimann's upstage-downstage distinction might be attributed in part to the dearth of adequate terminology for describing certain dramaturgical dynamics. In studies of early English drama, spatial metaphors have long been used to describe the phenomenology of theatre. As early as 1944, S. L. Bethell asserted that "[d]eliberate emphasis upon the unreality of the play world...reinforces the double consciousness of play world and real world, and at the same time...distances the play as play and produces intimacy with the audience for the actor as actor rather than as character."[28] Spatial terminology has often been applied rather loosely; Weimann's use, by contrast, is incredibly specific. In grounding the immaterial, evanescent dynamics of performance in the concrete terminology of physical space, Weimann's use of *locus* and *platea* offers an appealing alternative to such slippery dramaturgical concepts as "ironic distance" and "dramatic intimacy."

Emphasis on the spatial aspect of Weimann's theory might also derive from the centrality of the "fourth wall" as an interpretive paradigm. When Weimann posits a "difference between the imaginary landscape inscribed in the story and the physical, tangible site of its production" and argues that drama could "constitute at best an 'indifferent boundary' between them,"[29] he reinscribes the barrier separating actors and playgoers even as he argues for its permeability. The upstage *locus* is associated with "Romantic obsession with character," the downstage *platea* with the breaking of theatrical illusion.[30] Weimann's more recent work, coauthored with Douglas Bruster, exhibits similar critical tendencies when it describes prologues as "interactive, liminal, boundary-breaking entities" that help usher audience members across the "threshold" between the world of the playhouse and the world of the play.[31] In Weimann's work, the *locus* constructs an invisible line separating actors from spectators, whereas the *platea* dissolves it, but the ontological status of that line remains unchanged. The stress placed upon the spatial component of Weimann's theory is encouraged by the pervasiveness of this conceptual paradigm.

Reading the *locus* as "upstage" and the *platea* as "downstage" is also particularly appealing because it transposes alien, medieval notions of space onto architectural forms more familiar to modern playgoers. The *OED*'s first recorded use of the word *upstage* is dated 1870, and *downstage* does not appear until 1898.[32] These terms grew out of the architectural specificities of proscenium arch theatres. The rear, elevated portion of a raked platform stage might appropriately be referred to as "upstage," but this same word cannot be applied with any degree of rigor to early modern playhouses. We might imagine that "upstage" in the outdoor amphitheatres was closer to the facade and that to move "downstage" was to walk between the posts to the "front" edge of the platform closest to the standing spectators in the yard. However, such an imaginary reconstruction is based on our own visual paradigms and conceptions of theatre. Modern theatres are constructed around sightlines. Audience members with the best vantage points for viewing a performance—that is, those in box seats or in the center orchestra—are charged the highest prices. Early modern playhouses functioned under a very different set of cultural assumptions. At the reconstructed Globe today, seats are "priced according to visibility."[33] Tickets for the front rows of the lowest gallery across the yard from the stage are £37.50 each—the most expensive category of seats in the house. In Shakespeare's day, those same seats were sometimes "associated rather with the standers in the yard"[34] and were much less desirable than the Lords' Rooms, which are priced at only £25 today. The fact that the Lords' Rooms in the original Globe should now be considered less desirable than the lowest gallery suggests something of the gap between modern and early modern conceptions of theatre. The shape, location, and architectural features of playhouses will certainly produce dramaturgical dynamics, but understanding the ways in which they do so requires historicizing bodily experiences and cultural discourses around space.[35] Our own implicit assumptions about visuality and theatre are only the tip of the iceberg, given the complex ways in which physical perception and sensation interact with social formations to produce theatrical effects. When we take such differences into account, dispensing with the upstage-downstage aspect of Weimann's formulation seems more and more appropriate.

Andrew Gurr has attempted to revise the spatial component of Weimann's theory by rearticulating *locus* and *platea* in terms of center and periphery: "The official speakers stood in the centre, while the commentators and clowns prowled around the flanks." In *Richard III,* he argues, the title character, "crouching at the stage edge and speaking in soliloquy to the crowd at his feet" at the beginning of the play, eventually moves "to occupy the centre of the stage" when he becomes king.[36] However, replacing the upstage-downstage binary with a center-periphery model does little to address the problem of physical proximity. Given the shape and layout of early modern amphitheatres, it is difficult to know how to define "proximity" at all. In Shakespeare's playhouse, where there was seating in the galleries as well as in the yard, the "above" portion of the stage and the area of the main platform closest to the facade would have been closer to some audience members than the so-called "downstage" area traditionally assigned to the *platea*. Audience members were also distributed horizontally, surrounding the thrust stage on three—or sometimes even four—sides. The stage at the Fortune was about 43 feet wide, and the dimensions at the Globe were probably similar. The stage at the Rose was just a bit smaller— 36 feet, 9 inches at its widest point, tapering to about 26 feet, 10 inches at the front.[37]

Figure 1.1 Sketch of the view from the Lords' Rooms at the Globe: "downstage left" as seen from "stage right" second gallery. © Erika T. Lin 2012.

Given both the horizontal and the vertical distribution of playgoers, being closer to some audience members meant being significantly farther from others. Actors located in what we might describe today as "downstage left" would be significantly "upstage" when seen from the perspective of spectators on "stage right" (figure 1.1). Even if one might make a sociological argument for the overall dramaturgical unity of the audience's response, one cannot make a very convincing case for the unity of their literal physical locations. Defining *locus* and *platea* in terms of the distance between performers and spectators becomes very problematic.

Revising *Locus* and *Platea*: Space, Sight, Sound

I have been focusing here on stage geography not because Weimann's theory can be reduced merely to its spatial component but because exploring this aspect of his work suggests useful avenues for reconceptualizing the performance medium. I would like to turn now to an examination of some specific examples from Shakespeare's plays. In analyzing these scenes, I will begin with the use of stage space and its implications for *locus* and *platea*. My ultimate goal, however, is to map out an alternative model for theorizing theatrical performance, one that builds on Weimann's concepts and revises them for a more precise understanding of the elements that might have been privileged by early modern performance.

In *King Lear*, when Edgar leads the blind Gloucester to the cliffs of Dover, Edgar speaks to the audience directly in numerous asides, but Gloucester does not. Weimann argues that the *platea* is the site of actor-audience interaction, so his theory would assign Edgar to the *platea* and Gloucester to the *locus*. However, is Edgar actually physically closer to the audience? The scene requires Edgar to be right next to Gloucester as he leads him; perhaps they are even physically touching. At one point, Gloucester says to Edgar, "Set me where you stand" (TLN 2460; 4.6.24), suggesting that at this particular moment Gloucester will quite literally stand in the same location on the stage as Edgar. Although Gloucester is in the *locus* and Edgar is in the *platea*, both occupy the same space on the platform stage.

In *All's Well That Ends Well*, when Parolles is "ambushed" by his fellow soldiers and made to think he has been captured by the enemy, the spatial aspect of *locus* and *platea* also fails in interesting ways. Upon entering the scene (TLN 1936; 4.1.23), Parolles speaks directly to the audience in soliloquy, an action that, according to Weimann's formulation, should bring him closer to spectators in terms of stage location as well as emotional connection. However, Parolles's soliloquy is continually interrupted by the Second Lord's asides. These asides might be addressed either to playgoers or to the other soldiers. If addressed to the audience, we might interpret the Second Lord and Parolles as dramaturgically parallel. Both share the same degree of affective intimacy with playgoers since both speak directly to the audience; both are therefore located in the theatrically privileged *platea*. However, the scene requires that Parolles be unable to see the Second Lord. His back must be toward the Second Lord and the other soldiers, and his face must be toward the audience. The most obvious way to stage this scene is to place the Second Lord next to the playhouse facade and Parolles next to the edge of the stage. In this scene from *All's Well That Ends Well*, two characters residing in the *platea* are situated in different locations on the stage. In the episode from *King Lear*, Edgar and Gloucester, two characters with differing degrees of theatrical authority, are positioned in the same location on the stage. Not only is there no correlation between theatrical authority and stage geography in these two scenes, but the dynamics of performance run directly counter to Weimann's theory.

Of course, there is another way to imagine the scene from *All's Well That Ends Well*: all of the actors could be located near the edges of the stage. Parolles might be, say, "downstage left," facing the audience on that side of the playhouse. The Second Lord and his soldiers would be located on the opposite end of the platform—what we might call "downstage right." Such a configuration would support Weimann's formulation: both Parolles and the Second Lord are in the *platea*, and both are equidistant from the audience. However, when Parolles is blindfolded by the other soldiers (TLN 1980; 4.1.67), he seems to move out of the *platea* and into the *locus*. This shift takes place both dramaturgically (he no longer speaks directly to the audience) and physically (because his back need not be facing the others, he may now be placed farther away from the edge of the stage). Yet, at least initially, one of the soldiers must be physically touching Parolles in order to blindfold him. As in the scene with Edgar and Gloucester, even though the location of the two characters onstage is essentially the same, their dramaturgical dynamics are not equivalent. When the soldiers return again with Parolles in act 4, scene 3, Parolles is blindfolded. Regardless of where he stands, he cannot see the other characters. Both he and the other characters may now be situated anywhere on the stage, and there are no further textual clues about these locations. In both of these episodes, spatial distinctions between *locus* and *platea* are complicated by the dynamics of spectatorship.

Indeed, the issue of sight throws quite a wrench into the works. In scenes such as the ones I have been discussing, in order to watch the *locus* character without being seen, the *platea* character must be either *literally* "upstage" (that is, closer to the facade) or *effectively* "upstage" for part of the audience (that is, the *platea* character will be farthest from playgoers who are directly in front of the *locus* character). Furthermore, in scenes where one character is blind, the need for that character to be touched (here, led or blindfolded) means that *locus* and *platea* spatial distinctions cannot be literalized since two characters will, at least momentarily, inhabit the same part of the stage.[38] Although it is clear that we cannot correlate dramaturgical authority with Weimann's ideas about stage space, scenes that contradict Weimann's theory in these ways also suggest some useful directions for revising the concepts of *locus* and *platea*. I want to turn now to a closer examination of the dynamics of spectatorship. From here on in, I will use the terms *locus* and *platea* without implying any spatial considerations but instead as shorthand to indicate the dramaturgical dynamics that Weimann associates with each term.

In *Shakespeare and the Popular Tradition in the Theater*, when Weimann discusses act 5, scene 2 of *Troilus and Cressida*, he seems to admit that spectatorship is an important factor in *locus* and *platea*. In this scene, "Cressida's meeting with Diomedes is watched from a distance by Troilus and Ulysses, who likewise are being watched by Thersites."[39] Thersites, Weimann argues, is more in the *platea* than the other characters because he "acts from a more nearly neutralized place where he can watch and hear the others but cannot be watched or heard by them."[40] In his more recent work, Weimann again points to the importance of the visual for the dramaturgy of this scene:

> In the performed event, certain characters, such as Cressida and Diomed [*sic*], *represent* a fairly self-contained action, presumably in front of the *locus* provided by Calchas' tent. At the same time, there is at least one performer who, not being "lost" in the representation, *presents* it and, through the "abuse of distance" (*Henry V* 2.0.32), views it in perspective. In doing so, the player playing Thersites remains unobserved and is not overheard by these characters or, for that matter, those intermediate personages, Troilus and Ulysses, who hide and watch.[41]

Both in his earlier book and in his more recent one, Weimann's reading of this scene highlights certain implicit aspects of his formulation. Stage geography, social legitimacy, and actor-audience interactivity are not the only important factors; *locus* and *platea* are also determined by whether a character is watching or being watched.

In *King Lear,* then, Edgar is more in the *platea* than Gloucester not only because Edgar interacts more with the audience but also because Gloucester is blind and Edgar can see. Edgar can observe Gloucester but cannot, in turn, be seen by him. In *All's Well That Ends Well,* the Second Lord is more in the *platea* because he sees Parolles but cannot be seen himself. In both of these episodes, the dramaturgical implications of spectatorship are literalized through the inclusion of blind or blindfolded characters. However, the same dynamics apply in scenes that do not involve physically impaired vision—in *Twelfth Night,* for instance, when Sir Toby, Sir Andrew, and Fabian spy on Malvolio reading the letter (act 2, scene 5), and in *Love's Labor's Lost,* when each of the four lords betrays his love for one of the ladies of France and then hides to observe the next confession (act 4, scene 3).[42]

Weimann's discussion of the scene from *Troilus and Cressida* suggests that sound also contributes to the dynamics of *locus* and *platea*: it is important that Thersites can be neither seen nor heard. In *King Lear,* because Edgar's asides cannot be heard by Gloucester, he does indeed seem to be more situated in the *platea*. In *All's Well That Ends Well,* even if the Second Lord's asides are addressed to the other onstage characters and not directly to the audience, he can hear Parolles but cannot be heard himself and is therefore located in the *platea*. Likewise, Toby, Andrew, and Fabian's comments to one another from the boxtree and Berowne, the King, and Longaville's asides to the audience all situate them more in the *platea* than the object of their observations. What is particularly interesting is that, in all of these cases, the dynamics of sight and sound seem to take precedence not only over upstage-downstage distinctions but also over the privileges granted to actor-audience interactivity. In other words, even if the character being watched and heard communicates directly with the audience in the tradition of the *platea*—as Malvolio in *Twelfth Night,* each successive lord in *Love's Labor's Lost,* and Parolles in *All's Well That Ends Well* do—that character still functions as a *locus* character. Being watched and heard apparently puts one in the *locus*. In the dynamics of sight and sound, it seems that *platea* characters are the active doers of the action, and *locus* characters are the passive receivers of the action. The difference between *platea* and *locus* in theatrical practice is the difference between subject and object.

Or is it? Act 2, scene 3 of *Much Ado About Nothing* raises some interesting questions. Here, the gulling of Benedick positions him as the one who watches and hears the other men. In the corresponding women's scene (act 3, scene 1), the same dynamics apply to Beatrice. On the surface, these two scenes appear to be the reverse of the other ones I have been discussing: the person being gulled is the one who hides and watches. Beatrice and Benedick are the active "subjects"; the characters on whom they eavesdrop are the passive "objects." However, in both of these scenes, the people being scrutinized are not only well aware of their secret observers but have, in fact, manufactured the situations for the express purpose of being overseen and overheard. Benedick may spy on the Prince, Claudio, and Leonato, and Beatrice may eavesdrop on Hero and Ursula, but their obliviousness to the fact that they, too, are being observed situates them more firmly in the *locus*. Modern theories of "the gaze" contend that the object of the gaze is disempowered; the privileged subject is the one doing the watching. In the early modern theatre, however, being the object of observation was actually a powerful position. During spectacles and pageants, monarchs consolidated their authority by exposing themselves to the gaze of their subjects. Status-conscious gallants sought out the envious glances of those too poor to afford their finery. In early modern England, being the subject of the gaze was not necessarily better than being its object. Merely being watched or heard does not situate one in the *locus;* rather being watched or heard *unawares* does.[43]

So far I have been grouping sight and sound together as I explore their theatrical ramifications, and it does seem that in many cases sound contributes to the dynamics of *locus* and *platea* in precisely the same ways as sight. In *All's Well That Ends Well,* Parolles is situated in the *locus* as a result of not being able to "look back," but his *locus*-like orientation is compounded by his inability to, shall we say, "hear back." His fellow soldiers speak an imaginary foreign language to make Parolles believe they are "some band of strangers i'th aduersaries entertainment" (TLN 1926–27; 4.1.14–15). Indeed, before the Second Lord allows one of the soldiers to serve as "Interpreter" (TLN 1918; 4.1.6), he asks whether Parolles will recognize the soldier's voice: "Art not acquainted with him? knowes he not thy voice?" (TLN 1920–21; 4.1.8–9). It is only when the answer comes back in the negative that the Second Lord agrees to let him serve as translator. From the *locus,* Parolles can be heard, but he does not properly "hear back." In the scene from *King Lear,* Gloucester's inability to "hear back" likewise situates him in the *locus.* After Gloucester has supposedly fallen down the precipice, Edgar pretends to be a passerby who happens upon the older man's body at the base of the cliffs. Edgar's speech patterns here—at least as they are represented in the playtext—do not differ noticeably from those earlier in the scene. Although these lines might have been inflected differently in performance, such variations in tone are usually recorded orthographically in early modern published playtexts.[44] When Edgar speaks to Oswald toward the end of this same scene, the text registers a change in his voice as he slips into and out of "peasant" dialect. There is no indication that Gloucester notices any of these inconsistencies. His hearing appears to be just as impaired as his vision, and this obliviousness positions him more firmly in the *locus.* Edgar can look at Gloucester, but the older man cannot, in turn, "look back." Edgar hears everything that Gloucester says, but his father cannot accurately "hear back."

But what does it mean to not "hear back"? Sound envelops the listener. Rather than emanating from one particular fixed point, it comes to the listener from multiple and indeterminate angles. Whereas the ability to see is primarily dependent on direction, the ability to hear is primarily dependent on distance. "Hearing back" per se is not actually possible.[45] In the scenes from *King Lear* and *All's Well That Ends Well,* the problem is really one of mistaken identity: Parolles imagines he has been kidnapped by the enemy; Gloucester believes his son is poor, mad Tom. "Hearing back," then, might more appropriately be described as the ability to accurately determine the relationship between someone's voice and that person's identity. In the episode from *King Lear,* however, Gloucester doesn't simply misidentify Edgar but also mistakenly thinks he is at the cliffs of Dover. At the beginning of the scene, Edgar asks Gloucester, "Hearke, do you heare the Sea?" (TLN 2435; 4.6.4). Not more than 20 lines later, Edgar contradicts himself, saying, "The murmuring Surge, / That on th'vnnumbred idle Pebble chafes / Cannot be heard so high" (TLN 2455–57; 4.6.20–22). Gloucester lets this inconsistency go unremarked and blindly trusts (or should I say "deafly trusts"?) the beggar who is leading him. The gulling scenes from *Much Ado About Nothing* function in a similar way. Benedick can easily and accurately identify the Prince, Claudio, and Leonato, and Beatrice has no trouble recognizing Hero and Ursula; in a different sense, though, both characters are unable to "hear back." Beatrice and Benedick believe that the conversations they overhear are genuine. They are unable to perceive them for what they "truly" are—key elements in an elaborate prank. To "hear back," then, not only requires the ability to correctly determine characters' identities but also depends on properly interpreting aural signifiers. A consideration of sight and sound has allowed us to revise how we define *locus* and *platea*: the more accurately characters can relate what is presented visually or aurally on the stage to what that presentational element "really" signifies within the theatrical representation, the more those characters are in the *platea*.

An Alternative Model of Theatrical Authority

Let's return now to the scene from *King Lear* in order to further nuance this model of theatrical performance. In the episode at the cliffs of Dover, Edgar misleads Gloucester into thinking they are near the precipice by describing at length what Gloucester cannot see:

> Come on Sir,
> Heere's the place: stand still: how fearefull
> And dizie 'tis, to cast ones eyes so low,
> The Crowes and Choughes, that wing the midway ayre
> Shew scarse so grosse as Beetles. Halfe way downe
> Hangs one that gathers Sampire: dreadfull Trade:
> Me thinkes he seemes no bigger then his head.
> The Fishermen, that walk'd vpon the beach
> Appeare like Mice: and yond tall Anchoring Barke,
> Diminish'd to her Cocke: her Cocke, a Buoy
> Almost too small for sight. The murmuring Surge,
> That on th'vnnumbred idle Pebble chafes
> Cannot be heard so high. Ile looke no more,
> Least my braine turne, and the deficient sight
> Topple downe headlong. (TLN 2445–59; 4.6.11–24)[46]

Here, the *platea*-like Edgar uses the same technique to deceive Gloucester that early modern actors used to create the world of the play: he constructs imaginary space by describing it through words. Gloucester, unaware of imagined space, seems likewise unaware of the actual space of the theatre. His obliviousness both to the actual performance event and to the representational strategies of real-life actors is here contrasted with Edgar's canny awareness and adept deployment of theatrical conventions. In foregrounding these differences, the play grants Edgar more dramaturgical authority; it situates him in the *platea*. Theatrical privilege, then, is not only about the accurate interpretation of aural and visual signifiers but is also a function of the way verbal cues construct imaginary space. We might revise our model as follows: the more characters are aware of the playhouse conventions through which visual, aural, and verbal cues onstage come to signify within the represented fiction, the more they are in the *platea*.

But what should we make of the end of this scene? When Lear appears at the cliffs of Dover, Gloucester demonstrates truly remarkable hearing abilities. Upon the king's entrance, he first declares, "I know that voice" (TLN 2542; 4.6.95), and then adds, "The tricke of that voyce, I do well remember: / Is't not the King?" (TLN 2552–53; 4.6.106–7). His astuteness is surprising: Lear, as far as we can tell from the playtext, sounds nothing like himself at all. The king now sounds mad, significantly madder than when Gloucester left him at the end of act 3, scene 6. This episode resonates with the beginning of the scene. When Gloucester declares that he does not hear the sea, Edgar insists that the older man's hearing must be impaired:

> [*Edg.*] Hearke, do you heare the Sea?
> *Glou.* No truly.
> *Edg.* Why then your other Senses grow imperfect
> By your eyes anguish.
> *Glou.* So may it be indeed.
> Me thinkes thy voyce is alter'd, and thou speak'st
> In better phrase, and matter then thou did'st.
> *Edg.* Y'are much deceiu'd: In nothing am I chang'd
> But in my Garments.
> *Glou.* Me thinkes y'are better spoken. (TLN 2435–44; 4.6.4–10)

Edgar's dismissal of his father's perceptual abilities only emphasizes the fact that, here at least, Gloucester hears quite accurately. The actor playing Edgar no longer adopts the discontinuous exclamations of Poor Tom; he *does* speak "[i]n better phrase, and matter."

The dynamics of voice intersect with questions of costuming in this scene. When Gloucester notices the change in Edgar's voice, Edgar responds, "Y'are much deceiu'd: In nothing am I chang'd / But in my Garments" (TLN 2442–43; 4.6.9–10). Gloucester's awareness of Edgar's vocal shift initially moves the older man into the *platea*, but Edgar then trumps his father by calling attention to his change in clothing.[47] In a theatre that makes extensive use of doubling, switching costumes is the same as switching characters. In fact, Edgar has already done so prior to this scene—and has played on the audience's uncertainty about it. Jean MacIntyre and Garrett Epp argue that such ambiguity rarely occurs in early modern drama:

> When a play's clothing cues are not accurate about sex or status, the audience can follow the play's action only if it is told that already familiar characters wear changed costumes.... Edgar announces his plan to disguise himself as Poor Tom (in 2.3) several scenes before he actually appears in his new costume, feigning madness (3.4); he maintains this disguise throughout that scene and well into the next before speaking as Edgar in one brief "aside" and the soliloquy that closes the scene (3.6). Few characters ever maintain so radical a disguise for more than one full scene, however, before somehow reminding the audience that they are indeed in disguise.[48]

In drawing attention to Edgar's costume changes and in connecting them with his multiple identities, the play reaffirms Edgar's *platea* status. The references to Edgar's vocal shifts serve a similar purpose. On the early modern stage, both costume and voice could constitute identity. In the anonymous play *Look About You*, characters repeatedly disguise themselves by adopting both the clothing and the speech impediments of other characters.[49] In *Twelfth Night*, Feste's change in voice fools Malvolio into thinking he is conversing with Sir Topas. At the scene at the cliffs of Dover, then, Edgar's reference to his own "chang'd...Garments" draws on a performance tradition where clothing and voice functioned as theatrical signifiers. Edgar's skillful description of the nonexistent ocean vista and his ironic allusions to costume and voice work together to align him more closely with the playhouse audience. Of all the characters in this scene, Edgar is the one who most often deploys the performance conventions that playgoers themselves used to interpret the play. The "proximity" to the audience that Weimann sees as the hallmark of *platea* characters might be better understood in terms of theatrical signifiers: the more a character articulates awareness of the playhouse conventions upon which audience members relied and the more he or she can manipulate those conventions within the represented fiction, the more that character is in the *platea*.

In order to nuance our ideas about *locus* and *platea* even further, I want to analyze one final example, this one from *1 Henry IV*. The references to costume in the scene from *King Lear* suggest that, in reformulating Weimann's concepts, the theatrical signifiers at stake include not only visual, aural, and verbal cues but also material objects. An episode toward the end of *1 Henry IV* suggests that theatrical signifiers also include material *subjects*—that is, the bodies of actors. In act 5, scene 4, when Prince Hal is locked in battle with Henry "Hotspur" Percy, the two men are interrupted by the entrance of Douglas. Falstaff, who has been watching Hal and Hotspur while trying to keep out of the conflict, is reluctantly forced into combat. The stage direction reads, "*Enter Dowglas, he fights with Falstaffe, who fals down as if he were dead. The Prince killeth Percie*" (TLN 3040–41; 5.4.76.s.d.). Immediately after the fight, Hal gazes upon the "dead" bodies of Hotspur and Falstaff and delivers a soliloquy. Both actions position the prince in the *platea*: he addresses the audience directly, and he looks upon bodies that are unable to "look back." However, shortly after Hal exits the stage, "*Falstaffe riseth vp*" (TLN 3076; 5.4.110.s.d.), revealing that he was not actually dead but was merely feigning death. Although earlier confined to the *locus,* Falstaff's revelation now situates him in the *platea*. Because he possesses a more accurate picture than Hal of what "really" happened during the fight, Falstaff's dramatic authority supersedes that of the prince. His speech also highlights another convention of early modern theatre. When Falstaff speaks directly to the audience, he confides his fear that Hotspur might not really be dead:

> I am affraide of this Gun-powder *Percy* though he be dead. How if hee should counterfeit too, and rise? I am afraid hee would proue the better counterfeit: therefore Ile make him sure: yea, and Ile sweare I kill'd him. Why may not hee rise as well as I[?] (TLN 3086–91; 5.4.121–26)

Falstaff's lines draw attention to the fact that, in the early modern playhouses, *all* "dead" people were, in fact, counterfeiting. Cadavers could not be literally presented onstage; the body of the actor stood in for the corpse.[50] Prince Hal may speak directly with the audience, and he may gaze upon bodies that cannot gaze back, but Falstaff's articulation of how bodies act as signifiers in theatre situates him more firmly in the *platea*.

And now we can reformulate Weimann's theory more completely. Rather than seeing *locus* and *platea* as functions of stage geography, social legitimacy, or actor-audience interactivity, it seems most useful to reconceptualize them in terms of the way presentational elements in performance come to signify within the represented fiction. Regardless of their status within the represented fiction of the play, those characters who articulate the most awareness of this theatrical semiotics and who showcase their ability to manipulate such signifiers are privileged by the performance medium. Because this theatrical semiotics *is* the system by which playgoers create meaning in the early modern playhouse, Weimann is right that what is privileged in performance is a function of the actor-audience relationship. However, Weimann is wrong in suggesting that certain figures might be understood specifically as *platea* characters.[51] Certain scenes or parts of scenes can also foreground theatrical conventions, even if characters within them do not. The feigned storm scene in act 4, scene 1 of *The Two Noble Kinsmen*, for example, draws attention to the phenomenological impossibility of distinguishing between a fake storm and a "real" storm on the bare platform stage. It emphasizes the necessity of verbal cues, actors' movements, and props in signifying what cannot be presented literally on the stage. So while certain characters utilize the *platea* techniques more often, the terms *locus* and *platea* inherently describe presentational dynamics of performance, not characters. A theory of what is privileged in early modern theatrical performance might best be formulated, then, as follows: regardless of *who* is socially privileged within the world of the play and regardless of *what* is privileged, thematically or otherwise, in a text-based analysis, moments in these plays that foregrounded the process by which elements presented onstage came to signify within the represented fiction were *theatrically privileged*.

If embedded in the signifying practices of the early modern theatre was an entire system of social relations and cultural understandings specific to that time, then theorizing the relationship between the presentational and the representational is a necessary first step to enriching both our conceptions about Shakespeare's theatre and our interpretations of early modern history and culture. With a fuller sense of the topography of performance, let us now turn to a deeper analysis of these theatrically privileged moments.

Part II

Theatrical Ways of Knowing

Chapter 2

Staging Sight: Visual Paradigms and Perceptual Strategies in *Love's Labor's Lost*

Shakespeare's *Love's Labor's Lost* opens with the king of Navarre and three of his lords firmly forswearing women, but when the princess of France and her three ladies come to town, the courtiers' resolve promptly crumbles. In a complicated scene at the end of act 4, each of the lords, unaware that he is being observed, recites a poem revealing his love for one of the ladies of France. In reverse order, each then steps forward to chastise his compatriots—only to have his own hypocrisy revealed.

This episode poses some peculiar challenges for theatrical performance, challenges that point to crucial overlaps between theatrical modes of perception and those found elsewhere in early modern culture. Each of the lords must be positioned onstage so that he may spy on the others while remaining blissfully unaware that his own confession has already been witnessed. Unless carefully arranged, the blocking of the scene quickly renders it implausible. As Bernard Shaw once put it, we have an "absolutely impossible situation," with

> Biron hiding in the tree to overlook the king, who presently hides to watch Longaville, who in turn spies on Dumain; as the result of which we had three out of four gentlemen shouting "asides" through the sylvan stillness, No. 1 being inaudible to 2, 3, and 4; No. 2 audible to No. 1, but not to 3 and 4; No. 3 audible to 1 and 2, but not to No. 4; and No. 4 audible to all the rest, but himself temporarily stone deaf.[1]

As Shaw's comments suggest, the scene must be orchestrated so that sensory perception functions in credible ways, yet the staging requirements of this highly schematic episode are daunting. The four men are situated in analogous positions on the stage and engaged in analogous activities. They are to some extent interchangeable—Shaw refers to them simply as numbers—yet the narrative requires that playgoers be able to differentiate who can and cannot be seen or heard by each of the other characters.

In today's theatre, when actors deliver asides, they frequently hide, move away from one another, or at least turn their heads to face the audience. In addition, spotlights are sometimes illuminated to isolate speakers onstage. Such gestures and lighting cues are visual signifiers used to represent aural phenomena taking place within the imaginary world of the play. So long as these symbolic markers are present, convention dictates that asides cannot be heard by other characters, regardless of how loudly an actor speaks. This disjunction between presentational signifier and representational signified, between what can be heard in the actual playhouse and what can be heard within the imaginary world of the play, is something we take for granted. Sound, in other words, does not need to function mimetically in order for it to be theatrically credible.

Visual dynamics onstage, however, require a greater degree of verisimilitude. Today's performance conventions, inherited from late nineteenth-century theatre, dictate that if actors can see one another, so can their characters. Stage space and fictional space are here collapsed into each other, and the same physics govern them both. The production of *Love's Labor's Lost* that Shaw describes flouted this convention—to disastrous effect—when Berowne attached himself to the trunk of the property tree "in an attitude so precarious and so extraordinarily prominent that Dumain (or perhaps it was Longaville), though supposed to be unconscious of his presence, could not refrain from staring at him as if fascinated for several seconds."[2] Because the staging made it impossible to maintain the visual paradigms that Shaw and other playgoers expected, the plausibility of the dramatic representation was undermined. These boundaries of believability may be stretched for theatrical effect, but the fundamental principles underlying them must nevertheless be preserved. In one 1985 Royal Shakespeare Company (RSC) production, for example, Berowne

> jumped up on the pedestal with [a statue of] Eros and made his shape conform to that of the headless statue. The King rolled under the garden bench and placed a potted plant—"this bush"—in front of his face as he lay there. Longaville...jumped onto the umbrella table, opened the umbrella, and tilted it to shield himself from Dumaine's view.[3]

Rather than offering convincing modes of subterfuge, the RSC production humorously exaggerated the scene's inherent situation comedy. Yet by substituting symbolic obstructions for actual ones, it maintained the underlying conventions governing stage representations of visual perception. Sight must operate according to mimetic paradigms. In order to indicate that the lords are hidden, some sort of physical barrier is required—at least a statue, a potted plant, or an umbrella, if not an entire tree.

Such visual dynamics exert a powerful influence over imagined stagings of the episode from *Love's Labor's Lost*. Even though theatrical conventions governing sound are not terribly realistic, it is difficult to believe that sight, too, might have functioned in nonverisimilar ways on Shakespeare's stage. When reconstructing how the spying scene was originally performed, scholars thus often try to mitigate its artificiality. As Miriam Gilbert puts it, "IV.iii...does require that all four men be on stage at the same time and that, at least to the audience, it look faintly plausible that they do not see each other."[4] In trying to rescue the play, modern-day critics articulate values that contrast interestingly with those of their eighteenth- and nineteenth-century counterparts. These earlier accounts embrace contradictory viewpoints, condemning the play's overall artifice even while praising its exceedingly artificial eavesdropping scene. Charles Gildon, for instance, declared in 1710 that *Love's Labor's Lost* was "one of the worst of *Shakespear's* [sic] Plays, nay I think I may say the very worst"; at the same time, he admitted, "The Discovery of the King's, *Longavile*'s, and *Dumain*'s Love is very prettily manag'd, and that of *Biron* by *Costard*'s mistake, is a well contriv'd Incident."[5] William Hazlitt remarked in 1817 that "[i]f we were to part with any of the author's comedies, it should be this," yet he singled out the eavesdropping episode as "[t]he scene which has the greatest dramatic effect."[6] These conflicting opinions suggest a tension between two different coexisting value systems and the disparate epistemological assumptions that undergird them. Believing that plays should function as internally coherent representations of the real world, one interpretive mode finds *Love's Labor's Lost* lacking. Foregrounding the scene's fine craftsmanship and performance potential, the other celebrates its complexity of form. The implausibility of the scenario is, in this sense, not a liability but a delight.

This chapter explores what counted as a theatrical signifier in early modern England by analyzing the semiotics used to represent the act of seeing.[7] Rather than impose anachronistic ideas by assuming that verisimilitude was required for onstage action to be theatrically credible, I examine sixteenth- and seventeenth-century artistic and architectural practices as well as scientific and religious discourses to uncover the visual paradigms taken for granted by actors and playgoers alike. English artists and architects were not known for the technical prowess and aesthetic innovations that brought fame to their European counterparts. Because they tended to draw on established conventions instead of showcasing creative novelties, their images, artifacts, and buildings offer a record of visual paradigms that extended beyond the elite to those lower in the social hierarchy. By contrast, learned treatises on the physiology of vision and on the moral and spiritual implications of sight circulated primarily among the more well-to-do members of society. Some of the theories they espoused were idiosyncratic to their authors and did not reflect widespread popular beliefs. Yet, reading between the lines, we can detect in these writers' habitual ways of thinking about sight certain fundamental attitudes and discourses that permeated early modern culture at all levels. In the theatre, these visual modes influenced not only the content of plays but also the formal mechanisms through which that content was conveyed. They shaped not only *what* playgoers saw but also *how* they saw.

In elucidating the performance dynamics of sight, I organize my analysis around four key factors: (1) hierarchies, both social and moral, embedded in the use of stage space; (2) idealized modes of spectatorship produced by linear perspective, surface patterning, and notions of representational depth; (3) the impact of affective piety and discourses of idolatry on actor-audience identification; and (4) the performativity of visuality, with special attention to the cultural valences of invisibility. The spying episode in *Love's Labor's Lost* offers an especially compelling site for investigating these issues because it enacts the process of spectatorship rather than merely thematizing it. In requiring that each actor indicate unambiguously whom he can and cannot see, the scene's narrative structure allows us to isolate and historicize the theatrical signifiers used to represent vision. Moreover, by repeatedly signaling that specific figures onstage are visible while others are not, the play rehearses the interpretive paradigms required for theatrical literacy. In doing so, it not only trains spectators to distinguish intentional theatrical signifiers from mere "background noise" but also naturalizes the visual paradigms underpinning those conventions. Even as it represents the act of seeing, the episode simultaneously shapes what counts as perceivable both inside and outside the playhouse.

In mobilizing and reworking broader visual modes, the performance medium functioned as a discursive practice. It inculcated playgoers into certain ways of thinking and being by weaving those standards into the semiotics required for its own intelligibility. Such moral and social norms were reinscribed all the more powerfully for being transmitted implicitly in theatrical form rather than communicated directly in representational content. Onstage actions and spectator practices were ultimately more influential than verbal instruction and rhetoric. In this way, theatre not only depicted material reality but also constructed the interpretive principles through which that reality was to be understood.

Social and Moral Hierarchies of Stage Space

When scholars try to reconstruct how the eavesdropping episode in *Love's Labor's Lost* was originally performed, they often propose "solutions" to make the scene's visual dynamics accord more with our own. Because Berowne is the first one to appear onstage and must be able to oversee the entire action without being detected, the usual assumption is that he was located above and behind the others, perhaps in the branches of a property tree.[8] Modern directors also frequently imagine Berowne located "above and behind." Ralph Koltai, the set designer for John Barton's 1978 RSC production, described his main problem as "avoiding 'a set about a tree.'" The solution, however, still required Berowne to be situated above the stage: the actor was to climb "a ladder-like support placed just at the proscenium opening, stage right."[9] Both scholars and directors tend to believe that characters are more likely to look down and in front than up and behind. The underlying assumption is that visual dynamics onstage operate according to paradigms of verisimilitude—a mode bound up with notions of theatre as an aesthetic practice that requires an "artistically" designed set to produce and maintain its representational frame. The dynamics of sight within the imaginary world of the play are thus collapsed with those in the actual playhouse.

In early modern England, however, would an elevated hiding spot for Berowne have been necessary—or even dramaturgically likely? Property trees in Shakespeare's theatre were generally used for allegorical or spectacular effect. Early modern theatrical producer Philip Henslowe recorded three property trees in his *Diary*: "j baye tree," "j tree of gowlden apelles," and a "Tantelouse tre."[10] Not one of these trees is "generic"; all were intended for particular characters, scenes, or plays. This assortment of trees was not unusual for the early modern stage. As Alan Dessen and Leslie Thomson have shown, property trees were used only for very specific purposes—in dumb shows, for instance, or for special effects.[11] To bring one onstage for the sole purpose of hiding Berowne does not fit with this theatrical paradigm. The notion that a property tree might have formed part of the background seems even more unlikely given early modern drama's blatant disregard for scenic realism. Although Miriam Gilbert speculates that a tree might have been there "from the beginning as part of the 'outdoor' setting,"[12] Dessen and Thomson note that property trees are rarely, if ever, used in scenes that take place in the woods or forest.[13] Although other plays do sometimes require certain figures to climb "trees," stage directions in such instances might just as well indicate a stage post or other architectural feature rather than actual theatrical props.[14] Moreover, no stage direction instructing Berowne to climb a tree appears in either the quarto or folio versions of *Love's Labor's Lost*. The *Riverside Shakespeare*'s direction for the moment when Berowne hides—"*He stands aside, [climbing into a tree]*" (4.3.20.s.d.)—ultimately derives from John Payne Collier's 1858 edition. The stage direction at the moment that Berowne reveals himself—"*[Descending and advancing.]*" (4.3.149.s.d.)—is based on Samuel Johnson's 1765 and 1768 editions. It is telling that theories regarding property trees in this scene did not emerge in the editorial tradition until the eighteenth and nineteenth centuries. Not only were ideas about set-dressing in this later period markedly different from those in Shakespeare's day, but the play itself was, in fact, no longer being performed. The years between 1604 and 1839 include not even a single reference to a production of *Love's Labor's Lost*. Indeed, it was, as Miriam Gilbert notes, "conspicuously, the *only* play of Shakespeare's not performed between 1700 and 1800."[15]

Although the use of a property tree in the eavesdropping scene is rather improbable, another location that scholars sometimes propose for Berowne—the Lords' Room, or gallery, above the main platform stage—is supported by more solid evidence.[16] Nevertheless, the meaning of that location differs from the meanings often assigned to it today. Immediately after Dumaine's entrance, Berowne declares

> All hid, all hid, an old infant play,
> Like a demie God, here sit I in the skie,
> And wretched fooles secrets heedfully ore-eye. (TLN 1412–14; 4.3.76–78)

Given that the canopy overhanging the stage was known as "the heavens," Berowne's reference to sitting "in the skie" fits well with a location in the gallery above the main acting platform. Positioning Berowne here makes sense if we take into account the legacy of medieval place-and-scaffold theatre, where highborn characters were situated in physically high spaces. During such performances, as Robert Weimann notes, "[a]s a rule, it was the more highly ranked persons who sat on the scaffolds: God the father, the 'King' in *The Pride of Life,* Decius (enthroned as in the Fouquet miniature)."[17] When Berowne explicitly likens himself to a "demie God," his comment calls to mind this performance tradition. Rather than assuming that Berowne was positioned in the gallery so as to remain undetected—an assumption that inappropriately projects paradigms of verisimilitude onto Shakespeare's stage—we would do well to attend to the specific theatrical practices Berowne invokes. His comments suggest that early modern stage geography reflected not visual realism but status, with the high "demie God" situated both socially and morally above those referred to as "wretched fooles"—a phrase that itself has both worldly and spiritual connotations.

In addition, Berowne's reference to "an old infant play" may have alluded to performance activities that combined the sacred and the secular. Most editors have glossed the remark as a continuation of the beginning of the line, which refers to the children's game known as "all hid."[18] However, Robert Weimann suggests that "an old infant play" could also have meant

> the older, but less artistically developed mystery plays (see *OED* "Infant": "In its earliest stage, newly existing, ungrown, undeveloped, nascent..."") in which a demigod (a pun on the fact that the actor who played *Deus* was indeed mortal) sat in the "heavens" looking down upon and judging the actors.[19]

Although early modern actors would not necessarily have adopted a teleological narrative treating medieval drama as "undeveloped," there is indeed evidence that Berowne's "old infant play" may refer to popular theatrical customs—in particular, dramatic renditions of Herod's Slaughter of the Innocents, such as those by the Wakefield master, or role-playing associated with the Feast of the Holy Innocents (December 28).[20] Like other holidays celebrating Christ, the apostles, and the evangelists, this feast day survived the Reformation relatively intact.[21] Its popular Lord of Misrule tradition continued unabated well into the seventeenth century. In France, this custom was associated with the *sociétés joyeuses,* who were in charge of organizing dramatic entertainments and whom E. K. Chambers described as the "frivolous counterparts of religious *confréries* or literary *puys.*"[22] Two of the most well documented of these *sociétés* integrated the term *infant,* or *enfant,* into their names: the late sixteenth-century *l'Infanterie Dijonnaise* and the Parisian *Enfants-sans-Souci.*[23] In English, the term *infanterie* appears to have had similar associations with group performance and entertainment. David Klausner notes that, although it literally meant "infantry," the word could be "used fig[uratively] and with an ironic pun on the nonce-sense *troop of infants.*"[24] His gloss refers to the anonymous pamphlet *Old Meg of Herefordshire,* in which the term *infanterie* describes a group of elderly morris dancers.[25] Indeed, the earliest reference in the *Oxford English Dictionary* to the term's military connotations is 1579; its other definition, "Infants collectively, or as a body. Now *jocular,*" dates to 1616.[26] Berowne's line about the "old infant play," then, draws upon these various connotations. Combined with his subsequent remark likening himself to a "demie God," it calls forth associations with traditional dramatic practices.

These performance customs involved visual paradigms radically different from our own. Today, accurate vision is understood in physiological terms—the "correct" 20/20 standard of eye exams. In the scene from *Love's Labor's Lost,* the mechanics of sight are subsumed within a broader symbolic system that renders the physical meaningful. What was important was not the individual's corporeal experience but his or her status within a community. Vision was not primarily a biological function but an expression of social hierarchy.[27] This hierarchy was not only social but moral. In medieval performance, the scaffolds used for God the father were also used for seating highborn members of the audience. Ordinary spectators gathered around the flat green, or "place," which was the principal acting area for devils.[28] Class status and moral status were collapsed into each other, and vertical position onstage was used to signify both. Locating Berowne in the gallery above the stage might thus serve as an appropriate comment on what it means to be "brought low." In order to chastise the friends he refers to as "wretched fooles," Berowne must descend from a position associated with moral and social superiority. Once he places himself on the same level as the other men, however, the "hypocrisie" that he "step[s]...forth to whip" (TLN 1488; 4.3.149) is revealed to be his own.

The fact that Berowne is ultimately shown up by the Clown is thus most appropriate. In breaking their vows, the lords have compromised their moral status, a change here likened to social decline and literalized through physical descent. At the end of the scene, the Clown Costard's parting statement just before he exits the stage likewise collapses social and moral decline. "Walk aside the true folke, & let the traytors stay" (TLN 1561; 4.3.209), Costard says. And indeed, throughout the play, he and Jaquenetta repeatedly serve as foils to the King, Berowne, Longaville, and Dumaine. In the opening scene of the play, Costard's affair with Jaquenetta is introduced immediately after the noblemen swear their oaths. The lords' aristocratic ideals are thus immediately transgressed by the lowborn. Jaquenetta's presence in the later eavesdropping scene is entirely superfluous to the narrative, but it serves to underscore parallels between the noblemen and the Clown. Wooing the French princess and her ladies, Berowne and his fellows have debased themselves, just as the Clown does with his wenching. Berowne's comment that "you three fooles, lackt mee foole, to make vp the messe" (TLN 1552–53; 4.3.203) is but the last in a string of references to the men as "fools." The use of this term associates the nobles specifically with the lowborn Costard as well as with the lustful tendencies generally ascribed to the clown figure.

This way of conceptualizing stage space—as social and moral hierarchy—is predicated on a semiotics of vision that might be described as indexical not iconic, where the signifier does not resemble the signified but rather gestures toward it. Although such visual modes are often ascribed to the medieval past, they remained quite popular after the Reformation. In the Protestant broadside "A godly meditation day and night to be exercised" (ca. 1600), for example, the deity is positioned at the top of the page amid clouds, an echo of Berowne's sitting "[l]ike a demie God...in the skie" (figure 2.1). Hell is located at the bottom of the page and is represented in its traditional form as the flame-filled mouth of a beast. The same correspondences between physical position and moral status can be seen in amateur theatrical practices. Although visual evidence from English religious drama is scarce, extant documents from the Continent are more plentiful. Renward Cysat's stage plan for the second day of the 1583 Passion Play in Lucerne (figure 2.2), for example, adopts a visual language similar to the English Protestant broadside.

Figure 2.1 William Rogers, "A godly meditation day and night to be exercised" (ca. 1600). © The Trustees of the British Museum. All rights reserved.

Reproduced with changes by Franz Leibing in 1869, it exemplifies the distance between early modern visual paradigms and the nineteenth-century ones that still inform our own practices today. This copy of the original sixteenth-century plan includes in the middle of the page an inset drawing that reproduces a portion of Martin Martini's 1597 view of Lucerne—as if Leibing's readers would need an isometric view in order to visualize the theatrical arrangement (figure 2.3).[29] The early modern image upon which this addition is superimposed, by contrast, maps physical space according to moral hierarchies. At one end is the mansion marked "Heaven," where the "Father eternal and the 7 angels" reside. At the opposite end, in the lower left-hand corner, is the hell-mouth, here inverted, with two large eyes and a full set of sharp, pointed teeth. Above it are written the words "street stand Hell"; below it, "Lucifer and the 8 devils."[30] The sixteenth-century plans for the Donaueschingen Passion Play also situate God at the top of the page and relegate hell to the bottom.[31] Such images adopt a mode of visuality that privileges status and degree over the mechanics of sight. Because these theatrical documents derive from amateur religious drama and exhibit visual paradigms alien to those most familiar today, they are frequently relegated to the medieval past, even when they are, in actuality, contemporaneous with Shakespeare. Berowne's comments may accord well with a position in the gallery, but the meanings associated with that location differ significantly from those in modern productions. Early modern visual paradigms, these documents suggest, emphasized social and moral hierarchies over verisimilitude.

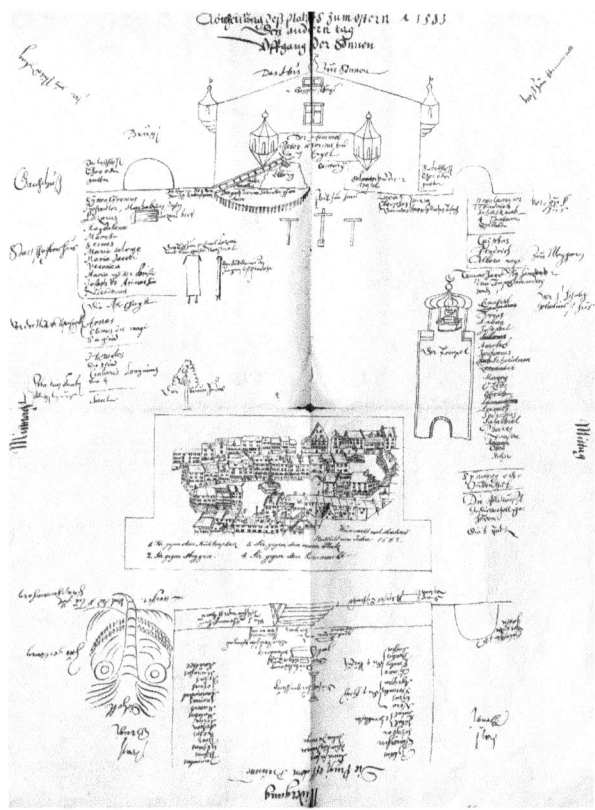

Figure 2.2 Stage plans for Lucerne Passion Play (1583). Reproduced from Franz Leibing, *Die Inscenirung des zweitägigen Luzerner Osterspieles* (Elberfeld, 1869). With the assistance of Special Collections and Archives, George Mason University Libraries.

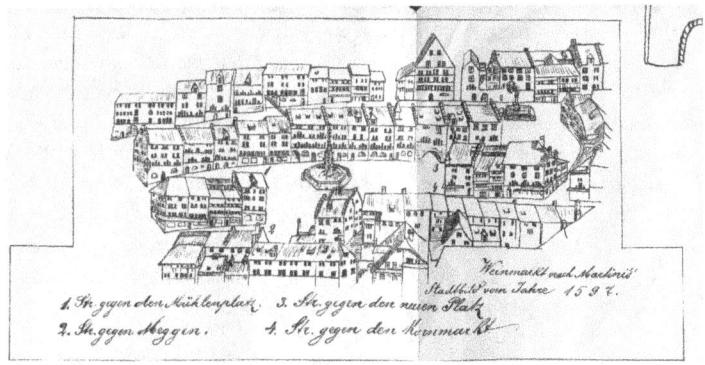

Figure 2.3 Detail of nineteenth-century additions to stage plans for Lucerne Passion Play (1583). Reproduced from Leibing, *Die Inscenirung des zweitägigen Luzerner Osterspieles*.

Linear Perspective, Surfaces, and Representational Depth

Situating Berowne above the main platform stage further falls prey to ahistorical theatrical assumptions if we imagine the scene from a particular spectator's point of view. The idea that Berowne would be hidden from the others were he in the gallery immediately above the platform stage conceptualizes the edge of the thrust stage farthest from the facade as its "front," with the facade and stage gallery functioning as the imagined proscenium's scenic backdrop. The other characters, it is assumed, would have played to the audience "down in front," oblivious to Berowne's position "behind" them. This imaginative reconstruction of original staging exemplifies the ways in which the theatrical paradigms associated with the proscenium arch theatres commonly found in auditoriums today can, unintentionally and unconsciously, infiltrate our thinking. The playhouse facade has traditionally been described as essential for the staging of scenes of interior space.[32] However, this facade would be most visible to audience members seated in the galleries directly across the yard. Although we know well that spectators in Shakespeare's theatres surrounded the stage on at least three sides, the playgoer is nevertheless imagined as situated in the "center orchestra" position, the same location as the ideal viewer in our own theatres today.

Similarly, scholars often imagine the King and Longaville as located behind the two stage pillars because this position allows them to remain hidden during soliloquies delivered by other characters.[33] Such reconstructions take for granted that soliloquies were spoken near the edge of the stage in close physical proximity to audience members. The unstated assumption is that standing playgoers in the yard gathered primarily at the "front" part of the thrust stage, as they might in a proscenium arch theatre.[34] Yet when we consider the vertical distribution of playgoers, other possible stage locations also seem plausible. When actors performed to spectators at the "sides" of the stage, they played both to the standers in the yard and to the customers in the galleries. We might imagine that positioning Berowne on the upper stage makes him harder for the other lords to spot because they are less likely to "look up" than they are to "look around," but the physical locations of spectators suggest otherwise. In fact, Derek Peat proposes that actors may have been *more* likely to perform to playgoers in the galleries and *less* likely to perform to those in the yard. In an Elizabethan theatre, he argues, there was an important audience above the stage in the Lords' Room, and "the actors, mindful of economic values and the benefit of court performances, were unlikely to ignore this part of their audience." He notes that, unlike "theatre in the round," where "the best seats are everywhere and anywhere[,] ... in an Elizabethan theatre I suspect the best seats were behind the stage in the lords' room."[35] Taking such factors into account when reconstructing where the King and Longaville were placed onstage complicates what it means to be "behind" the two stage pillars.

The problem of what it means to be "behind" is really an issue of sightlines: where the viewer is located and which direction the actor is, as a result, facing. This way of conceptualizing the issue, however, begs the question of the cultural meanings embedded in visual modes. In our own theatrical settings, the most expensive seats are the ones with the best sightlines. All other locations are understood to be less desirable because the spectators there do not watch the play from the ideal spot. The "center orchestra" model thus privileges the position of the viewer, the subject of the gaze. Moreover, actors are expected to face this idealized spectator. Such modern visual paradigms, where the use of stage space is governed by the mechanics of sight, are especially evident in proscenium arch theatres, but they also apply to other architectural formations, such as theatre-in-the-round. Director Stephen Joseph, who founded the Theatre-in-the-Round in Scarborough in 1955, insisted that, although audience members should be seated on all sides, the actual playing space should be rectangular rather than circular. As David Wiles describes,

> Joseph...castigates the circle on two practical grounds. First is focus. He argues that the circle is not vectored and has but a single strong point, namely the centre, which makes it a less interesting space to play in. He makes an analogy with the interior of a lighthouse, saying that lighthouse-keepers are known to go mad because they have no point of orientation. Secondly, he remarks that the circle is unsympathetic to the spaces which plays most commonly represent: rooms, roads, fields and so forth.[36]

The two arguments Joseph makes both emphasize the mechanics of visual perception. His first takes the issue of visual focus as a geometrical proposition, not a moral or social one. As we shall see later, mathematical interpretations of sight and the related emphasis on sightlines are common today but were still quite foreign to early modern English sensibilities. Joseph's second argument—that a round playing area would not facilitate the depiction of rooms, roads, and so forth—takes for granted that the use of theatrical space should operate according to the same rules of physics that govern real life. The pervasiveness of visual paradigms derived from proscenium arch staging is amusingly parodied in a cartoon by Ionicus, which Wiles reprints.[37] The image depicts spectators in a circular theatre just before a show begins. A male playgoer sits with a program in his left hand and a small, cardboard proscenium frame in his right. As he holds the frame up to his face in preparation for watching the performance, the female spectator sitting next to him—presumably his wife—leans over to her friend to whisper, "He doesn't like theatre-in-the-round." No matter the physical space, the cartoon implies, the most inflexible audience members will insist on habitual viewing practices. The fact that a handheld frame could be enough, however, tellingly underscores similarities between staging for the proscenium arch theatre and staging for other modern spaces, including theatre-in-the-round.

Early modern actors and playgoers proceeded from a different set of initial theatrical assumptions. For them, Berowne's descent from a position of moral and social superiority was just as "true" as a verisimilar representation of the physical dynamics of vision, if not more so. A theatrical representation of universal principles did not necessarily mean representing *physiological* reality. Flesh was ephemeral; only the world of the spirit was truly universal. The audience members with the best sightlines were those who stood in the yard—the lowest position in the vertical hierarchy. More privileged spectators did not need to see the play so much as *be* seen. During one performance at Christ Church, Oxford, in 1566, for example, the "populus" stood on the floor around the stage, the more noteworthy spectators sat on top of scaffolds built along the walls, and Queen Elizabeth's throne of state was placed at the back of the stage *facing* the audience.[38] These same theatrical values persisted during James I's reign. When the king visited Christ Church, Oxford, in August 1605, he attended some plays staged in a novel way. Some of his courtiers were seated in the front row of the auditorium. Rather than valuing the fact that they had the best sightlines, these honored guests, as John Elliott puts it, "complained that they could not now be seen by the rest of the audience as well as they could before."[39]

The problematic tendency to locate an imaginary ideal viewer in Shakespeare's theatre as situated in the "center orchestra" position is much indebted to the dominance of fixed-point perspective in Italian Renaissance art. This visual paradigm, and the spatial understandings that come with it, have important implications for how we conceptualize performance. Frequently credited with inventing linear perspective, Filippo Brunelleschi's paintings were meant to be so realistic that, as his student Antonio Manetti put it, "the spectator felt he saw the actual scene when he looked at the painting." It is telling that, to create such effects, Brunelleschi insisted that a perspective painter should "postulate beforehand a single point from which his painting must be viewed."[40] His comments sound remarkably similar to theatrical paradigms that imagine the ideal viewer as located in a single position from where the stage action is best watched. Moreover, like theatrical paradigms favoring playgoers in the "center orchestra" location, perspectival artistic practices privilege verisimilitude as a representational paradigm.[41]

Although Italian visual models such as Brunelleschi's are, by now, quite familiar, they were not nearly so commonplace in early modern England. Theories of linear perspective were primarily of interest to those in the upper echelons of English society. The ninth Earl of Northumberland was able to lend Sir John Holles 11 books on architecture by authors such as Alberti and Serlio, who were famous for their applications of mathematical perspective. Most people, however—including even master builders and carpenters—had neither the time nor the resources to pursue such innovations.[42] The houses of English aristocrats built during this period often appear odd when compared to Italian models. They had irregularly placed windows, towerlike turrets that projected over the roofline, and heavy, projecting bays[43]—all of which fail to accord with the Italian visual modes that are more familiar today.

Perspectival stage sets were equally scarce in early modern England. Inigo Jones's experimental use of linear perspective in the theatre was only just being introduced to the court in the early seventeenth century.[44] Jones was the exception rather than the rule: the playwright George Chapman wrote in a dedicatory epistle that Inigo Jones was "our only Learned Architect."[45] Jones's innovations in the theatre were not always well received. The plays presented to King James at Oxford in 1605—which, as I mentioned earlier, caused considerable grumbling among his courtiers—were meant to showcase Jones's new perspective scenery. During the performances, the king was placed on an "isle" in the center of the room—the best seat in the house and the ideal viewing location for the perspectival stage set. But James was apparently as dissatisfied as his courtiers. Not caring that he alone was positioned in the ideal viewing location, the king complained that he could not hear. His comments resonate with the famous early modern pronouncement that, in the presence of "An excellent Actor," one may "sit in a full Theater, and you will thinke you see so many lines drawen from the circumference of so many eares, whiles the *Actor* is the *Center*."[46] Sightlines are irrelevant; it is *sound*lines that matter here— and the very oddity of this neologism highlights the strangeness of the concept for us. Yet actors performing in the newly reconstructed Globe Theatre in London have pointed to the centrality of sound as a compensatory technique for playgoers' periodic inability to see a speaker's face.[47] Italian ideas about space and vision are by now so firmly established that it is an innovation for actors to realize how theatres such as the Globe complicate issues of sight. In Shakespeare's England, however, these visual paradigms were only just beginning to filter their way into the popular consciousness.[48]

Early modern English visual paradigms also evince a taste for surface patterning. Today our own spatial sensibilities privilege theatrical depth: the play world is thought of as every bit as three-dimensional as the real-life playhouse. Shakespeare's performance paradigms, by contrast, may well have emphasized two-dimensional surfaces. Embroidered tapestries in this period were essentially woven pictures, yet, as art historian Lucy Gent has argued, their "close stitches" presented images "without any suggestion of looking through a transparent window."[49] This same visual paradigm informed English paintings, which (unlike Italian Renaissance art) shared the "flatness" of medieval paintings, what Erwin Panofsky has described as "material surface covered with lines and colour which could be interpreted as tokens or symbols of three-dimensional objects."[50] Inscriptions on paintings were not set off by a cartouche or device, but instead drew attention to the surfaces of images. Today these inscriptions seem a bit odd since they interrupt the illusion of depth. In early modern England, however, they were thought of as valuable design elements, just as proverbial sayings and religious verses painted directly onto the surfaces of houses were a common form of interior wall decoration. Poems and phrases were written along the edges of walls or positioned in frames painted directly on the surfaces above mantelpieces. While such practices might seem like graffiti to a viewer today, there was nothing illicit about the activity in early modern England. The patterns created in this way offered textured patterns pleasing to the eye.[51]

Indeed, paintings in general were appreciated as decorative "wall-cladding,"[52] calling attention to surfaces through intricate patterns. As Lucy Gent describes,

> [M]any English paintings of the period are worked out as large surfaces; the Hardwick portrait of Queen Elizabeth is seven feet high; the Drury portrait discussed by Ellen Chirelstein above is nearly eight feet high. Such pieces seem conceived as versions of tapestry and do not match a tradition of the painting as an autonomous art object.[53]

Moreover, artists and house painters were thought of as one: George Gower, an accomplished portrait painter, was also in charge of the repetitive patterning used to decorate the royal palaces in 1581; Sampson Strong, who painted the founders of Christ Church, Oxford, was hired by them to paint doors and organs in 1605 and 1607–8.⁵⁴ Like painters, those who built houses were considered craftsmen, not architects. Indeed, as Caroline van Eck has pointed out, the term *architect* was not introduced into printed English until 1563 and was used then to refer specifically to "an outsider, called in by a patron desirous to build in the classical taste he had acquired...on the Continent."⁵⁵ The taste for surface ornament can also be seen in the widespread practice of hanging broadside sheets and woodcuts on walls as decoration. As Tessa Watt has convincingly shown, these inexpensive products of print culture were accessible not only to the elite but to people at all levels of society. Moreover, they were prized not only for their verbal content but also for their visual appeal. Their physical format drew attention to surfaces through the use of intricate borders, variety of fonts, and even the arrangement of text in pleasing visual patterns.⁵⁶ The outsides of buildings were also decorated in ways that drew attention to their surfaces. Brick, for example, was an ornament as well as a building material. It was interwoven with white stone, enhanced by paint via a process known as "russetting," and organized into a diaper pattern with dark bricks juxtaposed against lighter ones.⁵⁷ Embroidered tapestries, wall paintings, cheap print, and fancy brickwork—all of these modes of ornamentation suggest that English art and architecture valued surface, color, and pattern, as opposed to Italian visual paradigms emphasizing perspective and proportion.

These examples of the way visual culture was integrated into everyday life suggest a way of seeing at odds with modern paradigms. Influenced by Italian linear perspective, our own visual sensibilities privilege depth; we view two-dimensional art in terms of the imaginary three-dimensional space located "inside" the picture. Such visual paradigms lead many modern directors to think of blocking in terms of "stage pictures," with the proscenium arch serving as a framing device.⁵⁸ The artifice of the spying scene in *Love's Labor's Lost* thus becomes a problem compounded by the challenges of blocking it realistically—a problem directors often seek to amend by varying the position of the four men onstage. For early modern spectators, however, visuality was less about depth and illusionary space and more about seeing the surfaces themselves. Such visual paradigms change how we think about staging the episode. Rather than placing the lords in different locations onstage, arranging the men in a symmetrical fashion would more directly support the hierarchical meanings embedded in the scene, emphasizing the lords' similarities and the fact that all are equally forsworn. Moreover, staging the episode in this way would underscore its repetitive and formulaic narrative structure. The visual symmetry of the lords' physical positions onstage would highlight the scene's artifice rather than efface it. For early modern playgoers trained in reading images for their surfaces, such performance choices might have been not denigrated as unrealistic but praised for offering pleasing patterning.

Delight in surface patterning, however, should not be mistaken for lack of emotional engagement. Differences between early modern and modern notions of surfaces reflect different understandings about the materiality of visual perception. Contemporary quantum mechanics describes light as both wave and particle, but that particle, a *photon,* is defined as having no mass. Light, though a material object, is thus imagined as immaterial. Optics is often thought of as a geometric science, a series of abstract representations of an insubstantial substance. The privileging of sightlines in the modern theatre reflects this mathematical notion of visuality. Imaginary dotted lines connect the spectator to the performer, and theatrical spaces are constructed accordingly. Yet in early modern England, vision was not understood in such abstract terms, nor were surface and depth mutually distinct categories. Bruce Smith has described how sound in this period was not only something one heard but something one felt, a haptic experience resonating between and within bodies.[59] For early modern playgoers, the sense of sight was also a kind of variation on touch. Susan Foister has argued that engraving and painting were understood as branches of sculpture and that the vocabulary distinguishing between them was ambiguous. Foister notes that Holland's translation of Pliny, for example, makes reference to "[t]he honour of flat picture in old time." As Foister puts it, "[P]icture, or portraying, was assumed first of all to be three-dimensional and therefore had to be qualified as being flat."[60] In early modern England, surface and depth were not ontologically separate categories. One could quite literally "see it feelingly" (TLN 2593; 4.6.149), as Gloucester in *King Lear* puts it.

Even Renaissance perspective manuals were much more tactile and material in how they imagine visuality than we normally give them credit for. Leon Battista Alberti, often seen as the most influential theorist of abstract perspective in this period, describes this visual mode using material metaphors. In his *Della pittura*, when discussing practical techniques for drawing according to the principles of linear perspective, he states, "Nothing can be found, so I think, which is more useful than that veil which among my friends I call an intersection. It is a thin veil, finely woven, dyed whatever colour pleases you and with larger threads [marking out] as many parallels as you prefer."[61] A veil that has color, that is dyed, that feels "finely woven" is not as abstract as the geometric grid famously reproduced in Dürer's 1538 text, *Vnderweysuug* [sic] *der Messung* (figure 2.4). Even Dürer's grid, however, is presented as a material object, its wooden frame turned sideways and thus foregrounded for the viewer, who can see the lines within that frame only at an angle. From the point of the view of the artist within the image, the three-dimensional woman is flattened into two dimensions through the device of the grid. From the

Figure 2.4 Draftsman drawing a nude (woodcut). Albrecht Dürer, *Vnderweysuug* [sic] *der Messung* (Nuremberg, 1538), Q3v. By permission of the Folger Shakespeare Library.

actual viewer's perspective, however, the artist's model is as rounded and real as the artist himself. Having the wooden frame bisect the print calls attention to the visual symmetry within the image between the model and the artist: from the vantage point of the real-life viewer, both figures within the woodcut are equally material and concrete. Dürer's print plays with the question of perspective by calling attention to the difference between representation and presentation, between what takes place in the imaginary world within the image and what takes place in the actual viewer's experience. That difference highlights the corporeality of vision by presenting the voluptuous figure of the woman as well as the male artist's active role in mediating that sensuous experience. In a situation where one may look but not touch, looking *is* a form of touching.

Just as art and architecture privileged material surface over imaginary depth, devotional practices, too, stressed the materiality of not only visual images but also the act of seeing. Religious woodcuts that served as wall decorations after the Reformation were heirs to inexpensive prints originally meant for meditation.[62] Traditional understandings of vision as a form of ingestion were also essential to spiritual incorporation into the community. For Catholic believers, seeing the Host was equivalent to eating it. Communion was received only at Easter. During the rest of the year, the Eucharist was ingested not through the mouth but through the eyes, at the moment immediately following the consecration when the priest held the wafer over his head. The parallel between seeing and eating is vividly exemplified in an English verse homily dating from around 1400 in which a Jew witnessing the elevation miraculously sees replicas of the Christ child fly from the priest's hands to "lihte bi-twene vche monnes honde"; all spectators then eat their images of the child.[63] Beholding the Eucharist was also credited with all sorts of mystical properties, including the ability to improve digestion.[64] To facilitate the viewing of the Host, rood screens separating the congregation from the altar had small holes, known as eye squints, cut out of them. In larger churches, people ran from one chapel to another to catch glimpses of multiple sacrings.[65] As Miri Rubin notes, the elevation was originally so popular that it was understood as the only essential ritual during the service: "[P]eople ran into the church at the sound of the elevation bell. Requirements to remain until the end of the mass abound."[66] Protestant Reformer Thomas Becon complained that "[w]hen the Bell once ryngs (if they can not conueniently see) they forsake their seates and runne from altare to altare, from Sakering to Sakering, peeping here and touting ther, and gasing at that thing, which the pilde-pate Priest holdeth vp in hys handes."[67] Numerous sources also repeated the derisive caricature of worshippers who insist that their neighbors "stoop down before," demand that their priest "hold up higher," and declare loudly, "I thank God I see my Maker today."[68] Although the Reformation abolished many traditions associated with the Eucharist, the visual paradigms undergirding popular investment in the elevation were apparently more difficult to displace.

Just as devotional practices emphasized that visual experiences could profoundly change the viewer, so, too, did scientific explanations of optical phenomena. Images mattered, so to speak, because they were in fact *matter*. Extramission theories of vision, as Lucy Gent so aptly puts it, "saw the eye as the source of rays exploring the world 'rather as fingers palpate objects.'"[69] Such theories were the basis for such common poetic tropes as the disabling power of the beloved's gaze—the woman whose eyes are so beautiful that they are like Cupid's arrows piercing the male lover's heart. Intromission theories of vision at this time were also profoundly material. According to this view, all objects emitted *visual species,* tiny particles that were exact, miniature copies of the objects themselves.[70] Sight occurred when these particles flew into the eye of the beholder, where they impressed themselves upon the soft matter, or *spirit,* within the eye in the manner of a seal upon wax.[71] Even light itself had an impact on the viewer. As David Lindberg notes, Henry of Langenstein (also known as Henry of Hesse)—whose fourteenth-century treatise *Questiones super perspectivam* was published in 1503—thought of rays of light "not as mathematical lines but as pencils or pyramids of radiation" that always have width.[72] In contrast to the evanescent substance we associate with the perspectivist tradition and subsequent theories of optics, light for many early modern people was concrete, physical matter.

Cultural beliefs about the nature of sight and the visual practices these attitudes engendered have important implications for performance. In professional theatres today, actors and audience members are often physically separated from one another. In early modern England, spectatorship was itself a form of bodily contact, paralleling other forms of interactivity between playgoers and performers that theatre historians have often noted. Whereas theatrical spectatorship today is imagined as fundamentally passive and receptive—a playgoer, we say, "takes in" a show—in early modern England watching a play was understood as a much more active and material process. Through the power of the gaze, viewers might literally touch what they saw. Moreover, they could be physically changed by the object of their vision. Modern ideas about stage space and the mechanics of blocking are radically different from these early modern conceptions of sight.

Affective Piety, Idolatry, and Actor-Audience Identification

Spectatorship in Shakespeare's theatre was thus embedded in a larger nexus of beliefs about the power of vision to reshape bodies and souls. These same understandings also promoted the concept of affective piety, wherein contemplation of visual images was thought to generate feelings within the worshipper that would be of spiritual benefit. Although devotional practices related to the sacramental gaze were officially proscribed by Protestant Reformers, images were still thought of as powerful affective vehicles. Their seductive charms were still dangerous temptations to be actively guarded against. In *Love's Labor's Lost,* the perils of visual worship are vividly depicted in the lords' attitudes toward their ladies. Longaville adopts the traditional language of courtship when he recites a poem referring to his lady as a "Goddesse" (TLN 1398; 4.3.63). His protestations of love are, however, described by Berowne as a kind of idolatry:

> This is the liuer veine, which makes flesh a deity.
> A greene Goose, a Coddesse [i.e., goddess], pure pure Idolatry.
> God amend vs, God amend, we are much out o'th'way. (TLN 1407–9; 4.3.72–74)

In Berowne's view, Longaville's adoration has an inappropriate object: by treating passionate desire as love, he mistakenly substitutes the physical for the spiritual. This emphasis on idolatry continues later in the scene, when Berowne, in turn, declaims on his lady:

> Who sees the heauenly *Rosaline*,
> That (like a rude and sauage man of *Inde*.)
> At the first opening of the gorgeous East,
> Bowes not his vassall head, and strooken blinde,
> Kisses the base ground with obedient breast? (TLN 1570–74; 4.3.217–21)

When Berowne compares himself to a heathen worshipper making obeisance to the sun, his language draws on discourses conflating Catholicism with paganism. Indeed, antitheatricalists, such as Stephen Gosson and John Northbrooke, condemned the playhouse as idolatrous specifically because of its purported origins in pagan Greece and Rome.[73] Moreover, when the King derides Berowne for loving a lady who is "blacke as Ebonie" (TLN 1596; 4.3.243), Berowne compares Rosaline to an image made of wood:

> *Berow*. Is Ebonie like her? O word diuine?
> A wife of such wood were felicitie.
> O, who can giue an oth? Where is a booke?
> That I may sweare Beauty doth beauty lacke,
> If that she learne not of her eye to looke:
> No face is faire that is not full so blacke.
>   *Kin*. O paradoxe, Blacke is the badge of hell,
> The hue of dungeons, and the Schoole of night:
> And beauties crest becomes the heauens well.
>   *Ber*. Diuels soonest tempt resembling spirits of light. (TLN 1597–1606; 4.3.244–53)

When Berowne asserts that a "wife of such wood were felicitie," he situates the language of erotic love within the discourse of idolatry. The King's response calls attention to this comparison by describing such adoration as devilish.

In all of these passages, the female body is imagined as the idol that dangerously ensnares the male viewer. This notion informs not only the fictional narrative of the play but also its performance dynamics. In early modern England, Protestant Reformers attacked images of female saints for bringing "a certain whorish bravery into the service of God: the worship wherof they make to be Carnal."[74] At the same time, as Bob Scribner has shown, the seductive power of images could be used to good effect. With their eroticized allegories of Death with a maiden and voluptuous images of Eve at the Fall, Protestant artists sought to "induce sexual arousal in order to condemn the viewer for his sinful response."[75] By drawing on the discourse of idolatry, the scene from *Love's Labor's Lost* functions in a similar way to implicate viewers in the action onstage. The performance dynamics of the episode encourage playgoers to identify with Berowne, who serves as the onstage spectator and therefore their counterpart within the fictional world of the play. However, by invoking the dangers of idolatry, the scene also explicitly cautions the audience not to make the same mistake that Berowne does. Playgoers should not worship what they see, should not make the mistake of collapsing signifier into signified.

Within the representational narrative, this theme is played out in the lords' illicit love affairs; in the world of the playhouse, it is woven into the semiotics of performance. The modulation of audience identification and disidentification in this scene reflects in particular on early modern controversies over affective piety. In pre-Reformation England, saints were often perceived of not as distant holy men and women but rather as friends and intimates, what Julian of Norwich referred to as "kynd neyghbour[s] and of our knowyng."[76] As Eamon Duffy has shown, certain saints were thought to be particularly helpful for specific afflictions, their power "spring[ing] from the fact that they themselves had shared the sufferings of their clients."[77] This sense of empathy worked both ways. Meditating on woodcut "images of pity," or *Pietàs,* which depicted Mary holding the dead body of Christ, allowed Catholic believers to be moved more intensely by the experience of the Passion. By identifying with the suffering of the mother whose son has been tortured and killed, they could come to a deeper understanding of the deity's love and compassionate sacrifice and could appreciate more readily the bond of kinship that made Christ their "blessed brother."[78] The mode of visuality encouraged by such practices was referred to in sixteenth-century woodcuts as "devoutly" or "pytously beholdyng."[79]

Protestant Reformers, in contrast, argued that viewers should not empathize with Christ's bodily torment but contemplate their own sins. The appropriate response to images of the Passion was not sorrow but "fear and trembling."[80] As Duffy explains, Reformers "placed the efficacy of the Cross not in the sufferings of Christ's humanity, but in the eternal will of God which had decreed that the crucifixion should be effective for the salvation of sinners. Christ's obedience, not his sufferings, interested Calvin."[81] The performance dynamics of the spying episode in *Love's Labor's Lost* are informed by the tension between the visual modes espoused by pre- and post-Reformation believers. Whereas one famous account by an early modern eyewitness of a performance of *Othello* records that Desdemona on her deathbed "entreated the pity of the spectators by her very countenance,"[82] the reaction of audience members to *Love's Labor's Lost* was most likely not "pity" but mirth. In a 1598 poem lamenting unrequited love for a lady, Robert Tofte states, "*Love's Labor Lost,* I once did see a Play, / Ycleped so," and, "To euery one (saue me) twas *Comicall.*" He adopts the traditional language of the spurned lover, claiming that although the play "to others seemede a iest," for him "[t]was I that Griefe (indeed) did beare in brest."[83] While Tofte implies that he empathized with the noblemen lovers in the play, his conceit only works because it presumes that others did not do so.

Playgoers who take to heart the feelings of the King, Berowne, Longaville, and Dumaine will find Tofte more sympathetic than Shakespeare. However, my point is not simply that, as a genre, comedy distances its audience in order to promote laughter over sympathy but that the performance dynamics of the spying episode explicitly modulate the interplay of audience identification. On the one hand, playgoers are led to identify with the lords because they, like the audience, are spectators. The scene's nested structure—with characters spying on each other and then revealing themselves in a predictable, well-ordered sequence—foregrounds the act of watching. On the other hand, the episode's overt artifice makes it difficult for the audience to forget that what they are watching is not real. Instead of drawing playgoers into the fictional universe and leading them to identify with characters, the narrative is arranged schematically. Each of the lords mimics the actions of the others, reads aloud cliché poetry, and offers unoriginal declarations of love—all making the scene feel more formulaic. In this sense, the episode in *Love's Labor's Lost* strongly resembles the one in *As You Like It* where Silvius declaims on "what 'tis to loue" (TLN 2490; 5.2.83) to the repeated chorus of "And so am I for *Ganimed*," "And so am I for *Rosalind*," "And so am I for no woman" (TLN 2507–9; 5.2.100–102). In both episodes, symmetry and repetition work against any actual idealization of the love object. Idolatrous erotic tendencies are contained by representing the actions of characters as farcical echoes of one another. The performance dynamics of the eavesdropping scene from *Love's Labor's Lost* thus lead the audience to both identify and disidentify with the noblemen. Playgoers are encouraged to adopt the subject position of adoring spectator at the same time that the scene's deployment of artifice serves as an implicit caution against overzealous devotion.

It is telling, then, that Berowne's description of Longaville's poem as "pure pure Idolatry" (TLN 1408; 4.3.73) is spoken in an aside to the audience. Playgoers are here encouraged to identify with the onstage spectator, Berowne, who voices (at least temporarily) the dangers of "the liuer veine, which makes flesh a deity" (TLN 1407; 4.3.72). When Berowne, too, is revealed to be in love, the performance dynamics shift to hold playgoers at arm's length. For the remainder of the scene, he does not address the audience in asides nor does he assume the position of privileged onstage spectator. Instead, he idolatrously declares, "Is Ebonie like her? O word diuine? / A wife of such wood were felicitie" (TLN 1597–98; 4.3.244–45), and equivocates that "[i]t is religion to be thus forsworne. / For Charity it selfe fulfills the Law: / And who can seuer loue from Charity" (TLN 1714–16; 4.3.360–62). The audience is asked to identify not with Berowne as was the case earlier in the scene but rather with the Clown and Jaquenetta. The undesirable presence of these clownish figures as spectators to Berowne's shame is repeatedly foregrounded:

> [*Ber.*] O dismisse this audience, and I shall tell you more.
> *Dum.* Now the number is euen.
> *Berow.* True true, we are fowre: will these Turtles
> be gone?
> *Kin.* Hence sirs, away.
> *Clo.* Walk aside the true folke, & let the traytors stay. (TLN 1556–61; 4.3.206–9)

Because the scene's structure emphasizes symmetry and repetition, it prompts the audience to anticipate Berowne's downfall before it actually occurs. The question is not *if* he will be exposed but *when* and *how* that revelation will occur. At the entrance of the Clown and Jaquenetta, the device becomes clear. The only remaining spectators for the scene, and thus for Berowne's humiliation, are the Clown, Jaquenetta, and actual playgoers. The result is that audience members are encouraged to ultimately disidentify with even Berowne in favor of the lowborn figures who function in the dramaturgically liminal space between actor and audience. The Clown's parting line ("Walk aside the true folke, & let the traytors stay") may well have been spoken to playhouse spectators in imagined solidarity.

The joke, however, is that, when the Clown departs, the real-life audience remains, their status as "true folke" compromised by their willingness to watch the subsequent love plot unfold. The lords are "traytors" principally because they violate their oaths, but they also commit treason in another sense: in their idolatrous love for their ladies, they are too much like Catholics, who were often executed as traitors for violating political, rather than religious, law.[84] Playgoers, who do not "[w]alk aside" but rather "stay" to watch the rest of the performance, are likewise traitors in that they idolize the visual spectacle before them. The humor of the Clown's parting comment lies in its inversion of accepted hierarchies: treason implied both social and moral descent, yet the Clown and Jaquenetta (supposedly of the lowest status) are the only "true folke" remaining in the playhouse.[85] Theatre allows for reversals in both worldly and spiritual degree. In order to maintain their superiority, however, the Clown and Jaquenetta must "[w]alk aside," leaving the performance event that turns traditional order upside down. Playful inversion is temporary; audience members are idolatrous if they take it too much in earnest.

The Performativity of Visuality

This emphasis on the moral ramifications of seeing has implications as well for theatrical representations of visibility and invisibility—whether or not something *can* be seen. According to Reformers, the most heinous idol of popish worship was the Eucharist itself. Despite such radical polemic, however, Protestant and Catholic popular beliefs were not quite so far apart from each other as they might initially seem. As Christopher Marsh has observed,

> [F]our centuries have driven into us the importance of a fierce and fundamental divide between Protestantism and Catholicism. This divide is given physical expression in the streets of modern Belfast .... The Reformation chasm yawns large in our minds as we look back, and it is therefore wise to remember that, in the parishes of mid-sixteenth-century England, it was something new and peculiar, a distinction that had to be learned rather than simply inherited.[86]

Marsh's emphasis on the need to learn new religious distinctions is important. As behavioral psychologists will attest, external actions can often precede internal belief. Although the mind will adjust eventually, it takes time and practice to revise deep-seated notions. For the vast majority of early modern laypeople, new doctrines surrounding the Eucharist would have been experienced first as changes to familiar ritual practices; only later would their new meanings have been internalized. Unsettling the visual paradigms at their core would have been an even longer process.

Although debates over transubstantiation divided worshippers, both Protestants and Catholics believed that the Eucharist was spiritually efficacious. For Reformers, however, what gave the Host its power was not the fact that the bread *was* Christ but rather the *distance* between signifier and signified. Calvin insisted,

> The nature of the Sacrament is therefore canceled, unless, in the mode of signifying, the earthly sign corresponds to the heavenly thing. And the truth of this mystery accordingly perishes for us unless true bread represents the true body of Christ. Again I repeat:... visible bread must serve as an intermediary to represent that spiritual bread—unless we are willing to lose all the benefit which God, to sustain our weakness, confers upon us.[87]

It was only because the bread could symbolize Christ's body without actually being the deity that the Eucharist could be ritually efficacious.[88] It was a divinely given equivalence: the presence of the symbol equaled the presence of the thing itself, even though the symbol was itself not equal to the thing. Or, as Calvin put it, "by the showing of the symbol the thing itself is also shown... if the Lord truly represents the participation in his body through the breaking of bread, there ought not to be the least doubt that he truly presents and shows his body."[89] The bread, in other words, was not God, but it was *through* bread that communion with God could be effected. It is tempting to oversimplify theological differences by saying that Catholics believed in transubstantiation and Protestants in purely symbolic memorial representation. However, Calvin's comments suggest that the actual doctrinal complexities were much more subtle. The theory of "consubstantiation," espoused by Wycliff and Luther, complicated the situation further. Whereas transubstantiation posited that the substance of bread was converted to the substance of the body of Christ even as its appearance, or "accidents," remained unaltered, consubstantiation affirmed that the substance of the bread coexisted with the substance of the body of Christ. This theory did not critique the principle of the real presence of Christ but simply alleged that bread was indeed there in substance along with the holy body.[90] For many people in early modern England, such fine distinctions would have been beyond them. It would have been difficult to parse the difference between, on the one hand, a sign being efficacious in and of itself and, on the other hand, a sign's status as holy mystery rendering it efficacious. The reformed religion was not so spiritually bankrupt as to assert that the Eucharist was an empty signifier. The notion that God's Sacrament was still efficacious, just differently so, would, I suspect, have been good enough for most people.

This ritual efficacy becomes especially significant when we consider early modern theatre's use of speech acts. In *As You Like It,* when Rosalind says, "[t]his is the Forrest of *Arden*" (TLN 797; 2.4.15), her words transform the bare platform stage into an imaginary forest. Verbal cues of this sort had a long theatrical tradition. At the beginning of the fifteenth-century play *Mankind,* for instance, the first speaker declares, "Mercy is my name" (line 18), his speech act transforming the person of the actor into the allegorical representation of mercy.[91] Theatrical conventions here echo the performativity of Eucharistic practices in both pre- and post-Reformation England. Both traditions posited a discrepancy between appearance and reality. For Catholic believers, numerous stories emphasized that, where communion bread was concerned, visual perception was unreliable. "The Host," as Eamon Duffy frankly states, "did not look like the thing it was."[92] What appeared to be bread might really be the body of Christ. Stories in which the communion bread would turn into bloody hunks of meat ultimately described unbelievers; once converted, the formerly faithless would see flesh resume the comforting appearance of bread. In the Croxton *Play of the Sacrament,* for example, Eucharistic bread stolen by Jews bleeds when stabbed with their daggers. When it is subsequently thrown into an oven, Jesus bursts out of the oven and convinces the Jews to convert to Christianity.[93] In another story, a doubting monk sees a loaf of bread transformed into the Christ child, who is then stabbed and dismembered by an angel of God. Bleeding flesh resumes the appearance of bread only after the monk declares his belief.[94] This emphasis on the unreliability of vision extended back to early Christian writings, where doubts expressed by the disciples during the Last Supper were viewed as evidence of their inability to grasp the mystery unfolding in front of their eyes *except* through an act of faith. Seeing the Host literally—as flesh, not bread—was a sign of lack of belief. Only doubting Thomases needed ocular proof. While the Reformation had a profound effect in many arenas, changes in Eucharistic practices and doctrine did not alter this fundamental epistemological problem. Like their Catholic predecessors, Protestants believed that the physical sense of sight was inadequate for determining the actual truth of the Sacrament. They reasoned that it was God's word upon which the faithful should rely. Mere bread could only become a symbol of the Host through the speaking of ritual words.

These Eucharistic practices and the visual logics they espoused have important implications for the staging of the scene from *Love's Labor's Lost.* Communion was a performative act, its spiritual benefits granted to the communicant only after the bread had undergone a process of transformation. Although Catholics believed in a literal transformation, whereas Protestant Reformers adopted a more complex line of reasoning, both groups required that the Host be properly consecrated before it could be spiritually efficacious. The ritual words spoken by the celebrant were essential to this process. Believers readily assumed that their eyes were less reliable than their ears: the holy transformation occurred even when visual evidence might suggest otherwise. Despite the prevalence of such devotional beliefs, it is difficult for modern scholars to imagine that visuality in the scene from *Love's Labor's Lost* might have worked in a similar way. When the King declares that he has been "closely shrouded in this bush" (TLN 1474; 4.3.135), early modern playgoers would neither have required nor expected to see an actual "bush." The representational fiction is produced performatively through his speech act. Early modern playgoers would have found alien Bernard Shaw's complaint, quoted at the beginning of this chapter, regarding an extraordinarily prominent Berowne on the trunk of the tree. Trained through years of observance of the Eucharist, where the words "Hoc est corpus meum" turned simple bread into consecrated

Host, audiences who heard Berowne declare that he has concealed himself might well find that statement fully adequate. So long as his words indicate that he should be invisible, *actors* playing the lords could have looked directly at Berowne in the upper gallery without their *characters* seeing him—and without the audience experiencing any contradiction in this fact. Indeed, the plot of the spying scene and the blocking requirements that result from its nested structure make it difficult for the actors *not* to see each other.

Moreover, as Alan Dessen has pointed out, early modern dramatic texts rarely use the term *aside* in its modern, theatrical sense. Rather, *aside* is most often used as an adverb to modify a verb, as in "speaks aside" or "stands aside."[95] The *OED* does not include the theatrical term in its current form as a noun until the eighteenth century.[96] Surveying stage directions in Shakespeare's quartos and First Folio, Dessen demonstrates that the term *aside* appears in its modern sense in only two instances: a "suspect" part of *Pericles* and a "bad" quarto of *The Merry Wives of Windsor*. In the quarto version of *Love's Labor's Lost,* stage directions indicate that Berowne "*stands a side*" (E2v; 4.3.17) and that the King "*steps a side*" (E3r; 4.3.39). These same stage directions appear in the Folio, though with *aside* spelled as one word—the standard by 1623. In this episode, the term *aside* is clearly used to designate not speech but physical movement. It indicates bodily motion rather than verisimilar action. In a world where sight was assumed to be deceptive and only true faith might allow one to see accurately, the particular gestures and conventions used to indicate theatrical asides would not necessarily have included averting one's eyes.

These performance dynamics reinforce the episode's thematic emphasis on "hypocrisie" (TLN 1488; 4.3.149). Positioning the figures onstage so that the actors are forced to see each other, even though their characters are supposedly concealed, emphasizes just how misguided the lords actually are. They think they see clearly, but in fact their eyes are, to use the early modern term, "bleared." By leading playhouse spectators to depend on spoken words in order to determine who counts as visible within the represented fiction, the scene serves as a warning to them not to rely too extensively on their eyes. Moreover, the performance dynamics of the episode also implicate playgoers in what it means not to *be* seen. The structure of the episode draws a parallel between onstage and offstage spectators. When the King asks, "Are wee betrayed thus to thy ouer-view?" (TLN 1513; 4.3.173), his comment is directed most literally at Berowne, but it applies also to the audience, who has watched all of the action unfold. Like Berowne, playgoers are able to see those characters who imagine themselves to be concealed. When Berowne's own confession is brought forth to his chagrin, the scene collapses the subject of the gaze with its object. Even though the lords think they are hidden, they are entirely visible to real-life spectators. Berowne's own humiliation reveals that he is not exempt from the gaze. Similarly, the scene suggests, playgoers should not be so arrogant as to think their own sins will go undiscovered. Just as early modern murder pamphlets emphasize that God, who sees all, will expose hidden crimes, the performance dynamics of this episode suggest playgoers are also being watched.[97] If they perjure themselves, as the noblemen do, they too will be exposed. The scene's performance dynamics thus serve as a caution against worldly pride.

Staging the episode so that actors can see each other but characters cannot underscores this message. Playhouse spectators are here implicated in what it means not to see accurately and are warned not to be presumptuous. Any smug satisfaction theatregoers might feel at the nobles' humiliation only makes them more like the lords. Although apparently omniscient viewers, they are also mortal, and God will witness their actions. The episode's thematic emphasis on the dangers of hypocrisy are integrated into its performance dynamics.

Beyond the particulars of *Love's Labor's Lost,* the visual paradigms I have been exploring also bear on the staging of invisibility in other early modern plays. Speech acts were not the only kinds of performative signifiers in the early modern theatre; visual signifiers also constructed what playgoers "saw" on the stage. Carrying a lantern, for instance, was a visual cue that playgoers should imagine a scene taking place at night.[98] Ironically, these same kinds of visible markers may also have been used, in conjunction with speech acts, to represent *in*visibility. Alan Dessen has convincingly argued that invisibility on the early modern stage did not require the use of special effects. The term *invisible* itself appears in only five stage directions from the period. The more common mechanism was simply to include relevant dialogue, as in *The Two Noble Ladies,* when Sinew remarks about an invisible spirit, "I hear him though I see him not."[99] In addition to dialogue, plays may also have relied on gesture to indicate that a character was supposed to be unseen. Dessen speculates that a marginal stage direction in Q2 of *Hamlet*—"It spreads his armes"—could have been part of the gestural vocabulary of Shakespeare's theatre. Rather than assigning this action to Horatio, Dessen argues that it could potentially refer to the ghost, as a way for the supernatural figure to indicate that it could now be seen.[100] Audible speech and visible gesture serve as theatrical signifiers of that which, within the fictional world of the play, cannot be perceived.

More striking still is the use of actual objects to represent invisibility. The most famous example is, of course, the note in Henslowe's *Diary* regarding the purchase of "a robe for to goo invisibell."[101] Barbara Palmer has speculated that this garment might have been made out of black fabric, "the intent being to blend in rather than stand out."[102] Palmer's engaging article presents a nice survey of medieval and early modern technologies for representing invisibility, but her emphasis lies on moments in plays where there are miraculous or magical disappearances. Accordingly, she proposes that special effects, such as fireworks, and theatrical devices, such as pulleys, could well have been used for staging invisibility. That such resources were available to early modern performers is well known. More run-of-the-mill scenes involving merely hidden spectators and asides to the audience would not have required them. However, the visual paradigms I have been surveying suggest that early modern culture did not privilege verisimilar modes of seeing. Rather than assuming that spectacular effects were used to make a play seem more "real," we would do well to contemplate how they might have signified iconographically on the early modern stage. In other words, instead of "blending in," invisibility might well have been performatively constructed through visual markers that "stood out" for reasons deeply embedded in the culture.

In particular, I propose that property nets might have been used to represent invisibility in the early modern theatre. Stage directions from the period include a number of examples of property nets. Although their appearance in plays is usually in the context of catching fish or trapping people,[103] nets were also commonly associated with obstructed vision. The *OED* notes that to "dance (also march, walk, etc.) in a net" meant "(a) to act with practically no disguise or concealment, while expecting to escape notice; (b) to do something undetected."[104] This meaning of the term *net* is employed by Philip Stubbes in his famous *Anatomie of Abuses* when he criticizes those who host church ales for their "pretensed allegations, wherby they blind the world, and conueigh themselues away inuisibly in a clowd. But if they daunce thus in a net, no doubt they will be espied."[105] John Hind's *Eliosto Libidinoso* also uses *net* in this sense when he describes the lovers, Eliosto and Cleodora, as so transparent in their affections that "all the Court (though they poore soules thought to daunce in a net, and not be seene) perceiued how entirely they loued, and liked each other."[106]

Examples of this use of the term *net* may also be found in the dramatic tradition. In *The Spanish Tragedy,* for instance, Hieronimo declares that the murderer Lorenzo "[m]archt in a net, and thought him selfe vnseene."[107] In John Heywood's *Play of Love,* the Vice figure behaves "[l]yke as a foole myght haue iettyd in a net / Beleuyng hymselfe saue of hym self onely / To be perceyued of no lyuyng body."[108] This connection between nets, invisibility, and the Vice also appears in *Mankind,* first performed in the late fifteenth century. When the Vice figure, Titivillus, says, "Ever I go invisibull—it is my jett— / Ande befor his ey thus I will hange my nett / To blench his sight" (lines 529–31), he becomes invisible to the character Mankind. Terms such as *this* or *thus* often signal moments where, as Alan Dessen puts it, "the meaning of a line or phrase is (presumably) to be completed or fulfilled by a motion or action from the speaker," as in the classic example from *Hamlet* when Polonius says, "'Take this from this, if this be otherwise' (II.ii.156) where the first *this* refers to 'head,' the second to 'shoulders,' and the third to 'this situation.'"[109] In Titivillus's line from *Mankind,* then, the phrase "thus I will hange my nett" is suggestive: the use of an actual property net would make sense of the action implied by the gestic *thus*. Speech, gesture, and prop here work together; visual and verbal signifiers combine to construct Titivillus's invisibility.

The use of property nets to signify invisibility may seem counterintuitive to us, but this kind of theatrical signifer accords well with early modern conceptions of visuality. Its significance would lie not only in its physical enactment of a verbal expression but also in its literalization of failures of vision. Nets have holes that enable the eyes of captives to roam free, but since nets also immobilize their victims, that freedom is merely an illusion. Moreover, nets can themselves be hidden, catching their victims unawares—a different mode of visual deception. The use of nets to mark invisibility would involve the adoption of a theatrical signifier whose material form was at odds with that which it represents. Although it works counter to verisimilar theatrical modes, we should not discount it for that reason alone. Using a concrete object to mark the failure of sight is no more odd than using lanterns to signify nighttime. In the early modern playhouse, light could signify dark; the visible, invisibility. In understanding sight onstage as performatively produced, the semiotics of early modern performance foregrounded both the vulnerability of human vision and the need for spiritual grace.

* * *

Rather than assuming that scenes of spectatorship, such as the one from *Love's Labor's Lost,* were necessarily strained and artificial, we would do well to attend to the historically specific cultural practices that shaped visual logics when the play was first performed. Just because the episode pushes the boundaries of believability today does not mean that it would necessarily have done so in the early modern theatre. Reconstructing the cultural specificity of such visual paradigms has important ramifications not only for our understandings of performance but also for critical interpretations from both literary and theatrical perspectives. Thematic readings of *Love's Labor's Lost* might describe the dynamics of sight in terms of the lords' self-absorption (only when they learn their lesson at the end of the play are their eyes opened) or the shallowness of their love (the men mistake their masked ladies for one another while the women can see through the Muscovite disguises). Theatrical readings of the eavesdropping scene might follow in the same vein (the lords' inability to see one another on the stage underscores how love has blinded them; the heightened artifice of the scene reflects the artificiality of their feelings). However, such readings are biased by our own theatrical semiotics and visual modes.

Indeed, what becomes evident from an analysis of early modern visuality is the extent to which Shakespeare's theatre may have adopted a kind of *allegorical* logic when it represented the act of seeing. Rather than treating vision as a biological experience to be represented mimetically, early modern performance used it to point indexically toward a range of social and cultural issues. Tessa Watt has convincingly argued that the Reformation did not merely tolerate allegorical visual paradigms but actually encouraged their growth. The first English emblem book, she notes, was printed in 1586, and "[t]he most frequent image of the deity from the 1570s to the 1630s was the abstract Hebrew Tetragrammaton; [sic] although popular pamphlets on natural disasters or plagues often used the hand emerging from the clouds holding a rod or sword."[110] For Protestant publishers, she contends, allegory was a visual mode safe from accusations of idolatry.

Early modern theatre took advantage of this traditional way of seeing. It did not overturn pre-Reformation visual logics; it redeployed them. Although the Reformation disrupted certain modes of seeing and attempted to inculcate new ones, many Catholic and Protestant ideas about visuality were more similar to each other than either of them are to our own paradigms today. Alan Dessen's reading of a stage direction from *The Tide Tarrieth No Man* offers one way in which we might interpret allegorical modes of signification on the early modern stage. Dessen focuses on a moment in the play when "Courage and Greediness enter as though they saw not Christianity."[111] He notes that "[a] director today might seek to make this entrance more 'believable' by having Greediness and the Vice [Courage] looking the wrong way or by distancing the two sets of figures."[112] However, by staging the scene in the most "unrealistic" way possible, by presenting it so that "Greediness and Courage walk right through Christianity as if he did not exist," such a scene "tells the spectator, swiftly and emphatically, something important about [a character's] moral status or spiritual condition or way of life":[113]

> [T]he element of surprise in such moments, the initial *il*logic (when we first realize that Greediness...do[es] not see what we see), provides a theatrical *italics* that underscores the dramatist's point. Like an italicized phrase, such a device calls attention to itself and provides a clear signal that something of importance is happening, thus encouraging a thinking precisely on the event.[114]

Dessen's notion of "theatrical italics" is, in a sense, a kind of apolitical variation on Brecht's alienation effect. Brecht's goal was to foreground the artifice of the theatrical event, whereas Dessen's "italicized" moments serve to highlight primarily thematic points, but both require an "initial *il*logic," a jolt or disjunction.

However, devices similar to the one in Dessen's example call attention to themselves only if audiences expect that visual perception in the theatre will operate according to conventions of verisimilitude. We cannot take for granted that this was necessarily the case. Allegorical narratives such as *The Tide Tarrieth No Man* were popular in early modern England, but I suspect they were not "mere" allegory—or, to put it another way, their popularity was nourished by a culture where the physical, temporal, "profane" world and the invisible, eternal, "sacred" world were understood as intimately linked to one another. Although *The Tide Tarrieth No Man* was written in 1576, well after the various Protestant Reformations were underway, physical blindness remains a sign of moral blindness. The play demonstrates a kind of allegorical logic, where the physical world is but a key through which one might access the "true reality" of the spiritual world.

This movement between the everyday and the eternal, between the profane and the sacred, has implications for how theatrical signification worked on the early modern stage. To the extent that everyday life was itself allegorical, was a text in which believers might discover the markers of a (better) heavenly order, the line between mimetic representation and allegorical representation was necessarily blurred. In *The Tide Tarrieth No Man,* physical actions presented onstage signify both mimetically and allegorically. The action verisimilarly presents two people who must behave "as though they saw not" a third at the same time that it signifies a didactic or moral truth, not a fictional universe. The way to indicate allegorical significance *is* to resemble the thing itself. Early modern cultural understandings of the interpenetration of the sacred and the profane did not simply inform the fictional narratives of plays but were woven into the semiotics of performance, the material means through which theatre was created. It was not simply that stage geography might signify moral status or that invisibility might be performatively constructed through speech acts or visual markers, such as property nets. As we shall see in the next chapter, allegorical ways of thinking were so thoroughly integrated into early modern culture that they were not necessarily understood as different in *kind* from mimetic signifiers. A property net could be simultaneously a conventional way of marking invisibility, a mimetic representation of obstructed vision, and an allegorical signifier indicating spiritual entrapment. The ways in which these modes of understanding overlapped and intertwined was the result of varied and multilayered ideas about epistemology and semiotics in early modern England. The impact of such discourses on the interpretive frameworks that playgoers brought with them to the theatres is the subject of the next chapter.

Chapter 3

Imaginary Forces: Allegory, Mimesis, and Audience Interpretation in *The Spanish Tragedy*

> O pardon: since a crooked Figure may
> Attest in little place a Million,
> And let vs, Cyphers to this great Accompt,
> On your imaginarie Forces worke.
> Suppose within the Girdle of these Walls
> Are now confin'd two mightie Monarchies,
> Whose high, vp-reared, and abutting Fronts,
> The perillous narrow Ocean parts asunder.
> Peece out our imperfections with your thoughts:
> Into a thousand parts diuide one Man,
> And make imaginarie Puissance.
> Thinke when we talke of Horses, that you see them
> Printing their prowd Hoofes i'th'receiuing Earth:
> For 'tis your thoughts that now must deck our Kings.
>
> —Shakespeare, Prologue to *Henry V*

When the Prologue to Shakespeare's *Henry V* calls upon spectators to "[p]eece out our imperfections with your thoughts," he invokes a familiar trope: audience members must use their imaginations to compensate for deficiencies in theatrical performance. This model of dramatic practice is predicated on the assumption that verisimilitude is the representational ideal. Theatre, it presumes, aims for a facsimile of reality. By supplementing onstage actions with mental pictures, audiences "fill out" the material inadequacies of the playhouse, so as to make the fiction seem more "real." For early modern spectators, however, "[p]eece[ing] out" the actor's "imperfections" was not always quite so simple.

Take, for instance, *The Two Noble Ladies,* a play first performed at the Red Bull Theatre in 1622. The theatrical techniques used in this play might seem unusual to modern eyes. In one episode, two soldiers drown in the Euphrates River—a challenging moment to stage in a theatre privileging verisimilitude. The early modern approach to this problem suggests a different performance paradigm at work: the stage directions read, "*Enter two Tritons with silver trumpets,*" "*The Tritons seize the soldiers,*" and "*The Tritons drag them in sounding their trumpets.*"[1] For this scene to be intelligible, playgoers had to mobilize allegorical modes of interpretation. Far from simply enhancing the action to make it more "real," spectators had to engage in an act of translation, turning an onstage signifier (Tritons with trumpets) into a fictional signified (drowning in the Euphrates). At the same time, audiences could not rely *only* on allegorical interpretation to make sense of the scene. Certain theatrical signals needed to be taken quite literally. The Tritons' costumes, for instance, were probably represented mimetically: Henslowe's *Diary* includes records for "j sewtte for Nepton" and "Nepun [*sic*] forcke & garland."[2] Correct allegorical interpretation of the scene depended on accurate perception of mimetic resemblance: in order for the actors to "read" as Tritons, their garments had to fall recognizably within the boundaries of an iconographic tradition—a tradition that was itself intended allegorically. The episode from *The Two Noble Ladies* thus raises some intriguing questions. How did playgoers navigate from onstage action to fictional representation? What interpretive paradigms did they apply to the layers of signification in between—the actual garments worn onstage signifying Tritons' robes, the robes indicating that these particular actors are supposed to be Tritons, the Tritons traditionally representing water, water therefore indicating the Euphrates River—so that the action of Tritons dragging the soldiers offstage would thus signify drowning in the Euphrates River?

Instead of assuming a priori that playgoers used their imaginations in order to make what happened in the theatre seem more real, this chapter will interrogate what exactly counted as "real" in early modern performance. Allegory, I contend, was not merely a convenient way for actors to depict situations, such as drowning in the sea, that would otherwise be difficult to stage. Rather, it was one of the underlying cultural logics that shaped basic theatrical literacy, that allowed onstage actions to be intelligible *as* representations. Early modern playgoers lived in a universe where everyday life was understood as intimately linked to eternal verities, where signs of the latter were constantly present in the former. This way of thinking encouraged what, from our modern perspective, might seem like contradictory beliefs: reality was both profoundly physical and inherently illusory, both fixed and malleable, both concrete and abstract. These cultural understandings shaped not only the content of plays but also the semiotics of performance. Theatrical signifiers, I argue, were understood both literally and figuratively; they were at once a reflection of the material world and an index to universal, abstract truths. Mimesis was itself always already allegorical.[3]

The interpenetration of these two seemingly disparate representational modes problematizes evolutionary models of theatre history, which often associate allegory with medieval religious theatre and verisimilitude with the "secular" drama of Shakespeare and his contemporaries.[4] Yet even a cursory glance suggests that allegory was flourishing not only in civic pageants and court masques but also in the public theatres. The Jacobean *Two Noble Ladies* was not a throwback to medieval drama but part and parcel of a continuing allegorical tradition. Personifications of the seven deadly sins, who regularly appeared in plays such as *Doctor Faustus,* were not anachronistic medieval remnants but an essential component of early modern drama. As Roslyn Knutson has shown, morality plays appeared "on stage and/or in print throughout the years of *Henslowe's Diary.* Strange's Men, for example, performed *A Looking Glass for London and England* in 1592, and the play was printed in 1594, 1598, and 1602."[5] Allegorical figures also featured prominently in other genres. In Shakespeare's histories, we have personifications such as Rumor in *2 Henry IV;* in his romances, characters such as Time in *The Winter's Tale.* In domestic tragedies, a genre famous for its deployment of realistic settings and contemporary geographic details, are figures named Homicide, Avarice, and Truth.[6] If, as Frederick Kiefer so aptly puts it, "abstractions commonly mingle with people on the Elizabethan stage,"[7] how did audience members negotiate that diversity? And how did the performance medium reconcile such seemingly contradictory representational modes?

Thomas Kyd's *The Spanish Tragedy* serves as an especially useful case study for addressing such questions. Not only does it feature allegorical characters, but its metatheatrical structure also foregrounds matters of audience interpretation. The dramatic narrative is organized around a series of plays-within-plays: (1) the frame story, in which the ghost of Don Andrea and the allegorical figure Revenge watch and comment on the unfolding action; (2) the main plot of the play, which takes place at the Spanish court and involves the murder of Horatio and Hieronimo's subsequent revenge; and (3) the inset entertainments presented for the court, which include a number of masques as well as the culminating tragedy of "Soliman and Perseda." I turn to the "Soliman and Perseda" episode at the end of this chapter, when I examine early modern ideas about semiotics and language. However, my discussion begins with a detailed consideration of the frame narrative, in particular the opening scene, in which the metatheatrical structure of the play is introduced, and the moment at the end of act 3 when Revenge falls asleep and then stages a dumb show. These episodes have sometimes been considered strangely superfluous, given that the main action of the play ultimately centers not on Andrea's revenge but rather on Hieronimo's. Analyzing the frame narrative in relation to cultural discourses about dreams, ghosts, and demons, however, suggests that it is integral to the play's exploration of theatrical interpretation. Moreover, attending to its performance dynamics offers insight into the function of plays-within-plays in early modern drama more generally. Metatheatrical moments, I contend, did not serve as self-conscious commentary on "the reality of illusion and the illusion of reality,"[8] as most scholars would have it. What was at stake for early modern spectators was not the aesthetics of representation (art as a reflection of life), but the spiritual implications of negotiating theatre as a semiotic system (art as an allegorical index of larger truths). Plays-within-plays, I argue, articulated broader anxieties about interpreting seemingly real sensory experiences, and these epistemological challenges and their moral consequences were not merely thematized within the drama but enacted in performance.

Sensory Perception and Interpretation in *The Spanish Tragedy*

For early modern theatregoers, proper interpretation of performance depended first and foremost on accurate perception: in order to know what onstage signifiers meant, audience members had first to see and hear them correctly. In chapter 2, I examined how visual paradigms outside the playhouse shaped what counted as perceivable in the theatre; here, I want to push that argument further to consider what early modern accounts of eyes and ears suggest about the nature of interpretation itself. These cultural conceptions had important implications for the moral and epistemological challenges of theatrical interpretation, as we shall see in *The Spanish Tragedy*'s attention to visual uncertainty in its frame narrative and its treatment of aurality and performative language in the "Soliman and Perseda" episode.

In early modern England, the base physicality of the sense organs was a factor that rendered visual and aural information spiritually unreliable. The problem was, as Bob Scribner puts it, "how do we apprehend supernatural reality, trapped as we are in material being?"[9] For late medieval Catholics, one solution to this problem was the sacramental gaze, a mode of seeing through which viewers came to experience divine or saintly presence through acts of "pytously beholding."[10] Affective piety of this sort could be found in attitudes toward the elevation of the Host during mass as well as in the cult of images, where proper devotion toward images of saints led not only to spiritual benefits but also sometimes to material manifestations of the holy persons.[11] With the Protestant Reformation came a theological shift: divine truth, church officials proclaimed, could no longer be accessed through the embodied experience of viewing. In lieu of images was the Word of God, to be experienced through the ears, not the eyes. As I argued in chapter 2, even when sacramental seeing came to be understood as suspect, devotional practices rooted in affective piety nevertheless profoundly shaped the actor-audience dynamics of the public theatre. Widespread ideas about visuality that had undergirded earlier religious beliefs continued to persist. Protestant iconoclasts did not so much find images irrelevant as fear their power to be devilish.[12] Sensory perception was still understood as a way to access the supernatural; it was simply that the moral valences were inverted. For both Catholics and Protestants, the eye provided information about the spirit world; whether the spirits at issue were good or evil was the question.

Both pre- and post-Reformation writers emphasized that the physical senses were not merely symbolic of enlightenment or damnation but rather a literal link between everyday life and the supernatural realm. This way of understanding sensory perception can be seen in a mid-fifteenth-century account of a church robber. The story concerns a thief who, because he had stolen from the church, was unable to see the Eucharistic Host after it had been consecrated. The man soon realized that the problem was not the "febyllnes of hys brayne" but rather that he "lackyd grace." According to the narrative, after the thief confessed his crimes, he was able to "see that blessyd sacrament well inowe."[13] Physical blindness is here not merely symbolic of moral degeneration but is rather the concrete manifestation of a spiritual malady. In treating the material world as closely entwined with the supernatural one, Protestant Reformers were not so different from their Catholic predecessors. Famous for their discussions of hearing, they too understood sensory experiences as indexical embodiments of higher truths. Their writings suggest that religious shifts resulted not in a straightforward transition from visual symbol to the literal word but in significant crossover between the allegorical interpretation of images and biblical exegesis in the vernacular. Richard Brathwaite's *Essaies vpon the Fiue Senses*, for instance, stresses that the ear is not meant for listening to profane music or participating in everyday conversation but is "an edifying sence, conveying the fruit of either morall or diuine discourse to the imagination."[14] Brathwaite's text expresses a familiar sentiment: the Word of God will raise up the faithful; obstinate unbelievers who fail to listen are inevitably damned. Because such pronouncements were so common among Protestant Reformers, it is easy to take for granted the relationship they describe between the physical and the spiritual worlds. Salvation, it appears, was a kind of one-way street: holy words flow into the ears of receptive believers and lead them to redemption.

However, this familiar view sometimes obscures more subtle and complex beliefs. In early modern England, the path of edification ran in both directions: the material world was not merely an inert signifier pointing to the signified of the spiritual world; changes in the physical conditions of everyday life were also seen as having very real consequences in the spiritual realm. For example, in *The Boring of the Eare*, a treatise on the proper behavior of parishioners when listening to sermons, Stephen Egerton states that criminals whose ears are cut off suffer not only bodily punishment but also potential peril to their souls:

> The next punishment vnto death by our Nationall law, is losing the eares. And certainly whose eares or hearing God hath suffered to be taken away, they are in a dangerous or desperate case, because the Word is the sauour of life vnto the right hearer, and the sauour of death vnto him that heareth not as hee ought.[15]

Egerton shifts abruptly from addressing the material world, where ears are parts of the human body, to discussing the spiritual effect of losing those biological organs. Punishment that is applied to the physical body has serious consequences in the moral realm. A similar logic may be found in the opening lines of Brathwaite's treatise: "Though the *eye* of my bodie allude to the *eye* of my soule," he says, "yet is the eye of my soule darkned [*sic*] by the eye of my bodie."[16] As scholars have noted, references to the body that seem on the surface to be merely metaphorical were, for early modern writers, often quite literal descriptions of material reality.[17] Both Brathwaite's and Egerton's texts describe the physical world as not merely a descriptive signifier but also a performative one. Everyday life was a text in which believers might discover the signs of a higher heavenly order as well as a slate on which one could inscribe words that would lead to salvation or damnation. Material reality, in other words, did not merely represent spiritual truths; it actively affected them.

This fluidity between the sacred and the profane, between representation and causation, can be seen in the opening scene of *The Spanish Tragedy*, where the challenges of interpreting theatrical performance are tied to the vexed question of how to distinguish true visions from false dreams. The play begins with the ghost of

Don Andrea describing his heroic death in battle and his subsequent travels in the underworld. At the end of this long speech, Andrea says to Revenge,

> Forthwith (*Reuenge*) she [Proserpine] rounded thee in th'eare,
> And bad thee lead me through the gates of Hor[n]:
> Where dreames haue passage in the silent night.
> No sooner had she spoke but we were heere,
> I wot not how, in twinkling of an eye.
>   *Reuenge.*
> THen [*sic*] know *Andrea* that thou art ariu'd,
> Where thou shalt see the author of thy death:
> *Don Balthazar* the Prince of Portingale.
> Depriu'd of life by *Bel-imperia*:
> Heere sit we downe to see the misterie,
> And serue for *Chorus* in this tragedie.[18]

Andrea's speech alludes to the belief that dreams could be divided into two categories: those from the gates of ivory were supposed to be false dreams; those from the gates of horn, true visions. Early modern writers inherited this model of the twin gates of sleep from classical texts, particularly *The Odyssey* and *The Aeneid*.[19] The timing of Andrea's reference to the gates of horn is significant. Prior to this point in the play, spectators may reasonably assume that the figures onstage will be characters in the main plot. It is only at this moment that the metatheatrical structure of *The Spanish Tragedy* becomes evident, as if the invocation of the gates of horn magically calls the play into being. The allusion is described as spoken by Proserpine to Revenge. It serves as a kind of speech act, miraculously transporting Revenge and Andrea to the "heere" of the theatre. This movement in space is accompanied by a movement in time: the play shifts from narration of Andrea's past to the "thou art ariu'd" of the theatrical present. The space and time of the fictional play and those of the actual playhouse here converge and become one, situating both fictional spectators and actual playgoers as viewers of the action to come.

That it is the reference to the twin gates of sleep that produces this conjunction is noteworthy. The concept itself is allegorical: it transforms an abstract binary—true vision, false dream—into the concrete form of two parallel doors, as is illustrated vividly in an image from Michel de Marolles's *Tableaux du Temple des Muses* (figure 3.1). At the same time, the way in which this allegorical concept is deployed in *The Spanish Tragedy* renders *mimetic* interpretation problematic. By referring to the gates of horn immediately before Revenge and Andrea "sit...downe to see the misterie," the play constructs the action at the Spanish court as true vision, not false dream. The play-within-the-play, it seems to suggest, should be understood as "real," as an accurate depiction of a fictional universe. However, referring to one half of the twin gates of sleep simultaneously calls to mind the other. Why should it be necessary to affirm that the play within is true? The deployment of the dream metaphor in this scene raises the specter of its opposite: by insisting that the events at the Spanish court may be taken at face value, it reminds the audience that not all visions are necessarily reliable. Like false dreams, seemingly real theatrical representations may in fact be deceptive.

Figure 3.1 "The Palace of Sleep." On the right are the gates of horn, through which true visions appear; on the left, the gates of ivory, representing false dreams. Michel de Marolles, *Tableaux du temple des muses* (Paris, 1655), plate lviii. By permission of the Print Collection, Miriam and Ira D. Wallach Division of Art, Prints, and Photographs, the New York Public Library, Astor, Lenox, and Tilden Foundations.

This distrust of surface appearances seems well warranted given subsequent developments in the play. When Hieronimo murders Balthazar and Lorenzo through his staging of "Soliman and Perseda," the Spanish King and Portuguese Viceroy are initially deceived into applauding the entertainment. Only afterward, during Hieronimo's epilogue, does the onstage audience come to the grim realization that those stabbed within the play are, in fact, "actually" dead. The convention of using a play-within-the-play to effect "real" murder later became a staple of revenge tragedy. Familiar as we are with the genre, it is not surprising that the challenges of interpreting mimetic theatrical action are thematized in this episode. At the time Kyd wrote *The Spanish Tragedy*, however, the device was still a novelty,[20] and it is striking that these same issues are, from the beginning of the play, woven into the semiotics of performance itself. By invoking the epistemological difficulty of interpreting dreams at the very moment when the metatheatrical frame comes into being, the opening sequence with Andrea and Revenge exhorts audiences not to jump too quickly to conclusions about the actions they see onstage. Mimetic resemblance is not to be trusted. What *counts* as real in the ensuing drama, the play seems to suggest, may not be what *seems* to be most real on the surface.

The dangers of trusting too easily in mimetic representation are likewise integrated into the performance medium at the end of act 3. Here again, connections between epistemological questions thematized in *The Spanish Tragedy* and problems of signification in the actual playhouse arise at a moment when there is a shift from one representational mode to another. In the opening episode, the dream metaphor is used to transition from discursive description of the underworld to real performance event; at the end of act 3, it is invoked specifically when the play shifts from dialogue to direct audience address. When the ghost of Andrea discovers to his dismay that Revenge has fallen asleep, he cries,

> *Ghost.*
> Awake *Reuenge,* for thou art ill aduisde,
> Thsleepe [*sic*], away, what, thou art warnd to watch.
> *Reuenge.*
> Content thy selfe, and doe not trouble me.
> *Ghost.*
> Awake, *Reuenge,* if loue as loue hath had,
> Haue yet the power or preuailance in hell,
> *Hieronimo* with *Lorenzo* is ioynde in league,
> And intercepts our passage to reuenge:
> Awake *Reuenge,* or we are woe degone [*sic*].
> *Reuenge.*
> Thus worldlings ground what they haue dreamd vpon,
> Content thy selfe *Andrea,* though I sleepe,
> Yet is my mood soliciting their soules,
> Sufficeth thee that poore *Hieronimo,*
> Cannot forget his sonne *Horatio.*
> Nor dies *Reuenge* although he sleepe a while,
> For in vnquiet, quietnes is faind:
> And slumbring is a common worldly wile,
> Beholde *Andrea* for an instance how,
> *Reuenge* hath slept, and then imagine thou,
> What tis to be subiect to destinie. (I2v; 3.15.10–28)

This moment stands out as the only onstage action Revenge performs that is scripted in the playtext.[21] As in the opening sequence, we have the simultaneous deployment of allegorical and mimetic modes of representation. The notion that Andrea's revenge has been delayed is represented through the character Revenge falling asleep. Yet the allegorical signifier itself (sleep) is represented mimetically—that is, although the action is meant to be interpreted symbolically, it *resembles* real-life slumber. As in act 1, scene 1, the overlap between allegory and mimesis is associated with the epistemological quandaries of interpreting dreams.

The episode also works toward similar ends as the opening sequence in that both scenes associate the challenge of interpreting dreams with the difficulties inherent in decoding theatrical performance. When Andrea exhorts Revenge to awake, the latter declares that his slumber should not be read as a sign that he has forgotten the injustices perpetrated at the Spanish court. Before Revenge makes clear his intentions, however, he prefaces his explanations with a statement that is directed more toward the audience than Andrea: "Thus worldlings ground what they haue dreamd vpon." Revenge's declaration that mortals base their beliefs on what is merely a dream is not simply a natural extension of the dominant motif of sleep in this scene; it is used specifically to caution against misinterpreting stage action. Andrea's anxiety over the fact that "*Hieronimo* with *Lorenzo* is ioynde in league, / And intercepts our passage to reuenge" is based not only on what he has seen of the play-within-the-play but also on his misapprehension of what Revenge's sleep means. Andrea's interpretations, Revenge suggests, are faulty because the allegorical figure's "quietnes is faind." Andrea here misunderstands Revenge's true intentions *not* because he has misconstrued the way allegory works—he correctly identifies that Revenge's sleep is significant—but because the mimetic signifiers pointing to the allegorical meaning are themselves problematic. It is, in other words, mimetic interpretation that is difficult here; allegorical interpretation only becomes troublesome because mimesis is deceptive. Given the metatheatrical structure—the events at the Spanish court are witnessed not only by Andrea but also by actual playgoers—Revenge's warning to Andrea also serves as a caution to the audience. Both on- and offstage spectators are characterized as gullible "worldlings" who must be careful not to misinterpret the meaning of the show.

In the remainder of the scene at the end of act 3, metatheatricality is further connected to the epistemological challenges posed by theatrical performance. Immediately following Revenge's comment, "Beholde *Andrea* for an instance how, / *Reuenge* hath slept, and then imagine thou, / What tis to be subiect to destinie," a dumb show is presented:

>   Enter a dumme shew.
>   *Ghost.*
>   Awake *Reuenge*, reueale this misterie.
>   *Reuenge.*
>   The two first the nuptiall Torches boare,
>   As brightly burning as the mid-daies sunne:
>   But after them doth *Himen* hie as fast,
>   Clothed in sable, and a Saffron robe,
>   And blowes them out, and quencheth them with blood,
>   As discontent that things continue so.
>   *Ghost.*
>   Sufficeth me thy meanings vnderstood,
>   And thanks to thee and those infernall powers,
>   That will not tollerate a Louers woe,
>   Rest thee for I will sit to see the rest.
>   *Reuenge.*
>   Then argue not for thou hast thy request. (I2v–I3r; 3.15.28–40)

When Andrea asks Revenge to explicate the meaning of the entertainment, he refers to it as a "misterie," the same term Revenge uses in the opening scene to refer to the action at the Spanish court ("Heere sit we downe to see the misterie, / And serue for *Chorus* in this tragedie" [A3r; 1.1.90–91]). In early modern drama, the chorus served not to echo theatrical action but to move the narrative along and assist in its explication. Both the dumb show and the main action of the play are imagined as nontransparent shows that require interpretation. Revenge's comment here at the end of act 3 indicates that the appropriate interpretive mode to deploy is allegorical. Staging a dumb show that needs to be interpreted allegorically immediately following an overtly allegorical moment in the play (Andrea's attempt to "awaken" Revenge) draws a parallel between the interpretive strategies that the characters must use to decipher the dumb show and the strategies expected of actual playgoers in interpreting their earlier exchange. This parallel between on- and offstage spectators would have been enhanced by the fact that act 4 most likely began immediately after this episode with no pause in the live performance.[22] By presenting act 4 right after Andrea declares that he will "sit to see the rest" and Revenge replies "thou hast thy request," this scene positions both fictional characters and actual audience members as joint witnesses to the subsequent stage action. Moreover, it implies that both must adopt similar strategies to decode performance. Rather than taking theatrical representation at face value, the play problematizes the reliability of mimetic signifiers onstage.

Dreams and Metatheatricality

That the difficulties involved in navigating between allegorical and mimetic modes of performance should be concentrated in the play's use of the dream metaphor as a metatheatrical device is especially fitting when we consider views about semiotics and epistemology in early modern texts on dreams and ghosts. Dream interpretation manuals contained long lists cataloging the often obscure meanings that corresponded to different dreams. Thomas Hill's *A Most Briefe and Pleasant Treatise of the Interpretation of Sundrie Dreames,* for instance, states, "To see thy house faire swept with a broome, signifieth the consumption of thy money."[23] Artemidorus's *Oneirocritica,* translated in English as *The Iudgement, or Exposition of Dreames,* notes that dreams about "[q]uinces signify heauines. Almonds, Walnuts, and Filberts, are trouble and anger."[24] These correspondences seem, if not entirely arbitrary, at least far from obvious to the average interpreter. Describing at length such varied and obscure meanings, dream interpretation manuals evince the signifying practices usually ascribed to allegory. As Angus Fletcher states in his foundational book, allegory is a mode characterized by "a peculiar doubleness of intention":[25]

> In the simplest terms, allegory says one thing and means another. It destroys the normal expectation we have about language, that our words "mean what they say."... Pushed to an extreme, this ironic usage would subvert language itself, turning everything into an Orwellian newspeak. In this sense we see how allegory is properly considered a mode: it is a fundamental process of encoding our speech.[26]

Early modern dream manuals foreground this duality: the true meaning of the dream lies beneath its surface and can only be unearthed through a process of interpretation. This doubleness was also essential to early modern understandings of the term *allegory* itself. In *The Alchemist,* for example, Ben Jonson highlights the distance between signifier and signified when he compares esoteric alchemical jargon to the indecipherable "mystick *Symboles*" of the Egyptians and to poetic fables "Wrapt in perplexed *Allegories.*"[27] Thomas Elyot's dictionary, first published in 1538 and subsequently reprinted numerous times through 1559, defined *"Allegoria"* as "a figure or inuersion of wordes, where it is in wordes one, and an other in sentence or meanynge."[28] This emphasis on the "otherness" of allegory's meaning, on the gap between signifier and signified, picks up on the contradiction inherent in the word's etymology. The prefix *allos* ("other") appended to the verb *agoreuein* ("to speak openly, to speak in the assembly or market") marks allegory's tendency to obfuscate meaning.[29]

Early modern dream interpretation manuals are structured around the explication of such hidden meanings. As such, they offer a perspective on drama's deployment of the dream metaphor that is different from what scholars typically assume. In the context of these manuals, to say that theatre is "like a dream" would be to say that theatre signifies something *other* than what it mimetically represents. The only hint in these texts that dreams might simulate life—that is, that the dream metaphor might serve the function usually ascribed to it by scholars of early modern drama—can be found at the beginning of the first book of Artemidorus's treatise. Here he distinguishes between two types of dreams: those that are "[s]peculatiue and agreeable to theire vision, As when a man dreames that the ship wherein hee is doth perish, & rising finds it to be true and saues himselfe with some fewe besides," and those that are "allegoricall, and by one thing signifie another."[30] It is noteworthy that his text is devoted entirely to the second kind of dream, the "allegorical" ones whose meanings are obscure. Dreams of the first kind are apparently not worth interpreting. Their meaning is self-evident. While it might be tempting to think of these dreams as mimetic representations, what is important, for Artemidorus, is not so much that the dream ship *resembles* the actual ship but that it marks an actual occurrence. Rather than serving as an image of external reality, the dream is the substantive reality itself. If such dreams are signifiers, in other words, they are signifiers that, like theatre, also function as embodied presence.

In early modern England, the semiotic import of dreams and the interpretive questions they raised were not morally neutral matters. Dream interpretation manuals suggest that the act of decoding such signifiers, even in seemingly secular contexts, was shot through with spiritual consequence. Texts on dreams are not overtly religious in theme. Most begin with introductory materials that situate dreams in relation to humoral theories of the body. The first step was to ascertain which dreams contained interpretable information. To eliminate dreams of no account, eating and drinking moderately were required, so as to avoid humoral imbalances. The translator of Artemidorus's treatise, for example, notes that "dreames of importa*n*ce" only arise late in the night because until then "all the sences, and corporall powers are occupied in digesting the supper."[31] However, digestion is only one factor necessary for obtaining true visions, for "a sober and quiet man may see dreams,

which are of import, not onely after midnight & [i.e., but] also in the day time."³²
The dreamer's moral condition, in other words, could apparently exempt him or her from the requirement of temperate eating.

Other texts likewise combine the moral and the physiological when outlining prerequisites for true dreams. Gonzalo's *The Divine Dreamer* states that

> many times a person going to his rest, not cloyed with bad affections, nor superfluity of food; but being vertuously minded, and healthfully disposed, his soule in sleeping may foresee things to come, for the soule, which of it selfe is divine and celestiall, being not offended with any evill cogitations, or over-bad meats, is at free liberty, and best performeth her actions when the body sleepeth, not being busied with any other matters.³³

Even as Gonzalo stresses the importance of healthful eating habits, he ties the physical condition of the body to the moral state of the soul. The power of prophesying through dreams, the author suggests, will only come to those who are "vertuously minded" and who avoid "bad affections" and "evill cogitations." In early modern usage, the word *bad* could denote not only the morally bankrupt but also the physically unwholesome, as in the "over-bad meats" described later in the passage.³⁴ The term *evil* likewise referred both to the wicked and to the unhealthy, as in Shakespeare's *Richard III* when the title character attributes the King's illness to "euill Diet" (TLN 147; 1.1.139).³⁵ Such ambiguity in usage suggests a slippage between the physical and the spiritual in early modern thinking about dreams that is akin to the dialectical relationship we saw earlier with regard to the senses.³⁶ Both kinds of virtue were necessary for accurate interpretation to take place.

The combination of physical and moral concerns in early modern English dream manuals produced a curious kind of circular logic. As we have seen, whether or not dreams contained interpretable signifiers depended on the dreamer's moral character. Yet, at the same time, the dreamer's moral character was precisely what was revealed through his dreams. Thomas Hill, for instance, states that the dreams of "wicked persons" revolve around their misdeeds:

> [T]he condition of the wickednesse, doth incline and dispose the person vnto the often considering and dreaming those wicked facts, which were done a good whiles before, in the day time, and then thought vpon and renewed in the dreame; for that such like do soone occurre vnto memorie: whereof, the unchast persons doe often dreame of women: the drunkards, of wines and other strong drinks: and the theeves, of robberies.³⁷

A similar kind of circular logic applied to the person of the interpreter. A dream's spiritual implications could only be assessed by an accurate interpreter, but it was precisely a person's spiritual condition that determined the accuracy of his interpretations. Hill's treatise notes that the "Expounder of Dreames must bee such a person...as leadeth a godly life."³⁸ Artemidorus's text likewise states that the proper interpreter must be "good, vertuous[,] pure, and cleane" and "exempt from humaine fragility"; when his "spirite is lesse bound, tyed and soyeld with the felloweshippe of the body," his readings will be correct.[39] Although authors and publishers of treatises on dreams had an obvious stake in emphasizing the honesty of their profession, it is nevertheless significant that correct exposition was tied not to features internal to the dream nor to cryptographic skill but to the moral character of the interpreter himself.

The contradictions in dream manuals reflected broader cultural ambivalence about the epistemological and moral valences of dreams. On the one hand, dreams were considered legitimate enough to be included in legal and medical cases. When the Gunpowder Plot conspirators were tried for treason, dreams were admitted as evidence in court.[40] When patients brought their ailments to doctors, dreams were a diagnostic tool. As Thomas Wright put it, "[W]ee prooue in dreames, and physitians prognosticate by them, what humour aboundeth."[41] On the other hand, dreams were viewed as potentially deceptive; their prognosticatory power might potentially be not religious revelation but demonic manipulation. As Stuart Clark describes, "True dreams were good dreams that came from God (or angels) and were spiritually improving, even revelatory, and might lead to conversion; false dreams were evil ones sent by the devil to tempt and corrupt."[42] The difficulty was sorting out which was which. In order to properly understand the spiritual meaning of a dream, it was first necessary to pinpoint its origin, yet determining that origin meant relying on the moral valences of its consequent effects. Dreams seemed to demand an allegorical mode of interpretation, but that process was epistemologically circular, working forward and backward at once.

Comparisons between plays and dreams were thus not merely benign musings on the aesthetics of representation. Acts of interpretation had important moral repercussions. Analyzing *The Spanish Tragedy* in light of dream manuals enables us to better understand the purpose of metatheatricality in early modern drama. Scholars have often taken the dream metaphor as commentary on the relationship between art and life. Jackson Cope's influential book, *The Theater and the Dream,* for instance, asserts that "[l]ife is a dream, but dreams are more real than life. The world is a theater, but the theater is more real than this world."[43] David Bevington suggests that sleep is increasingly "connected by Renaissance dramatists with the very business of writing and acting plays," and he associates this metatheatricality with "explorations of carnival inversion, indeterminacy of meaning, uncertainty as to the will of Providence, and the ironies of human lack of self-awareness"[44]—in short, with questions of epistemology. Yet Bevington takes for granted what metatheatricality *is*: references to sleep and dreams, he argues, serve as "a metaphor for the fluid boundaries between reality and illusion, life and art, theater and dream."[45]

This view of metatheatricality proceeds from the assumption that the representational strategies of the early modern playhouse were primarily mimetic. If dreams are images of real life, so the reasoning goes, then references to theatre as being like a dream must stem from preoccupations with what it means for drama to imitate life. Indeed, theories of metatheatricality in general tend to take mimesis as a given. For example, Lionel Abel asserts that "in the metaplay life *must* be a dream and the *world* must be a stage," and this view he sees as broadly applicable both to Shakespearean metatheatre and to later drama.[46] Scholarly accounts of specific plays-within-plays follow the same trajectory. Inset plays in comedies are often noted for their inability to sustain dramatic illusion, as in, for example, the rude mechanicals' performance in *A Midsummer Night's Dream*. Plays-within-plays in tragedies, by contrast, are seen as realistic—even overly realistic—in their theatrical depictions, as in *Hamlet* when "The Mousetrap" holds the mirror up to nature so well that Claudius recognizes his own image. Yet both comedies and tragedies are measured against the same yardstick: the dream metaphor, the *theatrum mundi* topos, and plays-within-plays are all assessed in relation to mimetic performance.[47]

Reading *The Spanish Tragedy* in conjunction with early modern dream manuals, however, complicates this perspective on metatheatricality. For early modern playgoers, the mimetic was always already the allegorical. Imitation of the visible world *was* a kind of allegorical embodiment. It both gave physical form to abstract concepts and served as an earthly manifestation of higher truths. Neither dreams nor drama could be taken at face value as mere reflections of reality; both had to be mined for their true significance. It was this issue—interpretation, *not* verisimilitude—that motivated comparisons between theatre and dreams. What was at stake was not whether a play was similar to real life but whether what seemed real could actually be trusted. Far from straightforward commentary on the illusoriness of life, metatheatricality functioned as a meditation on the challenges posed by early modern performance as a signifying system.

Ghosts, Demons, and Epistemologies of Performance

In the case of *The Spanish Tragedy*, the meanings generated by the ghost of Andrea and the allegorical figure of Revenge were conditioned not only by epistemological and moral dilemmas clustered around dreams but also by related beliefs about specters and demons. In early modern England, sleep was understood to be a liminal state that predisposed one to ghostly visitations, but the line between real spirits and illusory apparitions was a thin one, as can be seen in the overlap of the terms *phantom, phantasm,* and *fantasy*: all three derive from the same Greek and Latin roots signifying "ghost, apparition" as well as "mental image...figment, illusion."[48] This slippage is evident in Francis Kinnaston's *Leoline and Sydanis*. When the disguised Sydanis pays a nighttime visit to her beloved, he awakens suddenly from a dream to find her standing there. Sydanis claims that she is an "ayeriall Phantom,"[49] a phrase that plays on early modern beliefs that false visions were concocted of air or vapors acting as mirrors.[50] The irony is that she is actually a real person disguised as a spirit and thus entirely substantial. The unreliability of mimesis is here foregrounded and overlaid onto discourses of dreams and apparitions.

Nocturnal visions were also potentially problematic because they might be demonic illusions. Ghostly visitations were denounced as superstitious nonsense by Protestant Reformers, who denied the existence of Purgatory. Yet despite official doctrine, popular beliefs that spirits returned from the dead to convey warnings or offer portentous remarks remained widespread.[51] Regardless of confessional allegiance, however, all agreed that devils might impersonate the dead in order to damn the souls of those to whom they appeared.[52] Catholics and Protestants were further united in their disapproval of skeptics who attributed ghostly apparitions to natural causes or human tricks. John Deacon and John Walker's *Dialogicall Discourses of Spirits and Divels,* for example, condemns "those *godles Atheistes* now in our daies, who hold there are neither *Spirits nor Diuels.*"[53] Pierre le Loyer's *A Treatise of Specters* similarly avers that such beliefs belong to "all sorts of *Atheistes* whatsoeuer."[54] As Kristen Poole has argued, modern scholars have often placed undue attention on unusual figures, such as Reginald Scot, whose distrust of spectral visions resembles our own post-Enlightenment attitudes.[55] Most early modern people, however, believed that dismissing the existence of demonic spirits was both morally reprehensible and profoundly irrational. It made as little sense as discounting the presence of God—a fundamentally unthinkable position.

The dangers of demonic deception rendered dreams especially problematic, and these discourses informed early modern ideas about theatre's impact on spectators. Thomas Nash, for instance, describes the dangers of nocturnal isolation in terms related specifically to theatrical performance. "In the day," Nash writes, the devil "may smoothly in some mild shape insinuat, but in the night he takes vpon him like a tyrant.... This Macheuillian tricke hath hee in him worth the noting, that those whom he dare not vnited or together encounter, disioined and diuided, hee will one by one assaile in their sleepe."[56] Dreaming, he warns, renders one vulnerable to the devil's wiles because it is the quintessential individual experience. The sleeper must confront these visions alone, and the devil may thus divide and conquer. By referring to this epistemological difficulty as the devil's "Macheuillian tricke," Nash links demonic deception through dreams to theatre. As Jonas Barish has shown, antitheatrical discourses repeatedly imagined actors as Machiavels.[57] The devil is the ultimate actor; the convincingly mimetic representations he offers are dangerous because of their potential to deceive. In the public playhouses, interpretation was both communal and individual: theatre was experienced alongside other people, but decoding presentational signifiers was ultimately an individual experience. Nash's reference to the devil as a kind of "tyrant" is thus especially appropriate. As Marissa Greenberg has shown, in early modern England, unlike on the Continent, the notion of tragic catharsis was understood to have special applicability to tyrants.[58] Theatre's ability to "catch the Conscience of the King" (*Hamlet,* TLN 1645; 2.2.605) relied for its effects on differentiation between individual and group response: distinguishing the guilty from the innocent required that tyrants respond one way and just rulers another. As in dream manuals, where the spiritual condition of the dreamer determined interpretative accuracy, the moral integrity of the spectator is here crucial. Ascertaining the nature of nocturnal apparitions was, like decoding theatrical signifiers, a task dependent on individual sense perception and interpretation. Comfort in numbers was not possible where mimetic illusion was concerned. Proper interpretation was thus essential for guarding against the dangers of demonic deception.

Theatrical representations of ghostly visitations during sleep reflected these diverse beliefs about the nature of apparitions. Supernatural figures in some plays offer true visions. In *Cymbeline,* the ghosts in Posthumus's dream give him a book that prophesies correctly about England's ultimate triumph (TLN 3065–188; 5.4.29–150). In *Richard III,* the spirits of the murdered who visit Richard on the night before the final battle likewise predict his downfall at Bosworth Field (TLN 3561–637; 5.3.117–76). Both of these scenes depict ghosts as "real" spirits—that is, as the souls of actual people returned from the dead. In *Cymbeline,* they offer comfort; in *Richard III,* curses; but in both instances, their status is clear. However, in Thomas Goffe's *The Courageous Turk,* which was performed at Christ Church, Oxford, in 1619, Amurath the Turk retires to bed on the night before a battle, only to be visited by four figures who appear "*framed like Turkish Kings, but blacke, his supposed predecessors.*" These apparitions turn out to be devils impersonating the ghosts of past monarchs. Their goal is to torment Amurath, reminding him of his crimes and impending defeat, in much the same way as the ghosts in *Richard III* disturb his sleep on the eve of Bosworth Field.[59] Ghosts might be real spirits in the pre-Reformation vein, but they might also be malicious agents, producing false dreams that could lead a person to despair and damnation.

The frame narrative of *The Spanish Tragedy* toys with the audience's uncertainty about the status of ghosts and the possibility that they might be demonic. In the opening lines of the play, Andrea claims to be a "Courtier in the Spanish Court" (A2r; 1.1.4) who has traveled through the underworld. For modern readers, Andrea's ghostly status and identity are corroborated by stage directions, speech prefixes, and the *dramatis personae* list—an entire textual apparatus that lends legitimacy to his claims. Early modern readers perusing the 1592 quarto of the play would only have found partial confirmation of the figure's assertions. Speech prefixes in the frame narrative designate the stock character, "Ghost," rather than the personal name, "Andrea"—corroborating his status but not his identity. Spectators at the earliest performances of the play may have had the opposite problem from readers of the printed text: from Andrea's first appearance in courtly apparel, they would have been more certain of his identity as a courtier than of his status as a ghost. Their ability to identify Andrea would have been determined in part by their previous experiences with the story depicted in Kyd's play. *The Spanish Tragedy* was most likely the second half of a two-part play.[60] Henslowe's *Diary* records four instances in which the two plays were performed on consecutive afternoons.[61] For playgoers lucky enough to attend both showings, the person appearing at the beginning of *The Spanish Tragedy* would most likely have been identifiable as Andrea, especially assuming the same actor performed the role on both days. For those who saw only one of the plays, however, the identity of the figure onstage would not have been immediately obvious. This experience of a "one-off" showing appears to have been the norm for *The Spanish Tragedy*. Henslowe records 12 stand-alone performances of the play, three times as many as the number of "paired" showings. As Roslyn Knutson has demonstrated, playing companies were somewhat erratic about the scheduling of sequels.[62] Moreover, the subject of *The Spanish Tragedy*'s prequel is summarized in the opening sequence to the play, as if playgoers could not be counted on to be familiar with the plot.[63]

Even the subset of audience members who knew the first play, however, might have been misled because early modern costuming practices would have made it difficult to determine if Andrea was supposed to be alive or dead. Ghosts in the public theatres were only occasionally clothed in white winding-sheets. More typically, they were dressed to resemble the person while alive. In *Cymbeline,* for instance, the ghost of Posthumus's father is "*attyred like a warriour*" (TLN 3066–67; 5.4.29.s.d.). In *The Second Maiden's Tragedy,* the ghost appears "*in the same form as the [body of the] lady is dressed in the chair*"; the joke in this scene is that the corpse of the lady has been painted and propped up to look as if alive.⁶⁴ As Ann Rosalind Jones and Peter Stallybrass have argued, this tendency to clothe ghosts in particular and situated ways was tied very much to questions of identity. Without clothing, the anonymity of death would reduce all to the same, undifferentiated status, to the skull that Hamlet fails to recognize as Yorick. Only through the external marks of clothing could the injunction to remember be properly carried out.⁶⁵

The interpretive challenges posed by such costuming conventions feature prominently in *Hamlet*. Although modern audiences tend to take for granted that the ghost is Hamlet's father, early modern spectators seeing Shakespeare's play performed for the first time might not have been so sure. In the opening scene, Horatio, Marcellus, and Barnardo repeatedly express uncertainty about the ghost's identity. They do not refer to it as the ghost of the old king but, instead, call it "this thing" (TLN 30; 1.1.21), "this dreaded sight" (TLN 34; 1.1.25), "this Apparition" (TLN 37; 1.1.28), "this portentous figure" (1.1.109), and even this "Illusion" (TLN 127; 1.1.127).⁶⁶ Moreover, they use the pronoun "it," rather than "he." They do not report that the ghost *is* Hamlet's father but rather that it resembles him: the creature, they say, comes "[i]n the same figure, *like* the King that's dead" and "[l]ookes...*like* the King," "*like* the King," "so *like* the King / That was" (TLN 53, 55, 74; 1.1.41, 43, 58, 110–11; emphasis mine).⁶⁷ A few scenes later, when Hamlet sees the vision for himself, he questions whether the ghost is "a Spirit of health, or goblin damn'd," whether it brings with it "ayres from Heauen, or blasts from Hell," and whether it has "intents wicked or charitable" (TLN 625–27; 1.4.40–42).⁶⁸ The original staging might well have increased the audience's interpretive difficulties if the ghost spoke from beneath the stage when requiring Horatio and the others to swear. Because the platform's trapdoor was the location traditionally assigned to the hellmouth in medieval drama, the association of ghosts with this stage location would have linked them with the demonic. Playgoers evaluating the moral status of such figures onstage might have found it a complicated task to distinguish true spirits from devils.

Beyond stage geography, the moral and epistemological challenges posed by dreams and ghosts also inform Hamlet's famous "Oh what a Rogue and Pesant slaue am I" speech:

> Is it not monstrous that this Player heere,
> But in a Fixion, in a dreame of Passion,
> Could force his soule so to his own conceit
> That from her working, all his visage warm'd,
> Teares in his eyes, distraction in's Aspect,
> A broken voyce, and his whole Function suiting
> With Formes, to his Conceit? And all for nothing?
> For *Hecuba*?
> What's *Hecuba* to him, or he to *Hecuba*,
> That he should weepe for her? What would he doe,
> Had he the Motiue and the Cue for passion
> That I haue? (TLN 1591–1602; 2.2.551–62)

By comparing theatre to a "dreame of Passion," this speech connects the epistemological quandaries of interpreting sleeping visions to the problem of distinguishing true and false emotions in the playhouse. The First Player's ability to conjure up real tears "in a Fixion" is here constructed as "monstrous." Acting is condemned for its falsehood. Within the fictional narrative, Hamlet's goal is to emphasize that his feelings, unlike those of the First Player, are real. In the actual playhouse, however, this distinction collapses. By drawing attention to the supposed differences between himself and the First Player, Hamlet underscores the fact that he, too, is an actor—the actor playing Hamlet. As his use of the theatrical term *cue* highlights, Hamlet's supposedly genuine emotions are merely the performance of the actor's scripted part.

The epistemological challenges of interpreting onstage action are further foregrounded when Hamlet mentions the questionable status of the ghost:

> The Spirit that I haue seene
> May be the Deuill, and the Diuel hath power
> T'assume a pleasing shape, yea and perhaps,
> Out of my Weaknesse, and my Melancholly,
> As he is very potent with such Spirits,
> Abuses me to damne me. Ile haue grounds
> More Relatiue then this: The Play's the thing,
> Wherein Ile catch the Conscience of the King. (TLN 1638–45; 2.2.598–605)

The soliloquy here juxtaposes the player's production of false tears "in a dreame of Passion" with the devil's power over the "Spirits" of Hamlet's body—that is, over the biological imbalances producing his physical weakness and melancholy. Just as theatre is here understood as affecting the physiology of the body, so too does the devil work upon bodily humors.[69] Moreover, the problem of how to interpret the ghost is presented as the immediate impetus for the play-within-the-play. Both the problem of mimesis (how to interpret the First Player's tears) and the metatheatrical device of the conscience-catching play are here imagined as having spiritual consequences: for audiences charged with interpreting stage action, moral difficulties are intertwined with epistemological ones.

Similar issues inform the interpretation of the ghost in *The Spanish Tragedy*. In the opening scene, Andrea could have been read in a variety of ways: as a live person, a legitimate ghost, or a demonic impersonation. The convention that soliloquies involve characters speaking frankly and truthfully to the audience supports the figure's claims about his identity. Yet the subsequent references to the twin gates of sleep, figuring the play-within-the-play as a kind of dream, raise the possibility of deception: the figure declaring himself the ghost of Andrea might be not a friendly apparition but a malicious vision, conjured by the devil to damn a dreaming audience. The question of Andrea's status would have been reinforced for spectators familiar with Virgil. As Lukas Erne has shown, Kyd's opening scene revises Book VI of *The Aeneid* to conflate the rewards of Elysium with the punishments of Tartarus. The underworld from which Andrea's ghost comes to the audience is thus an in-between space, what Erne calls "a purgatorial place."[70] This spiritual liminality is analogous to the physical liminality of sleep: in both cases, the porous boundary between worlds is dissolved, rendering sensory experiences epistemologically uncertain and morally ambiguous. The abolishment of Purgatory in official

Protestant doctrine complicated things further by declaring all apparitions not walking souls but demonic illusions. In such a world, Andrea's status was critical. If the actor was supposed to represent the real spirit of a just avenger, then the play as a whole would be epistemologically reliable, and allegorical interpretations of it could be counted on to be morally sound. If, however, the actor was to represent an unjust avenger ambiguously presented to the audience as a true ghost, then the play would be a deceptive vision; allegorical interpretations of it could be misleading. Understanding the play correctly required first determining whether the figure in the opening scene was a proper spirit, returned from the dead to demand justice. In constructing spectators as dreamers and Andrea himself as a vision to be interpreted, *The Spanish Tragedy* draws a parallel between the ghost and the play-within-the-play. The same epistemological and moral challenges mobilized by the twin gates of sleep here cluster around the ghost as a theatrical signifier.

Representing apparitions onstage was particularly challenging in the early modern playhouse because discourses about the corporeal's relation to the spiritual also informed the semiotics of the actor's body onstage. In Shakespeare's *Twelfth Night*, for example, when Viola is reunited with her brother, she does not immediately rejoice in his survival but first points to his clothing and declares, "So went he [Sebastian] suited to his watery tombe" (TLN 2399; 5.1.234). The markers of dress, as Viola knows well, might signify a ghost returned from the dead. She then postulates that the figure might be not a true ghost but a demonic impersonation: "If spirits can assume both forme and suite / You come to fright vs" (TLN 2400–2401; 5.1.235–36). This scene is usually imagined as a moment of disbelief about identity that prompts the twins to offer subsequent corroborating evidence, such as the mole upon their father's brow and the date of their father's death (TLN 2408–14; 5.1.242–48). However, prior to this exchange, Sebastian first takes up the issue of whether or not he is a ghost. "A spirit I am indeed," he says, "But am in that dimension grossely clad, / Which from the wombe I did participate" (TLN 2402–4; 5.1.236–38). Punning on the word *spirit* as meaning both a disembodied ghost and a person's soul, Sebastian invokes the early modern trope of the body as like clothing temporarily covering the eternal soul. What is curious is that these lines not only adopt a familiar sartorial metaphor but also foreground the semiotics of the actor's body. The scene here draws attention to the way costumes signify the shape of the body beneath the clothes. The episode onstage involved two boy actors side-by-side, a juxtaposition underscoring the disparate ways in which the performers' bodies are to signify: although "[a]n apple, cleft in two, is not more twin / Then these two creatures" (TLN 2388–89; 5.1.223–24), one body is supposed to be female, the other male. This attention to theatre's signifying practices would have been accentuated if both actors wore similar costumes, as is suggested earlier in the play when Viola says that she dresses like her brother, who "went / Still in this fashion, colour, ornament, / For him I imitate" (TLN 1902–4; 3.4.381–83). The performance dynamics of the episode underscore the fact that embodying spirits is what actors do: they are the physical manifestations of characters' souls. Highlighting the issue of costume emphasizes that the resurrected Sebastian is bodied forth only when an actor is clad in costume. The Prologue to Shakespeare's *Henry V* draws attention to this ironic condition of theatrical performance when he refers to actors as "flat vnraysed Spirits, that hath dar'd, / On this vnworthy Scaffold, to bring forth / So great an Obiect" as "Warlike *Harry*" (TLN 10–12, 6; Prologue.9–11, 5). Actors are here described as spirits who still remain on earth; their job is to embody the dead. Players are thus in the awkward position of doing precisely the same thing as the devil: offering illusions of seemingly resurrected spirits.

In *The Spanish Tragedy,* then, the moral and epistemological challenges of theatrical representation as embodied practice come together especially in the frame narrative's representation of the ghost. When Andrea declares, "When this eternall substance of my soule, / Did liue imprisond in my wanton flesh: /.../ I was a Courtier in the Spanish Court" (A2r; 1.1.1–4), he draws on the same tropes about the duality of body and soul that we saw in *Twelfth Night*. Moreover, the interpretive challenge of this scene echoes the one that Viola experiences: costume as an identity marker onstage is unreliable if the living and the dead are identically clothed. Kyd, like Shakespeare, ironically highlights the actor's body onstage by negating the character's body within the fictional narrative. In theatre, actors must stand in for souls; the physical must stand in for the spiritual. Rather than naturalizing the relationship between signifier and signified, the scene draws attention to the gap between them. Verisimilar representation, it suggests, is impossible. Spectators cannot remedy imperfections in mimesis by using their imaginations. Their job is to treat theatrical signifiers as indexical markers gesturing toward signifieds whose literal embodiment is impossible. When flesh stands in for spirit, people must stand in for abstract concepts. The failure of mimesis requires the mobilization of allegorical interpretive practices.

Revenge and Allegorical Show

The challenges involved in interpreting the ghost of Andrea also extend to the allegorical figure of Revenge, whose moral valences were complicated by the fact that he might represent not only just punishment but also unjust retribution. These difficulties are foregrounded in the dumb show at the end of act 3, which follows immediately after the discussion of Revenge's "sleep." Two figures appear bearing torches; following them is a third, "[c]lothed in sable, and a Saffron robe," who blows out the torches and "quencheth them with blood" (I2v; 3.15.34–35). Although Revenge subsequently glosses one of these figures as Hymen, traditionally dressed in a saffron robe, and refers to the burning brands as "nuptiall Torches" (I2v; 3.15.30, 32), early modern spectators might well have read the action as an allegory of vengeance bound up with the classical Furies. As Frederick Kiefer has shown, Revenge was frequently associated with these mythical creatures, who were said to avenge the murder of loved ones. Conventionally imagined as women dressed in black robes and sometimes covered in blood, the Furies also carried steel whips and torches steeped in blood or gore.[71] Between the sable black clothing, the orange-red robe, and the bloody torches, the persons in the dumb show shared significant iconographic resonances with these classical figures, resonances that would have been reinforced by the cultural and theatrical connotations of torches. Fire was associated especially with revenge, and the torches traditionally assigned to the Furies grew out of this tradition.[72] In the playhouse, torches were also used to signify a nighttime setting,[73] underscoring the action of Revenge asleep and situating the dumb show as a kind of dream vision. Torches were, moreover, connected to the revelation of hidden crimes. The title page to the 1615 quarto of *The Spanish Tragedy* vividly illustrates this notion: when Hieronimo discovers his dead son hanging in the arbor, he carries a burning torch (figure 3.2). These varied cultural and theatrical associations with torches underscore connections among the murder of Horatio, the inset dumb show, Revenge's sleep, and the lighting of the playhouse stage. Metatheatrical frames here map across and collapse into one another.

That the character Revenge is here connected to the Furies is also noteworthy because it associates the allegorical figure with hell. When Revenge explains the meaning of the dumb show, Andrea expresses his gratitude, saying, "[T]hanks to thee and those infernall powers, / That will not tollerate a Louers woe" (I3r; 3.15.37–38). The proximity of Andrea's comment to Revenge's explanation suggests that these "infernall powers" could potentially be the figures just presented

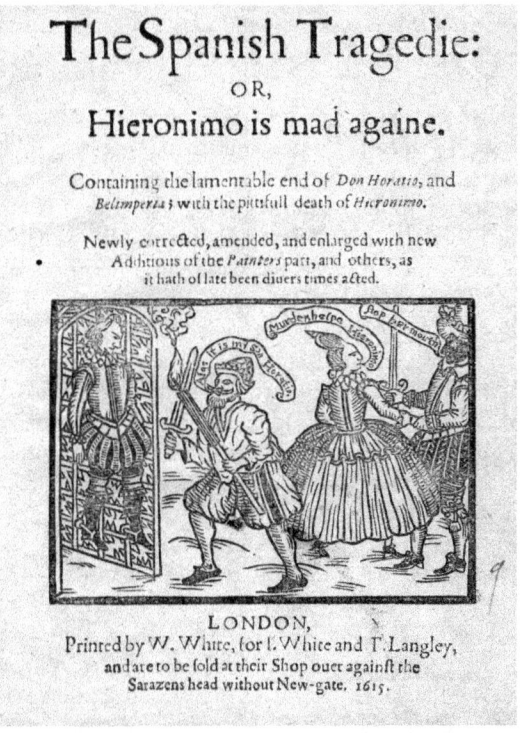

Figure 3.2 The torch Hieronimo carries is associated with the revelation of hidden murder. Thomas Kyd, *The Spanish Tragedie* (London, 1615), title page. By permission of the Folger Shakespeare Library.

in the dumb show. Earlier in the play, Andrea describes the underworld as a place where "bloudie furies shakes [sic] their whips of steele" (A3r; 1.1.65). This association had wider currency in early modern England. Pierre le Loyer, for example, deems the Furies a species of female devil; he refers to them as "euill Spirits," and he specifically styles them "Infernal Furies,"[74] an echo of Andrea's phrase. Connecting Revenge to the classical Furies positions the allegorical figure, and by extension vengeance, as potentially problematic: taking God's justice into one's own hands, the play suggests, could possibly result in eternal damnation. Significantly, Andrea's line also comments on the audience's experience. If spectators in the early modern theatre were, like Andrea, grateful for Revenge's explanation of the dumb show, then Andrea's thanks to "those infernall powers" problematizes playgoers' feelings of gratitude by calling their moral valences into question. On the one hand, spectators who believed they were seeing the Furies would have had their assumptions reinforced: the dumb show does indeed signify vengeance; their readings are, in this sense, correct. On the other hand, the reliability of playgoers' interpretive practices is undermined by the fact that the principle figures within the dumb show turn out not to be the Furies after all. Spectators who have too willingly jumped to conclusions, based on costumes and action, about the identity of the figures onstage are warned to be more wary. Attending to theatre's mimetic aspects, the play suggests, is important but not sufficient; allegorical meaning depends upon, but also exceeds, what appears at first glance to be self-evident.

The moral difficulties exemplified in Revenge's association with the Furies are intensified by the allegorical figure's link to the theatrical Vice. Connections between the two can be seen in both the dramatic and iconographic traditions. John Pikering's *Horestes,* for example, includes a Vice who pretends to be Patience and Courage but finally reveals his true identity, Revenge.[75] Both figures were also associated with the dagger, a small, easily concealable weapon connoting hidden revenge and secret murder.[76] These overlaps between Revenge and the Vice make particular sense in the context of *The Spanish Tragedy*'s hybrid form, which combines classical drama with aspects of Christian morality plays.[77] More importantly, however, associations between the Vice and Revenge also shape the performance dynamics of Kyd's play. Just as the Vice serves to bridge the gap between actor and audience, so too Revenge in *The Spanish Tragedy* connects spectators to the main plot of the play through the device of the frame narrative. Just as the Vice shares his secret stratagems with playgoers, Revenge confides to the audience his plans for the downfall of Andrea's enemies. In this sense, Kyd's play builds on early modern university productions of classical tragedies, in which each act began with a dumb show whose moral meaning was explicated by a chorus after the intervening action.[78] Unlike academic plays, however, *The Spanish Tragedy* complicates audience interpretation by rendering the choric figure morally suspect. The audience, like Andrea, must rely on Revenge to "reueale this misterie" (I2v; 3.15.29), yet Revenge is repeatedly associated with the Furies and with hell. In undermining his moral authority as "*Chorus* in this tragedie" (A3r; 1.1.91), the play situates him firmly in the Vice tradition. Although Revenge mediates between the audience and the main action of the play, he does not embody their moral struggle so much as he produces it. It is Andrea who serves as the audience's representative onstage. He, like playgoers, must navigate the treacherous waters of interpreting theatrical performance and must discern whether to trust Revenge. The psychomachia of the morality drama is here woven into the frame narrative's metatheatricality, with Andrea as a kind of Everyman figure and Revenge as the Vice.

Yet Andrea's role as the audience's onstage representative is complicated by his problematic position as a ghost situated at the gates of sleep. Indeed, Revenge earlier says that "we" (A3r; 1.1.90)—that is, both the allegorical figure and the ghost—will function as chorus to the ensuing action. In this sense, spectator identification with Andrea is itself called into question: like Revenge, he, too, is an ambiguous figure. These moral and epistemological difficulties would have been heightened if, at the beginning of Kyd's play, the allegorical character and the ghost both appeared from the trapdoor below the stage, the playing area traditionally associated with hell.[79] Audience interpretations might also have been complicated by costume. Frederick Kiefer's iconographic analysis suggests that Revenge was often clad in military gear—specifically, wearing a helmet and breastplate.[80] If Andrea was likewise dressed in armor, he and the allegorical figure might seem interchangeable in this episode: both might be the ghosts of soldiers returning from the dead. Indeed, Kiefer notes that allegorical characters are nearly always identified through dialogue in order to ensure that playgoers understand the visual symbolism,[81] yet here Revenge is onstage for nearly the entirety of Andrea's long speech before his allegorical meaning is made clear. Audience identification is thus troubled by the status of the figures onstage, both of whom are positioned as epistemologically unreliable and morally suspect apparitions.

The dynamics I have been tracing in *The Spanish Tragedy* suggest how the semiotic density of theatrical signifiers onstage complicated early modern playgoers' interpretive work. Such issues were not merely thematized in the play but integrated into its performance dynamics through the device of metatheatricality. Questions about the moral status of the ghost and the allegorical figure arise at moments in which representational fiction and presentational action converge: in the dumb show and its explication at the end of act 3 and in soliloquies where actors speak directly to playgoers. By conflating acts of interpretation within the fictional narrative with the interpretive work performed by real-life spectators, the frame narrative uses plays-within-plays and direct audience address to instruct theatregoers in strategies for making sense of onstage action. Holding the mirror up to nature did not produce a neutral reflection; it offered a way to grapple with the challenges of theatrical interpretation. We tend to associate epistemological uncertainty (whether something was real or not) with the issue of mimetic representation, and we tend to associate moral uncertainty (whether something was good or not) with the issue of allegorical representation. For early modern audience members, however, theatrical interpretation was simultaneously a mimetic and an allegorical endeavor. Questions of epistemology and moral interpretation were inseparable. By using metatheatricality to raise fundamental questions about the nature of interpretation, *The Spanish Tragedy* enacts the very uncertainty that it describes—as if trying to represent the epistemological and moral challenges of the semiotics of performance poses such difficulty that the result is an endless regression of representational frames that resist interpretive certainty.

Language, Performativity, and Material Semiotics

In the "Soliman and Perseda" episode at the end of Kyd's play, these interpretive difficulties are mapped onto issues of metatheatricality through the play's meditation on the materiality of different kinds of signifying systems. The entertainment Hieronimo stages at the end of *The Spanish Tragedy* has been much studied in terms of the failure of language. Scholars have argued that, when Hieronimo reveals Horatio's corpse and then later bites out his own tongue, visual presentation ultimately substitutes for the explanatory power of words, which are represented as inadequate.[82] Critical attention to verbal signification, however, has obscured the way the episode negotiates the epistemological challenges of the semiotics of performance. The linguistic signifier is, in its ideal form, a "pure" marker, whose job is to point to a referent. Although the meanings and connotations generated by a given word may be compromised by its physical form—say, the font in which a book is printed—the signifier itself is, in theory, unadulterated by its referent. In the case of theatrical performance, however, the signifier necessarily exists in a bodily form. It is true that words are always material—there is ultimately no abstract *logos* outside of the physical forms and ideological structures through which language is produced. However, theatrical signifiers are *by definition* imagined as embodied.

The material form of a theatrical signifier bears a complex relationship to its referent: the signifier might literally resemble the signified, as when an actor lies down to represent sleep (icon); it might imply the signified by representing some related thing, as when a torch signifies night (index); or it might offer a signifier completely divorced from the signified, as when a saffron robe signifies marriage (symbol). These three possibilities are not discrete semiotic modes but rather sketch out a continuum along which any given signifier might fall. Moreover, they are not mutually exclusive but overlapping modalities. In Charles Sanders Peirce's foundational work on semiotics, language is the quintessential symbol; only in a partially pictorial language, such as Chinese, does it sometimes shade into icon or index. Theatrical performance, by contrast, routinely makes use of each of these semiotic relations and often mobilizes more than one at the same time.[83]

The tensions generated between language and embodied performance, between a semiotic system imagined as pure and one in which the signifier is necessarily tainted by its referent, are articulated in the "Soliman and Perseda" episode at the end of *The Spanish Tragedy*. Before that play-within-the-play even begins, however, the contingency of signifying systems is raised as an issue when Hieronimo asks his actors to perform their roles in multiple languages:

Each one of vs must act his parte,
In vnknowne languages,
That it may breede the more varietie.
As you my Lord in Latin, I in Greeke,
You in Italian, and for because I know,
That *Bel-imperia* hath practised the French,
In courtly French shall all her phraises be. (K1v; 4.1.172–78)

Balthazar protests that "this will be a meere confusion, / And hardly shall we all be vnderstoode" (K1v; 4.1.180–81). The play's emphasis on confusion and on being understood is reiterated at the end of the scene, when Hieronimo declares, "[N]ow shall I see the fall of Babilon, / Wrought by the heauens in this confusion" (K1v; 4.1.195–96).[84] As David Bevington notes in his edition of the play, aside from being "an apocalyptic sign of approaching Last Judgement," the fall of Babylon "also suggests the Tower of Babel (Genesis xi), and indeed the two were widely confused; the English Bibles of the Renaissance called Babel 'Babylon' except in Genesis x and xi" (4.1.195n). The Tower of Babel in early modern England symbolized, among other things, the folly of human pride. Hieronimo's reference to the Tower of Babel in this scene fits well with the play's emphasis on revenge: just as God exerted his all-powerful will at Babel, so too will he demonstrate his mightiness when he smites Balthazar and Lorenzo so that divine justice can be served.[85]

The Babel trope also fits in with *The Spanish Tragedy*'s attention to questions of theatrical embodiment. Early modern references to Babel slip smoothly and easily between the Tower and its close cognate, Babylon, in ways that tie Babel to theatre itself. One of William Crashawe's sermons, for instance, attacks theatre as "*a Bastard of Babylon,* a daughter of error and confusion, a hellish deuice (the diuels owne recreation, to mock at holy things)."[86] This notion of Babel/Babylon as that which produces sinful bodily delight can also be seen in Richard Brathwaite's account of hearing in *Essaies vpon the Fiue Senses,* when he compares worldly pleasure to "an impudent strumpet" who deludes innocent listeners. "*Babels* subversion," he argues, "proceeded from the height of her sinner," and "her serpentine embraces, adulterate affections, and obsequious delights" can result in nothing but "death and ruine." He refuses to let his "*eare* be intangled with her soules staine" or "prostitute her *attention* to so odious a subiect."[87] Brathwaite's text calls to mind both the Tower of Babel and the whore of Babylon, conflating the two references and gendering ambition. Just as the Tower of Babel fell because the heights it attempted were sinful, so will worldly pleasures lead to damnation. God's punishment of humanity at Babel is, in this sense, a condemnation of the flesh. That divine discipline should be effected through the confusion of tongues is thus appropriate: if, in Brathwaite's account, the body in general and the ear in particular are problematic sites of pleasure, then what better than to punish the body with embodiment, to cast down transcendent language so that it must henceforth be fettered by material form?

In *The Spanish Tragedy,* when Hieronimo refers to "the fall of Babilon," his comment ties the physicality of language to the problem of embodiment in theatrical performance. On a thematic level, the play here presents a connection between pride and revenge: if justice is simply state-sponsored revenge, effected by those in power and sanctioned by God, then Hieronimo's revenge is just in that it mirrors the divine punishment meted out at Babel in response to human ambition. On the level of performance, this overlap between Babel/Babylon and Revenge is extended to the theatrical medium itself: it is the play-within-the-play that Hieronimo says will *cause* the fall of Babylon and, thus, effect both his revenge and God's justice. In treating metatheatricality as the agent of revenge, the play identifies the allegorical figure with the inset play: the onstage spectator here collapses into the onstage performance, and both are imagined as produced through the material body. The use of multiple metatheatrical frames in Kyd's play extends these connotations outward into the actual playhouse event: audience members are not separate from dramatic representations of ambition and vengeance but morally implicated in them.

This moral complicity is interwoven with the epistemological difficulties of interpreting performance. When Hieronimo refers to "the fall of Babilon," he calls to mind not only the dangers of an ambition that, in Macbeth's words, "ore-leapes it selfe" and thus "falles" (TLN 501–2; 1.7.27–28), but also cultural understandings of Babel as the mythic site of lost semiotic unity. For early modern playgoers, all of humanity once spoke the same language prior to the Tower's fall. This nostalgia for a perfect language can be seen in many texts from this period, but I will focus my attention here on some excerpts from John Bulwer's *Philocophus: or, The Deafe and Dumbe Mans Friend* (figure 3.3), which offers an especially clear articulation of the issues at stake. Bulwer is better known for his more famous works, *Chirologia*,

Figure 3.3 Frontispiece to John Bulwer, *Philocophus: or, The deafe and dumbe mans friend* (London, 1648). By permission of the Folger Shakespeare Library.

Figure 3.4 Seeing with the ears and hearing with the eyes. Detail from frontispiece to John Bulwer, *Philocophus: or, The deafe and dumbe mans friend* (London, 1648). By permission of the Folger Shakespeare Library.

or, The Naturall Language of the Hand and *Chironomia, or, The Art of Manuall Rhetoricke*, which have often been cited as evidence of a gestural language used by early modern actors.[88] In *Philocophus*, he turns from hand-based sign language to the practice of lipreading. Although its subject matter is thus fascinatingly unique, the text participates in an ongoing conversation about the nature of language and expresses sentiments found across early modern discussions of the written and spoken word.[89] The interplay between seeing language and hearing it is underscored in the row of figures at the bottom of the frontispiece to Bulwer's text. In the lower right corner, one of the heads has eyes in his ears; the other has an ear in place of his eye (figure 3.4). What it means to "see" through sound or "hear" through sight is central to Kyd's final play-within-the-play, in which the visual and the aural become two epistemological modes at odds with each other.

Bulwer's treatise distinguishes between two different kinds of language. On the one hand, it imagines words as immaterial, idealized, abstract concepts that precede all forms of physical expression. On the other hand, it describes words as concrete, material manifestations—in sound, in writing, and in bodily gestures. For Bulwer and other early modern writers, the perfect semiotic system was something that was "truly and properly mentall," something "produced *intellectually* onely, without *Matter* or *Motion*."[90] Bulwer privileges this abstract, immaterial language by referring to it as the "Word":

> Indeed that Word which sounds outwardly, is but the *signe* of that which *appeareth* inwardly, and to that rather doth the name of the Word appertaine: For, that which is *framed and delivered by the Mouth,* is but *Uox Verbi,* and is so called in respect of the other, from which it hath the *Derivation and Apparencie,* and there may be a *Word* (a *Mental one*) without *pronunciation,* but there cannot bee *pronunciation* or any Vocall representation of the Mind by any utterance of Discourse, without a *Word*.[91]

For Bulwer, true language is "inward" and located in the "Mind"; speech is but the imperfect representation of that idealized "Word." Compared to speech, writing was thought of as even one more step removed from the perfect semiotic system. David Browne's *Calligraphia,* for example, notes,

> Writs or Letters are the Symboles of Voyces or Wordes, (howsoever it may bee thought that the Voyce beeing invisible cannot bee represented by anie externall Signe) the Voyces Symboles of the Conceptions of the Minde, and the Conceptions of the Minde, Images of thinges which bee outwith the Minde: and that both of Divine Writs and Humane.[92]

In Browne's view, written language is the last step in a process of signification that begins with "thinges," moves from there to "Conceptions of the Minde," is translated into "Voyces," and finally (and most imperfectly) turned into "Writs or Letters."

This notion of language as mediated and attenuated, as an imperfect embodiment of idealized things, informs Bulwer's account of the Tower of Babel. In his discussion of the incident, he does not attribute the confusion of tongues to God's need to punish unseemly human ambition. Rather, Bulwer blames the loss of the ideal semiotic system on the materiality of language itself. He suggests that "the originall roote of the diversity of languages" is that "*words* are compounded of *vowells* and *consonants*,"[93] and

> this happens according to the scituation of the Regions wherein men live, to be more inclined to some *vowels,* or *consonants* then others: whence it comes to passe without any further worke, *vowels* and *consonants* were by little and little changed, and such a diversity ensued, that men no more understood one another: and this might happen without *confusion of tongues,* of which (according to some) there is no very firme ground in the sacred text; for whereas they were at *Babell* of one *lippe* and word, it is thought to imply no more; but that they were all of one *minde,* and resolved to remaine united together; so that there needed no more to confound their *tongues,* then to disperse them into severall *Countreys*.[94]

Human ambition to reach heaven through the Tower of Babel is here presented as being of unified mind, a view appropriate to a notion of true language as transcendent and mental. Shifts in spoken language, by contrast, are associated with fracture and the malleability of phonemes, the end result of which is the multiplication of worldly languages.

Although Bulwer imagines gradual changes in pronunciation as caused by the "Regions wherein men live," he nevertheless insists on the primacy of the sounds of the English language, which he refers to as "*natures Alphabet*":[95]

> [A]ll *tongues* are not necessarily tyed to take in all the *Letters of natures Alphabet*... B is not used by the *Chinoys,* and the *Tartars* cannot pronounce it, and the *Chinoys,* as it is sayd, cannot pronounce R. The *Brasileans* cannot pronounce the Letters, L. F. R. the reason whereof being demanded made answer, because they had amongst them neither Law, Faith, nor Rulers.[96]

Even as Bulwer highlights differences in pronunciation, he also subordinates all other vernaculars to his own. The variety of human phonetic systems is here collapsed into a single, unified language. That that language is English parallels what happens in *The Spanish Tragedy*. In both the 1592 and 1602 quartos, the "Soliman and Perseda" episode, which supposedly takes place in multiple foreign languages, is printed in English. The inset play is preceded by a note that reads, "*Gentlemen, this play of* Hieronimo *in sundrie Languages, was thought good to be set downe in English more largely, for the easier vnderstanding to euery publique Reader*" (K3r; 4.4.10.2–4).

It is difficult to determine how this scene was originally staged. David Bevington suggests that "presumably the original performances were in English throughout. Audiences readily accept the convention that they are 'hearing' other languages."[97] J. R. Mulryne and Janette Dillon instead follow S. F. Johnson in claiming that the play was performed in multiple languages. Mulryne believes that "[s]ince the audience has already heard the play's 'argument' they might well have been content to listen to 'unknown languages', provided they were not given too much of them and provided the action that accompanied them was highly explicit and stylised."[98] Dillon takes this position one step further, arguing that the audience's understanding of verbal content was less important than its experience of language as pure sound: "The confusion of languages, as sound effect, functions as jarring music might do on film at the moment of killing, freezing the event as image in order to compel the spectator into a deep engagement with its horror."[99] Carla Mazzio and William West suggest that staging "Soliman and Perseda" in multiple languages would be consistent with the play's themes and cultural contexts. Mazzio declares that the sundry languages device signals *The Spanish Tragedy*'s "engagement with contemporary debates about language," especially contemporary ambivalence about linguistic borrowing and fusion, and that "its importance in terms of the play as a whole cannot be overstated."[100] West argues that this device intentionally generates confusion in both on- and offstage audiences: as they "struggle to follow the babble of tongues, . . . they miss the deadly and serious work that is taking place." The confusion, he contends, thus enables a "new dramaturgy of action."[101]

At the heart of this debate lie disagreements about the semiotics of performance as well as the relative authority of language as communication and as spectacle. If theatrical signifiers are "iconic" in Peirce's sense of the term—that is, physically resembling the things they signify—then ideally the play-within-the-play would be spoken in sundry languages. However, the effect of this technique would be, ironically, to privilege language as embodied sound, as spectacle not communication. If theatrical signifiers are what Peirce calls "indexical," pointing toward referents that they do not resemble, the result is the reverse: staging the play in English foregrounds language as a functional semiotic system through which meaning is conveyed. Both of these staging options situate linguistic and theatrical signifiers as in tension with each other. If the play is performed in sundry languages, then the meaning-making function of language is subordinated *in order for* language to serve as embodied spectacle. If the play is performed in English, language continues to be viable as a semiotic system, but only at the cost of the presentational side of performance. Either solution foregrounds fractures and disjunctions in semiotic systems. The unified—and unitary—modes of signification prior to Babel's fall are no longer recuperable.

The paucity of external evidence about the staging of the inset play also involves a different semiotic problem: how did what was presented on the page signify with regard to what actually happened in the playhouse? I will return momentarily to the ways in which the note to the "*publique Reader*" complicates the status of the printed text as a record of spoken performance, but first let me take the quartos on their own terms. Printing conventions used in early modern drama support the idea that the "Soliman and Perseda" episode was performed in English. In published playbooks, foreign dialogue is usually presented in the original language, rather than being translated into English—as in the scenes from Shakespeare's *Henry V,* when Katherine speaks in French, and in Dekker's *The Shoemaker's Holiday,* when Lacy/Hans speaks in a kind of pseudo-Dutch. *The Spanish Tragedy* contains numerous examples of this printing convention. At the end of act 2, scene 6, after Hieronimo discovers the dead body of his son Horatio, he offers 14 lines of Latin as a spoken dirge, lines that are not translated into English in the published quartos. Shorter allusions to Italian, French, and Latin sayings also appear in the play, all represented in their original languages without any comment.[102] In the 1592 quarto, these foreign language selections are printed in italics, setting them off from the dialogue of the play, which is rendered in roman type. The letter that Hieronimo reads aloud at 3.7.32 is also printed in italics (F4r), marking it as a set piece to be distinguished from the rest of his soliloquy. The "Soliman and Perseda" episode, by contrast, is printed in roman, integrating it into the main action.[103] The numerous instances of untranslated foreign languages included in the quarto, together with the typographical conventions used to set off these selections, suggest that Hieronimo's climactic inset play was performed in English. If it had indeed been performed in French, Italian, Latin, and Greek, it would likely have been printed in those languages and differentiated from the main text through the use of italics.

In addition to publishing conventions, patterns internal to the dramatic representation also point to a performance of "Soliman and Perseda" in English. Unlike *The Spanish Tragedy,* other early modern plays that include foreign languages usually integrated explanations in English into the same scene. In Shakespeare's *Henry V,* for example, Pistol's amusing exchange with the French soldier in act 4, scene 4 is punctuated by proper translations performed by the Boy. Katherine's exchange with Alice earlier in the play is entirely in French, but its subject is an English-language lesson about the parts of the body, and the words were no doubt also accompanied by actors' gestures. If the "Soliman and Perseda" episode had actually been performed in sundry languages, it would not have been difficult to integrate into the scene this sort of concurrent explication. At the beginning of the entertainment, Hieronimo gives the Viceroy a "booke" (K3r; 4.4.10.s.d.) or "plot" (K3v; 4.4.33) containing the "argument of that they shew" (K3r; 4.4.10). At two moments during the performance, the King, the Viceroy, and the Duke of Castile interrupt the play. Rather than force audience members to rely on Hieronimo's explanations several scenes earlier, it would have been quite straightforward to have onstage spectators gloss the story as it unfolded. Instead, their interjections merely identify who is playing whom—a necessary explication for real-life playgoers, since

Balthazar, Lorenzo, and Bel-imperia have all changed costumes. That the sundry languages episode might have been performed entirely in English is not without precedent. As Janette Dillon points out, Robert Wilson's *Three Lords and Three Ladies of London* includes a scene with two heralds, one Spanish and one English. Their exchanges are initially in English, "lead[ing] the audience into the assumption that the different languages must be *imagined* for speakers of different nationalities,"[104] but they later switch to foreign vernaculars, which are included in the printed playtext in their original.

If the "Soliman and Perseda" episode was performed in English, Hieronimo's earlier comments about Babylon take on added poignancy. Scholars have typically read the use of sundry languages as emblematic of semiotic fracture, the breakdown of language as a signifying practice.[105] Such readings address the action taking place within the fictional universe of Kyd's play: the multilingual court performance represents the collapse of the mythical, idealized language prior to Babel's fall. Attending to the play's performance dynamics, however, tells a slightly different story. When "Soliman and Perseda" is presented, the diversity of imperfect worldly languages is collapsed into comprehensible English. The play may *represent* the dissolution of linguistic clarity, but it *enacts* the fantasy that that lost semiotic unity might be recuperated in vernacular English. In this sense, the sundry languages device positions theatrical performance as the means through which the gap between signifier and signified might be bridged. The disjunction that cannot be healed in the linguistic realm is redirected to the realm of performance. Rather than viewing the stage as problematic because it demands that signifiers be embodied, the enactment of the play-within-the-play positions the materiality of theatrical signifiers as its strength.

At the end of "Soliman and Perseda," then, Hieronimo's declaration, "Heere breake we off our sundrie languages, / And thus conclude I in our vulgare tung" (K4r; 4.4.74–75), should not be read as a transparent indicator of performance practices. If the play-within-the-play were performed in English, these lines would serve to highlight the theatrical semiotics through which foreign vernaculars are represented onstage. The printed note that the play was "*set downe in English more largely, for the easier vnderstanding to euery publique Reader*" (K3r; 4.4.10.s.d.) would replicate this performance dynamic in the medium of print. Not only might it remind readers who had already seen the play of the representational strategies used in their earlier playhouse experiences, but it also simultaneously foregrounds the text's own signifying practices, the process of translating from stage to page, from spoken language to written language. In attempting to reproduce the experience of performance in book form, the note to the reader in the quarto edition thus ironically delegitimizes its own medium. Performance with its oral dimension is imagined as primary; the printed text, as secondary. The centrality of embodiment in theatre's signifying system gives it the power to repair the damage of Babel; the dissolute, derivative medium of the book can only echo that power by calling attention to its own material form.

From this vantage point, we can now revisit the relationship of allegorical to mimetic modes of performance, implicated so fully in early modern drama's deployment of metatheatricality. Thomas Wilson's *Christian Dictionarie* characterized allegory as "[a] sentence consisting of sundry strange and borrowed speeches, which sound one thing, and couertly shewes forth another"[106]—a definition that connects allegory to anxiety over the incorporation of "sundry" foreign words into the English language. A proponent of linguistic borrowing, Richard Mulcaster expresses similar sentiments in *The Elementarie* when he refers to a foreign word as "a metaphor," relocated from its original setting to a new place where it can be "more properlie vsed."[107] His argument, like Wilson's, hinges on the displacement of language. As with allegory, foreign words that enter into English are characterized at first by a marked distance between signifier and signified. Once the word has become familiar, however, that distance diminishes; or, as Mulcaster puts it, "when the foren word hath yeilded it self, & is receiued into fauor, it is no more foren, tho of foren race, the propertie being altered."[108] Mulcaster's phrasing emphasizes the alteration of the word itself. The signifier that was once foreign is fundamentally changed. It is not simply that the semiotic *relation* has been naturalized; rather, the word is imagined as itself transformed. As in theatrical allegory, the signifier that is *allos*, or "other," comes to embody the signified; originally born "of foren race," it becomes native.

The performance of sundry languages in *The Spanish Tragedy* draws on these intersecting discourses about allegory as linguistic foreignness, and it imagines the degree of foreignness in terms of the distance between signifier and signified. In staging the multiplicity *of* languages, the play grapples with the problem of the multiplicity *in* language as a semiotic system. The "Soliman and Perseda" episode does not point to the failure of theatrical signification, however: whereas language is debased by its materiality (its diversity a function of the fall of Babel), theatrical signifiers are powerful precisely because they are embodied. Allegorical figures, such as Revenge, can be used to represent abstract concepts. One need not rely on language; embodied performance is an alternative. When Hieronimo reveals the corpse of Horatio during his epilogue, the implication is not simply that ocular proof trumps discourse—or that the visual is more persuasive than the verbal—but that the body of the actor is an icon of the explanation in "our vulgare tung," the English that serves as a fantasy of the recuperation of a universal language. Hieronimo's words as he displays the body follow a pattern we have seen before in this play:

> See heere my shew, look on this spectacle:
> Heere lay my hope, and heere my hope hath end:
> Heere lay my hart, and heere my hart was slaine:
> Heere lay my treasure, heere my treasure lost:
> Heere lay my blisse, and heere my blisse bereft. (K4r; 4.4.89–93)

Within the fictional representation, the passage marks the extremities of a father's grief over his murdered son. The repetition of the word "heere," however, gestures toward the performance context. It is not simply that the corpse substitutes for the explanatory force lacking in the verbal medium; rather, the actor embodies semiotic presence, the convergence point of signifier and signified that was taken away from humanity at Babel. Metatheatricality here asserts the value of the performance medium. In dramatizing the act of audience interpretation—including its moral difficulties and epistemological challenges—the play offers a kind of manifesto.

Theatre, it suggests, can effect spiritual change in its spectators, for embedded within performance is the potential to enact the overcoming of postlapsarian semiotic disjunction.

Moreover, if the problem after the Tower of Babel was an interruption to language's descriptive function (it being no longer clear what a given word refers to), then theatrical performance circumvents this difficulty through its use of linguistic performatives. Through speech acts, theatre can call into being an entire world, can create embodiment. When Hieronimo says, "Heere breake we off our sundrie languages, / And thus conclude I in our vulgare tung" (K4r; 4.4.74–75), his lines are simultaneously descriptive (foreign languages, he indicates, have been represented by English) and performative (all subsequent English shall now be declared to actually represent English again). He draws attention to theatre's semiotic system while also calling into being the imaginary world. The fact that Hieronimo's lines take place immediately after the play-within-the-play mirrors Revenge's comments to Andrea in the opening scene: "Heere sit we downe to see the misterie" (A3r; 1.1.90). The "here" in both of these instances gestures to the now, the present time of the playhouse converging with that of the fictional representation. "Here" performatively creates the very thing it describes.

* * *

Returning to the Prologue to *Henry V*, then, we can see a different purpose for the metatheatrical commentary at the beginning of Shakespeare's play. Calling upon the imaginative capacity of the audience to "[p]eece out our imperfections with your thoughts" has usually been understood as a gesture toward verisimilitude as a representational ideal. However, rather than reading this moment as a comment on theatre's failure or inability to live up to its mimetic aspirations, one might instead consider it in the light of the climactic play-within-the-play in *The Spanish Tragedy*. By calling attention to the modes of representation used in the "Soliman and Perseda" episode, the sundry languages device foregrounds theatre's semiotic conventions. In the Prologue to *Henry V*, a similar dynamic occurs. The moment may seem on the surface to draw attention to theatre's deficiencies, but what it does is offer a speech act that constructs the very world it enjoins audiences to imagine. "Thinke when we talke of Horses, that you see them / Printing their prowd Hoofes i'th'receiuing Earth," the Prologue says. But that is precisely what he is doing: he is actually *talking* of horses. The act of speaking turns words into embodied beings: the Prologue (person) speaks the prologue (language) in order to create horses (things). In speech acts, theatre motivates the collapse of allegory and mimesis: the signifier is self-identical with the signified. The semiotic unity before the fall of Babel is recuperated.

To the extent that "Soliman and Perseda" gestures toward the fantasy of semiotic resolution as effected through performance, it offers a kind of answer or response to the epistemological and moral challenges put forward in the Revenge-Andrea narrative. In both cases, metatheatricality is imagined not as a mirroring device commenting on the similarity of art and life but as an endless regression of frames that foregrounds the act of interpretation itself. Performance here produces both semiotic fracture and recuperation—as if metatheatricality sets up interpretation as a problem specifically so that it might reenact the process through which the disjunction of signifier and signified might be resolved. This compulsive rehearsal of the epistemological difficulties attendant on theatre suggests that whatever closure Hieronimo's play offers is only temporary. When the play-within-the-play is done, Andrea demands further tortures for his enemies in the underworld. Revenge agrees to fulfill the ghost's request: "For heere, though death hath end their miserie, / Ile there begin their endles Tragedie" (L2v; 4.5.47–48). The return to the metatheatrical signals a kind of perpetual repetition. The "heere" of the theatre is juxtaposed with the "there" of hell. One "end" has been achieved; the next "begin[s]." Though the action in the real-life playhouse concludes, the "Tragedie" to come will be "endles."

In the context of the play and its performance effects, this closing gesture does not break down the fourth wall so much as it reinscribes playgoers as living in a postlapsarian universe. The materiality of language is a problem, a symptom of the Fall. The materiality of theatre is its strength, the means through which the original and originary breakdown in signification can be repaired. But theatrical embodiment—and the linguistic speech acts that produce and performatively constitute embodiment—cannot be the perfect semiotic system because they must be interpreted by fallen spectators. The recursive cycle of interpretation continues ad infinitum until the second coming. When Andrea declares that the events of the main plot of *The Spanish Tragedy* "were spectacles to please my soule" (L2r; 4.5.12), he calls upon a notion of spectacle as itself problematically dual. On the one hand, this emphasis on presence—on the being-ness of theatre and on its power to call-into-being—was a kind of religious ecstasy: it was the power of the Host, through which salvation could take place, and the power through which semiotic unity might be regained. On the other hand, that same presence was a seductive temptation through which the devil might work upon the souls of playgoers. To understand this dichotomy, we must turn now to the nonreferential aspects of early modern performance. The affective impact of presentational spectacle is the subject of the next two chapters.

Part III

Experiencing Embodied Spectacle

Chapter 4

Dancing and Other Delights: Spectacle and Participation in *Doctor Faustus* and *Macbeth*

In 1588, the Lord Admiral's Men were paid £20 for presenting before Elizabeth "twoe Enterludes or playes" and for "showinge other feates of activitye and tumblinge." In 1590/91, "George Ottewell and his Companye the Lorde Straunge his players" were paid a similar sum for two plays and "other feates of Activitye."[1] In addition to performances at the court, the *Records of Early English Drama* (REED) volumes also note numerous payments for such activities to professional players traveling in the provinces.[2] As Philip Butterworth has noted, the phrase *feats of activity* in early modern usage referred to acts of physical skill, such as tumbling, vaulting, and "rope-dancing"—that is, balancing acts performed on a tight or slack rope (figure 4.1).[3] Although Shakespeare and his contemporaries are best known today for their scripted drama, records of payment such as these suggest that both representational theatre and spectacular physical displays were offered by the same performers at the same events and to the same audiences.

In order to understand early modern drama, then, we need to pay closer attention to how such feats of activity were understood. Although many plays featured displays of physical skill, the peculiarities of printed dramatic texts tend to efface these nonverbal experiences. Take, for instance, dancing and music—two kinds of skilled entertainment that were frequently integrated into representational drama. Among the 500 or so extant plays performed by professional actors between 1580 and 1642, there are nearly 350 references to the word *dance* in stage directions alone, as well as numerous other allusions to the names of specific dances. When compared to the roughly 380 instances of the word *fight*, a stage direction that is quite common, it becomes clear that dances were extensively integrated into the drama.[4] Dances take a significant amount of time to perform, and they dominate the physical space; yet a single, short stage direction such as "they dance" is read quickly, occupies only a tiny portion of the printed page, and fails to capture the fullness and vibrancy of the

Figure 4.1 Tumbling, rope-dancing, and other feats of activity. Johann Amos Comenius, *Orbis sensualium pictus* (1659; repr., London, 1685), 266 [S5v]. By permission of the Folger Shakespeare Library.

embodied experience. The colorful flash of costumes in the afternoon sunlight, the intricate patterns produced by choreographed movements, the masterful precision with which actors leap into the air—these are all lost.

The same difficulty is evident in the countless references to onstage music, including instrumental accompaniment to dances and also stand-alone arrangements and songs. When Autolycus sings in *The Winter's Tale,* the dramatic text at least prints some of the ballads he performs, but in *1 Henry IV,* when Glendower's daughter sings in Welsh, the stage direction "*Heere the Lady sings a Welsh Song*" (TLN 1790; 3.1.244.s.d.) offers no additional clues to the words or tunes presented. The scene's narrative thematics thus easily overshadow its experiential component: it is easier to explore, say, the political alliances represented within the play than to reconstruct the evanescent sensations associated with the floating cadences of the boy actor's voice. References to music in printed playbooks are paltry placeholders for the rich aural textures of the original performance and the cultural meanings such moments invoked and produced.

This chapter analyzes the ephemeral, yet crucial, affective responses generated by displays of physical prowess in the public theatres. I begin at the most basic level by surveying early modern descriptions of viewer experiences of spectacle, both inside and outside the playhouse. With regard to extratheatrical spectacles, I pay particular attention to travel narratives, a genre whose emphasis on foreign customs encouraged detailed descriptions of unusual physical feats. However, references to spectacular bodily displays can also be found in a wide range of other documents, including medical treatises, religious works, satirical poems, and translations of classical works. Early modern accounts of spectacle repeatedly refer to the "pleasure" and "delight" of beholding feats of activity. Though the meaning of these terms seems obvious at first, historicizing them suggests a very different story: far from indicating straightforward enjoyment, they signal complex cultural attitudes toward spectacle as both healthful and dangerous, both stimulating and seductive.

Examining early modern viewer responses to spectacle also offers surprising insights into the affective experiences produced by watching such displays and the consequences of these experiences for the beholder. From a post-Benjamin, post-Brecht perspective, it is easy to take for granted modern notions of spectacle as that which dazzles viewers and renders them passive.[5] Early modern accounts of bodily feats, by contrast, imply that spectators were thought of as active participants even when they merely watched the show.[6] Their complicity in the onstage action was related to the physiological and moral changes these performances were believed to engender in them. As recent scholarship on the early modern passions has shown, emotions in this period were not understood as primarily individual or autonomous reactions to external stimuli but were deeply bound up in the social order.[7] Admiration for displays of physical skill, I contend, were likewise not merely personal responses but the material means by which cultural norms were constructed *through* the affective experiences generated in performance.

These complex attitudes toward and experiences of spectacle and spectatorship were not merely disseminated in dramatic narratives but were integrated into performance practices. In the second half of my chapter, I move from early modern responses to spectacle more generally to an analysis of two scenes in particular: the devils' dance in the contract-signing episode in *Doctor Faustus* and the witches' dance after the procession of Banquo's descendants in *Macbeth*. Both of these scenes draw crucial parallels between on- and offstage spectators that shed light on the performance medium's relation to the cultural discourses I discuss in the first half of the chapter. These episodes, I argue, not only cite notions of spectacle circulating outside the playhouse but also enact them. Moreover, they offer particular insight into what happened at the convergence point of dramatic representation and onstage presentation: in order to represent onstage dances, actors had to actually dance.[8] Spectacles of this sort existed in a kind of double space: even as they operated within a given play's fictional narrative, they also served as legitimate entertainments in their own right. Jean Alter refers to these complementary aspects of theatre as its "referential" and "performant" functions: theatre as semiotic system, employing both mimetic and nonmimetic forms of representation, and theatre as spectacular show, akin to sports or the circus.[9] Onstage dances are one kind of theatrical action in which the referential and performant functions come together. These entertainments operated within the fictional world of the play as part of the dramatic narrative, but, for both characters and playgoers, they were also pleasing shows, inherently enjoyable to behold. Other kinds of spectacle on the early modern stage served different purposes inside and outside of the representation: processions represented the monarch without royalty actually being present, and swordfights were staged without the intent to harm.[10] Dances as entertainment, however, had the same function for fictional spectators as they did for real-life playgoers.

Scenes involving onstage dances thus serve as especially useful case studies of the historically specific workings of the performant function in theatre. Jean Alter defines the performant function in terms of spectacular displays that go beyond the norms of everyday life and existing expectations. As he explains in relation to sports and the circus, spectators admire acts even if an athlete has only exceeded a previous record by a few inches or a circus performer uses trained animals instead of wild ones.[11] The excellence of the performer—"excellence" in the sense of "that which excels"—generates wonder and admiration, and it is these qualities that constitute the performant function. In early modern performance, however, similar acts did not necessarily produce the same reactions. How then should the performant function be defined? If we take its contrast to the referential function as our starting point, we can see that the performant function can also be applied to less obviously spectacular aspects of stage practice. Props, costumes, playing spaces, special effects, the presence of the actor's body—in early modern England, all of these operated as theatrical signifiers, of course, yet their sheer material existence onstage also generated dramaturgical effects that exceeded their semiotic meanings. As scholars have recently shown, the London playhouses were not simply venues for acting but also sites where valuable objects were circulated and exhibited.[12] An ornately carved cup, a jeweled crucifix, or an embroidered handkerchief might function as props operating within a dramatic narrative, but they might equally serve as luxury items displayed for the delectation of viewers.

The affective impact of these objects certainly differed from those produced by feats of bodily prowess. Each object generated unique effects that grew out of its particular materials of construction, its modes of production and distribution, and the cultural discourses that surrounded it. Investigating all of these various objects in their myriad glory is not only impractical but devolves into an ever-more-detailed account of individual items. Doing so certainly has its benefits—thick descriptions offer valuable insights into the complexities of history and culture—but does not allow us to step back enough to isolate the performant function as a variable for study and examine its consequences *across* the varied individual instances that constitute theatrical performance. Examining onstage dances enables us to zero in on what happened in early modern theatrical practice when onstage presentation and dramatic representation converged. It thus offers a useful way to historicize the nature of the performant function itself beyond the individual meanings and materials that might attach to any given object, gesture, or experience that was presented onstage. By analyzing the performance dynamics of dance, we therefore learn not only about a single cultural practice but also about the workings of theatre as a whole.

The Language of Playhouse Spectacle

To understand what it meant for early modern spectators to view feats of activity, let us begin by examining the terminology most commonly used by writers of the period to describe reactions to bodily displays. Sixteenth- and seventeenth-century texts often recount responses to theatrical and extratheatrical spectacles that seem familiar on the surface. Bodily feats are frequently described as "recreations" that are "pleasing" or "delightful," especially to the eyes. Upon further interrogation, however, such terminology reveals cultural sensibilities and audience reactions that differ significantly from our own.

Contemporary references to playgoing frequently use the terms *pleasure* and *delight* to describe viewer responses to theatrical spectacles. Richard Vennar's *Apology*, for example, refers to plays as "a daily offring to the God of pleasure, resident at the Globe on the Banke-side."[13] John Florio's English-Italian conversation book, *First Fruites*, notes that people go to "the Bull, or else to some other place" to see "Comedies" because "euery ma*n* delites in the*m*" and "[t]hey please me also wel."[14] Although modern readers may associate "Comedies" with certain kinds of dramatic narratives, early modern spectators knew this genre as one that offered physical entertainments. Comedies were showpieces for clowns, performers famous for their displays of bodily feats. Will Kemp, for instance, was known to have been a very athletic actor. Shortly after he left the Lord Chamberlain's Men, he danced the morris from London to Norwich supposedly in nine days, a publicity stunt recorded for posterity in *Kemps Nine Daies Wonder*. His replacement, Robert Armin, was known for another physical skill: singing.[15] Clowns also elicited laughter through comic gestures and face-pulling as well as broader onstage movements, such as "leaping"—a term associated also with dancing. In addition, the clown's first onstage appearance frequently foregrounded his physical skill. The routine involved a comically protracted entrance that began with only the performer's head peeping out from behind a curtain at the back of the stage. The technique was a mainstay of Richard Tarlton's repertoire.[16] By contrast, accounts of playgoers' laughter as a result of jokes or other verbal phenomena are significantly more limited. Although some evidence exists that obscenity and puns were popular with playgoers, Matthew Steggle has demonstrated that "[a]ccounts of audience reaction contain very little which directly links particular sorts of verbal effect to audience laughter, and those accounts which do are almost always dismissive about the value of the effect."[17] Even if these sources present only a partial picture, it is notable that what early modern writers found worthy of comment with regard to the laughter of theatregoers were the physical routines displayed during comedies. And this genre was, moreover, exceedingly popular. As Roslyn Knutson has noticed in her careful dissection of Henslowe's *Diary*, "[T]he Admiral's men were offering two or three comedies per week for every tragical history or tragedy."[18]

The notion, implicit in Florio's account, that the appeal of comedies lay in their function as presentational entertainment, is made explicit in other early modern references to playgoing. In his famous tract, *Playes Confuted in Fiue Actions*, Stephen Gosson remarks that "in Comedies delight beeing moued with varietie of shewes, of euentes, of musicke, the longer we gaze, the more we craue."[19] Theatregoers are here depicted as "moued" not by narrative but by spectacular acts. Moreover, their "delight" is described as the product of diverse stimuli working on the "gaze." Even "musicke," as Andrew Gurr notes, is in this passage imagined as seducing the eyes.[20] In *The Trumpet of Warre*, Gosson again uses the term *delight* to describe playgoers' reactions to spectacle. "[I]n publike Theaters," he writes, "when any notable shew passeth ouer the stage, the people arise vp out of their seates, & stand vpright with delight and eagernesse to view it well."[21] The most popular aspect of theatre, he suggests, is its function as visual spectacle—a feature he finds problematic.

Such an attitude may be unsurprising coming from an antitheatricalist such as Gosson, yet playwrights themselves adopted similar rhetoric when they sought to elevate their own works above the lowest common denominator. This tendency is, of course, most famously exemplified by Ben Jonson, who repeatedly stressed that his plays were not for base beholders but discerning auditors.[22] Other writers also tried to distance themselves from the public taste for spectacle. For instance, the commendatory verses to Philip Massinger's *The Bondman* use the same word Gosson deploys, *delight,* when asserting that "[h]ere are no *Gipsie Iigges,* no *Drumming stuffe,* / *Dances,* or other *Trumpery* to delight, / Or take, by common way, the common sight."[23] William Davenant's prologue to *The Unfortunate Lovers* echoes these sentiments when he describes viewers at the early outdoor playhouse known as the Theatre to be "[g]ood easie judging soules, with what delight / They would expect a jigge or Target fight."[24] Davenant here refers to spectators at the Theatre 20 years prior to his Caroline play, and he distinguishes them from the Blackfriars audiences for whom his tragedy would be performed. Both Massinger and Davenant imply that if discriminating listeners are to distinguish themselves from the "common" standers in the yard, they must attend to more than displays of physical skill. Ironically, however, their comments also suggest that it was precisely such visual spectacles that most "delight[ed]" the masses. When the Prologue to Shakespeare's *Henry V* calls on theatregoers "[g]ently to heare, kindly to iudge our Play" (*Henry V,* TLN 35; Prologue.34), the association of hearing with gentility foreshadows the class distinctions that underlie later Jacobean and Caroline references to playgoer reactions.[25] What is noteworthy here is that auditors could only claim social superiority if the majority of playgoers focused more on the spectacular aspects of theatre than on the subtleties of poetry. Indeed, as Gabriel Egan has recently shown, received scholarly opinion that early moderns used the phrase "to hear a play" more often than "to see a play" is, in fact, incorrect: drawing on statistics compiled through the *Literature Online* (LION) searchable full-text database of early modern literature, Egan demonstrates that preference for the visual turn of phrase exceeds the aural by more than 12 to 1.[26] When William Lambarde mentions how "such as goe to *Parisgardein,* the *Bell Sauage,* or *Theatre,* to beholde Beare baiting, Enterludes or Fence play, can account of any pleasant spectacle,"[27] then, it is telling that drama is sandwiched between references to presentational entertainments styled as "pleasant spectacle." It is not simply that there were two kinds of playgoers focused respectively on the aural and the visual but that those who valued the latter were more widespread.

The word *show,* or *shew* as it was often spelled in early modern England, is also significant as a term that was frequently used to refer to theatrical spectacles. The prologue to Davenant's *News from Plymouth,* acted at the Globe in 1635, notes that "each Spectator knows / This House, and season, does more promise shewes, / Dancing, and Buckler Fights, then Art, or Witt."[28] The prologue to Shirley's *Doubtful Heir* makes a point of apologizing to Globe spectators for offering "No shews, no dance and what you most delight in, / Grave understanders, here's no target fighting."[29] In all of these instances, "shews" are associated specifically with presentational bodily feats. Like *pleasure* and *delight,* the term also particularly implied the visual dimension. In the prologue to Jonson's *The Staple of News,* the pleasures of the eye are imagined specifically in opposition to the pleasures of the ear:

> For your owne sakes, not his, he bad me say
> Would you were come to heare, not see a Play.
> Though we his *Actors* must prouide for those,
> Who are our guests, here, in the way of showes,
> The maker hath not so; he'ld haue you wise,
> Much rather by your eares, then by your eyes.[30]

Jonson's denigration of spectacular acts as "showes" reflects broader cultural understandings of the term *show* as implying visuality. In John Lyly's *Euphues and His England*, for instance, Philautus warns gentlewomen of the dangers of suitors who "attempt with showes to please their Ladies eyes."[31] This example from Lyly gestures toward connections between the terms *show* and *please*. The word *show* was also associated with *delight*. In John Hind's prose romance *Eliosto Libidinoso*, Amasias laments how his love for Florinda has made him unable to enjoy worldly pleasures:

> Good God! how vnsavory seeme those sweet meates vnto me, wherein I was wont to delight? how vnpleasant are the sports wherein I was woont to take pleasure? how con bersome [*sic*] is the companie, which was woont to content me? no game pleaseth me, no triumphs, no shewes, no hawking, no hunting, yea, nothing vnder the Sunne doth solace me. And would I know the cause why I have not a contented mind? The exquisite parts of Florinda do so diversly distract my minde that onely her sight is sweet, onely her societie is comfortable, onely her presence is delightfull vnto me.[32]

In this passage, *delight* is linked to physical nourishment and activity: to the eating of sweetmeats, the sports of hunting and hawking. It is also connected specifically with presentational spectacles, with "triumphs" and "shewes." *Tarltons Newes out of Purgatorie* draws on these intersecting discourses when the speaker mentions that even though he "sawe as rare showes, and heard as lofty verse," after the departure of the famous clown Tarlton, "the wonted desire to see plaies left me" and "I inioied not those woonted sports."[33] Distinguishing the seeing of "showes" from the hearing of verse, early modern writers underscore the notion that the popularity of displays of physical skill onstage lay in the pleasures they offered to the eye.

Recreating Bodily Pleasures

The same terms used to describe theatrical spectacle were also deployed in early modern accounts of bodily feats outside the playhouse. The English translation of Jan Huygen van Linschoten's travel narrative, *Itinerario*, for instance, mentions that the "leaping and dauncing" of Brazilian children were "most wonderfull and verie pleasant to behold."[34] In contrast to playwrights seeking to distinguish listeners from viewers, however, extratheatrical writers without a stake in such distinctions sometimes emphasize that the enjoyment of spectacle comes from the integration of visual and aural phenomena. The 1603 English translation of Plutarch's *Moralia*, for example, notes that "we take pleasure to heare the organs and instruments of musicke sound pleasantly; we delight to heare birdes singing sweetly; we behold with right good will, beasts playing, sporting, dauncing, and skipping featly."[35] In this text, the eyes and the ears are equally the means through which "pleasure" and "delight" are experienced. Indeed, the two perceptual modes are analogized: the delights of hearing music and birdsong are imagined as similar in kind to the enjoyment derived from watching animals "playing, sporting, dauncing, and skipping featly." Travel narratives describing the dances of foreign inhabitants also mention the aural working in conjunction with the visual. For example, José de Acosta's account of the Americas states that the "Mittote," a Mexican dance involving music, was performed with "so goodly an order and accord, both of their feete and voices, as it was a pleasant thing to beholde."[36] The emphasis on "order and accord" fits with Renaissance notions of musical harmony and consonance as exemplifying measure and moderation, both values expressing proper cosmic and worldly hierarchies.[37] In Acosta's text, it is the balanced integration of music and movement that produces a delightful sensory feast.

This same combination of aural and visual sensory experiences characterized early modern understandings of the experience of "beholding." Central to accounts of displays of physical skill both inside and outside the playhouse, "beholding" was not simply a passive "taking in" of performance. According to the *OED*, it could also imply a more active process of thinking. In early modern usage, the term *behold* retained the connotations of its etymological root word, *hold*. Indeed, as the *OED* puts it, "[t]he application to watching, looking, is confined to English."[38] *Behold* could thus denote the notion of "holding to" a particular attitude or belief, as in one example from 1525 stating, "Euery man behelde the same oppynyon."[39] In Middle English, the term also designated the mental processes that went into the formation of those beliefs.[40] Descriptions of dances as "pleasant to behold" thus extend beyond visual perception to encompass a more wholistic experience of contemplation and cognition.[41] Indeed, if "beholding" involved the integration of seeing and hearing along with other cognitive and affective processes, then early modern playwrights' tendency to separate out the eyes and the ears starts to make more sense: it was only because aural and visual spectacle *were* intertwined that writers found it necessary to denigrate "beholders," thus defining through opposition a class of more privileged "hearers."

That the value of bodily feats is often attributed to "pleasantness" is also telling, given that early modern meanings of this term implicate the spectator in the action being viewed. The most readily accessible sense of the phrase "pleasant to behold" is that presentational performances were inherently enjoyable. However, in early modern usage, *pleasure* had more ambivalent connotations. The *OED* offers numerous examples from about 1450 onward of the word *pleasure* as referring to "[t]he indulgence of physical, esp. sexual, desires or appetites; sensual or sexual gratification."[42] The contradictory valences of the term extend further back in time as well. According to the *Middle English Dictionary*, the word *pleasure* could signify both spiritual satisfaction and "sensual pleasure; sexual satisfaction."[43] *Pleasaunte* could mean, on the one hand, "[p]leasing or acceptable to God; in accordance with the divine will" and, on the other, merely "[p]leasing to the senses."[44] Like *pleasant,* the word *delight* had contradictory valences as well, and the two words were sometimes used interchangeably. In Adriano Banchieri's satirical work, *The Noblenesse of the Asse,* the author refers to Cairo as offering "many pleasant iestes, especially such as teach Cammels, Asses and Dogges to daunce, a sight very pleasing to behold."[45] His source is Leo Africanus, whose English translator referred to these spectacles as "delightfull to behold."[46] *Delight* seems rather innocuous when viewed from a modern perspective, but, like *pleasure,* its early modern usage also implied sensuality and seduction. The term was derived from the Latin *delicere,* meaning "to entice away, allure," as well as from *delectare,* "to allure, attract, delight, charm, please."[47] In Middle English, to *accomplishen, don,* or *performen delite* was "to have sexual intercourse," and the term also referred specifically to "the second stage of sin, pleasure in the contemplation of sin, desire to sin."[48] By the late sixteenth century, the word *delite* began to be spelled *delight* because it was erroneously believed to derive from the word *light,* also associated with promiscuity.[49] In Spenser's *Faerie Queene,* for instance, the unchaste Malecasta who climbs into Britomart's bed "cleeped was the Lady of delight."[50] Both *pleasant* and *delight* serve as linguistic registers of cultural ambivalence surrounding the response evoked by presentational spectacles; their sensual and sexual valences foreground the centrality of the body as both producer and receiver of spectacle.

Descriptions of theatrical spectacle sometimes make explicit the sensual connotations that are registered implicitly on the linguistic level. Thomas Nash's *Pierce Penilesse,* for example, groups theatre with other carnal enjoyments when he describes how young gallants and soldiers "do wholy bestow themselues vpou [i.e., upon] pleasure, and that pleasure they deuide (howe vertuously it skils not) either into gameing, following of harlots, drinking, or seeing a Playe."[51] As in extratheatrical accounts, the word *pleasure* here refers not merely to amusements in general but to the joys of the flesh in particular. That the sexual connotations of the term are linked specifically to playgoing can further be seen in Richard Brathwaite's satirical portrait of well-to-do female spectators, whose viewing of plays are, in his text, associated with their lustful attention to men:

> But now you'r seated, and the Musick sound
> For th'Actors entry; pleasures doe abound
> In ev'ry Boxe; sometimes your eye's on th'Stage,
> Streight on a lighter Object, your loose *Page,*
> Or some phantastike *Gallant,* or your *Groome* ....
> Thus you in painted joyes mis-spend your dayes
> More to your *Suiters* than your *Makers* praise.[52]

In this passage, "th'Stage" and other "loose" and "lighter Object[s]" both attract the playgoer's gaze. The licentiousness implicit in the histories of the words *pleasure* and *delight* are here made explicit: performance stirs up erotic pleasure, and spectators' bodily desires are channeled through their eyes.

Cultural ambivalence toward spectacle in part derived from early modern paradigms of vision as itself a form of bodily congress between the beholder and the object of his or her vision. Displays of physical prowess not only focused attention on the body of the performer but also activated anxieties about the permeability of the body of the viewer. Like other orifices, the eyes were understood as vulnerable to penetration and, thus, potential physical corruption. As I discussed in chapter 2, early modern science imagined seeing as a profoundly material, even haptic, experience. According to extramission theories of vision during this period, the eye shot out rays to explore the world much as fingers reach out to touch objects. According to intromission theories of vision also current at this time, sight occurred when tiny particles that were exact miniature copies of objects flew into the eye of the beholder.[53] Both extramission and intromission theories of vision imagined seeing as a form of bodily penetration, whether the beholder was *doing* the penetrating or *being* penetrated.

Such ideas about the nature of visual perception help explain why early modern moral treatises express as much concern about *watching* dancing as engaging in it. John Northbrooke's *A Treatise wherein Dicing, Dau[n]cing, Vaine Plaies...Are Reprooued* imagines dances as moving spectators through their eyes. Citing Ludovicus Vives, Northbrooke declares,

> Or what woman nowe a dayes ([*sic*] that is sadde and wise, wilbe knowne or seem to haue skil in dauncing. For what chastitie of body and minde can be there, where they shall see so many mens bodies, and haue their mindes enticed by the windowes of their eyes, and by the meanes of the most subtill artificer the Diuell.[54]

In Northbrooke's account, performer and spectator are not only parallel but are indeed one and the same. The woman, who will "seem to haue skil in dauncing," is also the spectator, who "shall see so many mens bodies." Watching is a form of participation. The eyes are imagined as "windowes," not because they offer a glimpse of the internal subject as they might in a modern account but because they are vulnerable openings through which the spectator might be "enticed." Anxiety about spectacle and the consequent compromising of the beholder is here expressed through the gendering of the viewer as female.[55] Eyes in this text are imagined as orifices through which the spectator's body might be penetrated as she quite literally "takes in" the show. By treating watching as an almost sexual activity, early modern texts position viewers as knowingly and culpably participating in those bodily acts that they witness.

In contrast to lascivious dances, which are imagined as dangerously seductive, dances performed in praise of God were thought of as holy and laudable. For example, in *Brief Conclusions of Dancers and Dancing*, John Lowin—an actor who joined the King's Men in 1603 and later wrote this rather Puritan tract—vigorously objects to "the vsage of such *Dances,* as are onely effected for the pleasure of our eyes," but sanctions so-called "godly" dances.[56] Lowin's printer, John Orphinstrange, echoes these sentiments. In the opening epistle to the reader, Orphinstrange defends against accusations of dance as a "vaine and friuolous" subject by arguing that it is "of it selfe...altogether serious, and of a great moment."[57] He insists that the treatise is based "vpon the word of GOD it selfe" and that the dances of "holy men and women" can be safely "before our eyes heere erected" because they are intended for the praise of God.[58] What is striking, though, is that in order "to praise and laud the immortall worker of their triumphs," dancers must do what Lowin and Northbrooke believe might also potentially corrupt spectators: they will "stirre vp the people...by the actiuones [sic] and agilitie of their bodies in Dances."[59] In defending the subject of the treatise, Orphinstrange states that the text is "not framed according to the pleasure of the eye, but for the comfort of the heart."[60] In this, he constructs the treatise itself as a godly dance and readers as viewers, moved by the actions "before [their] eyes heere erected" to praise God.[61] What serves as the moral justification for the text is not that it is different *in kind* from its subject but rather that its *purpose* is holy.

This conflation of printed text and spectacle, of reader and spectator, can also be found in Leo Africanus's famous account of his travels in Africa. The mode of reporting on the customs and manners of foreign peoples in early modern travel narratives might be understood as adopting an early version of the anthropological gaze, with the European spectator as privileged subject and the foreign performer as the object of study. However, Leo Africanus's text suggests something of the potential for slippage between subject and object, viewer and performance. When he relates the exploits of a particular dancing ass in the suburbs of Cairo, he introduces the anecdote by describing the place where these tricks were performed as typical of those kinds of entertainments: "Hither after Mahumetan sermons and deuotions, the common people of Cairo, togither with the baudes and harlots, do vsually resort; and many stage plaiers also, and such as teach camels, asses, and dogs, to daunce: which daucing is a thing very delightfull to behold."[62] Following a rhetorical formula similar to other travel narratives we saw earlier, this passage describes the dancing animals as "very delightfull to behold." Where it differs from the other texts, however, is in its portrayal of the spectators. In other travel narratives, the reader straightforwardly imagines the performance from the privileged perspective of the narrator. In this one, the reader's identification with the narrator is complicated by the fact that the other spectators are, in fact, "the common people of Cairo, togither with the baudes and harlots." The comparison is underscored by a marginal note, which was added to the 1600 edition, presumably for the English reader's benefit: "These asses are somewhat like to Banks his curtall, that plaid his prizes all England ouer."[63] The reference is to a trained horse who performed tricks across the country in the 1590s and subsequently traveled on the Continent as well. Readers who have witnessed the feats of the famous animal, appropriately named Morocco, are here likened to the "Mahumetan" people delighted by the dancing ass. The line between the European spectator as the subject of the gaze and the foreign spectacle as its object is blurred in this English edition of Leo Africanus's work. Moreover, in conflating reader of text with spectator of bodily feats, the printed text almost comes to stand in for the physical spectacle itself. As in Orphinstrange's preface to Lowin's treatise, the seduction of viewers through their eyes complicates the position of the reader, whose eyes must stick to their proper course—the text— and not stray toward the spectacles the text portrays.

This conflation of enacted performance and printed text as spectacle can also be seen in the pamphlet *Maroccus Extaticus,* which supposedly transcribes a conversation between Banks and his horse, Morocco (figure 4.2). The animal was well known for doing tricks, such as guessing the number of coins in a spectator's purse, but he was also famous for his physical stunts, such as performing the dance known

Figure 4.2 Printed text as spectacular feat. *Maroccus Extaticus. Or, Bankes bay horse in a Trance* ([London], 1595), A4v. Reproduced by permission of the Huntington Library, San Marino, California.

as the Canaries.[64] The imaginary dialogue recorded in the pamphlet deploys the language of "play" when the trainer Banks states at the outset that he intends to "recreate my selfe awhile with your horsemanship."[65] The animal responds that he is "as like[,] master[,] to shew you some horse plaie as ere a nag in this parish."[66] This passage calls to mind the horse's bodily feats and ties those acts to the witty banter in the printed text: the subsequent rhetorical "plaie" in the pamphlet is offered up as a performance equally as entertaining as Morocco's usual shows. Moreover, the passage refers to the horse's antics as a way to "recreate my selfe"—a term related to *recreation,* also used in other early modern texts to refer to spectacle.

In travel narratives, the word *recreation* as applied to foreign spectacles shares the ambivalence inherent in early modern understandings of *pleasure* and *delight.* José de Acosta's account of natives in the Americas, for example, refers to the dance called the Mittote as "a recreation and pastime for the people."[67] His usage here echoes that found in early modern texts describing dance as beneficial. John Playford's famous *The English Dancing Master,* for instance, refers to ancient writers who "commend it to be Excellent for Recreation, after more serious Studies, making the body active and strong, gracefull in deportment, and a quality very much beseeming a Gentleman."[68] At the same time, in addition to these positive meanings, the term *recreation* also had more problematic connotations. Acosta specifically notes, "We have not discovered any Nation at the *Indies,* that live in comminalties, which have not their recreations, in plaies, dances, and exercises of pleasure," and he describes Peruvian dances as not only "sportes of recreation" but also "superstitions, and kindes of idolatries."[69] The ambivalence we saw earlier surrounding the word *pleasure* is here associated with *recreation* as well.

Although today *recreation* refers to leisure entertainments, in early modern parlance the term also encompassed the act of perception itself—a usage that concurs with references to spectacle as pleasant or delightful "to behold." Christiaan van Adrichem, for example, describes Jerusalem's ancient "Amphitheater" as

> a place inuironed with scaffoldes and stages, capable of fourescore thousand men, where the people were woont to behold their games.... Wherein, to recreate the beholders, wrastlers and sword players, shewed many feates of actiuitie: and sometimes, Lyons, Leopardes, Bulles, Beares, Bores, Wolues, and other exceeding wilde and fierce beasts, fought one with another, and sometime condemned men were cast vnto these to bee deuoured, and captiues taken in warre.[70]

What does it mean to "recreate the beholders"? Early modern usage of the phrase seems to suggest a notion of refreshment. For example, in John Banister's anatomical treatise, a section marked off by the marginal note "Why the eyes being weary we winke" describes the uvea, or inside lining of the eye, as having a range of pigments "[b]y the which varietie of colours the weryed eyes are recreated, & therfore we shut the eyes, to the ende that after quiet resort of the visible spirites, these coulours may newly be refreshed."[71] Helkiah Crooke's *Mikrokosmographia* similarly states that eyelids "recreate the sight, least [*sic*] at one time too great a number of spirits should be exhausted; for if the eyes should be so long open as wee are awake, they would be wearied, and many things falling vpon their coates would offend them."[72] In the phrase "recreate the beholders," then, the implication seems to be that viewers' tired eyes are revived by spectacular acts—a meaning that concurs with the *OED*'s third definition of *recreate* as a transitive verb.[73]

This healthful refreshment implicit in the phrase "recreate the eyes" is not separate from the notion of recreation as seduction, as can be seen in early modern descriptions of precious gems. John Maplet's natural history, *A Greene Forest,* for example, includes a section on sapphires in which he writes, "[I]t is good (if it be not otherwise ouerlaide) to the eiesight, and that nothing in the whole worlde, doth more recreate or delight the eies than the *Smaradge* & *Sapphir* doe."[74] Robert Chester's poem, *The Anuals of Great Brittaine,* also known as *Loves Martyr,* likewise describes "Skie colour'd *Saphire*" as that which "doth delight and recreate the Eyes."[75] The use of the phrase "recreate the eyes" in these nonperformance contexts is instructive. The beauty of sapphires "is good...to the eiesight," but the lure of worldly gems is bound up with the ambivalence of "delight." In this sense, the sparkling of jewels corresponds to the attractions of spectacular entertainments: both are appealing to the eyes, yet in this way both are also potentially dangerously seductive.

Such moral consequences are not unrelated to the spiritual challenges of allegorical interpretation, which I discussed in chapter 3. In *The Arte of English Poesie,*

George Puttenham argues that "deuices"—or emblems—"insinuat some secret, wittie, morall and braue purpose presented to the beholder, either to recreate his eye, or please his phantasie, or examine his iudgement, or occupie his braine."[76] Puttenham's turn of phrase, "recreate his eye," speaks to the similarities between watching spectacle and interpreting allegory: both modes of experiencing performance implicate the viewer in the action being viewed in a quite physical way with real moral consequences. Such notions of the implications of taking in performance resonate with another now-obsolete meaning of *recreation*: "refreshment by eating; nourishment; a meal."[77] I argued in chapter 2 that Eucharistic notions of vision as a kind of ingestion helped shape the semiotics of perception on the early modern stage. In descriptions of spectacle as "recreating the eye," we see another facet of this same issue: the notion of visual delights as bodily refreshment had moral implications for the viewer. For an early modern text to say that a particular entertainment served as "recreation," then, underscores not its function as leisure but its rejuvenating properties as well as its physiological and spiritual consequences.

The stimulating effects of spectacle can also be found in Simon Goulart's *Admirable and Memorable Histories Containing the Wonders of Our Time*. In a section titled "Agilitie and Force," Goulart compiles various anecdotes regarding spectacular displays of physical skill. One of the accounts, from a source describing *"things done at Constantinople, at the Circumcision of* Amvraths *Sonne in the yeare.* 1582," details the feats performed by a rope-dancer:

> At this feast of the Turkish Circumcision, many dancers vpon the roape made goodly proofes of their dexterity: but there was one which wonne the spurres from all the rest. I knowe no man but was rauished, seeing him runne so swiftly, with so good a grace, and without stay. An ancient *Poet* said in one of his Commedies, that the vulgar sort were amazed to see one that went vpon a Roape. But if this *Poet* had seene one like vnto this, hee would haue beene amazed for he mounted vpon Roapes tied vnto Piramides, to the heighest that might be seene, with such celerity as any one would haue thought they had beene steppes or degrees: then hee came downe back-wards, or vpon his belly, hauing no other support but a small staffe which serued him as a Counterpeze. Sometimes hee leaped vpon the Roape with both feete, sometimes with one, then imbracing the Roape with both his feete, he hung downe-ward, and turning about, raised himselfe againe. Hee did slide with a strange resolution, from the toppe vnto the bottome, and that which I esteeme most in this agilety, at night he would tie six naked Cymiters to either foote, and continued his sport by torch-light with such admiration and applause of all the world, as if happely any of the Spectators had desire to sleepe, this man by his admirable agility did presently awake him. So as by the generall consent of great and small in this sollemne Assembly, he was called the chiefe maister of his art.[78]

Several aspects of this passage deserve comment. First, as in the references to "recreation," the "admiration and applause" of spectators is explicitly associated with alertness. Even those who felt sleepy, the text implies, would be awakened by the energizing qualities of the performer's feats. Second, it is the "dexterity," "grace," and "agility" of the rope-dancer, along with his ability to move "swiftly" and "with...celerity," that causes this admiration. The stimulating effects engendered in viewers are here tied specifically to the performer's physical prowess, not to other features of the show.

Third, as a result of this performance, viewers are described as "rauished" and "amazed." *Ravished* in early modern usage primarily referred to violent seizure of goods, personal violation, and rape. In addition, it also signified what the *OED* refers to as being "[t]ransported in spirit or with some strong emotion; entranced, enraptured, captivated."[79] The term implies that the intense reactions of spectators are, in some sense, against their will. Feelings elicited by spectacle are imagined as an undesirable response. This sense of an external force taking over the viewer is also present in the word *amazed,* here associated with a reference by an "ancient *Poet*" to the "vulgar sort." In relegating such reactions to the lower classes, this attitude concurs with the Renaissance valuing of moderation and measure. Moreover, the rhetorical point seems to be that the performer's skill overcomes the viewer's reluctance: even those, like the classical playwright, who try *not* to have a strong reaction, will be "amazed" by the performance. In early modern usage, the word *amaze* denoted confusion and was often linked with its etymological antecedent, *maze*.[80] It could also signify being struck, either figuratively ("terror-stricken, terrified, alarmed") or literally, in the sense of a physical blow, as one of the *OED*'s quotations makes clear: "She strake hir head so hard against the wall, that she fell downe amazed."[81] In early modern usage, both *ravished* and *amazed* seem to imply violence, confusion, terror, and physical harm. The same contradictory valences found in *pleasant* and *delight* are evident here: spectacle engenders involuntary disturbance of the physiological, emotional, and social realms.

Amaze, ravish, pleasant, and *delight*—all of these words serve as linguistic registers of cultural ambivalence surrounding both presentational spectacles and the powerful responses they evoked in early modern viewers. Shakespeare's plays, especially those later in his career, have sometimes been interpreted as overwhelming passive playgoers with their spectacular shows. Early modern accounts of extratheatrical spectacle, however, suggest that *pleasure, delight,* and other related terms marked a kind of alertness and activeness that extended beyond the physical to the emotional, social, and spiritual. These texts describe spectacle as eliciting an intense reaction that defies Renaissance proscriptions for moderation. Moreover, their sensual and even sexual valences foreground the centrality of the body as both producer and receiver of spectacle.

Devilish Delight in *Doctor Faustus*

Such attitudes toward and experiences of spectacle were woven into theatrical performance on three different levels. First, the terminology used in these texts to refer to viewer responses to spectacle is notably similar to the kind of language found in the plays of Shakespeare and his contemporaries, where reactions of onstage spectators to presentational shows are often described as involving *pleasure* and *delight*. Second, the same ambivalence we saw earlier in accounts of bodily feats is depicted within the dramatic fiction, both in terms of narrative plot and in terms of characters' responses. Third, and most important, are the ways in which cultural attitudes toward spectacle were not merely represented onstage but integrated into actor-audience dynamics. Analyzing the devils' dance in *Doctor Faustus* and the witches' dance in *Macbeth* suggests key ways in which attitudes toward spectacular bodily displays outside the playhouse were not simply transmitted *through* dramatic narratives but embedded *in* the medium of performance itself.

In the contract-signing episode in *Doctor Faustus*, the dance of the devils takes place in conjunction with a moment of heightened suspense. The scene centers on a crucial question: Will Faustus actually go through with the bargain that will damn him to hell for all eternity, or will he be saved just in the nick of time? The stage business here is very involved, as if to increase audience excitement and anticipation. Faustus first cuts his arm to get the blood that will serve as ink with which to write. When he does, however, his blood congeals, and Mephistopheles must fetch a chafer of coals to heat it until it thins. Faustus then signs the contract, but just before he agrees to hand it over to Mephistopheles, there is another delay as the words *homo fuge* suddenly appear on his arm:

> *Faust. Consummatum est*: this byll is ended,
> And *Faustus* hath bequeath'd his soule to *Lucifer*.
> But what is this Inscription on mine Arme?
> *Homo fuge*, whether should I flye?
> If vnto heaven, hee'le throw me downe to hell.
> My sences are deceiu'd, here's nothing writ:
> O yes, I see it plaine, euen heere is writ
> *Homo fuge*, yet shall not *Faustus* flye.
>   *Meph.* I'le fetch him somewhat to delight his minde.
>   *Exit.*
>   *Enter Deuils, giuing Crownes and rich apparell*
>   *to Faustus: they dance, and then depart.*
>   *Enter Mephostophilis.*
>
>   *Faust.* What meanes this shew? speake *Mephostophilis*.
>   *Meph.* Nothing *Faustus* but to delight thy mind,
> And let thee see what Magicke can performe.
>   *Faust.* But may I raise such spirits when I please?
>   *Meph.* I *Faustus*, and do greater things then these.
>   *Faust.* Then *Mephostophilis* receiue this scrole,
> A Deed of Gift, of body and of soule.[82]

The episode is a curious one. It is not altogether evident *why* Mephistopheles should choose this moment to bring on the dancing devils. The stage direction does not indicate the form of this dance, and the stage business seems oddly out of sync with the rest of the scene. A modern reader is likely to wonder, as Faustus does, "What meanes this shew?" (B-text, B4v; 2.1.83). When we consider the cultural connotations of spectacle, however, the action begins to make more sense. The entire rhetorical thrust of the episode centers on the question of whether or not Faustus will go through with the contract. When Faustus has finally signed the deed, the scene presents a critical moment of delay: Faustus becomes suddenly indecisive about handing over the contract to Mephistopheles. It is at this point that Mephistopheles states that his goal is to "delight" Faustus's mind, an act of seduction that he effects through the power of spectacle. This subsequent show makes Faustus eager to stage similar spectacles whenever it might "please" him and ultimately convinces him to surrender the scroll. *Pleasure* and *delight*'s joint associations with spectacle and with bodily seduction are here mapped onto what Jean Alter would call theatre's referential function.

The cultural attitudes registered on the linguistic level work in tandem with the play's performance dynamics. As the onstage spectator, Faustus is in a position that mirrors that of the actual playgoer. The spectacle that seduces him is the very one that theatre audiences have paid to see. The devils in *Doctor Faustus* use two kinds of visually appealing "shew" to entice Faustus: they give him "*Crownes and rich apparell*," and they perform the onstage dance. Within the fictional narrative, these spectacles function toward the same end: both contribute to Faustus's seduction. In the actual playhouse, their effect on spectators was more complex. The crowns and costly clothing are, within the imaginary world of the play, valued as precious objects; for theatregoers, however, they served primarily as spectacle. Their spectacular quality depended in part on their actual value and material characteristics: aristocratic clothing given to servants as livery was sometimes sold to acting companies for use onstage,[83] and in such instances, the social prestige of the garments combined with the expensive fabrics out of which they were constructed to produce a kind of multisensory feast, mobilizing not only visual spectacle, as fake velvet or artfully applied metallic paint might, but also tactile spectacle, as audiences imagined touching the sumptuous cloth themselves.[84] At the same time, the spectacle of the crowns at least, if not also the clothing, was a result of the semiotics of performance: costumes presented onstage were spectacular because they were supposed to *signify* valuable objects. To adopt Alter's terms, the "*Crownes and rich apparell*" simultaneously mobilized both the referential and the performant functions in the service of pleasure and delight.

By contrast, the devils' dance served as the same kind of "shew" for both Faustus and actual playgoers. In both play and playhouse, its primary function was spectacular entertainment resulting from nonreferential physical display. The complicity of both on- and offstage viewers in the spectacle of dance is underscored in the 1604 A-text. This version of the play includes a line not in the B-text: when Mephistopheles assures Faustus that he, too, will be able to "raise vp spirits," Faustus responds, "Then theres inough for a thousand soules" (A-text, C1r; 2.1.88).[85] This remark might be understood not only as a general exclamation but also as a metatheatrical reference to actual playgoers. Public theatre performances typically attracted approximately a thousand customers. In his *Epigrammes,* Sir John Davies quips, "[A]s we see at all the play house dores, / when ended is the play, the daunce, and song: / A thousand townesmen, gentlemen, & whores, / Porters & seruingmen togither throng."[86] The same number appears in *The Roaring Girl* when Sir Alexander wittily alludes to spectators at the Fortune Theatre as having "a thousand heads."[87] Modern estimates concur with these early modern references, with typical attendance projected to have been around half capacity in theatres that held 2,500 to 3,000 spectators.[88] Referring to the dance as "inough for a thousand soules" implies that, like the fictional protagonist, playgoers may also have sold their souls for devilish spectacle. The tension between the two kinds of display, exemplified by the rich apparel and the dance, can be understood in relation to the contradictory valences of "pleasure" and "delight." The sparkling crowns and sumptuous clothes "recreate" (that is, refresh) the eye of the beholder even as they are explicitly imagined as sinful temptations. The dance more overtly seduces the viewer by presenting a bodily feat.

In situating both Faustus and theatregoers as delighted spectators of the same diabolical dance, the scene suggests that merely watching displays of physical prowess is itself potentially dangerous. The problematic status of the act of beholding comes to the forefront in *Doctor Faustus* just before the appearance of the dancing devils. When Faustus notices *homo fuge* written on his flesh, he wonders whether his "sences are deceiu'd." Is the inscription on his arm actually there? And if so, should it be interpreted as an exhortation to seek God's mercy or as a demonic incitement to despair? Faustus's confused reaction is here tied to uncertainty about the act of seeing. Much is at stake: the fate of his eternal soul hangs in the balance. These morally weighty questions are not confined to the dramatic representation but are woven into the semiotics of performance. Unless the suddenly vanishing bloody writing was staged through a special effect, playgoers must take Faustus at his word about what he "sees." Faustus's speech, in other words, produces an imagined visual effect. Just as the fictional narrative foregrounds Faustus's struggle to interpret the message on his arm, the performance dynamics of the scene highlight the strategies actual playgoers might deploy to make sense of theatre. For both onstage and offstage spectators, the unreliability of the visual is foregrounded.

The invisible inscription *homo fuge* serves as a counterpoint to the visual splendors of the "*Crownes and rich apparell*" and the devils' dance to come. After the latter display, when Mephistopheles claims that the spectacle means "[n]othing *Faustus* but to delight thy mind / And let thee see what Magicke can performe," his lines belie the presentational impact of the action: the "shew" means "[n]othing" only insofar as it does not itself symbolize anything in particular, does not or cannot have an "argument" in the early modern sense of the term. Its enactment most certainly does mean something, since it is this show that problematically "delight[s]" Faustus—a point that the crucial word "but" in Mephistopheles's construction "[n]othing...but" cannot help but underscore. The verbal assertion that the spectacle is "[n]othing" is undermined by the onstage action, concretely and materially visible to playgoers. Like Faustus, theatregoers, taken in by a show of something, are asked by the devil to disregard it as nothing. If the word *nothing* was, as many scholars believe, a homonym for the word *noting* in early modern pronunciation, then its resonances are all the more striking: it is spectators' failure to note, or notice, the manipulations of the devil that leads to their moral complicity in and with the onstage action.[89] The performative force of words to construct the dramatic representation is subsumed within and beneath the presentational spectacle. Moreover, it is the sheer presence of that spectacle that, in turn, gives meaning not only to the representation (Faustus is ultimately seduced by the show) but also to the presentation (so, too, is the audience).

By contrast, in the *homo fuge* episode immediately preceding the show, the verbal undermines the visual. What is invisible, the play suggests, must be produced through the power of words. Through onstage speech, writing comes into being within the representational narrative. Far from "[n]othing," Faustus's speech act calls the words on his arm into being, from *no* thing into *some* thing.[90] The presentational dimension of theatre here takes a backseat to the representational. A similar dynamic informs the reading of the contract that takes place later in the scene after the devils' show. Because playgoers cannot literally see what, if anything, is written on the property scroll, they must take the actor at his word.[91] Modern actors know that *not* reading words off a page makes it is easier to speak the speech trippingly onstage. Whether or not the same was true for early modern players, the moment aims to enhance the audience's curiosity: they may crane their necks to catch a glimpse of what is on the document, but what they cannot see, they must perforce hear. If writing was viewed in early modern England as a mediated and imperfect representation of speech, as I discussed in chapter 3, here that hierarchy is reversed. This onstage reading raises all sorts of questions, not only about the efficacy of speech but also about the status of vision. As Andrew Sofer argues, there was a fine line between "hollow" theatrical speech acts and efficacious performatives that could cause changes in the real world, and it was the blurriness of this distinction that led to the well-known stories about "one devell too many" appearing alongside the actors in *Doctor Faustus*.[92] Beyond this linguistic dimension, however, this episode also has implications for early modern conceptions of vision: if reading the deed is a speech act in the playhouse that brings words into being on the page within the dramatic fiction, then what is the status of sight? Are theatre's spectacular displays to be understood as representational visions conjured up by actors or as truly delightful shows in real life? In its handling of these questions, the play posits a "both/and" kind of answer: like speech acts in the play, vision also may be efficacious outside the theatrical representation. Just as reading and conjuring in the play skirt the edge of dangerously meddling with real demonic powers, seeing involves spectators in the act of judging, in sorting out what they "really" see from what they think they see as well as distinguishing recreational spectacle from delightful seduction.

In juxtaposing all of this stage business in a single scene, the play calls attention to the nature of theatrical performance. When watching a play, what does it mean to "see it plaine"? In the *homo fuge* episode, speech operates as a form of spectacular magic that makes the invisible visible. Within the play's fiction, this power may be a sign of divine intervention, but in the playhouse it is an actor's trick. In the reading of the contract, speech is likewise the means through which invisible writing on the page is made visibly manifest to the playhouse audience. Within the representation, doing so has authority—it binds Faustus permanently to the devil—but in the playhouse, the bond's efficacy is undermined if the words on the page are invisible. These moments, which bracket the devils' show, raise questions about the moral consequences of the referential function's ability to *produce* vision and, thus, about the way the performant function should be interpreted. To what extent is the material spectacle of the devilish show actually there? If it delights playgoers' eyes, is that experience efficacious in the real world, causing real seduction to occur? Or if it is "mere" theatrical spectacle, does it mean, as Mephistopheles says, "[n]othing"?

Playgoers' imaginative complicity in the semiotics of performance, in the epistemological difficulties of interpreting and experiencing the performant function, implicates them in Faustus's moral dilemma.

Ambivalence and Amazement in *Macbeth*

The problematics of spectatorship that inform *Doctor Faustus* are also central to *Macbeth* and have attracted a good deal of scholarly attention.[93] When situated in relation to early modern ambivalence about spectacle, however, what it means to "see" takes on new meanings that implicate playgoers through the play's performance dynamics. In act 4, when the protagonist demands to know "Shall *Banquo*'s issue euer / Reigne in this Kingdome?" (TLN 1646–47; 4.1.102–3), the witches adopt the same diction as we saw previously in *Doctor Faustus*: "Shew" (TLN 1652–54; 4.1.107–9), they each cry in sequence before saying in unison, "Shew his Eyes, and greeue his Hart, / Come like shadowes, so depart" (TLN 1655–56; 4.1.110–11). The stage direction immediately following calls for *"A shew of eight Kings, and Banquo last, with a glasse / in his hand"* (TLN 1657–58; 4.1.111.s.d.). When faced with the procession of future monarchs who are not his own descendants, Macbeth cries out that the vision "seare[s] mine Eye-bals" (TLN 1660; 4.1.113). He demands of the witches, "Why do you shew me this?" (TLN 1663; 4.1.116), and he is appalled at Banquo's line stretching out ad infinitum in the "glasse, / Which shewes me many more" (TLN 1666–67; 4.1.119–20). "Horrible sight," he concludes, "Now I see 'tis true, / For the Blood-bolter'd *Banquo* smiles vpon me, / And points at them for his" (TLN 1669–71; 4.1.122–24). The witches' and Macbeth's comments all connect the procession of kings to the language of spectacle and spectatorship.

What is noteworthy about this moment in the play is not just the linguistic resonances of what it means to see a "shew," but also the way these verbal echoes are enacted in the performance medium. The problematic nature of what it means to rely on one's vision is, even at this initial moment after the procession, tied to the complexities of spectacular display, for Macbeth's reaction to the dramatically striking *"shew of eight Kings"* serves as the immediate impetus for the witches' dance. Wondering whether what he has seen is in fact "true" (TLN 1669; 4.1.122), Macbeth then inquires of the witches, "What? is this so?" (TLN 1671; 4.1.124). The first witch responds,

> I Sir, all this is so. But why
> Stands *Macbeth* thus amazedly?
> Come Sisters, cheere we vp his sprights,
> And shew the best of our delights.
> Ile Charme the Ayre to giue a sound,
> While you performe your Antique round:
> That this great King may kindly say,
> Our duties, did his welcome pay.   *Musicke.*
>   *The Witches Dance, and vanish.* (TLN 1671–80; 4.1.124–32)

The fact that Macbeth "[s]tands...thus amazedly" when faced with Banquo's descendants causes the sisters to "shew the best of our delights." Like the terms *shew* and *delight, amaze* also had problematic valences, connoting confusion and terror, as we saw in early modern accounts of extratheatrical spectacle. In this dramatic context, then, Macbeth's "amazed" reaction to the procession might be understood less as stunned silence than as horrified bewilderment. It is to remedy this reaction that the first witch proposes to "Charme the Ayre to giue a sound" while her sisters perform their "Antique round."

The "sound" produced by the witches to accompany their "round" also connects their dance to the show of Banquo's descendants that immediately precedes it. As Amanda Winkler has pointed out, "The act of singing was literally imbedded within the word incantation (*cantare*), reflecting the belief that sound and song were essential tools of the magician's and the witch's trade."[94] The word *shew*, which conjures the procession of kings, is intoned three times by the witches individually before being repeated in unison by all of them. This rhythmic reiteration combined with the meter and rhyme in the subsequent line ("Shew his Eyes, and greeue his Hart, / Come like shadowes, so depart") suggest that the thrice-repeated "Shew" and the verses immediately following may have been chanted or sung onstage. In the speech just prior to the dance, the first witch's request to "Charme the Ayre" may therefore have drawn a parallel between the "sound[s]" of the procession and of the dance.[95] Similarities between the "horrible sight" of Banquo's descendants and the "Antique round" would thus be underscored not only in the visual register but also in the aural one. Both are stage spectacles "shew[n]" by the witches to witnesses, onstage and off, who are eager to behold them.

However, the effects of these two shows are different from each other. Whereas the procession produces confused amazement, the dance is aimed at generating "delight." This seemingly positive motivation nevertheless retains in the performance medium the more ambivalent moral connotations present in the word's etymological history. In particular, the witches turn to spectacle in order to relieve Macbeth of his trepidation and bewilderment—a strategy much like the one Mephistopheles adopts in *Doctor Faustus* when the magician doubts his decision. In *Macbeth,* as in the earlier play, it seems at first glance as if the dance is meant to entertain the protagonist and to alleviate his terror and confusion. However, its actual effect is to cause Macbeth to damn himself by inciting him to kill Macduff's family. After the witches' dance, Macbeth determines that he will no longer delay but that "[t]he very firstlings of my heart shall be / The firstlings of my hand" (TLN 1700–1701; 4.1.147–48). He decides to go to Macduff's castle and "giue to th'edge o'th'Sword / His Wife, his Babes, and all Vnfortunate Soules / That trace him in his Line" (TLN 1704–6; 4.1.151–53). The dance performed for Macbeth thus serves two purposes. On the one hand, it is entertainment, to "cheere...vp his sprights." On the other hand, this dance has the power to corrupt, delighting the protagonist and then inciting him to commit foul deeds. As we saw earlier, the early modern terms used to describe viewer responses to spectacle encode within them ambivalence about the moral implications of beholding such performances. Here, we see such cultural understandings playing themselves out within the narrative, in theatre's referential function.

Ideas about spectatorship as potentially problematic also inform the performance dynamics of this scene. When the first witch declares her hope that, in response to their dance, "this great King may kindly say, / Our duties, did his welcome pay," the play explicitly cites the overlap between the fictional king in the dramatic narrative and real spectators in the London playhouse.[96] As the onstage spectator, Macbeth's position mirrors that of the audience: both are engaged in watching and interpreting spectacular performance. Just as the scene draws attention to Macbeth's struggle about whether to trust what he has seen and heard, the performance dynamics of the play foreground the strategies required of actual playgoers interpreting perceptual acts in the theatre. Witness, for example, the witches' exit after the procession and dance. The stage directions "*The Witches Dance, and vanish,*" together with Macbeth's subsequent lines, suggest that, within the fictional representation, the witches' departure takes place instantaneously. Scholars have posited a variety of staging possibilities for this exit, ranging from flying machines to the use of a trapdoor.[97] However, the term *vanish* did not necessarily signal a special effect. As Alan Dessen and Leslie Thomson point out, stage trickery was primarily used only "when an object rather than an actor *vanishes*"; in "situations involving two or more figures," a trick disappearance, they suggest, is particularly unlikely.[98] In *Macbeth,* the term *vanish* may well have signaled "a fictional situation where a disappearance is important for the narrative but the playgoer actually sees one or more figures exit."[99] Indeed, in *The Devil's Charter*—a King's Men play performed at the Globe in 1606, the same year *Macbeth* was presented there—one stage direction reads, "*He goeth to one door of the stage, from whence he bringeth the Ghost of Candie ghastly haunted by Caesar pursuing and stabbing it, these vanish in at another door.*"[100] When "vanish"-ings were performed in this way, audience members had to imagine a disappearance that was not performed with any degree of verisimilitude. In *Macbeth,* then, even though within the fictional world of the play the witches' vanishing takes place instantaneously, the actors playing the witches may well have remained in full view of the audience while supposedly disappearing. Correctly interpreting theatrical semiotics at this moment in the play requires that playgoers determine which onstage actions count as signifiers. To what extent should they trust what they see and hear? Like Macbeth, they may find their eyes and ears unreliable.

The material conditions of early modern theatre reinforced these performance dynamics. Public theatre stages in early modern England were fairly large. The stage at the Globe, where *Macbeth* was performed, measured about 43 feet wide.[101] Actors who were called upon to "vanish" would have required some amount of time to move to the exit doors. Moreover, since early modern stage practice typically involved fast-paced speaking with few pauses, the actor playing Macbeth may well have spoken his lines—"Where are they? Gone?"—before the witches had actually left the stage. As J. L. Styan noted some years ago, pauses in Shakespeare's plays are carefully marked and serve specific theatrical purposes, as when Brutus in *Julius Caesar* pointedly states during his speech in the Forum, "I pause for a reply."[102] Pauses in between lines and pauses for entrances and exits were not standard practice.[103]

The material circumstances of the public theatre that undergirded the semiotics of performance thus supported the disjunction between onstage presentation and fictional representation at this moment in the play. Like Macbeth, audience members had to disregard what they saw presented before them in order to imagine that the witches had disappeared. For both onstage and offstage spectators, the unreliability of the senses is foregrounded.

This parallel between actor and audience continues when Macbeth questions Lennox after the witches have left the stage:

> *Macb.* Where are they? Gone?
> Let this pernitious houre,
> Stand aye accursed in the Kalender.
> Come in, without there.   *Enter Lenox.*
>   *Lenox.* What's your Graces will.
>   *Macb.* Saw you the Weyard Sisters?
>   *Lenox.* No my Lord.
>   *Macb.* Came they not by you?
>   *Lenox.* No indeed my Lord.
>   *Macb.* Infected be the Ayre whereon they ride,
> And damn'd all those that trust them. I did heare
> The gallopping of Horse. Who was't came by?
>   *Len.* 'Tis two or three my Lord, that bring you word:
> *Macduff* is fled to England.
>   *Macb.* Fled to England?
>   *Len.* I, my good Lord. (TLN 1681–96; 4.1.133–43)

As in his speech after the procession of Banquo's descendants, Macbeth here questions the reliability of sensory perception. Where have the witches gone? Did Lennox see them go by? Were the sounds that Macbeth heard indeed their horses? The protagonist's questions have important implications for the ensuing narrative: if the witches and their apparitions are real and Macbeth believes what he sees, then his actions will lead him to further murder and damnation. Spectacle and spectatorship within the world of the play are thus imagined as having serious moral consequences. Moreover, Macbeth's questions stress the perceptual strategies of actual playgoers. Paralleling onstage and offstage spectators in this way, the play implicates theatregoers in the same kinds of moral dilemmas that the fictional protagonist faces: if their understanding of what happens in the theatre depends upon sight and sound, they, too, must be careful in their interpretation of stimuli received through such fallible senses. Indeed, if the actors playing the witches exit through the same door through which Lennox enters, the two sets of actors would have passed by each other in full view of the audience. Thus, Macbeth's question to Lennox—"Came they not by you?"—and Lennox's insistence that they did not would foreground the interpretive acts required of real-life audience members. The medium of performance here enacts the very difficulties it simultaneously represents: questions of sensory perception were not merely thematized within the fictional narrative but were embedded in the signifiers that constituted performance itself.

That the epistemological and moral difficulties generated by this moment in the play extend to the playhouse audience suggests how cultural discourses about spectacle were transmitted and produced through performance, problematizing both the bodily displays presented onstage and the very experience of beholding spectacle. In *Doctor Faustus* and *Macbeth*, the ambivalence seen earlier in accounts of bodily feats outside the theatre are integrated into performance dynamics within the playhouse. Both scenes position fictional characters and actual playgoers as delighted viewers who derive pleasure from spectacular entertainment. At the same time, theatregoers' seduction by presentational performance is imagined as parallel to characters' seduction by devils and witches. The performant function in early modern theatre was clearly experienced as powerfully *affective* in its ability to move theatregoers, physiologically and emotionally. It was thus also crucially *effective*: what was displayed and how it was displayed could produce genuine moral and epistemological change.

* * *

That the responses induced in spectators by bodily feats had the potential to extend beyond the individual to shape the larger world complicates the issue of what constitutes "active" or "passive" theatrical spectatorship. In "A Short Organum for the Theatre," Bertolt Brecht referred to pleasure as absolutely central to theatre,[104] but he differentiated it from the visual and aural effects that spectators of his day experienced. Early twentieth-century playgoers, he complained, "stare rather than see, just as they listen rather than hear. They look at the stage as if in a trance.... Seeing and hearing are activities, and can be pleasant ones, but these people seem relieved of activity and like men to whom something is being done."[105] He refers to such spectators as "sleepers" and likens the hypnotic effect of the stage to control by "witches and priests"[106]—a telling comparison given our early modern examples of spectacle. In Brecht's manifesto, the trancelike effects produced by spectacle isolate individuals, obscure modes of production, mystify social hierarchies, and naturalize inequitable distribution of material resources. Theatregoers' passivity enforces their separation, renders them autonomous persons incapable of collective action. They are not just naturally indisposed toward political critique but are transformed by theatrical spectacle into slack-jawed subjects in whom imaginary *feelings* of agency supplant the actual ability to effect change.

This physical and social impassivity, however, differs from early modern notions of spectacle as involuntary seduction. The emotional and physiological responses of sixteenth- and seventeenth-century playgoers were inscribed within a universe where cosmic social and moral hierarchies were understood to be reflected on the level of the individual. True agency rested not with mere mortals but with God. However, this belief in the interconnections between microcosm and macrocosm meant that proper Christians were held accountable for replicating divine order on earth. Though spectacle was a kind of seduction or ravishment, the fact that beholders responded involuntarily did not absolve them of responsibility. Spectators were called upon to be faithful, to guard against demonic incursions. Whereas the "motionless" and "detached" viewers of Brecht's era "seem relieved of activity and like men to whom something is being done," playgoers in Shakespeare's theatre were socially and morally culpable for their actions and reactions despite their inability to control them.

Given such understandings of the universe, why would early modern spectators have subjected themselves to such displays? One answer lies in ideas about audience in medieval religious theatre. In the earlier drama, playgoers were central to the biblical narrative, as they played the part of crowd, whether saved at the Crucifixion or condemned at the Last Judgment. Morality plays likewise involved the audience in their emphasis on the trials and tribulations of the Everyman figure, who served as the onstage representative for actual playgoers.[107] Early modern plays also gave weight to the spectator as participant, but sometimes that central importance is eclipsed by modern assumptions about theatrical spectatorship. Though *Doctor Faustus* has often been discussed as a play in the morality tradition, *Macbeth* and other of Shakespeare's more famous tragedies tend not to be. Yet in the scenes I have analyzed, the parallel between playgoers and characters is critical to the way the performance medium integrates within itself broader attitudes toward spectacle and spectatorship. This conjunction suggests that, even in plays with more fully "fleshed-out" tragic protagonists, traces still exist of these figures as onstage representatives for the audience. In the notion that spectacle seduces the playgoer, we see multivalent early modern discourses coming together with traditional theatrical practices. The commonplace that devils and vices in the medieval drama offered spectacular delights leading to the temptation and fall of both on- and offstage beholders is here reproduced, extended, and revised in the theatre of Shakespeare and his contemporaries.[108]

Were delightful shows only to be guilty pleasures, then, heartily repented after the fact? Although anxiety about spectacle does reflect antitheatrical tendencies in early modern culture, the other side of the coin was the notion of spectacle as healthful and refreshing. These seemingly contradictory attitudes toward spectacle were grounded in the same underlying premise about the interconnectedness of the universe and the subject's place within it. The very characteristics that made spectacle potentially problematic could also render it socially and theatrically beneficial, reinforcing group identity and producing an engaged audience deeply invested in the show. This notion of participatory spectatorship as a positive force for the solidification of communal bonds can be seen especially clearly in an account of a masque performed before James I in 1618. As Orazio Busino (chaplain to the Venetian embassy) describes, watching feats of physical prowess encouraged viewers to participate in the action:

> Finally they [the knights in the masque] danced the Spanish dance once more with the ladies, and because they were tired began to lag; and the King, who is by nature choleric, grew impatient and shouted loudly, "Why don't they dance? What did you make me come here for? Devil take all of you, dance!" At once the Marquis of Buckingham, his majesty's favourite minion, sprang forward, and danced a number of high and very tiny capers with such grace and lightness that he made everyone admire and love him, and also managed to calm the rage of his angry lord. Inspired

> by this, the other masquers continued to display their powers one after another, with different ladies, concluding with capers, and lifting their goddesses from the ground. We counted 34 capers in succession cut by one knight, but none matched the splendid technique of the Marquis.[109]

Buckingham's display of physical skill impresses spectators, but rather than making them awestruck observers, it contributes to the communal nature of the event. The affective potential of spectatorship is present for *all* of the viewers: "[E]veryone admire[s]" Buckingham's prowess and "love[s] him," James's impatient rage is calmed, and, inspired by the impressive feat, the other masquers leap up to "display their powers" themselves.

Watching spectacle was thus powerful in two different directions. Done properly and eliciting the right responses, it was rejuvenating "recreation," necessary and good not only for the individual viewer but also for the community and society as a whole. Yet in that potential benefit, there was also a danger. For displays of bodily feats to have positive effects, they had to penetrate beholders and strongly affect them. Having the force to move viewers so deeply meant spectators might more easily succumb to their sensations, might be enticed by their senses. This notion of spectacle as simultaneously beneficial and detrimental may have contributed to the popularity of playgoing in early modern England. Both healthfully refreshing and dangerously seductive, performance would be inescapably compelling. Part of the allure of theatre may have been the complex ways in which spectators were pulled into the action onstage. Such participatory notions of spectatorship suggest the need to rethink common assumptions about playhouse practices. Rather than imagining actor-audience contact as taking place primarily during soliloquies, asides, and interpolated stage business by figures such as clowns, we should pay more attention to the potential for interaction during other moments onstage. If displays of physical prowess did not dazzle spectators into passivity but rather implicated the viewer in the action being viewed, then even when playgoers were "merely" watching, they were, in the early modern theatre, actively involved.

This ability to pull the spectator into the action onstage may have been crucial to the role that theatre played in the establishment and reproduction of social forms. Even if playgoers had to defend against the potentially evil influences of spectacle, their being implicated in the show may also have fostered social responsibility, reinforcing a sense of communal identity. Connecting viewers to performers through the very act of spectatorship, spectacles may also have constituted the audience as *jointly* impacted by the effects of what they saw, bound together by the shared experience of beholding spectacle—and thus "beholden" to one another.[110] When we talk of "spectatorship," then, we are dealing with not just straightforward acts of perception through which theatre as our object of study becomes visible, but a whole range of cultural beliefs that shaped the performance medium, which in turn reshaped the culture itself. With a fuller sense of the theatrical and cultural implications of displays of physical prowess, I turn now to a very different kind of spectacle. Dances were situated at moments in the performance of a play when representation and presentation came together, the convergence point of what was enacted on the playhouse stage and what was signified by those actions within the fictional story.

What happened when representation and presentation were at their furthest from one another? Stage violence functioned as spectacle, but dramaturgically it was the opposite of dance: severed limbs could not be literally presented onstage. The way early modern theatre negotiated this phenomenological constraint is the subject of the next chapter.

Chapter 5

Artful Sport: Violence, Dismemberment, and Games in *Titus Andronicus*, *Cymbeline*, and *Doctor Faustus*

One of the most bizarre episodes of dismemberment in early modern theatre occurs in *The Tragical Reign of Selimus*. When Acomat tortures Bajazet's ambassador Aga, he "[p]uls out his eyes" and "cut[s] of[f] his hands,"[1] as the stage directions tell us. He then commands Aga,

> [*Aco.*] Now in that sort go tell thy Fmperour [*sic*]
> That if himselfe had but bene in thy place,
> I would haue vs'd him crueller then thee:
> Here take thy hands: I know thou lou'st them wel.
>   *Opens his bosome, and puts them in.*
> Which hand is this? right? or left? canst thou tell?
>   *Aga.* I know not which it is, but tis my hand. (F3r; lines 1432–38)

The word *bosom*, in early modern usage, referred not only to a part of the body but also to the "part of the dress which covers the breast; also the space included between the breast and its covering," and it was specifically "[c]onsidered as the receptacle for money or letters, formerly answering to modern use of 'pocket.'"[2] This grotesque bit of stage business underscores Aga's loss of agency: the ambassador's hands no longer carry out Bajazet's will but are themselves objects to be carried. The literalness of this exchange is accentuated when Aga subsequently returns home. He calls upon Bajazet and his lords to "witnesse" his bodily mutilation, then says, "VVitnesse the present that he sends to thee, / Open my bosome, there you shall it see" (F3v; lines 1476–77, 1485–86). The stage direction reads, "*Mustaffa* opens his bosome and takes out his hands" (F3v; lines 1487–88). The messenger becomes the message itself; the emissary *is* the missive. The language in *Selimus* echoes the more famous instance of dismemberment in Shakespeare's *Cymbeline*. When the clownish prince,

Cloten, is decapitated by the princely clown, Guidarius, the latter declares, "I haue sent *Clotens* Clot-pole downe the streame, / In Embassie to his Mother; his Bodie's hostage / For his returne" (TLN 2480–82; 4.2.184–86). The humor in the line rests in the mobility of the severed head: separated from the body, it acts as an ambassador to the Queen. Like Aga's hands in *Selimus,* the severed head in *Cymbeline* complicates the distinction between subject and object. In both plays, body parts are imagined as independent entities, separated from their erstwhile owners and transformed from persons into things.

These fascinating episodes serve as potent synecdoches for dismemberment in the early modern theatre more generally. In both instances, the seemingly excessive violence foregrounds the semiotics of representing bodily mutilation in the playhouse. Aga's hands and Cloten's head are like theatrical props even within their fictional narratives: separate and mobile entities, they are objects that must be transported, just as the props used to represent those body parts must be carried on- and offstage. Moreover, bodies and body parts are, like props, imagined as interchangeable. In *Selimus,* Acomat taunts Aga by saying, "Which hand is this? right? or left? canst thou tell?" Holding up the hand and perhaps turning it back and forth in front of Aga's face, Acomat draws attention to what the blind man cannot see but playgoers can: left and right hands are inverses of each other. Just as many property hands look alike, Aga's fictional hands are indistinguishable from one another. In *Cymbeline,* Cloten's body is likewise portrayed as interchangeable: the head Guiderius bears is much like any other property head, and the prince's mutilated trunk comes to be mistaken for Posthumus.[3] Rather than trying to naturalize the material conditions that circumscribed performance, *Selimus* and *Cymbeline* play upon—and play up— those theatrical conventions.

This tendency to foreground severed limbs, rather than glossing over them, is found repeatedly in early modern drama. In this chapter, I demonstrate how the wildly improbable stage business around dismemberment in early modern plays drew on broader cultural attitudes and practices that were then revised through the act of performance. Like Aga's hands or Cloten's head, actors were both subjects and objects in the theatre: even as they represented people within the dramatic representation, their bodies operated as material signifiers onstage. Rather than effacing this phenomenological condition, however, early modern plays repeatedly highlighted it. In imagining actors' bodies as objects that could be transported, circulated, even tossed and thrown, scenes of dismemberment foregrounded the semiotics of theatre itself. Though we might at first assume that such self-conscious displays produced a kind of Brechtian alienation effect, distancing theatregoers by making the play seem less real, what is striking about such episodes is how often they *fail* to foreground questions of verisimilitude. Rather than questioning whether body parts appear real or fake, early modern plays drew attention to the ontological status of the actor's body by highlighting precisely those parts that were missing within the fictional representation but present onstage. In doing so, the performance medium did not simply rework or refract broader cultural concerns; rather, it expressed contradictions between ideas about the body inside and outside the playhouse.

Dismemberment serves as a particularly useful site for investigating the relationship between theatre as a representational system and theatre as a spectacular entertainment in its own right: it offered up *as* presentational spectacle physical mutilation that could not literally *be* presented. Stage violence pushed theatre's representational abilities to their limit: short of killing off all the actors, theatre had to use its own semiotic system to mobilize the affective power of spectacular entertainment. In this chapter, I analyze the peculiar depictions of dismemberment that arose as theatrical practices clashed with broader cultural beliefs and institutions. Outside the playhouse, violently mangled bodies were much on display in relation to judicial punishment, religious martyrdom, murder investigations, and violent sports, such as football and animal baiting. Focusing in particular on *Titus Andronicus, Cymbeline,* and *Doctor Faustus,* I argue that spectacles of dismemberment served as what the Duke of Vanholt in the B-text of *Faustus* refers to as "Artfull sport"[4]—onstage actions that functioned not only as fictional representations but also as real-life games and festive play. Theatrical dismemberment, I contend, was in this sense a kind of efficacious performance, reinscribing paradigms of social integration that lay at the heart of the violence of stake, scaffold, and sport. By examining the presentational dynamics of dismemberment, we can thus see not only how cultural discourses shaped early modern theatre but also how the medium of performance—through which those discourses were transmitted—authorized, revised, and ultimately produced broader social attitudes, practices, and institutional formations.

Justice, Martyrdom, Murder, and the Actor's Body

In Shakespeare's *Titus Andronicus,* when two of Titus's sons have been framed for murder and are condemned to die, Titus is tricked into cutting off his own hand in exchange for their release—but his sons are, nevertheless, subsequently executed. The audience and Titus both discover this fact when a messenger arrives carrying *"two heads and a hand"* (TLN 1382; 3.1.233.s.d.). During this scene, Titus's daughter Lavinia appears onstage mutilated—she has already had her hands cut off and her tongue cut out—and Titus himself is also missing a hand. At the end of the scene, Titus asks his family to help him remove these body parts from the stage:

> [C]ome Brother take a head,
> And in this hand the other will I beare.
> And *Lauinia* thou shalt be employd in these things:
> Beare thou my hand sweet wench betweene thy teeth[.] (TLN 1428–31; 3.1.279–82)

This grotesque bit of stage business makes modern audiences and readers very uncomfortable. Even though the First Folio and all early quarto editions of the play indicate that the mutilated Lavinia should carry the hand out between her teeth, directors frequently cut this portion of the scene.[5] Editors, for their part, often alter the speech so that Lavinia carries out the hand between her arms instead: omitting the rest of the third line after "employd," they change the fourth line to read "Bear thou my hand, sweet wench, between thine arms."[6] Editors have justified this reading through reference to the quarto versions of the play, in which the relevant lines are:

> Come brother take a head,
> And in this hand the other will I beare,
> And *Lauinia* thou shalt be imployde in these Armes,
> Beare thou my hand sweet wench betweene thy teeth[.] (1594 Q1, F3r)

This editorial practice follows the dubious tradition first put forth in the mid-nineteenth century when, as Eugene Waith describes,

> W. A. Wright (Cambridge edition) made the ingenious suggestion that the line in the manuscript copy ended at "employed"; that someone had written "arms" over "teeth" in the following line as a possible alternative to a ludicrous piece of business, but failed to cross out "teeth."[7]

For both directors and editors of the play, the stage action required in this episode seems to require emendation because it goes beyond the bounds of believability—not to mention good taste.

Scholars have tried to make sense of this episode in a number of ways. Traditional interpretations have focused on dismemberment as a symbol of political upheaval: with Saturninus on the throne, Rome is without its proper "head"; the grotesque inappropriateness of Lavinia carrying the hand in her teeth mirrors the disorder of a universe where Rome, the epitome of civilization, is but "a wilderness of Tigers" (TLN 1190; 3.1.54). More recently, scholars have analyzed the scene in relation to early modern cultural discourses. Studies have included, for instance, fascinating discussions of severed hands in relation to ideas about agency or as an outgrowth of fantasies about gestural languages in encounters with racialized peoples in the New World.[8] From a performance perspective, however, severed limbs were first and foremost theatrical props. When *Titus Andronicus* was first performed, there were no stage crews, no blackouts, no curtains to lower between scenes. Any properties that were brought onstage had to be carried off in full view of the audience. Homer Swander points out that in modern productions when a character dies onstage, "the body disappears with as little fuss as possible, most members of the audience hardly noticing at the time and, later, not remembering at all."[9] In the scene from *Titus Andronicus,* however, the way in which the stage gets cleared is the opposite of quiet. When Titus instructs his brother Marcus to take a head, says that he himself will take another, and tells Lavinia to carry the hand out in her teeth, the play grotesquely foregrounds both the action of removing the props and the fact of dismemberment itself. Forcing Lavinia to transport a hand—as opposed to, say, a head—emphasizes that she herself does not have hands. Her mutilation is further highlighted by the fact that hands are normally used to carry objects, but in this case, a hand is itself the object being carried. The stage might easily be cleared by having Marcus—who still has both his hands—carry more than one item. Instead, the play draws attention to the dismemberment and to the theatrical necessity of clearing the stage.

When Lavinia carries out the severed hand in her mouth, justice—or the lack of it—plays a particularly important role. The scene begins with a procession of judges and senators to the place where Titus's sons are to be executed for a crime that the audience knows they did not commit. Early modern theatregoers were no strangers to spectacles of the scaffold, and the performance dynamics of this moment reflected actual social practices. As Susan Amussen points out, spectators at real state violence sometimes "came to support, rather than condemn, the victims, who were seen as martyrs."[10] In the 1630s, for example, a crowd cheered John Lilburne as he was led through the streets for punishment; others expressed support for William Prynne, who, as one spectator wrote in his diary, "endured his mutilation with much courage."[11] The patent injustice of the conviction of Titus's sons puts audience members in the position of such dissenting witnesses, actively resisting the spectacle rather than sanctioning it. Playgoers are interpolated into the fictional story: hapless bystanders watching the execution procession, they are in the same spectatorial position as Titus, who garners their intense sympathy. Moreover, Shakespeare's play draws attention to the act of seeing when Titus explicitly enjoins his family, "Looke *Marcus,* ah sonne *Lucius* looke on her" (TLN 1252; 3.1.110). His words direct not only the Andronici but also actual theatergoers to gaze upon the disfigured Lavinia. Both on- and offstage spectators are here called upon to bear witness to the mutilation of Titus's daughter as they just have to the procession of his sons.[12] This emphasis on witnessing is heightened when Titus reads his daughter's physical gestures as if she were a text: "Marke *Marcus* marke," he says, "I vnderstand her signes, / Had she a tongue to speake, now would she say / That to her brother which I said to thee" (TLN 1287–89; 3.1.143–45). The line's punning repetition draws attention simultaneously to the marks upon Lavinia's mutilated body and to the act of attentive watching. "Marke[ing]" is both productive and receptive, both writing and reading, both inscription and interpretation.

When the two heads and the hand are subsequently brought onstage, discourses of judicial punishment and comparisons between playgoers and scaffold witnesses underscore interconnections between the dramatic narrative and its performance dynamics. In early modern England, dismemberment was the standard punishment for a range of crimes, and the body parts of offending criminals were often displayed prominently in public. Their heads were spitted on pikes at the city gates and their hands nailed to posts in the marketplace.[13] In order to get to the Globe or Rose theatres (where *Titus Andronicus* was originally performed), playgoers had to cross over London Bridge, where the heads of convicted criminals were displayed on pikes, as Visscher's 1616 view of London illustrates (figure 5.1). When the Swiss doctor Thomas Platter visited England in 1599, he specifically made mention of these heads in his diary:

> At the top of one tower almost in the centre of the bridge, were stuck on tall stakes more than thirty skulls of noble men who had been executed and beheaded for treason and for other reasons. And their descendants are accustomed to boast of this, themselves even pointing out to one their ancestors' heads on this same bridge, believing that they will be esteemed the more because their antecedents were of such high descent that they could even covet the crown, but being too weak to attain it were executed for rebels; thus they make an honour for themselves of what was set up to be a disgrace and an example.[14]

Figure 5.1 Dismembered heads on pikes above London Bridge. Detail from Claes Jansz. Visscher's panoramic view of the city of London (1616). Courtesy of the Library of Congress.

As Platter's account suggests, dismembered heads would have been associated specifically with treason. And in Shakespeare's play, treason is precisely the crime for which Titus's sons have been condemned.[15]

In post-Reformation England, treason was not simply a secular crime; it was also related to religious dissent. As Peter Lake and Michael Questier put it, "The basic thrust of Catholic resistance involved a determination to affirm their status as martyrs, men of conscience punished for their religious convictions, against the equally determined efforts of the authorities to type them as traitors."[16] In *Titus Andronicus,* Lucius specifically draws on this discourse when he says to Lavinia, "Speake gentle sister, who hath martyr'd thee?" (TLN 1220; 3.1.81). The strong cultural association between bodily mutilation and martyrdom meant that, when Catholics wrote pamphlets describing the execution of their brethren, they spelled out the dismemberment in gory detail, whereas pamphlets written by Protestants glossed over those same aspects of the executions.[17] For example, when a priest named Everard Hanse was executed, Catholics described in particular the drawing out of his bowels, while the Protestant version of the same event said simply that he suffered "due pains of death and execution." Catholics mentioned that the priest's genitals were cut off, while Protestants euphemistically referred to the hangman doing his duty. Catholic appropriation of dismemberment took place literally as well as figuratively: throughout this period, the body parts of Catholics who were executed for treason were repeatedly stolen as religious relics. An account of William Hart's execution at York in 1583, for instance, notes that "portions of his flesh were cut off"[18] and that his head and the head of another

Catholic named Richard Thirkill were stolen from the prison wall where they were displayed. After the execution of Robert Sutton in 1587 at Stafford, his arm and shoulder were carried off by local Catholics. Miracles were often attributed to such dismembered parts. Robert Sutton's forefinger and thumb, for example, which he used to celebrate the mass, supposedly remained undecayed even a year after his death. Protestant aversion to describing the details of Catholic deaths was an attempt to circumvent both textual and physical appropriation. Dismemberment was supposed to be a terrible punishment, but Catholics tried to integrate it into a discourse of martyrdom even as Protestants sought to prevent them from doing so.

Both Protestant authorities and Catholic recusants could agree on one thing, however: the body was the site of tremendous power. Associations between dismemberment and martyrdom extended beyond confessional divides, as can be seen most notably in Foxe's *Acts and Monuments,* which valorized Protestant martyrs who suffered torture and mutilation. Moreover, state officials dismembered and displayed the bodies of criminals specifically because it was believed that certain burial rites were necessary for the well-being of the dead.[19] The lack of proper funeral arrangements is precisely what is at issue in *Titus Andronicus,* both at the beginning of the play, when Titus's sons disobey him and he declares that they will lie unburied, and at the end, when Tamora's body is condemned to be eaten by beasts and birds.[20] The abrogation of appropriate rituals to care for the bodies of the dead was a terrible fate, and early modern judicial practices reflected and reinscribed such beliefs. Hanging, drawing, and quartering was the worst possible punishment not only because of the horror of dismemberment but also because the mutilated body was left to rot in the open air. As Sir Edward Coke describes, the final and most important part of the punishment was to have "the quarters set up in some high and eminent place, to the view and detestation of men, and to become a prey for the fowls of the air."[21] This very sensibility underlies William Harrison's reference to this practice as the "greatest and most grievous punishment used in England for such as offend against the state."[22] Ironically, these same cultural conceptions of the body allowed Catholics to reappropriate dismembered parts and situate them in a different discourse, one that portrayed severed limbs and heads as the relics of martyrs, not the remains of criminals. The interlocking judicial and religious practices surrounding treason and martyrdom constantly reaffirmed the physical body's immanent power by enacting through dismemberment the imaginary reintegration of a fragmented social body. Criminals were reincorporated into the community through the pity shown by sympathetic crowds, and martyrdom transformed the part into the whole by granting powers to severed limbs that exceeded those of the victim while alive. Dissolution of bodily wholeness ironically enabled the performative enactment of communal identity and cohesion.

Notions of the body as the locus of charismatic power also informed onstage dismemberment in contexts less overtly judicial than *Titus Andronicus.* In Shakespeare's *Cymbeline,* when Imogen wakes up next to the headless corpse, the body she discovers is not that of a condemned criminal but, she believes, the victim of a murder.

Mistaking Cloten's decapitated body for her husband, Posthumus, she repeatedly draws attention to his missing head:

> Oh *Posthumus,* alas,
> Where is thy head? where's that? Aye me! where's that?
> *Pisanio* might haue kill'd thee at the heart,
> And left this head on. (TLN 2642–45; 4.2.320–23)

And, in case anyone missed the point, the Roman general enters shortly thereafter, saying, "Soft hoa, what truncke is heere? / Without his top?" (TLN 2680–81; 4.2.353–54). As in *Titus Andronicus,* the repeated references to the missing head foreground the mutilated body rather than naturalizing it within the fictional story.

The sensational quality of this episode is not unlike those found in early modern murder pamphlets. One 1624 pamphlet, *The Crying Murther,* for example, describes on its title page the

> *cruell and most horrible bu[tchery] of Mr. Trat, curate of old Cleaue; who was first mu[rthered] as he trauailed vpon the high way, then was brought home to hi[s house] and there was quartered and imboweld: his quarters and bowels b[eing af]terwards perboyled and salted vp, in a most strange and fearefull manner.*[23]

Such graphic accounts of death and dismemberment are a form of cheap print whose veracity modern readers might doubt. However, as John Langbein notes, "the pamphlets appeared quite rapidly after the events—occasionally even before trial or execution of sentence" and were relatively accurate: "The witchcraft pamphlets, the only ones to have attracted much scholarly attention, have been regularly verified when checked against surviving legal records."[24] Legal documents, in other words, are no less "fictional" in their own way than popular pamphlets. Both reflect the agendas of the authors/authorities that produced them. Indeed, the rhetorical strategies used in murder pamphlets echo those found in records of testimony presented before coroners and magistrates. As Malcolm Gaskill puts it, court depositions do not offer "bland, dispassionate description, stripped bare of narrative structure and embellishments"; like pamphlets, these documents "were one-sided literary forms which sought to persuade rather than inform."[25] Moreover, in both genres, dismemberment was not "mere" representation. Despite the fact that legal documents and murder pamphlets purported to record actual events, whereas stage dismemberment specifically could not be real, both printed and theatrical accounts of murder constantly drew attention to those mutilated parts, underscoring the power of bodily presence.

This emphasis on presence is central also to early modern practices used to discover the perpetrators of crimes. Pamphlet literature, like revenge tragedy, often invoked the trope that "blood will out," that God's justice will triumph and expose murderers to their rightful punishment. One account describes a girl who, like Lavinia, has her tongue cut out to prevent her from revealing her brother's murderers. In court, however, she miraculously recovers the ability to testify because "with

God nothing is impossible."[26] Not only do murder pamphlets repeat this platitude often, but they do so by attributing miracles specifically to the bodies of victims. In this sense, murder pamphlets rework and extend martyrological discourses that depend upon a magico-religious notion of the body as the potent site of God's justice and divine revelation. These ideas about the power of the dismembered body informed related judicial practices in addition to murder literature. Cruentation, the belief that the corpse of a murdered person would bleed anew in the presence of its murderer, was institutionalized in the practice of judicial corpse-touching, or the "ordeal of the bier." Not merely a superstitious holdover from medieval England, corpse-touching was practiced throughout the sixteenth and seventeenth centuries and continued well into the eighteenth.[27] This popular belief was also represented onstage, as in Shakespeare's *Richard III,* when the title character woos Anne before the corpse of Henry VI, which bleeds in Richard's presence. Just as early modern punishment and ideas about martyrdom were founded on the premise that the body was a locus of charismatic power, so, too, were discourses about the bodies of murder victims.

When dismemberment was represented onstage, then, its associations with punishment, martyrdom, and murder heightened the sense that the body was serious, important, and powerful. At the same time, early modern theatre traded on its ability to *erase* the actor's body: in order for plays to be intelligible at all in a repertory theatre where actors doubled roles, the actor's body had to become *un*important so that his costumes and props could indicate identity. We see this tension played out in *Cymbeline* when Imogen discovers the headless corpse. In that episode, both semiotic systems are imagined as dangerously—and amusingly—unstable at the moment that Imogen misidentifies the corpse. Bodies, like clothes, can apparently be exchanged. The humor in this scene is made all the more pointed by the fact that early modern playgoers themselves risked making precisely the same mistake as Imogen. By staging the misinterpretation of the very signifiers that audiences themselves used to decode performance, the play calls attention to gaps and fissures in theatre's own semiotic practices. Spectators are admonished to remember that both kinds of identity markers can be read in multiple ways.

The problem dramatized in this episode—how to identify a faceless body—is found in many early modern murder pamphlets. In *Three Bloodie Murders,* one corpse is rendered unrecognizable by his mutilation: "[W]hether by reason his face, was so grieuously disfigured with cuts, or otherwise, I know not, but there hath not been any yet heard of, that could either tell his name, or the place of his dwelling."[28] In *The Cry and Reuenge of Blood,* when a murder committed years before is finally discovered, the author remarks that "had their flesh not bene wasted, and countenance remayned, this might have giuen some light to discerne their qualitie and condition; and so to have made some way for the finding out of the murtherers."[29] In early modern England, the use of lay investigators was common in cases where identification was difficult, and "searchers" were sometimes employed to examine the bodies of the dead for signs that might indicate the cause of death.[30] Reflecting these actual investigatory practices, murder pamphlets likewise indicate that when victims cannot be identified by their faces, their bodies must be searched for special marks or signs of who they were. In *The Crying Murther,* neighbors finally determine that "in all likelihood it was Mr. *Trat* their olde Curate that was murthered, there being one of his fingers knowne by a secret marke vnto them."[31] In *The Cry and Reuenge of Blood,* positive identification of one of the bodies is made when the mother, asked "what markes she could discouer to own them," is able to remember "two teeth broken out of his vpper iaw by a former accident, and the scull being searched approues the same; and so both markes concurring vpon the same carcase...vndoubted conclusion was made, that, that carcase was her sonne Iohns."[32] The identification of the victim here is specifically attributed to "the wisedome of God," who enables the "outward tokens" of identity to remain.[33] These physical "markes," a word deployed in *Titus Andronicus* and found also in other murder pamphlets, construct the body as a text, a material sign system to be interpreted.

In Shakespeare's *Cymbeline,* however, when Imogen reads the marks on the headless body, she *mis*identifies the corpse:

A headlesse man? The Garments of *Posthumus?*
I know the shape of's Legge: this is his Hand:
His Foote Mercuriall: his martiall Thigh
The brawnes of *Hercules*: but his Iouiall face—
Murther in heauen? How? 'tis gone. (TLN 2630–34; 4.2.308–12)

The dead body here is deceptive because it is dressed in "[t]he Garments of *Posthumus,*" perhaps even that "mean'st Garment" (TLN 1111; 2.4.133) that earlier in the play Imogen emphatically swore to value more than Cloten. The irony of the moment depends on the power of clothing as a marker of identity: dressed properly as a prince, Cloten's body would presumably have been easily recognized. Yet the scene also implies that sartorial signifiers can be deceptive in more than one way: because the corpse's "Iouiall face" is missing, Imogen places too much stock in the clothes he wears and ends up misreading the body. Pointing to his leg, hand, foot, thigh, and "brawnes"—a term referring to arms, calves, or buttocks, as well as more generally to rounded muscles[34]—she insists that she recognizes the signs of her husband's flesh. Both clothes and body parts here fail to function properly as markers of identity; a mistake in one semiotic system occasions the breakdown of the other. The episode highlights the potential for slippage between two different strategies through which audiences made sense of what they saw onstage. On the one hand, in a repertory system where doubling roles was common, costumes were crucial semiotic markers through which playgoers identified characters. For such a system to work, spectators had to ignore the actor's body and instead pay attention to his dress. On the other hand, actors were the physical incarnations of characters. Their corporeal presence was required in order to represent persons within the fictional world of the play.

The ironies attendant on this episode would have been heightened if, as Stephen Booth proposes, both Cloten and Posthumus were played by the same performer.[35] Yet even if this was not the case—and we have no historical evidence on the doubling of these roles—one of the two actors may well have played the corpse. Although English evidence is scarce, Continental sources suggest that dummies were used primarily for what regular actors could not perform. The 1536 Bourges

Acts of the Apostles burns several bodies onstage, and the 1580 Modane Antichrist play requires "two dummy bodies to rip up or saw through the middle, from which shall come out entrails and blood."[36] In a Provençal Passion play from the late fifteenth or early sixteenth century, a dummy is flown across the stage, and after it lands, an actor appears from behind a curtain to take its place.[37] A 1499 French Saint Lawrence play even involves a dummy being drawn and quartered onstage by horses, after which "angels come to look for the soul among the pieces."[38] All of these instances suggest that dummies were used to produce spectacular effects beyond actors' capabilities.

The converse was also true: where actors would suffice, there was no need to spend money on props. The technology to represent onstage beheadings with live actors was apparently available. In Massinger and Dekker's *The Virgin Martyr*, Dorothea is beheaded onstage, as are Sir John in Fletcher and Massinger's *Sir John Van Olden Barnavelt* and Herod in Markham and Sampson's *Herod and Antipater;* all three characters are alive and speaking until the very moment their heads are struck off.[39] Similarly, in the B-text of *Doctor Faustus,* the conjurer's "*false head*" (B-text, F1v; 4.2.37.s.d.) is struck off; the decapitated corpse remains to frighten the other characters. Although dummies were not usually made of wax, which was very expensive, their creation involved not insignificant time, money, and talent. The decapitation scene in a late sixteenth-century Majorca Saints Crispin and Crispinian play refers to "dummies filled with straw," but somewhat earlier is a property list for a 1429 play of Saint George, written in French and most likely performed in Turin, that records the creation of dummy heads using "11 ells of cloth," "two lbs. of white paint (*blanc de puillie*)," and other items such as wigs and glue.[40] Looking at sixteenth-century French sources, John Spalding Gatton concludes that dummies were "straw-filled figures or mannequins first sculpted in stone (*en pierre*), then carefully copied in cardboard (*en carton*), and finally painted to resemble the actor."[41] The Modane and Bourges plays suggest that dummy bodies and body parts may have been made from animal flesh, but this practice was not widespread. In the professional theatres, such props would decay and need to be replaced. *The Rebellion of Naples* does include a stage direction for "a false head made of a bladder fill'd with bloud," but it seems more likely that the bladder was intended to burst upon decapitation for a special effect.[42]

Given such performance conditions, references in *Cymbeline* to Cloten's missing head seem like they would have drawn attention to the actor's body as itself a theatrical technology, one that, like costumes or props, can be crafted or duplicated. Yet, in this, the actor's body comes to be subject to the same difficulties as costumes and props: all are mobile and multiple and can be exchanged or doubled—or misread. Not concerned with verisimilitude as such, with whether the body looks real or fake, the play foregrounds the convergence point (or perhaps I should say divergence point) of character and actor: the body parts missing within the fictional representation but present in real life. The performer's body is here not an incarnation of a fictional person but a demarcation of negative space within the dramatic representation—Cloten's absent head. Similarly, in *Titus Andronicus,* the hands and tongue of the character Lavinia are mutilated, but the hands and tongue of the actor playing Lavinia are whole. When Lavinia carries the severed hand out between her teeth, the action highlights the very parts of her body that are both "there" and "not there" at the same time, the hands and tongue that are missing in the play but present in the playhouse. Any ambiguity around theatrical signals in such scenes can result in unconventional spectator responses, as was made strikingly clear in one 1994 *Titus Andronicus* performed by the Atlanta Shakespeare Company. The production cast as Lavinia an actor, Sarah Lancaster (now Sarah Onsager), who actually has a prosthetic hand and lower arm (figures 5.2 and 5.3). Onsager agreed to take off her prosthetic for the production, and when audience members realized what they were seeing, a number of people fainted and had to be carried out of the theatre.[43] For playgoers in early modern England, the performance medium likewise depended on being able to distinguish dismemberment in jest and in earnest. Semiotic clarity about the interplay between bodily presence and absence was crucial if the jokes recorded in playtexts were to work.

The peculiar valences of early modern stage dismemberment stand out in especially sharp relief when compared to earlier plays. The late fifteenth-century Croxton *Play of the Sacrament,* for instance, involves some elaborate stage business with a severed hand. When a group of Jews steals the Host, they subject it to a series of tests to see if it is really Christ. After stabbing it with their daggers, the bread bleeds. They then decide to boil it in oil, but the bread sticks to their leader's hand. To detach it, they nail the bread to a post and then pull hard, but when they do, his

Figure 5.2   Sarah Onsager as Lavinia and Jim Peck as Marcus in a 1994 Atlanta Shakespeare Company production of *Titus Andronicus.* Photo by Atlanta Shakespeare Company.

Figure 5.3 Sarah Onsager as Lavinia and Stuart Culpepper as Titus in a 1994 Atlanta Shakespeare Company production of *Titus Andronicus*. Photo by Atlanta Shakespeare Company.

hand comes off. This entire sequence is performed onstage; as the stage direction reads, "*Here shall thay pluke þe arme, and þe hand shall hang styll with þe Sacrament*" (line 435).[44] They then throw the bread, attached hand and all, into the cauldron of oil, which turns into blood and boils over. Even though the Eucharist has remained whole throughout this business, the hand has been boiled "the fleshe from þe bonys" (line 626). The bread is then thrown into an oven, from which Jesus suddenly bursts out. He miraculously restores the severed hand to its owner and then turns back into bread, which the Jews return to the church. All are converted. The end. In the Croxton *Play,* the dismembered hand is presented in service to the overall message of the play: believe in Christ; the bread of the Eucharist really is God. This narrative emphasis, reinforced through elaborate stage business, makes sense in an overtly religious play performed in a pre-Reformation context, where tensions around the nature of the Eucharist were already beginning to surface. The actor's body is not at stake here; what matters is the ontological status of the Host.

In early modern theatre, by contrast, dismemberment focused attention on what we might call "theatrical ontology," what it meant for something to *exist* within the imaginary world of the play. By calling attention to the parts of the actor's body that are missing within the fictional narrative but present in real life, these plays highlight questions of theatrical presence and absence. What is at stake is the semiotics of the actor's body, how and when a physically palpable entity can be treated as significant within a dramatic representation. In *The Life of Drama*, Eric Bentley put forth one influential definition of theatre: "A represents X, while S looks on."[45] That is, an actor represents a character while a spectator looks on. This formulation takes for granted that theatre is a representational medium. For early modern audience members, however, such a definition was not to be taken for granted. As I discussed in chapter 4, players were often grouped together with acrobats and dancers—entertainers who traded on their bodily skill to perform "feats of activity." Actors offered presentational entertainments, such as dance, that were integrated into but also exceeded fictional narratives. In such a context, bodies onstage were never simply representations of characters but were crucially associated with spectacle. Or, to put it in Jean Alter's terms, described in chapter 4, their referential function was complicated by their performant function: actors' bodies were not just stand-ins for characters but were on display as examples of physical prowess that were entertaining for their own sake. The early modern theatre, then, was in the difficult position of needing to negotiate two radically different ways of understanding the body onstage. On the one hand, the performer's material presence enabled the display of bodily skill in the presentational entertainments with which theatre was most closely associated. On the other hand, early modern playing companies traded on the versatility of the actor. Even as the actor's physical presence was important, the ability to play multiple parts depended on his skill at erasing himself, at representing his own bodily absence. The constraints of commercial entertainment led to complex interplay between theatre's performant and referential functions that generated uncertainty about the status of the actor's body.

Notions of the body found in judicial punishment, religious martyrdom, and murder pamphlets can be understood in relation to these changing performance conditions. Beliefs about the immanent power of the body privileged physical presence, just as presentational spectacle did. Some scholars have suggested that with the Protestant Reformation came a shift away from medieval magico-religious conceptions of the body. Stephen Greenblatt, for example, has argued that earlier notions of bodily wounds as potentially sacred were transformed in early modern England into that which was "deeply suspect, bespeaking fraud, credulity, vain superstition, and, worst of all, a fall into pagan or demonic worship."[46] The new science of anatomy has also been cited as an example of increasing secularization that divested the body of its previous mystical power. However, to see this transition as a done deal by Shakespeare's time would be to mistake a *longue durée* process that extended over centuries for an immediate transition in worldview. As I argued in previous chapters, habits of thought derived from traditional popular religion strongly influenced early modern playgoers long after the Reformation. Similarly, it is easy to overestimate the importance of public dissections given the large number of Renaissance anatomy texts that still exist today. The fact was that anatomical demonstrations were not very common in England and, even among the learned at Oxford, were not offered until 1624.[47] Rather than attributing the peculiarities of early modern theatrical dismemberment to broader changes in ideas about the body, then, we would do well to consider how traditional beliefs in the body's inherent power might have clashed with shifting performance conditions. The performance medium, in other words, did not simply reflect existing cultural practices but contributed to them by offering representations of dismemberment that participated in ongoing discourses—including, as I discuss next, notions of violence as festive game.

Dismemberment as Playhouse Game

In one of the many episodes in *The Comedy of Errors* when Dromio of Ephesus is beaten as a result of mistaken identity, he protests to Adriana:

> Am I so round with you, as you with me,
> That like a foot-ball you doe spurne me thus:
> You spurne me hence, and he will spurne me hither,
> If I last in this seruice, you must case me in leather. (TLN 358–61; 2.1.82–85)

Dromio's lines highlight the ways in which the actor's body circulates as both subject and object within a discourse of violent sport. The servant is like a ball, bandied back and forth between his mistress and her husband, and he is beaten as contestants often were in the early modern game of football. The violence is a result of mistaken identity because of his outward appearance, or "case," a term that in Shakespeare's day meant both clothes and the body.[48] Dromio plays on these meanings when he insists that he must "case me in leather," with *case* here meaning "[t]o cover or clothe with the hide of an animal, etc. (Chiefly said with reference to armour.)"[49] and *leather* referring both to physical material out of which footballs were made and the protective gear needed for combat.

These interlocking puns play on the circulation of both identity and objects in *The Comedy of Errors* as a whole. The mistaken identities of the two sets of twins hinges on physical similarity of their bodies (within the fictional narrative) and their clothes (in the actual playhouse). Moreover, just as Dromio is imagined as a ball passed back and forth, objects such as purses, rings, and chains are repeatedly transferred from hand to hand throughout the play. The transposition of subject and object evident in the servant's speech is part of the play's larger portrayal of people as exchangeable for things. Egeon must forfeit his life unless he can raise a thousand marks. Subsequently Antipholus of Syracuse sends his own Dromio off with this exact amount of money to have it stored for them at the Centaur, and the seemingly misplaced sum causes the other Dromio to be beaten. In a pun worthy of *Titus Andronicus,* the missing gold marks cause the physical marks on the servant's body (TLN 246–51; 1.2.81–86). At the end of the play, "these errors" (TLN 1877; 5.1.389) are sorted out: by clarifying the disposition of the chain, the purse, the diamond ring, and the ducats that have gone astray, the looming shadow of Egeon's execution and the comic misidentifications of the two sets of twins are brought to a happy conclusion. Commercial exchange is the premise of the story, but here it is also the means through which that story is resolved. People, like commodities, are circulated in this economy. Subjects are, moreover, imagined not only as interchangeable, like the twins, but also as exchangeable *for* objects.

This transposition of subjects and objects echoes the performance dynamics of onstage dismemberment, a situation in which property heads and hands take the place of real actors' body parts. Props were objects separated out from their original contexts, possessing what Frances Teague has referred to as "dislocated function."[50] Employed in multiple plays, their actual purpose outside the playhouse was subsumed onstage into their function as theatrical signifiers: props were not simply objects but objects that represented objects. Yet *what* they represented—that is, *how* they signified onstage—changed from day to day. Like actors' bodies, theatrical props could signify in multiple ways, and different props—say, multiple rings or purses—might represent the same object within the fictional world of a particular play. When Dromio of Ephesus describes himself as a football cased in leather, he gestures toward this phenomenological condition: he is like an object not only within the play's fictional narrative but also onstage; his body is like a theatrical prop, a mobile signifier with multiple signifieds. Dromio's body is also likened to an exchangeable object that functions as sport. These complex and interwoven connotations resonate with the underlying violence of the play, in which both Dromios are repeatedly beaten, and they articulate the kinds of playing with the body that characterize scenes of dismemberment.

Scholars have noted that early modern culture displayed increasing anxiety about the mobility of signifiers, especially signifiers of identity. Thus, sumptuary laws attempted to nail down social distinctions, and popular pamphlets detailed the deceptive powers of "sturdy beggars" who used theatrical techniques to cozen unwary passersby.[51] Jean-Christophe Agnew has suggested that these concerns were the result of economic changes: the growth of a new commodity culture stirred up discomfort about exchangeability and interchangeability, and these fears manifested themselves as a desire for fixity.[52] Certainly such a reading makes sense of the emphasis on both economic transactions and identity exchange in *The Comedy of Errors,* which are at various points understood by characters in the play as intentional deception or sinister witchcraft. For the playhouse audience, however, confusion and exchange are the substance of theatrical entertainment: transposition of subjects and objects becomes a game for the audience. Stage violence was likewise associated with game and play. When Dromio of Ephesus compares himself to a football, his lines draw on broader cultural discourses where playing with identity was a kind of festive practice wrapped up with the violent sport of football, feats of martial prowess, and other bloody games, such as animal baiting.

These threads come together in *Titus Andronicus* when severed hands are imagined not only as portable and substitutable objects but exchangeable ones. In the scene that culminates with Lavinia carrying out her father's hand between her teeth, Aaron says,

> Let *Marcus, Lucius,* or thy selfe old *Titus,*
> Or any one of you, chop off your hand,
> And send it to the King: he for the same,
> Will send thee hither both thy sonnes aliue,
> And that shall be the ransome for their fault. (TLN 1297–1301; 3.1.152–56)

Aaron's instructions mark both the substitutability of the hand (it doesn't matter whose hand it is) and its exchangeability (the severed hand will ransom Titus's son). The hand, however, ends up being worthless currency: the promised exchange only produces more dismembered body parts—heads. Aaron highlights this fact when he says, "I goe *Andronicus,* and for thy hand, / Looke by and by to haue thy sonnes with thee: / Their heads I meane" (TLN 1348–50; 3.1.200–202). Within the represented fiction, the exchange of severed hand for severed heads, of part for more parts, is figured explicitly as a deceptive act:

> *Ti.* Come hither *Aaron,* I'le deceiue them both,
> Lend me thy hand, and I will giue thee mine,
> *Moore.* If that be cal'd deceit, I will be honest,
> And neuer whil'st I liue deceiue men so:
> But Ile deceiue you in another sort,
> And that you'l say ere halfe an houre passe.
>   *He cuts off Titus hand.* (TLN 1332–38; 3.1.186–91)

To "lend," "giue," "be honest"—these otherwise innocuous terms and phrases assume ambivalent valences when yoked with deception. Titus cuts off his own hand while Lucius and Marcus are away fetching an ax; his stated goal is to "deceiue them both." That Titus is himself deprived of his bargain by Aaron's further deception is, in this sense, quite just. The episode dramatizes both fair and unfair exchange: deceit for deceit, a father's hand for his sons' heads.[53]

While the mobility, substitutability, and exchangeability of body parts are imagined as entirely problematic and tragic within the represented fiction of Shakespeare's play, the performance dynamics of theatre present these actions in a more positive light—as play and sport, not as villainous deception. This association of dismemberment with games is made explicit when the messenger enters with the severed body parts and declares that Titus's hand has been rejected by the Emperor, who has made "[t]hy griefes, their sports" (TLN 1387; 3.1.238). While horrific within the narrative of the play, the moment highlights the position of playgoers, who have also paid good money to see Titus's griefs enacted for their sport. Audience sympathy for Titus at the beginning of the scene, when the procession situates them as dissenting witnesses to unjust punishment, here transitions to a more complex set of affective responses. Their initial identification with Titus may be enhanced by the dramatization of his pain and betrayal, even as their enjoyment *of* the experience of those feelings might align them more with the Emperor. Do playgoers really want to see Titus's sons returned to him alive? Surely spectacular dismemberment makes for the more entertaining action. Appropriately, it is Aaron who instigates this form of play: such actions build on the theatrical functions of the Vice figure as the traditional promulgator of songs, dance, and low humor and as the mediator between the playhouse audience and the dramatic representation.

In act 5, this overlap between dismemberment and sport is further associated with the Vice-like Aaron. When the Moor is captured, he describes Lavinia's mutilation in terms of cooking metaphors—a play on the banqueting theme for which the tragedy is most famous:

> [*Aron.*] 'Twas her [i.e., Tamora's] two Sonnes that murdered *Bassianus,*
> They cut thy Sisters tongue, and rauisht her,
> And cut her hands off, and trim'd her as thou saw'st.

> *Lucius.* Oh detestable villaine!
> Call'st thou that Trimming?
> *Aron.* Why she was washt, and cut, and trim'd,
> And 'twas trim sport for them that had the doing of it.
> *Luci.* Oh barbarous beastly villaines like thy selfe! (TLN 2206–13; 5.1.91–97)

The word "barbarous" in the Folio was spelled "barberous" in the Q1 version of the play, prompting some editors to suggest a possible pun on *barbers,* who were surgeons as well as hairstylists. That cutting Lavinia is compared to "trim sport" foregrounds connections between the cannibalistic feast later in the play and other communal pleasures, sexual and dramatic. Here as previously, spectators are in the awkward position of being likened to the play's villains, since Lavinia's mutilation is, shall we say, served up to them as sport in the playhouse. That they may later enjoy watching Chiron and Demetrius have their throats slit is small consolation morally speaking, since that enjoyment would be akin to the malicious glee of a figure such as Aaron, who is explicitly compared to a devil in this play.

When Aaron reveals his own role in the violence against Lavinia, he extends the metaphor of sport from feasting to festive games more generally:

> Indeede, I was their Tutor to instruct them.
> That Codding spirit had they from their Mother,
> As sure a Card as euer wonne the Set:
> That bloody minde I thinke they learn'd of me,
> As true a Dog as euer fought at head. (TLN 2214–18; 5.1.98–104)

In describing where Chiron and Demetrius learned their evil ways, these lines position the play's villains as winners at cards and bullbaiting. These games, moreover, become understood in terms of the young Goths' sexual and deadly violence, their "Codding spirit" and "bloody minde." The analogy between mutilation and sport is extended and elaborated in the subsequent lines, when Aaron says,

> I play'd the Cheater for thy Fathers hand
> And when I had it, drew my selfe apart,
> And almost broke my heart with extreame laughter.
> I pried me through the Creuice of a Wall,
> When for his hand, he had his two Sonnes heads,
> Beheld his teares, and laught so hartily,
> That both mine eyes were rainie like to his:
> And when I told the Empresse of this sport,
> She sounded almost at my pleasing tale,
> And for my tydings, gaue me twenty kisses. (TLN 2227–36; 5.1.111–20)

When the Moor states that he "play'd the Cheater for thy Fathers hand," he likens tricking Titus to dishonestly winning a card game. Upon this victory, Aaron "almost broke my heart with extreame laughter," the same response he has subsequently when Titus receives his sons' heads and Aaron "laught so hartily / That both mine eyes were rainie like to his." Dismemberment and cheating at cards are here imagined as producing the same response as spectatorship. In highlighting the act of beholding and the emotional reactions consequently produced, these lines draw attention to the actions and responses of real-life playgoers. They, too, are spectators who witness Titus's grief for the purposes of entertainment, just as Tamora finds the "sport" of the family's mutilation such a "pleasing tale." Moreover, whether audience members weeped or laughed—both potential reactions to scenes of dismemberment as subsequent stage history has shown—is treated as irrelevant when Aaron collapses the two in comparing his streaming eyes to Titus's own. Both within the narrative and in performance practice, laughter and tears were flip sides of the same coin, phenomenologically similar manifestations of intense emotion that align spectators with the Empress and the Moor.[54]

In the B-text of *Doctor Faustus,* dismemberment is likewise associated with sport. As in *Titus Andronicus,* severed limbs function within the dramatic representation as devilish deception, but in onstage presentation they are treated as game. This notion of dismemberment as itself a form of play is foregrounded repeatedly in the emphasis on severed body parts as props: theatre, the play suggests, is like other sports in making a game of the circulation of objects. The mobility and semiotic multiplicity of parts in *Doctor Faustus* feature prominently in two episodes, one involving Faustus's leg (in both the A- and B-texts) and the other involving his head (in the B-text alone). In the first episode, Faustus tricks the horse-courser by selling him a horse that turns into a bundle of hay. When the man, seeking a refund, returns to find the conjurer asleep, he accidentally pulls off Faustus's leg while attempting to wake him. This action is the same in both A- and B-texts. In the A-text, the stage direction reads, "*Pull him by the legge, and pull it away*" (A-text, E2v; 4.1.174); in the B-text, "*He puls off his leg*" (B-text, F3v; 4.4.37).[55] What happens next differs between the two versions of the play. In the A-text, the horse-courser promises to pay "fortie dollers more" to avoid being taken to the constable and then "*runnes away*" (A-text, E2v; 4.1.180–81, 185.s.d.), leaving behind the severed limb. The leg is then apparently magically reattached to Faustus's body: after the horse-courser's exit, the conjurer says, "What is he gone? Farwel he, Faustus has his legge againe, and the Horsecourser I take it, a bottle of hey for his labour" (A-text, E2v; 4.1.186–87). In the B-text, this stage business is made more elaborate. Here, the horse-courser comes to an important realization: having pulled off Faustus's leg means the doctor cannot chase him. The horse-courser declares, "[N]ow he has but one leg, I'le out-run him, and cast this leg into some ditch or other" (B-text, F3v; 4.4.40–42). He then exits with the severed limb. The B-text Faustus magically regenerates the leg after the man departs: "[H]a, ha, ha, *Faustus* hath his leg againe, and the Horse-courser a bundle of hay for his forty Dollors" (B-text, F3v; 4.4.43–45).[56] Both versions of the play focus attention on whether or not the leg exists and on the magical ability to make things appear or disappear, not on whether or not it looks like a real leg. As in the scenes of dismemberment from *Cymbeline* and *Titus Andronicus,* what is at stake is not verisimilitude but the problematic ontological status of the body onstage.

This episode spawns further business shortly thereafter in the play, when the horse-courser tells Robin, Dick, and the carter that he "tooke him [Faustus] by the leg, and neuer rested pulling, till I had pul'd me his leg quite off, and now 'tis at home in mine Hostry" (B-text, F4v; 4.5.51–53). In presenting the leg as a portable thing to be thrown into a ditch or stored in a hostelry, the B-text version of this scene reverses conventional understandings of subject and object. Instead of treating the leg as part of a person, it becomes an independent entity. Instead of being that which enables a person to walk or run—a sense foregrounded in the verb form of *leg*—the severed limb is itself an object which must be transported.[57] Whereas the body of the character is imagined as coextensive with that of the actor, the leg is here explicitly constructed as a theatrical prop. This aspect of dismemberment is underscored when, in a subsequent scene, Robin, Dick, the carter, and the horse-courser tease the magician about his missing limb:

> *Horse.* I mary, there spake a Doctor indeed, and 'faith Ile drinke a health to thy wooden leg for that word.
> *Faust.* My wooden leg? what dost thou meane by that?
> *Cart.* Ha, ha, ha, dost heare him *Dick*, he has forgot his legge.
> *Horse.* I, I, he does not stand much vpon that.
> *Faust.* No faith, not much vpon a wooden leg. (B-text, G2r; 4.6.75–81)

The clowns' repeated jokes about the "wooden leg" call to mind the inventory of props in Henslowe's *Diary*, which includes an entry for "Kentes woden leage."[58]

This association of Faustus's severed limb with theatrical props is reinforced as the episode continues and repeatedly draws attention to the numeric ambiguities surrounding the doctor's legs:

> *Cart.* And do you remember nothing of your leg?
> *Faust.* No in good sooth.
> *Cart.* Then I pray remember your curtesie.
> *Faust.* I thank you sir.
> *Car.* 'Tis not so much worth; I pray you tel me one thing.
> *Faust.* What's that?
> *Cart.* Be both your legs bedfellowes euery night together?
> *Faust.* Wouldst thou make a *Colossus* of me, that thou askest me such questions?
> *Cart.* No truelie sir, I would make nothing of you, but I would faine know that.
> *Enter Hostesse with drinke.*
> *Faust.* Then I assure thee certainelie they are.
> *Cart.* I thanke you, I am fully satisfied.
> *Faust.* But wherefore dost thou aske?
> *Cart.* For nothing sir: but me thinkes you should haue a wooden bedfellow of one of 'em.
> *Horse.* Why do you heare sir, did not I pull off one of your legs when you were asleepe?
> *Faust.* But I haue it againe now I am awake: looke you heere sir.
> *All.* O horrible, had the Doctor three legs. (B-text, G2r–G2v; 4.6.89–109)

As was the case earlier, the play here highlights the severed limb when Faustus is called upon to "curtesie," or "make a leg."[59] In addition, the emphasis on the leg as an object, or "thing," is echoed in the carter's demand to know "one thing" and his insistence that he "would make nothing of you" and asks "[f]or nothing." This punning reference to the severed limb is extended in the scene's attention to disparities in counting. "[N]othing," "one," "both," "three"—just how many legs does the doctor have? The semiotic excess produced by the fragmentation of the body is here comically attributed to numeric excess: the body must be whole, any multiplicity must be resolved into one, and thus if the horse-courser has one leg at home in his hostelry, the doctor must have had three legs to start. Just as the actor's body can signify more than one character, his body parts are also semiotically multiple. At once singular and plural, the severed limb is regenerated with extras to spare.

This stage business with the dismembered leg may seem superfluous to a modern reader, but its expansion from the A-text to the B-text suggests that, for early modern spectators, the scene was quite popular. Indeed, the episode itself subsequently compounded and multiplied. By 1723, John Thurmond's *Harlequin Doctor Faustus*, often cited as the first English pantomime, involved a scene with a usurer who, Shylock-like, demands Faustus's leg in place of his bond. After he cuts off the limb and carries it away, numerous other legs fly onto the stage; then, as the *Universal Journal* put it at the time, "the Doctor strikes a woman's leg with his wand, which immediately flies from the rest, and fixes to the Doctor's stump, which dances with it ridiculously."[60] Far from antithetical to the early modern version, the proliferation of parts in Thurmond's adaptation simply extends earlier emphasis on the severed leg as a mobile, substitutable, and nonunitary theatrical prop.

The association of dismemberment with the body as prop is further underscored when Faustus has his head cut off. Onstage decapitations in early modern plays are frequently marked simply with the stage direction *strike*.[61] Here, however, the text explicitly refers to a property head, which is the focus of subsequent stage business: "*Enter Faustus with the false head*" (B-text, F1v; 4.2.37.s.d.).[62] Immediately after "killing" the doctor, Benvolio, Frederick, and Martino repeatedly remark on this head:

> *Mar.* Strike with a willing hand, his head is off.
> *Ben.* The Deuil's dead, the Furies now may laugh.
> *Fred.* Was this that sterne aspect, that awfull frowne,
> Made the grim monarch of infernall spirits,
> Tremble and quake at his commanding charmes?
> *Mar.* Was this that damned head, whose heart conspir'd
> *Benvolio's* shame before the Emperour.
> *Ben.* I, that's the head, and here the body lies,
> Justly rewarded for his villanies.
> *Fred.* Come, let's deuise how we may adde more shame
> To the blacke scandall of his hated name.
> *Ben.* First, on his head, in quittance of my wrongs,
> Il'e naile huge forked hornes, and let them hang
> Within the window where he yoak'd me first,
> That all the world may see my iust reuenge.
> *Mar.* What vse shall we put his beard to?
> *Ben.* Wee'l sell it to a Chimny-sweeper: it will weare out ten birchin broomes I warrant you.
> *Fred.* What shall eyes doe?
> *Ben.* Wee'l put out his eyes, and they shall serue for buttons to his lips, to keepe his tongue from catching cold.

> *Mar.* An excellent policie: and now sirs, hauing diuided him, what shall the body doe?
> *Ben.* Zounds the Diuel's aliue agen.
> *Fred.* Giue him his head for Gods sake.
> *Faust.* Nay keepe it: *Faustus* will haue heads and hands,
> I call your hearts to recompence this deed. (B-text, F1v–F2r; 4.2.44–70)

Pointing to the various parts of Faustus's head, the three men describe the gory mutilation they would like to inflict upon it. Within the fictional representation, these grisly deeds are meant to "adde more shame / To the blacke scandall of his hated name." In the actual playhouse, though, such actions draw attention to the very thing-ness of the onstage head, which specifically *cannot* be that which it represents—the head that must be object not subject, prop not actor. This semiotic disparity is underscored when the headless corpse rises up. Faustus's body, signified by the actor, pointedly contrasts with his head, represented by the prop. This dichotomy is further highlighted when Frederick exclaims, "Giue him his head for Gods sake." The implication seems to be that the property head has been in circulation, passing back and forth among the men during the course of the scene. Whoever is currently holding the fake head—either Martino or Benvolio—is ordered to return it to Faustus. The magician, for his part, declines the offer, saying, "Nay keepe it." As with the dismembered leg in the episode with the horse-courser, the severed head is imagined as a portable object that can be tossed or thrown. In addition, the almost formulaic references to the various aspects of Faustus's head—his eyes, beard, and so forth—call to mind similar scenes in other plays where one character plays the straight man, asking a series of questions directing attention to different body parts, and the other devises witty answers in response to the first.[63] In this, the episode invokes a comic tradition in which disparaging remarks are viewed as a kind of game. Here, that dynamic gets extended: dismemberment becomes the occasion not only for verbal repartee but also for physical play or sport.

Football, Animal Baiting, and Festive Sport

Though there is ultimately no way to know if this scene was actually performed in this manner, the bizarre—but theatrically gripping—game of hot potato with Faustus's head may have borne a striking resemblance to early modern football. As David Underdown has shown, football took a number of forms in England at this time, and some varieties of the sport were closer to rugby than they were to soccer.[64] Ronald Hutton colorfully refers to the game as having "no clearly defined teams and effectively no rules; and goals, if they existed at all, were of secondary importance to the thrill of fighting for possession of the ball."[65] In his 1602 *Survey of Cornwall,* Richard Carew similarly describes the ball used in the game of hurling, a close cousin to football, as "an infernall spirit: for whosoeuer catcheth it, fareth straightwayes like a madde man, strugling and fighting with those that goe about to holde him."[66] Associations between dismemberment and football can also be found in the so-called Tapster Manuscript, which was a manuscript leaf discovered in 1988 attached to the inside back cover of an early modern edition of Homer's *Odyssey*. Primarily of interest for its relation to the Gadshill episode in Shakespeare's *1 Henry IV*, the document appears to be from an unknown play dated 1600 to 1620 and comprises a single scene that takes place in a tavern. After much drinking and tobacco, two thieves trick the tapster out of payment for his bill by offering, without intention to pay, a portion of the profit from an upcoming heist. After the tapster exits, one of the thieves declares "not one crosse of siluer that y^{ou} getst / [. . .] if thou dost chopp of this head of mine / to make a bottle or a footeball of / [D]id I not gull him finely of his beere" (lines 48–51).[67]

This association of decapitation with discourses of sport and drink helps us make sense of an episode in *Doctor Faustus* that has puzzled scholars. In the extended stage business with the severed leg in the B-text, one of the scenes when the horse-courser and his clownish fellows tease the magician about his missing limb opens with Faustus at the Duke of Vanholt's court. When the clowns enter, however, the ensuing action takes place in a tavern or alehouse. This shift in location troubles editors because it does not make sense within the fictional representation. In the previous scene, when the horse-courser tells his friends that he has Faustus's leg stashed in his hostelry, Bevington and Rasmussen note that "[t]he Hostess's welcome makes clear that the setting is a tavern" (B-text, 4.5.3–4n). In the subsequent scene, however, when they confront the conjurer, the editors state that "the clowns appear to think they have found Faustus in some tavern, but which one is not clear.... Evidently, Faustus has charmed their senses and wafted them here to amuse by their not knowing their 'place.'" For her part, the Hostess "is to be understood also as labouring under the delusion that Faustus has devised" (B-text, 4.6.60–68n). The editors display a marked urge to resolve the setting's apparent contradiction with the rest of the dramatic narrative and offer elaborate conjectures motivated by the need to interpolate this episode within a consistent fictional representation. If we think of the play in relation to its performance dynamics, however, such imaginative leaps are not necessary. When the horse-courser and his friends first bang on the gate, Faustus convinces the Duke to "let them come in" because they will be "good subiect for merriment" (B-text, G1v; 4.6.54–55).[68] Their subsequent conversation about the severed leg is figured as sport for the Duke and Duchess. The onstage noble audience here blends into the background by becoming one with the offstage audience: both experience the scene as merry sport. If jokes about Faustus's wooden leg take place in a drinking establishment and not at the Duke's court, the shift in setting is odd only if we insist on strict representational consistency. From a performance perspective, the presentational dynamics of the scene as well as dismemberment's associations with sport make the alehouse setting quite appropriate.

Associations between sport and dismemberment are also implied in the decapitation scene. After the headless Faustus rises up, he orders Benvolio, Frederick, and Martino to be carried off by devils. When the three men enter again later on, they appear, as the stage direction tells us, "*all hauing hornes on their heads*" (B-text, F2v; 4.3.0.s.d.). Horns were a stock feature of many early modern plays and were especially common in comedies. Of the seven plays included in Dessen and Thomson's *Dictionary of Stage Directions* that explicitly call for the use of property horns, the only two plays that are *not* listed as comedies in Harbage's *Annals of English Drama* are *The Brazen Age* (categorized as "Classical Legend") and *Doctor Faustus*.[69] In this episode, the stage business with the horns functions seriously within the play's representation: the three men would "rather die with griefe, then liue with shame" (B-text, F3r; 4.3.26). In its presentation, however, their very grief becomes comic sport for the audience, as was also the case for *Titus Andronicus*. Benvolio's fear that "[i]f we should follow him [i.e., Faustus] to worke reuenge, / He'd ioyne long Asses eares to these huge hornes, / And make vs laughing stockes to all the world" (B-text, F3r; 4.3.18–20) is shameful within the story but, onstage, might well add to the audience's sport.[70] When Benvolio, Frederick, and Martino reappear wearing horns, "their heads and faces" are "bloudy, and besmear'd with mud and durt" (B-text, F2v; 4.3.0.s.d.), underscoring associations with football. Indeed, early modern football was apparently quite violent and associated with getting beaten to a pulp. In Shakespeare's *King Lear*, for instance, when the steward Oswald is "strucken" and "tript" onstage, Kent refers to him as a "base Foot-ball plaier" (TLN 615–16; 1.4.85–86). A little later in the century, in Thomas Meriton's *The Wandering Lover*, one character boasts that he was "valourous" in a fight in which he had "my head beaten as soft as a Foot-Ball"; the scene then culminates in his onstage beating.[71] Football's association with theatrical violence accords with the opinion of non-dramatic writers, who repeatedly describe the game in terms of the broken bones, bruises, and mayhem it generated. In a section of his *Anatomie of Abuses* specifically marked "Great hurt, by Foot-ball play," for example, Philip Stubbes describes how sometimes players' "necks are broken, sometimes their backs, sometime their legs, sometime their armes, sometime one part thurst out of ioynt, sometime an other, sometime the noses gush out with blood, sometime their eyes start out."[72]

Despite football's detractors, authorities' attempts to regulate the sport repeatedly failed, in part because it was deeply integrated into the social fabric.[73] Stubbes's insistence that football "may rather be called a freendly kinde of fight, then a play or recreation. A bloody and murthering practise, then a felowly sporte or pastime,"[74] sounds suspiciously like an attempt to draw a distinction between football and healthful recreation that was not generally observed. Indeed, the sport was a kind of licensed festive observance, officially sponsored by cities and craft guilds in England and Scotland on Shrove Tuesday—that riotous holiday famous also for the sacking of the brothels and playhouses.[75] It is notable that the violence that characterized this day also included cockfighting, cock-throwing, or "cock-threshing"—that is, either stoning the bird or burying him up to his neck so that a blindfolded man could bludgeon him to death with a flail. Hutton has remarked that both football and the abuse of poultry "embodied... the intrinsic propensity of Shrovetide sports to express both violence and cruelty as part of the feast's cathartic role."[76] Though a presumption that "catharsis" was the goal of such festive violence oversimplifies the cultural structures and effects that motivated such practices, Hutton's comparison of these seemingly disparate popular pastimes is nonetheless appropriate: both were displays of physical strength, violent acts that were also athletic activities.

In this sense, football and cock-baiting might be understood as varied forms of festive combat—that is, martial activities that were an integral part of social gatherings and holiday observances. Cockfighting in early modern England was a practice sometimes imagined as analogous to martial valor among humans.[77] In addition to football and the mistreatment of chickens, municipalities also observed Shrove Tuesday with an array of other violent athletic pastimes, including bearbaiting (such as at Rye in the early sixteenth century), mock fights (such as assaults upon a "fort" at York in 1555), and playing for prizes (such as the "silver games" in Carlisle in the early decades of the seventeenth century).[78] Richard Carew explicitly uses military metaphors to describe the sport of hurling as "a pitched battaile, with bloody pates, bones broken, and out of ioynt, and such bruses as serue to shorten their daies; yet al is good play."[79] Situating football in relation to these other martial forms offers us a different perspective on Sir Thomas Elyot's reference to the sport as "nothynge but beastely fury, and extreme violence, whereof procedeth hurte."[80] Elyot's description criticizes football for its violence. In dehumanizing participants, however, his comment is not simply a figure of speech: like the baiting of animals, football blurred the line between man and beast, between athletic competition and sheer physical power, between honorable courage and bloody sport. Fighting was thus not mere disorderly behavior. In organized and sanctioned contexts, such as during Shrovetide, it allowed for the expression of communal values privileging bodily strength and skill as displayed in devolved forms of battle.[81]

This connection between football, martial valor, and bloody violence can also be seen in early modern accounts that refer—startlingly—to dismembered heads being used *as* footballs. Shaming rituals in the period were an integral part of judicial punishment, but they sometimes also resembled games and sports.[82] Football and dismemberment, too, could be combined as punishment or shaming ritual. Susan Amussen, for instance, describes a 1642 case in Dorchester in which Hugh Green, a Catholic priest, was drawn and quartered, and "some in the crowd showed their 'malice toward Catholics' by grabbing the head for a ghoulish game of football, which lasted from ten in the morning until four in the afternoon."[83] In the context of an execution, this gruesome use of a severed head is clearly meant as an insult, an added disrespect and further punishment of the criminal. At the same time, it was also sport, a form of entertainment that bridged the gap between games in our modern sense and early modern understandings of violence as communal observance.[84]

Similar instances associating dismemberment with football are found in other early modern texts. George Chapman's 1611 translation of *The Iliad*, for example, describes how Agamemnon kills Antimachus's son Hippolochus: "[A]s he lay, the angrie king, cut off his armes and head, / And let him like a football lie, for euerie man to spurne."[85] That this translation offers a uniquely early modern spin on the episode becomes particularly evident when we compare Chapman's version with a more recent edition. Rather than describing dismemberment as sport, modern translator Robert Fagles describes how Agamemnon kills Hippolochus "on the ground, / slashing off his arms with a sword, lopping off his head / and he sent him rolling through the carnage like a log."[86] Comparisons between football and dismemberment in battle can likewise be found in Richard Pike's pamphlet, *Three to One Being, an English-Spanish Combat,* which describes how "some of our Men...had there their Throates cutte; Some hauing their Braines beaten out with the stockes of Muskets; others, their Noses sl[i]c'd off; whilst some Heads were spurned vp & downe the Streets like Footeballs."[87] In both of these cases, the verb used to indicate this action is *spurn,* a word that, in early modern England, could be applied either figuratively to signal derogation or more literally to mean "to kick."[88] The use of this term in connection with football recalls Dromio of Ephesus's lines in *The Comedy of Errors,* discussed earlier, when he complains of being "like a foot-ball" for his master and mistress to "spurne…hence" and "hither." Even in battle, playing with a decapitated head is imagined not only as an insult to the victim but also as a community-building game.

Dismemberment's connection to football takes on additional interesting resonances with theatrical spectacle in Webster's *The White Devil* when Brachiano says, "Like the wild Irish I'le nere thinke thee dead, / Till I can play at footeball with thy head."[89] The sport's association with severed body parts was proverbially attributed to the supposedly bloodthirsty Irish. Richard Brathwaite, for example, in satirical commentary that compares English politics to theatrical tragedy, refers to the "Principal Actors" involved in political assassination as having "steel'd them with that wilde *Irish* antient resolution, Never to hold themselves secure from their Foe, till they might play at foot-ball with his head."[90] As Patricia Palmer has shown, such statements were forms of scapegoating, since the English were themselves guilty of atrocities with severed body parts during the Irish wars.[91] The gruesome practice of judicial head-hunting, for instance, was sanctioned by Elizabeth's officers, who offered bounty hunters monetary rewards for the heads of rebels. In fact, state papers still extant today include records that itemize the numbers of heads brought in along with the sums paid out.[92] *The White Devil* alludes to this practice when Francisco remarks that Monticelso's little black book of murderers must have been created for the purposes of blackmail, or "As th'Irish rebels wont were to sell heads, / So to make prize of these" (G2r; 4.1.80–81). Here, as in Brachiano's reference to football, severed heads associated with war are interpolated into a discourse of sport. The term "prize," which Francisco uses in reference to heads, was also commonly applied to staged weapons contests offered as popular spectacles both at parish celebrations and in London amphitheatres.[93] Like prizefighting, theatrical dismemberment was a kind of spectator sport in which performers' bodies were on display.

This association of dismemberment with other forms of violent game beyond football can be seen especially clearly in Fletcher's *The Island Princess.* When Ruy Dias attacks the city of Tidore toward the end of the play, the severed limbs that result from combat are described in terms of fighting and sport:

>   4. Are these the *Portugall* Bulls—
> How loud they bellow?
>   2. Their horns are plaguie strong, they push down Pallaces
> They tosse our little habitations like whelps,
> Like grindle-tailes, with their heeles upward;
> All the windowes ith' town dance a new trench-more,
> 'Tis like to prove a blessed age for Glasiers,
> I met a hand, and a Letter in't in great haste,
> And by and by a single leg running after it,
> As if the Arme had forgot part of his arrant,
> Heads flie like foot-balls every where.[94]

Though combat could be literally enacted onstage, stage props were required to represent severed parts. In scenes of dismemberment, actors' bodies entered into a theatrical economy where, like commodities, their inherent (use) value was displaced in favor of exchange value arising from the act of circulation. This circulation is, as we saw earlier in other plays, literalized in peculiar reversals of person and thing. In *The Island Princess,* references to the "hand," "single leg," and "Arme" as if they themselves were messengers enact this transposition of subject and object. Body parts here locomote on their own without the persons to whom they should be attached. This attention to severed limbs is extended in the lines that follow, when one townsman swears "By this hand" and another responds, "By this leg—Let me sweare nimbly by it, / For I know not how long I shall owe it."[95] The oath emphasizes the action now required of the townsmen: rather than engaging in combat with the strength of their hands, they must trust to the nimbleness of their legs in order to escape. The reference to severed heads as footballs in this passage thus appears amid extensive wordplay that stresses reversals of the regular order. The distance between subject and object collapses even as literal and figurative language converges. The overall effect of this rhetoric is not disorderly, however much the imaginary events it denotes are; the experience is, rather, one of sport, where the townsmen's witticisms are offered up for the pleasure of audience members. The reference to the "*Portugall* Bulls" and their "horns... [that] tosse our little habitations like whelps" further reinforce the episode's connection to sport. In the bloody practice of bullbaiting, dogs ("grindle-tailes") were often mangled and tossed into the air. Dismemberment is here associated not just with war but with animal baiting, which, like football, was connected with festive violence, especially at Shrovetide.

Even though literal dismemberment rarely occurred in the early modern baiting rings, both animal baiting and theatre were popular entertainments that played with the body in relation to violent spectacle. Public baiting events often culminated in a bear tied to the stake but began with similar baitings of bulls or of apes on horseback. Dogs, who were set loose to attack the animals, would score points for hits on the eyes, ears, and lips, and spectators wagered on the results.[96] Connections between baiting and playing were manifold. Both activities were grouped together with other kinds of "idle pastimes" in legal documents that restricted their use and in religious treatises that attacked their immorality. In addition, baiting rings and playhouses shared the same amphitheatrical structure, and some arenas were used for both. Paris Gardens was located right next door to the Globe itself. Moreover, baiting and playing became commercial enterprises with permanent locations around the same time, and they shared significant crossovers in terms of personnel, including Philip Henslowe and Edward Alleyn, who were also Masters of the Game.[97] Despite these significant interconnections, studies of early modern baiting and playing, other than the more strictly theatre historical accounts, have tended to focus on baiting as a literary metaphor or more recently baiting as indicative of early modern cultural discourses about humans and beasts.[98] The performance implications of animal baiting have attracted less attention,[99] yet examining this blood sport can offer useful insight into the relationship between dramatic representations of violence and actual violence offered as presentational spectacle.

Accounts of bearbaiting from the period tend to begin with a fairly neutral description of the actions comprising the event, only to shift suddenly from description to approbation. An entry in the diary of the Duke of Najera, who visited London in 1544, is typical:

> To each of the large bears are matched three or four dogs, which sometimes get the better, and sometimes are worsted, for besides the fierceness and great strength of the bears to defend themselves with their teeth, they hug the dogs with their paws so tightly, that, unless the masters came to assist them, they would be strangled by such soft embraces. Into the same place they brought a pony with an ape fastened on its back, and to see the animal kicking amongst the dogs, with the screams of the ape, beholding the curs hanging from the ears and neck of the pony, is very laughable.[100]

The Duke begins by outlining the events of the baiting ring in a straightforward manner, but he then comments that the mangling of animals was "very laughable"—a description quite jarring to modern sensibilities. Firsthand accounts by other early modern spectators follow a similar trajectory: they narrate what happens in a seemingly detached way, then suddenly declare that the violence was, as one writer puts it, "a sport very pleazaunt" and "a matter of goodly releef."[101] Referring to the animals' bloody contest as "plasant sport"[102] frequently makes modern readers squeamish in ways that resemble the audience reactions provoked by graphic dismemberment represented in modern theatres.

Scholars have long been curious about why spectators found displays of animal cruelty entertaining. Early modern accounts suggest that what was attractive about these events was the physical action itself. Writers often described the teeth, skin, and nails of the animal combatants,[103] and they imagined the baiting in terms of martial honor—the "valor" and the "fierceness" of the animals—thus embedding these blood sports in the same discursive network as football, combat, and dismemberment. Moreover, baiting was considered a profoundly physical experience for spectators as well as beasts. The snarls and screams of the animals combined with blood, dirt, and foul stench to produce a general onslaught to the bodily senses. John Davies describes the baiting ring Paris Garden as part of a satirical description of a law student:

> His Satten doublet & his veluet hose,
> Are all vvith spittle from aboue be-spread.
> When he is like a Fathers cuntrey hall,
> stinking vvith dogges, & muted al vvith hauks,
> and rightly too on him this filth doth fall,
> Which for such filthie spots his bookes forsake,
> Leauing olde Ployden, Dier & Brooke alone,
> To see olde Harry Hunkes & Sacarson.[104]

Bearbaiting, Davies implies, was a "stinking" affair in which the spectator's clothing was smeared with "spittle" and "filth." Brome's *The Antipodes* also describes bearbaiting in terms of its sound and stench when an old woman, whose eyesight is going, insists that she still loves bearbaiting and can

tell which dogge does best, without my Spectacles.
And though *I* could not, yet *I* love the noyse;
The noyse revives me, and the Bear-garden scent
Refresheth much my smelling.[105]

All of these accounts suggest bearbaiting was a profoundly physical experience, a simultaneously delightful and disgusting feast for the senses in which the spectator's own body was implicated.

Descriptions of baiting as bodily sensation provide a striking context for understanding the way dismembered bodies in the commercial playhouses negotiated between theatre as dramatic representation and theatre as an entertainment in its own right. Both bearbaiting and theatre were forms of popular entertainment, but the status of the body was different in each. In the baiting rings, blood and flesh were literally present, and the power of the body as spectacle was foregrounded. By contrast, in the playhouse, actors' bodies and props were required to represent dismemberment, and their spectacular potential could not rival that of the baiting rings next door. Violent spectacle could only come into being through a process of signification, and signification in the theatre was a practical problem: the same prop or the same actor—that is, the same body—could and did signify in multiple ways. In trying to come to terms with this difficulty, early modern drama generated scenes of dismemberment that highlighted their own theatricality. By calling attention to theatre's own semiotics—to the ways in which actors' bodies could signify onstage—and by emphasizing the experiences of spectators, such scenes underscored what the theatre could offer that other forms of entertainment could not: theatre could represent what could not literally be presented; it could *produce* spectacle. Comparisons between stage dismemberment and sport also point to an additional perspective on the social function of bloody spectacles. Though disorderly, festive violence was not antithetical to communal cohesion but essential for the reinscription of cultural values privileging martial prowess. Integrated into Shrovetide and other calendar rituals, football and animal baiting were bodily practices that undergirded and reproduced existing social formations. I have argued elsewhere that festive combat is characterized by reconciliation: after fighting, participants are reintegrated into the community, often through the sharing of food or drink.[106] Theatrical spectacles of dismemberment may have served a similar purpose by functioning as *enactments* of festive practices rather than simply representations of violence within the dramatic fiction, as ritual practices that reincorporated audience members into a communal whole through the staging of bodily fragmentation.

* * *

In *Doctor Faustus,* then, at the end of the tavern scene that jokes upon Faustus's missing leg, the Duke of Vanholt's concluding comments are particularly appropriate. As the onstage spectator who has witnessed the entire episode, his reactions may well have mirrored those of actual playgoers. Like other forms of festive violence in which fighting allows for reincorporation into the community, stage dismemberment is, as the Duke puts it, an "[a]rtfull sport [that] driues all sad thoughts away" (B-text,

G2v; 4.6.125). This way of looking at severed limbs and other forms of onstage mutilation—as socially efficacious communal observance that need not function as serious tragedy—suggests one reason why William Winstanley writing in 1687 might have described Marlowe's play as the "comedy of *Doctor Faustus,* with his devils and suchlike tragical sport, which pleased much the humours of the vulgar."[107] Analyzing stage dismemberment in terms of its performance dynamics allows us to make sense of many such episodes in early modern theatre that otherwise seem strange: the grotesque action of Lavinia's teeth clenching the severed hand in *Titus Andronicus,* Imogen's excessive comments on the headless corpse in *Cymbeline,* and the comic elaboration of the dismembered leg episode in *Doctor Faustus.* Thinking of theatre in this way has implications for how we understand a range of other plays in the canon. In attending to theatre's performant function, *King Lear* becomes not a play about the king who divides his realm between his three daughters but rather one centered on the body: Poor Tom's filth, Lear's increasing nakedness, the "vilde gelly" (TLN 2158; 3.7.83) of Gloucester's eyeballs. *Hamlet* becomes not a play about the internal struggles of a Danish prince but rather one focused on the corporeality of the actor playing the ghost, the grotesque postures of lovesick madness, and the excitement of the swordfight in the final act. *Doctor Faustus* becomes not a play about a man who sells his soul to the devil but rather one that sports with severed limbs and dancing devils. Indeed, the extraordinary popularity of that play can be ascribed directly to bodily spectacle: as John Melton wrote in 1620, playgoers went "to the Fortune in Golding Lane to see the tragedy of *Doctor Faustus*" because "[t]here indeed a man may behold shag-haired devils run roaring over the stage with squibs in their mouths, while drummers make thunder in the tiring-house and the twelve-penny hirelings make artificial lightning in their heavens."[108]

It is only with a play such as *The Duchess of Malfi* that we see the hint of a different, emerging discourse about dismemberment and performance, one that overlapped with existing discourses but that was not yet widespread. In Webster's play, after Ferdinand presents the Duchess with a severed hand and reveals the corpses of her husband and child, he informs the audience that the bodies are, in fact, fake:

> Excellent; as I would wish: she's plagu'd in Art.
> *These* [*sic*] presentations are but fram'd in wax.
> By the curious Master in that Qualitie,
> *Vincentio Lauriola,* and she takes them
> For true substantiall Bodies.[109]

In this passage, the emphasis on the ontological status of the actor's body is evident in the play's transposition of subject and object. The plot turns on the Duchess's mistake in treating as real persons what are merely wax figures: within the fictional narrative, that is, what seem to be persons are actually things. The irony of this moment would have been enhanced if, as is likely, the corpses were represented by actors. Given that the only physical mutilation required in the scene is Antonio's amputated hand, dummies would not have been economical or theatrically necessary. Using live performers to represent wax figures would also have highlighted Ferdinand's statement that his sister "takes them / For true substantiall Bodies," since that is indeed precisely what they would be. Whereas dismemberment is horrifying within the fictional world of the play, the performance dynamics of the early modern playhouse foregrounded theatre's own technologies. Doing so, as we have seen, drew attention to the ontological status of bodies onstage and turned theatre into a festive game with social functions akin to other violent sports in early modern England.

At the same time, in foregrounding the mechanism through which Ferdinand's deception is effected, *The Duchess of Malfi* pushes dismemberment into the realm of aesthetics. The title character is "plagu'd in Art" in three senses of the term: she is tricked by her brother's craftiness, she is duped by the artificial bodies, and the work he commissions is actually sculpture—that is, art. By stressing the role of the artist in producing an illusion, the episode constructs representational skill as a kind of presentational spectacle. Theatre's referential function is here put on display as a feat of activity. It is only with this increasing self-consciousness about the representational process as itself a form of bodily delight that we see the glimmers of a new discourse. *This,* the play suggests, is truly artful sport: taking true substantial bodies for characters. The imagination, it suggests, is more powerful than what is actually there; theatre as representation, it proposes, ought to trump theatre as spectacular entertainment. It was only much later that these early seeds grew into the naturalization of verisimilitude as a theatrical paradigm and only *then* that staging dismemberment might have produced a response closer to a Brechtian alienation effect. We cannot break down the fourth wall before it was erected. Analyzing the materiality of early modern performance, however, can open up new avenues for understanding the world before it was built.

Notes

Introduction: Materializing the Immaterial

1. Translation in Peter Meredith and John E. Tailby, eds., *The Staging of Religious Drama in Europe in the Later Middle Ages: Texts and Documents in English Translation* (Kalamazoo, MI: Medieval Institute, 1983), 105.
2. John Spalding Gatton, "'There must be blood': Mutilation and Martyrdom on the Medieval Stage," in *Violence in Drama*, ed. James Redmond (Cambridge: Cambridge University Press, 1991), 87.
3. See especially work associated with the *Records of Early English Drama* (REED) project, overviews of which are available in Audrey Douglas and Sally-Beth MacLean, eds., *REED in Review: Essays in Celebration of the First Twenty-Five Years* (Toronto: University of Toronto Press, 2006); and Peter Holland, "Theatre without Drama: Reading REED," in *From Script to Stage in Early Modern England*, ed. Peter Holland and Stephen Orgel (Basingstoke, UK: Palgrave Macmillan, 2004), 43–67.
4. See, for example, John H. Astington, *Actors and Acting in Shakespeare's Time: The Art of Stage Playing* (New York: Cambridge University Press, 2010); Jeremy Lopez, *Theatrical Convention and Audience Response in Early Modern Drama* (Cambridge: Cambridge University Press, 2003); Jennifer A. Low and Nova Myhill, eds., *Imagining the Audience in Early Modern Drama, 1558–1642* (New York: Palgrave Macmillan, 2011); Joanne Rochester, *Staging Spectatorship in the Plays of Philip Massinger* (Burlington, VT: Ashgate, 2010); and Charles Whitney, *Early Responses to Renaissance Drama* (Cambridge: Cambridge University Press, 2006).
5. See, for instance, Michelle M. Dowd and Natasha Korda, eds., *Working Subjects in Early Modern English Drama* (Farnham, UK: Ashgate, 2011); Valerie Forman, *Tragicomic Redemptions: Global Economics and the Early Modern English Stage* (Philadelphia: University of Pennsylvania Press, 2008); and Roslyn Lander Knutson, *Playing Companies and Commerce in Shakespeare's Time* (Cambridge: Cambridge University Press, 2001).
6. On performance as that which disappears, see Peggy Phelan, *Unmarked: The Politics of Performance* (London: Routledge, 1993); for a recent counterargument, see Rebecca Schneider, *Performing Remains: Art and War in Times of Theatrical Reenactment* (London: Routledge, 2011).
7. See, for example, Patricia Fumerton and Simon Hunt, eds., *Renaissance Culture and the Everyday* (Philadelphia: University of Pennsylvania Press, 1999); and Lena Cowen Orlin, ed., *Material London, ca. 1600* (Philadelphia: University of Pennsylvania Press, 2000).

8. Object-centered scholarship has thus been criticized by some for having a conservative streak. Although some working in this area have strong Marxist roots, the field as a whole has moved away from questions of political ideology and class conflict that informed the cultural materialism of the late 1980s and early 1990s. See Douglas Bruster, *Shakespeare and the Question of Culture: Early Modern Literature and the Cultural Turn* (New York: Palgrave Macmillan, 2003), 191–205; Crystal Bartolovich, "Oh, Dear, What Can the Matter Be? A Response to Peter Stallybrass's 'The Value of Culture and the Disavowal of Things,'" *Early Modern Culture* 1, no. 1 (2000), http://emc.eserver.org/1-1/bartolovich.html; and Hugh Grady, *Shakespeare's Universal Wolf: Studies in Early Modern Reification* (Oxford: Clarendon, 1996), 1–25. In theatre studies, Ric Knowles, *Reading the Material Theatre* (Cambridge: Cambridge University Press, 2004), usefully analyzes contemporary performance from a cultural materialist perspective.
9. See Judith Butler, *Gender Trouble: Feminism and the Subversion of Identity* (New York: Routledge, 1990); and *Bodies That Matter: On the Discursive Limits of "Sex"* (New York: Routledge, 1993). "Performativity" in Butler is not the same thing as performance. On the intersection between the two, see Andrew Parker and Eve Kosofsky Sedgwick, eds., *Performativity and Performance* (New York: Routledge, 1995); and W. B. Worthen, "Drama, Performativity, and Performance," *PMLA* 113 (1998): 1093–107.
10. On theatre as a semiotic system, see Marvin A. Carlson, *Theatre Semiotics: Signs of Life* (Bloomington: Indiana University Press, 1990); Keir Elam, *The Semiotics of Theatre and Drama*, 2nd ed. (London: Routledge, 2002); Erika Fischer-Lichte, *The Semiotics of Theater*, trans. Jeremy Gaines and Doris L. Jones (Bloomington: Indiana University Press, 1992); Patrice Pavis, *Languages of the Stage: Essays in the Semiology of the Theatre* (New York: Performing Arts Journal Publications, 1982); and Anne Ubersfeld, *Reading Theatre*, trans. Frank Collins (Toronto: University of Toronto Press, 1999). See also Jean Alter, *A Sociosemiotic Theory of Theatre* (Philadelphia: University of Pennsylvania Press, 1990), discussed further in chapter 4, and Nicholas Ridout, *Stage Fright, Animals, and Other Theatrical Problems* (Cambridge: Cambridge University Press, 2006), which analyzes semiotic crises onstage.
11. Michel Foucault, *The Archaeology of Knowledge; and, The Discourse on Language*, trans. A. M. Sheridan Smith (New York: Pantheon, 1972), 131.
12. Butler, *Bodies That Matter*, 250n5.
13. When I do use the term "Renaissance," I refer specifically to this humanist tradition. On the difficulties of both terms, see Jennifer Summit and David Wallace, eds., "Medieval/Renaissance: After Periodization," special issue, *Journal of Medieval and Early Modern Studies* 37, no. 3 (2007). On the cultural authority of drama as text versus performance, see W. B. Worthen, *Shakespeare and the Authority of Performance* (Cambridge: Cambridge University Press, 1997); Worthen, *Shakespeare and the Force of Modern Performance* (Cambridge: Cambridge University Press, 2003); Robert Weimann, *Authority and Representation in Early Modern Discourse*, ed. David Hillman (Baltimore: Johns Hopkins University Press, 1996); Weimann, *Author's Pen and Actor's Voice: Playing and Writing in Shakespeare's Theatre*, ed. Helen Higbee and William West (Cambridge: Cambridge University Press, 2000); and Nora Johnson, *The Actor as Playwright in Early Modern Drama* (Cambridge: Cambridge University Press, 2003).
14. See, in particular, Peter Burke, *Popular Culture in Early Modern Europe*, rev. ed. (Aldershot, UK: Ashgate, 1988); and Tim Harris, ed., *Popular Culture in England, c. 1500–1850* (New York: St. Martin's, 1995). On notions of the popular in theatre and performance studies, see Victor Emeljanow, "Editorial," *Popular Entertainment Studies* 1, no. 1 (2010): 1–5.

15. Burke, *Popular Culture*, xviii.
16. On historical phenomenology's theoretical premises and stakes, see Bruce R. Smith, "Premodern Sexualities," *PMLA* 115 (2000): 318–29; and Smith, *Phenomenal Shakespeare* (Chichester, UK: Wiley-Blackwell, 2010). For a good introduction to early modern affect studies more generally, see Gail Kern Paster, Katherine Rowe, and Mary Floyd-Wilson, eds., *Reading the Early Modern Passions: Essays in the Cultural History of Emotion* (Philadelphia: University of Pennsylvania Press, 2004). On the overlapping field of cognitive studies in theatre, see Evelyn B. Tribble, *Cognition in the Globe: Attention and Memory in Shakespeare's Theatre* (New York: Palgrave Macmillan, 2011). Other references are too numerous to note.
17. See, for example, Stephen Cohen, ed., *Shakespeare and Historical Formalism* (Aldershot, UK: Ashgate, 2007); Marjorie Levinson, "What Is New Formalism?" *PMLA* 122 (2007): 558–69; and Mark David Rasmussen, ed., *Renaissance Literature and Its Formal Engagements* (New York: Palgrave Macmillan, 2002). Working within and beyond historical formalism, see also Jean E. Howard, *Theater of a City: The Places of London Comedy, 1598–1642* (Philadelphia: University of Pennsylvania Press, 2007); and Henry S. Turner, *The English Renaissance Stage: Geometry, Poetics, and the Practical Spatial Arts, 1580–1630* (Oxford: Oxford University Press, 2006).
18. Among innumerable examples, see especially Zachary Lesser, *Renaissance Drama and the Politics of Publication: Readings in the English Book Trade* (Cambridge: Cambridge University Press, 2004); William H. Sherman, *Used Books: Marking Readers in Renaissance England* (Philadelphia: University of Pennsylvania Press, 2008); and Peter Stallybrass et al., "Hamlet's Tables and the Technologies of Writing in Renaissance England," *Shakespeare Quarterly* 55 (2004): 379–419.
19. Adam Fox, *Oral and Literate Culture in England, 1500–1700* (Oxford: Clarendon, 2000), 18.
20. Ibid., 14.
21. Peter W. M. Blayney, "The Publication of Playbooks," in *A New History of Early English Drama*, ed. John D. Cox and David Scott Kastan (New York: Columbia University Press, 1997), 385.
22. Ibid., 384; Fox, *Oral and Literate Culture*, 14; and Lesser, *Politics of Publication*, 20.
23. Douglas A. Brooks, *From Playhouse to Printing House: Drama and Authorship in Early Modern England* (New York: Cambridge University Press, 2000), 71.
24. Blayney, "Publication of Playbooks," 389.
25. W. R. Streitberger, "Personnel and Professionalization," in Cox and Kastan, *New History*, 337.
26. Roslyn Lander Knutson, *The Repertory of Shakespeare's Company, 1594–1613* (Fayetteville: University of Arkansas Press, 1991), 29–30; and Andrew Gurr, *The Shakespearean Stage, 1574–1642*, 3rd ed. (Cambridge: Cambridge University Press, 1992), 103–4.
27. Knutson, *Repertory*, 33.
28. Andrew Gurr, *Playgoing in Shakespeare's London*, 3rd ed. (Cambridge: Cambridge University Press, 2004), 24–25; and Gurr, *Shakespearean Stage*, 213.
29. Gurr, *Playgoing*, 69.
30. As a point of comparison, the National Safety Council reports that in 2007, the odds of dying in a motor vehicle accident were 1 in 88. National Safety Council, *Injury Facts*, 2011 ed., http://www.nsc.org/NSC%20Picture%20Library/News/web_graphics/Injury_Facts_37.pdf, accessed April 3, 2011.
31. Lukas Erne, *Shakespeare as Literary Dramatist* (Cambridge: Cambridge University Press, 2003). See also Erne, "The Popularity of Shakespeare in Print," *Shakespeare*

Survey 62 (2009): 12–29; and Zachary Lesser, Peter Stallybrass, and G. K. Hunter, "The First Literary *Hamlet* and the Commonplacing of Professional Plays," *Shakespeare Quarterly* 59 (2008): 371–420.
32. Lesser, *Politics of Publication*, 20.
33. Ibid.
34. Mary Thomas Crane, "What Was Performance?" *Criticism* 43, no. 2 (2001): 169–87.
35. John Rainolds, *Th'overthrow of stage-playes... Wherein is manifestly proved, that it is not onely vnlawfull to bee an actor, but a beholder of those vanities...* (London, 1599), A2v.
36. Francis Lenton, *Characterismi: or, Lentons leasures Expressed in essayes and characters...* (London, 1631), F4r, F5r.
37. Ben Jonson, *The alchemist* (London, 1612), A3r.
38. Translation in Tiffany Stern, "'On each Wall and Corner Poast': Playbills, Title-pages, and Advertising in Early Modern London," *English Literary Renaissance* 36 (2006): 66.
39. Charles Read Baskervill, *The Elizabethan Jig and Related Song Drama* (Chicago: University of Chicago Press, 1929), 6.
40. Bruce R. Smith, *The Acoustic World of Early Modern England: Attending to the O-Factor* (Chicago: University of Chicago Press, 1999), 158; emphasis in original.
41. William N. West, "When Is the Jig Up—and What Is It Up To?" in *Locating the Queen's Men, 1583–1603: Material Practices and Conditions of Playing*, ed. Helen Ostovich, Holger Schott Syme, and Andrew Griffin (Farnham, UK: Ashgate, 2009), 205.
42. Clare Williams, ed. and trans., *Thomas Platter's Travels in England, 1599* (London: Jonathan Cape, 1937), 166.
43. Thomas Dekker, *A strange horse-race at the end of which, comes in the catch-poles masque...* (London, 1613), C4v.
44. Transcribed in E. K. Chambers, *The Elizabethan Stage*, 4 vols. (Oxford: Clarendon, 1923), 4:340–41.
45. James Shirley, *Changes: or, Love in a Maze. A Comedie, As it was presented at the Private House in Salisbury Court, by the Company of His Majesties Revels* (London, 1632), H2r–H2v.
46. Peter Corbin and Douglas Sedge, eds., *Three Jacobean Witchcraft Plays* (Manchester: Manchester University Press, 1986), 13–14.
47. Alan Brissenden, *Shakespeare and the Dance* (London: Macmillan, 1981), 68.
48. John Russell Brown, *Shakespeare's Plays in Performance* (New York: Applause, 1993), 179–80.
49. I analyze this episode in more detail in chapter 4.
50. Frederick Kiefer, *Shakespeare's Visual Theatre: Staging the Personified Characters* (Cambridge: Cambridge University Press, 2003), 114–15; and Amanda Eubanks Winkler, *O Let Us Howle Some Heavy Note: Music for Witches, the Melancholic, and the Mad on the Seventeenth-Century English Stage* (Bloomington: Indiana University Press, 2006), 25–40.
51. Quoted in Vanessa Cunningham, *Shakespeare and Garrick* (Cambridge: Cambridge University Press, 2008), 50.
52. Winkler, *O Let Us Howle*, 40.
53. Garrick introduced further special effects for the witches (Cunningham, *Shakespeare and Garrick*, 51–52), and by Henry Irving's time, there were "some sixty witches who danced and flew in the air to the accompaniment of a full orchestra" (Brown, *Shakespeare's Plays in Performance*, 180).
54. Gurr, *Shakespearean Stage*, 177.

55. Ibid., 178.
56. John Forrest, *The History of Morris Dancing, 1458–1750* (Toronto: University of Toronto Press, 1999), 226.
57. John Fletcher and William Shakespeare, *The two noble kinsmen presented at the Blackfriers by the Kings Maiesties servants, with great applause* (London, 1634), G3v; 3.5.137.
58. Alan C. Dessen and Leslie Thomson, *A Dictionary of Stage Directions in English Drama, 1580–1642* (Cambridge: Cambridge University Press, 1999), 127.
59. Ibid.
60. Edmund Gayton, *Pleasant notes upon Don Quixot* (London, 1654), Mm3r.
61. Knutson, *Repertory*, 29.
62. For further discussion, see Erika T. Lin, "Popular Festivity and the Early Modern Stage: The Case of *George a Greene*," *Theatre Journal* 61 (2009): 271–97.
63. *Records of Early English Drama: Somerset*, ed. James Stokes, 2 vols. (Toronto: University of Toronto Press, 1996), 421.
64. Knutson, *Repertory*, 32. "For example, *Tasso's Melancholy* was introduced 'ne' on 11 August 1594 and scheduled a second time a week later (18 August); over the next nine months, it appeared twice in September, twice in October, once in November, once in December, twice in January, once in February, and once in May, at which time it was retired" (ibid.).
65. For the most recent work on this subject, see Phebe Jensen, *Religion and Revelry in Shakespeare's Festive World* (Cambridge: Cambridge University Press, 2008); and Paul Whitfield White, *Drama and Religion in English Provincial Society, 1485–1660* (Cambridge: Cambridge University Press, 2008).
66. Ronald Hutton, *The Stations of the Sun: A History of the Ritual Year in Britain* (Oxford: Oxford University Press, 1996), 248.
67. Philip Stubbes, *The anatomie of abuses contayning a discouerie, or briefe summarie of such notable vices and imperfections, as now raigne in many Christian countreyes of the worlde: but (especiallie) in a verie famous ilande called Ailgna...* (London, 1583), M2r. On the popular pamphlet's subsequent reprints, see Margaret Jane Kidnie, ed., *Philip Stubbes, The Anatomie of Abuses* (Tempe: Arizona Center for Medieval and Renaissance Studies, 2002).
68. I discuss these festive leaders at greater length in Lin, "Popular Festivity," 284–85.
69. Hutton notes that this task was generally undertaken in June, but in places such as Dorset and other locations in the south of England, the warmer climate meant that the work commonly began in May (*Stations of the Sun*, 323).
70. Leonard Tennenhouse, "Strategies of State and Political Plays: *A Midsummer Night's Dream, Henry IV, Henry V, Henry VIII*," in *Political Shakespeare: Essays in Cultural Materialism*, 2nd ed., ed. Jonathan Dollimore and Alan Sinfield (Ithaca, NY: Cornell University Press, 1994), 123–25.
71. On the *coranto*, see Brissenden, *Shakespeare and the Dance*, 113. On the *galliard* and *volta*, see Peter Walls, "Common Sixteenth-Century Dance Forms: Some Further Notes," *Early Music* 2 (1974): 164–65.
72. One 1611 court masque, for example, involved two dancing masters, paid £20 and £50 respectively—quite a large sum by any account but especially so when we consider that, for the same show, Inigo Jones and Ben Jonson were paid only £40 each. Chambers, *Elizabethan Stage*, 3:387; and Brissenden, *Shakespeare and the Dance*, 118n37.
73. Skiles Howard, *The Politics of Courtly Dancing in Early Modern England* (Amherst: University of Massachusetts Press, 1998), 70.

74. For recent work on contemporary performance that has aimed to redefine what counts as a theatrical event, see, for example, Vicki Ann Cremona et al., eds., *Theatrical Events: Borders, Dynamics, Frames* (Amsterdam: Rodopi, 2004); Temple Hauptfleisch et al., eds., *Festivalising! Theatrical Events, Politics and Culture* (Amsterdam: Rodopi, 2007); Hans-Thies Lehmann, *Postdramatic Theatre*, trans. Karen Jürs-Munby (London: Routledge, 2006); and Willmar Sauter, *The Theatrical Event: Dynamics of Performance and Perception* (Iowa City: University of Iowa Press, 2000). Although these scholars focus on performance activities that do not rely on dramatic narratives or scripts and although they consider the fluid relationship between spectating and performing, the historical context of their investigations is significantly different enough that many of their insights are not quite applicable to early modern theatre.
75. Foucault, *Archaeology of Knowledge*, 130.

1   Theorizing Theatrical Privilege: Rethinking Weimann's Concepts of *Locus* and *Platea*

1. Robert Weimann, *Shakespeare and the Popular Tradition in the Theater: Studies in the Social Dimension of Dramatic Form and Function*, ed. Robert Schwartz (Baltimore: Johns Hopkins University Press, 1978). The German edition was published in Berlin in 1967. See also Weimann's further development of his theories in "Bifold Authority in Shakespeare's Theatre," *Shakespeare Quarterly* 39 (1988): 401–17; and in *Author's Pen and Actor's Voice: Playing and Writing in Shakespeare's Theatre*, ed. Helen Higbee and William West (Cambridge: Cambridge University Press, 2000).
2. Weimann, *Shakespeare and the Popular Tradition*, 74.
3. Ibid., 74–76. In *Author's Pen and Actor's Voice*, Weimann describes the *locus* as embodying "localized, that is, spatially self-coherent representations. In Shakespeare's playhouse, there are a good many scenes that have a distinct, unmistakable setting (such as Macbeth's castle, Portia's Belmont, Gertrude's closet, Desdemona's chamber, Timon's cave, and so forth). They designate either a particular locality or a given place, such as a garden, bridge, court, gateway, or prison" (190).
4. Weimann, *Shakespeare and the Popular Tradition*, 74, 76, 80.
5. Ibid., 78.
6. Ibid., 212–13.
7. Ibid., 237, 228.
8. Although engaged in a very different kind of project, David Schalkwyk highlights this aspect of Weimann's work when he asserts that the "massive authority" of theatrical performance lies in its power to "represent, transform and limit the authority of a class who are also patrons and the pre-eminent audience of the theatre." David Schalkwyk, *Speech and Performance in Shakespeare's Sonnets and Plays* (Cambridge: Cambridge University Press, 2002), 34. Throughout this chapter, I use terms such as "authority," "privilege," and "foreground" interchangeably, despite their subtle variations in meaning. As Schalkwyk points out, one of the strengths of Weimann's work is its critique of class, a move that relies on fluidity between social and dramaturgical privilege. Since my goal here is to think through questions of theatrical signification, I temporarily bracket this important facet of Weimann's formulation in order to clarify the performance dimension.
9. Mark Fortier, *Theory/Theatre: An Introduction*, 2nd ed. (London: Routledge, 2002), 161.

10. Peter Thomson, *Shakespeare's Theatre*, 2nd ed. (London: Routledge, 1992), 57. For further examples, see Colin Counsell, *Signs of Performance: An Introduction to Twentieth-Century Theatre* (London: Routledge, 1996), 17–20; Penny Gay, "*Twelfth Night:* 'The Babbling Gossip of the Air,'" in *A Companion to Shakespeare's Works*, vol. 3, ed. Richard Dutton and Jean E. Howard (Malden, MA: Blackwell, 2003), 439–43; John Gillies, "Place and Space in Three Late Plays," in *A Companion to Shakespeare's Works*, vol. 4, ed. Richard Dutton and Jean E. Howard (Malden, MA: Blackwell, 2003), 186; and Arthur F. Kinney, *Shakespeare by Stages: An Historical Introduction* (Malden, MA: Blackwell, 2003), 15–16.
11. Wilheim Hortmann, *Shakespeare on the German Stage: The Twentieth Century* (Cambridge: Cambridge University Press, 1998), 394.
12. Yu Jin Ko, "A Little Touch of Harry in the Light: *Henry V* at the New Globe," *Shakespeare Survey* 52 (1999): 107–19. For additional instances, see Elaine Aston, *Feminist Theatre Practice: A Handbook* (London: Routledge, 1999), 95–96; Peter Donaldson, *Shakespearean Films/Shakespearean Directors* (Boston: Unwin Hyman, 1990), 5; Lorraine Helms, "Acts of Resistance: The Feminist Player," in *The Weyward Sisters: Shakespeare and Feminist Politics*, ed. Dympna C. Callaghan, Lorraine Helms, and Jyotsna Singh (Cambridge, MA: Blackwell, 1994), 102–56; Dennis Kennedy, "Shakespeare without His Language," in *Shakespeare, Theory, and Performance*, ed. James C. Bulman (London: Routledge, 1996), 133–48; and Loren Kruger, *Post-Imperial Brecht: Politics and Performance, East and South* (Cambridge: Cambridge University Press, 2004), 281–336.
13. David Scott Kastan and Peter Stallybrass, eds., *Staging the Renaissance: Reinterpretations of Elizabethan and Jacobean Drama* (New York: Routledge, 1991), 7.
14. Richard Helgerson, *Forms of Nationhood: The Elizabethan Writing of England* (Chicago: University of Chicago Press, 1992), 224.
15. Jean E. Howard and Phyllis Rackin, *Engendering a Nation: A Feminist Account of Shakespeare's English Histories* (London: Routledge, 1997), 105.
16. Louis Montrose, *The Purpose of Playing: Shakespeare and the Cultural Politics of the Elizabethan Theatre* (Chicago: University of Chicago Press, 1996), 209n2.
17. This diversity is made clear in the contributions to two Festschrift collections that have recently appeared in Weimann's honor: Bryan Reynolds and William N. West, eds., *Rematerializing Shakespeare: Authority and Representation on the Early Modern English Stage* (New York: Palgrave Macmillan, 2005); and Graham Bradshaw, Tom Bishop, and David Schalkwyk, eds., "The Achievement of Robert Weimann," special issue, *Shakespearean International Yearbook* 10 (2010).
18. In addition to studies already mentioned, see also Jean E. Howard, *The Stage and Social Struggle in Early Modern England* (London: Routledge, 1994); Steven Mullaney, *The Place of the Stage: License, Play, and Power in Renaissance England* (Chicago: University of Chicago Press, 1988); and Stephen Orgel, *Impersonations: The Performance of Gender in Shakespeare's England* (Cambridge: Cambridge University Press, 1996).
19. See, for example, Bernard Beckerman, *Shakespeare at the Globe, 1599–1609* (New York: Macmillan, 1962); James C. Bulman, ed., *Shakespeare, Theory, and Performance* (London: Routledge, 1996); Alan C. Dessen, *Elizabethan Stage Conventions and Modern Interpreters* (Cambridge: Cambridge University Press, 1984); Dessen, *Recovering Shakespeare's Theatrical Vocabulary* (Cambridge: Cambridge University Press, 1995); Dessen, *Rescripting Shakespeare: The Text, the Director, and Modern Productions* (Cambridge: Cambridge University Press, 2002); Michael Goldman, *Shakespeare and the Energies of Drama* (Princeton, NJ: Princeton University Press, 1972); Philip C. McGuire and David A. Samuelson, eds., *Shakespeare, the Theatrical Dimension*

(New York: AMS, 1979); J. L. Styan, *Shakespeare's Stagecraft* (Cambridge: Cambridge University Press, 1967); and Marvin Thompson and Ruth Thompson, eds., *Shakespeare and the Sense of Performance: Essays in the Tradition of Performance Criticism in Honor of Bernard Beckerman* (Newark: University of Delaware Press, 1989).

20. W. B. Worthen, *Shakespeare and the Authority of Performance* (Cambridge: Cambridge University Press, 1997), 154–55.
21. Ibid., 155–56. McGuire, for instance, describes theatrical performance as a way of "making physically present (of *realizing*) possibilities of perception and feeling that lie attenuated and frozen in the script." Introduction to McGuire and Samuelson, *Shakespeare, the Theatrical Dimension,* xx; emphasis in original.
22. See, in particular, Weimann's theoretically informed introduction to *Author's Pen* (1–17) as well as his discussion of Italian architecture and linear perspective (185–91).
23. Weimann, *Author's Pen,* 12; and Weimann, *Shakespeare and the Popular Tradition,* 216.
24. Kent Cartwright, for example, refers to Weimann's work on "blocking" and defines the *locus* as "the geographically specific middle and rear region of the Elizabethan stage" and the *platea* as "the generalized no-man's-land proximate to, and shared psychically with, the audience." Kent Cartwright, *Shakespearean Tragedy and Its Double: The Rhythms of Audience Response* (University Park: Pennsylvania State University Press, 1991), 39. For other similar instances, see Ruth Lunney, *Marlowe and the Popular Tradition: Innovation in the English Drama before 1595* (Manchester: Manchester University Press, 2002), 171; and Jeremy Lopez, *Theatrical Convention and Audience Response in Early Modern Drama* (Cambridge: Cambridge University Press, 2003), 58. Although both Lunney and Lopez concede that the upstage-downstage distinction should not be taken too literally, the spatial aspect of Weimann's formulation is, nevertheless, understood to be central to his work.
25. The quotation is Weimann's (*Author's Pen,* 193).
26. Michael E. Mooney, *Shakespeare's Dramatic Transactions* (Durham, NC: Duke University Press, 1990), xii.
27. Ibid., 19, xii; emphasis in original.
28. S. L. Bethell, *Shakespeare and the Popular Dramatic Tradition* (Durham, NC: Duke University Press, 1944), 37–38. For other early work on "dual consciousness" in English drama, see Maynard Mack, "Engagement and Detachment in Shakespeare's Plays," in *Essays on Shakespeare and Elizabethan Drama in Honor of Hardin Craig,* ed. Richard Hosley (Columbia: University of Missouri Press, 1962), 275–96; and Anne Righter [Barton], *Shakespeare and the Idea of the Play* (London: Chatto and Windus, 1962). See also Bernard Beckerman, *Shakespeare at the Globe,* especially his accounts of "localized" space (64–69) and stage illusion (157–68). Although not cited in *Shakespeare and the Popular Tradition,* Beckerman's work seems to play a significant role in *Author's Pen and Actor's Voice.* For accounts of "dual consciousness" contemporary with the English-language version of Weimann's earlier book, see Stephen Booth, "Doubling in Shakespeare's Plays," in McGuire and Samuelson, *Shakespeare, the Theatrical Dimension,* 103–31, later revised in Booth, *"King Lear," "Macbeth," Indefinition, and Tragedy* (New Haven, CT: Yale University Press, 1983); and Jackson I. Cope, *The Theater and the Dream: From Metaphor to Form in Renaissance Drama* (Baltimore: Johns Hopkins University Press, 1973).
29. Weimann, *Author's Pen,* 180.
30. Weimann, *Shakespeare and the Popular Tradition,* 251. In considering the social implications of "illusionistic" and "nonillusionistic" forms of theatre, Weimann also draws on Brecht's dichotomy of the "dramatic theatre" and the "epic theatre," the former Romantic and politically passive and the latter socially informed and politically active.

Although Weimann critiques Brecht's valorization of "convention and stylization," which he sees as "fall[ing] short of a sense of the complexity of Shakespearean dramaturgy" (250–51), his work resonates notably with Brecht's emphasis on the epic theatre's ability to deconstruct dramatic illusion. See Weimann, *Shakespeare and the Popular Tradition*, 249–52; and Bertolt Brecht, "The Modern Theatre Is the Epic Theatre," in *Brecht on Theatre: The Development of an Aesthetic*, ed. and trans. John Willett (New York: Hill and Wang, 1964), 33–42.

31. Douglas Bruster and Robert Weimann, *Prologues to Shakespeare's Theatre: Performance and Liminality in Early Modern Drama* (London: Routledge, 2004), 2. On liminality (à la Victor Turner and Arnold van Gennep), see ibid., 37–41; and Weimann, *Author's Pen*, 235–36, 240–45. In *Author's Pen*, Weimann also uses the term "threshold" when he associates the carnivalesque and marginalized place of the stage with the "spatial semantics in this threshold function of the *platea*" and with the "threshold functions" of characters located in "the downstage position of Launce and his dog,... Falstaff, Parolles, Thersites, Lucio, Autolycus, and others" (195). The term appears in Weimann's earlier work as well. See, for example, his statement that "between nonrepresentational speech and psychological realism there is a vast and often misunderstood threshold where the traditional and the modern mix rather freely" (*Shakespeare and the Popular Tradition*, 233–34). For his more recent explorations of notions of character along these lines, see Robert Weimann and Douglas Bruster, *Shakespeare and the Power of Performance: Stage and Page in the Elizabethan Theatre* (Cambridge: Cambridge University Press, 2008).

32. *Oxford English Dictionary* (*OED*) *Online*, 2nd ed. (1989), s.vv. "upstage, *adv.* and *adj.* (and *n.*)" and "down stage | down-stage, *adv.*," published online December 2011, http://www.oed.com/view/Entry/220184 and http://www.oed.com/view/Entry/57287.

33. This quotation, as well as the ticket prices I mention later, can be found on the Globe Theatre's website, http://www.shakespearesglobe.com/theatre/box-office/seating-plan-and-prices (accessed May 27, 2011).

34. Andrew Gurr, *Playgoing in Shakespeare's London*, 3rd ed. (Cambridge: Cambridge University Press, 2004), 24.

35. For further discussion of these issues, see, for instance, Gay McAuley, *Space in Performance: Making Meaning in the Theatre* (Ann Arbor: University of Michigan Press, 1999); and David Wiles, *A Short History of Western Performance Space* (Cambridge: Cambridge University Press, 2003). On London drama, civic pageantry, and performance in relation to the space of the city, see D. J. Hopkins, *City/Stage/Globe: Performance and Space in Shakespeare's London* (New York: Routledge, 2008). Weimann's concepts of *locus* and *platea* inform the book throughout, but Hopkins discusses them explicitly on 162–65. On early modern playhouse architecture, see John Orrell, *The Quest for Shakespeare's Globe* (Cambridge: Cambridge University Press, 1983); and Orrell, *The Human Stage: English Theatre Design, 1567–1640* (Cambridge: Cambridge University Press, 1988). On space and dramatic form more generally, see Jean E. Howard, *Theater of a City: The Places of London Comedy, 1598–1642* (Philadelphia: University of Pennsylvania Press, 2007); and Henry S. Turner, *The English Renaissance Stage: Geometry, Poetics, and the Practical Spatial Arts, 1580–1630* (Oxford: Oxford University Press, 2006).

36. Andrew Gurr, *The Shakespeare Company, 1594–1642* (Cambridge: Cambridge University Press, 2004), 47–48.

37. John Orrell, "The Theaters," in *A New History of Early English Drama*, ed. John D. Cox and David Scott Kastan (New York: Columbia University Press, 1997), 106–7, 109.

38. The performance dynamics in *The Merchant of Venice*, when Launcelot first meets up with Old Gobbo, are very similar to the scenes I have been discussing. In particular,

the two characters must be located in the same part of the stage when the blind father uses his fingers to explore his son's head and exclaims, "Lord worshipt might he be, what a beard hast thou got" (TLN 655; 2.2.93–94).
39. Weimann, *Shakespeare and the Popular Tradition,* 227.
40. Ibid.
41. Weimann, *Author's Pen,* 67; emphasis in original. For other accounts of the staging of this episode, see Douglas C. Sprigg, "Shakespeare's Visual Stagecraft: The Seduction of Cressida," in McGuire and Samuelson, *Shakespeare, the Theatrical Dimension,* 149–63; and Michael W. Shurgot, *Stages of Play: Shakespeare's Theatrical Energies in Elizabethan Performance* (Newark: University of Delaware Press, 1998), 183–98.
42. I discuss this latter episode in more detail in chapter 2.
43. For accounts of pageantry, spectacle, and the consolidation of royal power, see Stephen Orgel, *The Illusion of Power: Political Theater in the English Renaissance* (Berkeley: University of California Press, 1975); and Roy C. Strong, *Art and Power: Renaissance Festivals, 1450–1650* (Berkeley: University of California Press, 1984). Regarding gallants in the playhouses, see Gurr, *Playgoing,* 34–37, as well as Ann Rosalind Jones and Peter Stallybrass, *Renaissance Clothing and the Materials of Memory* (Cambridge: Cambridge University Press, 2000), 188. For essays challenging modern interpretations of subject and object, see Margreta de Grazia, Maureen Quilligan, and Peter Stallybrass, eds., *Subject and Object in Renaissance Culture* (Cambridge: Cambridge University Press, 1996).
44. I am thinking, for example, of *Love's Labor's Lost,* when the lords attempt to impersonate Muscovites, and of *Twelfth Night,* when Feste stages a conversation between himself and Sir Topas. In early modern England, printed books attempted to approximate spoken language as best they could. See Bruce R. Smith, *The Acoustic World of Early Modern England: Attending to the O-Factor* (Chicago: University of Chicago Press, 1999), 107–29.
45. For a more detailed examination of such phenomenological issues, see Smith, *Acoustic World,* 6–10.
46. For other discussions of this speech, see James Black, "*King Lear:* Art Upside-Down," *Shakespeare Survey* 33 (1980): 35–42; Alan C. Dessen, "Two Falls and a Trap: Shakespeare and Spectacles of Realism," *English Literary Renaissance* 5 (1975): 291–307; Alvin B. Kernan, "Formalism and Realism in Elizabethan Drama: The Miracles in *King Lear,*" *Renaissance Drama* 9 (1966): 59–66; Harry Levin, *Shakespeare and the Revolution of the Times: Perspectives and Commentaries* (New York: Oxford University Press, 1976), 162–86; Michael E. Mooney, "'Edgar I Nothing Am': 'Figurenposition' in *King Lear,*" *Shakespeare Survey* 38 (1985): 153–66; and Derek Peat, "'And that's true too': *King Lear* and the Tension of Uncertainty," *Shakespeare Survey* 33 (1980): 43–53. On related issues, see also Dessen, *Elizabethan Stage Conventions,* 130–55.
47. Michael Mooney argues that both this line and Edgar's vocal changes "mark stages in his attempt to regain his true identity" (*Shakespeare's Dramatic Transactions,* 142–43). He contends that Edgar's sharing of privileged knowledge with the audience situates him in the *platea.* Mooney's argument here complements mine, though our emphases are quite different. He focuses primarily on the audience's knowledge of events represented within the play; my argument centers on the scene's foregrounding of early modern theatre's own representational strategies.
48. Jean MacIntyre and Garrett P. J. Epp, "'Cloathes worth all the rest': Costumes and Properties," in Cox and Kastan, *New History,* 273–74. Note that Edgar's soliloquy in 3.6 appears only in the quarto version of the play.

49. *A pleasant commodie, called Looke about you. As it was lately played by the right honourable the Lord High Admirall his seruaunts* (London, 1600). The play was likely performed between 1597 and 1599.
50. Jody Enders discusses popular myths about supposedly real deaths onstage in *Death by Drama and Other Medieval Urban Legends* (Chicago: University of Chicago Press, 2002). For a discussion of early modern anatomy theatres and the spectacular display of corpses, see Jonathan Sawday, *The Body Emblazoned: Dissection and the Human Body in Renaissance Culture* (London: Routledge, 1995). I discuss in more detail the body of the actor as theatrical signifier in chapter 5. See also my reading of Arthur's dead body in Erika T. Lin, "'Lord of thy presence': Bodies, Performance, and Audience Interpretation in Shakespeare's *King John*," in *Imagining the Audience in Early Modern Drama, 1558–1642*, ed. Jennifer A. Low and Nova Myhill (New York: Palgrave Macmillan, 2011), 121–24.
51. On *platea* figures, the more clear-cut cases are in medieval drama; in Shakespeare and other later plays, there is more slippage between different dramaturgical modes. Weimann himself is interested in these kinds of transformations and changes; assigning characters to either *locus* or *platea*, however, sometimes obscures exactly how these modes are deployed in any given instance. In his earlier book, Weimann's list of *platea* characters includes "Launce and his friend Speed, most of the other Shakespearean clowns, the porters in *Macbeth* and *Henry VIII*, the gravediggers in *Hamlet*, Bottom in *A Midsummer Night's Dream*, the nurse in *Romeo and Juliet*, Richard Gloucester, Iago, the Fool, and, partly, Edmund in *King Lear*, Falstaff, Thersites, Apemantus, and—with some reservations—Aaron in *Titus Andronicus*, the Bastard Falconbridge in *King John*, and Autolycus in *The Winter's Tale*. Also belonging to this group are characters whose status within court groupings is temporarily changed or weakened as a result of real of feigned madness (Edgar, Lear, Hamlet, and, to a lesser extent, Ophelia)" (*Shakespeare and the Popular Tradition*, 224). Weimann's more recent book also includes the murderers in *Richard III*, the "rural fellow" in *Antony and Cleopatra*, Parolles, Lucio, and both "Launce and his dog" (*Author's Pen*, 195). Michael Mooney follows Weimann's lead in applying *locus* and *platea* to "the ways Shakespeare presented his tragic protagonists" (*Shakespeare's Dramatic Transactions*, 22). Emily C. Bartels also echoes Weimann's emphasis on *locus* and *platea* as applying specifically to characters: her "Breaking the Illusion of Being: Shakespeare and the Performance of Self," *Theatre Journal* 46 (1994): 171–85, argues that *platea* characters are, in fact, more coherent in their subjectivity than *locus* characters.

2 Staging Sight: Visual Paradigms and Perceptual Strategies in *Love's Labor's Lost*

1. Bernard Shaw, *Shaw on Shakespeare: An Anthology of Bernard Shaw's Writings on the Plays and Production of Shakespeare*, ed. Edwin Wilson (London: Dutton, 1961; repr., New York: Applause, 1989), 114. The production was staged in 1886.
2. Ibid.
3. Felicia Hardison Londré, "From a Theatregoer's Notebook: The RSC's *Love's Labour's Lost*," in *"Love's Labour's Lost": Critical Essays*, ed. Felicia Hardison Londré (New York: Garland, 1997), 411–14. The production, directed by Barry Kyle, starred Kenneth Branagh as the King. Similar visual conventions are evident in the film version Branagh

later directed, in which Alessandro Nivola as the King hides beneath a table and holds a tiny potted plant up to his face. Kenneth Branagh, *Love's Labour's Lost* (Shepperton, UK: Pathé Pictures et al., 2000), 35 mm film.
4. Miriam Gilbert, *Love's Labour's Lost*, Shakespeare in Performance (Manchester: Manchester University Press, 1993), 7.
5. Charles Gildon, "Critical Remarks on His Plays," in *The Works of Mr. William Shakespear [sic]*, ed. Nicholas Rowe, 7 vols. (1709–10; repr., New York: AMS, 1967), repr. in Londré, *"Love's Labour's Lost": Critical Essays*, 45–48.
6. William Hazlitt, *Characters of Shakespear's Plays* (London, 1817), repr. in Londré, *"Love's Labour's Lost": Critical Essays*, 61–63.
7. Although I focus on visuality, I have been influenced by scholarship on the other senses. See David Hillman and Carla Mazzio, eds., *The Body in Parts: Fantasies of Corporeality in Early Modern Europe* (New York: Routledge, 1997); Bruce R. Smith, *The Acoustic World of Early Modern England: Attending to the O-Factor* (Chicago: University of Chicago Press, 1999); Wes Folkerth, *The Sound of Shakespeare* (New York: Routledge, 2002); Elizabeth D. Harvey, ed., *Sensible Flesh: On Touch in Early Modern Culture* (Philadelphia: University of Pennsylvania Press, 2003); Gina Bloom, *Voice in Motion: Staging Gender, Shaping Sound in Early Modern England* (Philadelphia: University of Pennsylvania Press, 2007); and Holly Dugan, *The Ephemeral History of Perfume: Scent and Sense in Early Modern England* (Baltimore: Johns Hopkins University Press, 2011).
8. See, for example, Anne Righter [Barton], *Shakespeare and the Idea of the Play* (London: Chatto and Windus, 1962), 150–51; G. R. Hibbard, ed., *Love's Labour's Lost*, The Oxford Shakespeare (Oxford: Oxford University Press, 1990), 19; and J. L. Styan, *Shakespeare's Stagecraft* (Cambridge: Cambridge University Press, 1967), 31, 104.
9. Quoted in Barbara Hodgdon, "Rehearsal Process as Critical Practice: John Barton's 1978 *Love's Labour's Lost*," *Theatre History Studies* 8 (1988): 11–34, repr. in Londré, *"Love's Labour's Lost": Critical Essays*, 387–409, 392.
10. R. A. Foakes, ed., *Henslowe's Diary*, 2nd ed. (Cambridge: Cambridge University Press, 2002), 319–20.
11. Alan C. Dessen and Leslie Thomson, *A Dictionary of Stage Directions in English Drama, 1580–1642* (Cambridge: Cambridge University Press, 1999), 236.
12. Gilbert, *Love's Labour's Lost*, 8.
13. Dessen and Thomson, *Dictionary of Stage Directions*, 236.
14. Ibid.
15. Gilbert, *Love's Labour's Lost*, 21. See also Miriam Gilbert, "The Disappearance and Return of *Love's Labor's Lost*," in *Shakespeare's Sweet Thunder: Essays on the Early Comedies*, ed. Michael J. Collins (Newark: University of Delaware Press, 1997), 155–75. On property trees, see Werner Habicht, "Tree Properties and Tree Scenes in Elizabethan Theater," *Renaissance Drama* 4 (1971): 69–92; Bernard Beckerman, *Shakespeare at the Globe, 1599–1609* (New York: Macmillan, 1962), 81; E. K. Chambers, *The Elizabethan Stage* (Oxford: Clarendon, 1923), 3:89; and Andrew Gurr, *The Shakespearean Stage, 1574–1642*, 3rd ed. (Cambridge: Cambridge University Press, 1992), 189. Alan C. Dessen, *Recovering Shakespeare's Theatrical Vocabulary* (Cambridge: Cambridge University Press, 1995), 59–63, argues against Habicht's view that property trees were put onstage to enhance the "atmosphere."
16. See John Kerrigan, ed., *Love's Labour's Lost*, The New Penguin Shakespeare (Harmondsworth, UK: Penguin, 1982); and Harry Levin, "Sitting in the Sky (*Love's Labor's Lost*, 4.3)," in *Shakespeare's "Rough Magic": Renaissance Essays in Honor of C. L. Barber*, ed. Peter Erickson and Coppélia Kahn (Newark: University of Delaware Press, 1985), 113–30.

17. Robert Weimann, *Shakespeare and the Popular Tradition in the Theater: Studies in the Social Dimension of Dramatic Form and Function*, ed. Robert Schwartz (Baltimore: Johns Hopkins University Press, 1978), 78.
18. "All hid" followed rules similar to hide-and-seek or blind man's buff, as numerous editors note. John Davies calls the game "Wincke-all-hid" with a marginal gloss stating "A sport so called." John Davies, *Humours heau'n on earth with the ciuile warres of death and fortune...* (London, 1609), G2v.
19. Weimann, *Shakespeare and the Popular Tradition*, 229.
20. On this holiday and related performance traditions, see Clifford Davidson, *Festivals and Plays in Late Medieval Britain* (Aldershot, UK: Ashgate, 2007), 4–24; Thomas P. Campbell, "Liturgy and Drama: Recent Approaches to Medieval Theatre," *Theatre Journal* 33 (1981): 291–93, 299–301; Joel Fredell, "The Three Clerks and St. Nicholas in Medieval England," *Studies in Philology* 92 (1995): 181–202; and Nicholas Orme, "The Culture of Children in Medieval England," *Past and Present* 148 (1995): 70–73.
21. Ronald Hutton, *The Stations of the Sun: A History of the Ritual Year in Britain* (Oxford: Oxford University Press, 1996), 25.
22. E. K. Chambers, *The Mediaeval Stage* (Oxford: Oxford University Press, 1903), 1:374.
23. Ibid.
24. *Records of Early English Drama: Herefordshire, Worcestershire*, ed. David N. Klausner (Toronto: University of Toronto Press, 1990), 674.
25. *Old Meg of Hereford-shire, for a Mayd-Marian: and Hereford towne for a Morris-daunce. Or Twelue Morris-dancers in Hereford-shire, of twelue hundred yeares old* (London, 1609), B2r.
26. *Oxford English Dictionary (OED) Online*, 2nd ed. (1989), s.v. "infantry, *n.*" (defs. 1, 2), published online December 2011, http://www.oed.com/view/Entry/95236.
27. As Robert Nelson puts it, "In other places and times," vision could be "an ethical, a moral, theological, and even political issue," not primarily a biological one. Robert S. Nelson, ed., introduction to *Visuality Before and Beyond the Renaissance: Seeing as Others Saw* (Cambridge: Cambridge University Press, 2000), 1–2.
28. Weimann, *Shakespeare and the Popular Tradition*, 78.
29. I am grateful to Peter Kamber at Sondersammlung, Zentral- und Hochschulbibliothek, Luzern, for his assistance with Leibing's reproduction of Cysat's plan. Kamber notes that, in addition to the central inset, Leibing also included numerous other small variations from the original, although the overall plan remains the same.
30. Translations in Peter Meredith and John E. Tailby, eds., *The Staging of Religious Drama in Europe in the Later Middle Ages: Texts and Documents in English Translation* (Kalamazoo, MI: Medieval Institute, 1983), 300. For more on the Lucerne stage plans, see ibid., 283–85; John E. Tailby, "Die Luzerner Passionsspielaufführung des Jahres 1583: zur Deutung der Bühnenpläne Renward Cysats," in *The Theatre in the Middle Ages*, ed. Herman Braet, Johan Nowé, and Gilbert Tournoy (Leuven, Belgium: Leuven University Press, 1985), 352–61; and M. Blakemore Evans, *The Passion Play of Lucerne: An Historical and Critical Introduction* (New York: Modern Language Association of America, 1943).
31. For the Donaueschingen plans, see Chambers, *Mediaeval Stage*, 2:84; and A. M. Nagler, *The Medieval Religious Stage: Shapes and Phantoms*, trans. George C. Schoolfield (New Haven, CT: Yale University Press, 1976), 41. A more detailed discussion of staging may be found in M. Blakemore Evans, "The Staging of the Donaueschingen Passion Play," parts 1 and 2, *Modern Language Review* 15 (1920): 65–76 and 279–97. However, see Joseph A. Dane, *Abstractions of Evidence in the Study of Manuscripts and Early Printed*

Books (Farnham, UK: Ashgate, 2009), 41–49, especially 46–48, for a discussion of potential problems with Chambers's plans, including the one for the Donaueschingen Passion play. The play itself is usually presumed to have been performed around 1485, but the only extant manuscript of it is from the sixteenth century, and Nagler has argued that the plan was actually for the Villingen Passion play, also found in the Donaueschingen library but dating to about 1585 (*Medieval Religious Stage*, 36–47).

32. See David M. Bevington, *Action Is Eloquence: Shakespeare's Language of Gesture* (Cambridge, MA: Harvard University Press, 1984); and George R. Kernodle, *From Art to Theatre: Form and Convention in the Renaissance* (Chicago: University of Chicago Press, 1944), 130–53.
33. The Penguin editor John Kerrigan and the Oxford editor G. R. Hibbard both espouse this view, as does J. L. Styan, who declares that, in eavesdropping scenes, stage pillars would have served for "a mock hiding-place" (*Shakespeare's Stagecraft*, 103).
34. On the staging of soliloquies, see my argument about Weimann's influence in chapter 1. On the development of the "downstage" convention, see Edward A. Langhans, "The Post-1660 Theatres as Performance Spaces," in *A Companion to Restoration Drama*, ed. Susan J. Owen (Oxford: Blackwell, 2001), 3–18. For a useful corrective, see Smith, *Acoustic World*, 213–14, which argues that soliloquies were spoken from the middle of the platform, halfway between the stage pillars—the amphitheatre's most acoustically powerful position.
35. Derek Peat, "Looking Back to Front: The View from the Lords' Room," in *Shakespeare and the Sense of Performance: Essays in the Tradition of Performance Criticism in Honor of Bernard Beckerman*, ed. Marvin Thompson and Ruth Thompson (Newark: University of Delaware Press, 1989), 182, 185.
36. David Wiles, *A Short History of Western Performance Space* (Cambridge: Cambridge University Press, 2003), 165.
37. Ibid., 166.
38. John R. Elliott Jr., "Early Staging in Oxford," in *A New History of Early English Drama*, ed. John D. Cox and David Scott Kastan (New York: Columbia University Press, 1997), 71.
39. Ibid., 74.
40. Translations in David C. Lindberg, *Theories of Vision from Al-Kindi to Kepler* (Chicago: University of Chicago Press, 1976), 149.
41. On linear perspective and theatre, see also Kernodle, *From Art to Theatre*, 176–200.
42. Eric Mercer, *English Art, 1553–1625* (Oxford: Clarendon, 1962), 55.
43. Ibid., 36.
44. Elliott, "Early Staging in Oxford," 74.
45. Grammaticus Musaeus, *The divine poem of Musaeus. First of all bookes*, trans. George Chapman (London, 1616), A3r. On Jones's incorporation of English architectural practices into his classical designs, see Christy Anderson, *Inigo Jones and the Classical Tradition* (Cambridge: Cambridge University Press, 2007).
46. Thomas Overbury, *Sir Thomas Ouerburie his wife with new elegies vpon his (now knowne) vntimely death: whereunto are annexed, new newes and characters* (London, 1616), M2r.
47. Pauline Kiernan, *Staging Shakespeare at the New Globe* (New York: St. Martin's, 1999), 9, 133–34, 138–39.
48. For further examples, see Svetlana Alpers, *The Art of Describing: Dutch Art in the Seventeenth Century* (Chicago: University of Chicago Press, 1983); and Lucy Gent, ed., *Albion's Classicism: The Visual Arts in Britain, 1550–1660* (New Haven, CT: Yale University Press, 1995).

49. Lucy Gent, "'The Rash Gazer': Economies of Vision in Britain, 1550–1660," in Gent, *Albion's Classicism*, 379.
50. Erwin Panofsky, *The Life and Art of Albrecht Dürer*, 4th ed. (Princeton, NJ: Princeton University Press, 1971), 247.
51. Juliet Fleming, *Graffiti and the Writing Arts of Early Modern England* (Philadelphia: University of Pennsylvania Press, 2001).
52. Gent, "'Rash Gazer,'" 382.
53. Ibid.
54. Mercer, *English Art*, 152.
55. Caroline van Eck, ed., *British Architectural Theory, 1540–1750: An Anthology of Texts* (Aldershot, UK: Ashgate, 2003), 53–54.
56. Tessa Watt, *Cheap Print and Popular Piety, 1550–1640* (Cambridge: Cambridge University Press, 1991), 178–253.
57. Mercer, *English Art*, 91–95.
58. See Margreta de Grazia, "World Pictures, Modern Periods, and the Early Stage," in Cox and Kastan, *New History*, 7–21.
59. Smith, *Acoustic World*.
60. Susan Foister, "Sixteenth-Century English Portraiture and the Idea of the Classical," in Gent, *Albion's Classicism*, 171.
61. Translation in Lindberg, *Theories of Vision*, 150.
62. Watt, *Cheap Print*, 131.
63. Carl Horstmann, ed., *Minor Poems of the Vernon Manuscript*, 2 vols. (London: K. Paul, Trench, Trübner, 1892–1919), 1:175, quoted in Leah Sinanoglou, "The Christ Child as Sacrifice: A Medieval Tradition and the Corpus Christi Plays," *Speculum* 48 (1973): 499.
64. Eamon Duffy, *The Stripping of the Altars: Traditional Religion in England, c. 1400–c. 1580*, 2nd ed. (New Haven, CT: Yale University Press, 2005), 100.
65. Ibid., 95–102.
66. Miri Rubin, *Corpus Christi: The Eucharist in Late Medieval Culture* (Cambridge: Cambridge University Press, 1991), 152.
67. Thomas Becon, *The Worckes of Thomas Becon* (London, 1563), part III, fol. 44, quoted in Sinanoglou, "Christ Child," 498.
68. Thomas Cranmer, *The Works of Thomas Cranmer*, ed. John Edmund Cox, 2 vols. (Cambridge, 1844–46), 2:442, quoted in Duffy, *Stripping of the Altars*, 98; Becon, *Worckes*, part III, fol. 44, quoted in Sinanoglou, "Christ Child," 498; and John Foxe, *Actes and Monuments of John Foxe*, ed. Stephen Reed Cattley, 8 vols. (London, 1837–41), 6:361, quoted in Huston Diehl, *Staging Reform, Reforming the Stage: Protestantism and Popular Theatre in Early Modern England* (Ithaca, NY: Cornell University Press, 1997), 100.
69. Gent, "'Rash Gazer,'" 386. See also Robert S. Nelson, "Descartes' Cow and Other Domestications of the Visual," in Nelson, *Visuality*, 1–21.
70. Catherine Wilson, *The Invisible World: Early Modern Philosophy and the Invention of the Microscope* (Princeton, NJ: Princeton University Press, 1995), 20.
71. Katharine Park, "Impressed Images: Reproducing Wonders," in *Picturing Science, Producing Art*, ed. Caroline A. Jones and Peter Galison (New York: Routledge, 1998), 264.
72. Lindberg, *Theories of Vision*, 124–25.
73. Michael O'Connell, *The Idolatrous Eye: Iconoclasm and Theater in Early-Modern England* (New York: Oxford University Press, 2000), 19.
74. Robert Parker, *A scholasticall discourse against symbolizing with Antichrist in ceremonies* (Amsterdam, 1607), X3v, quoted in Diehl, *Staging Reform*, 160.

75. Bob Scribner, "Ways of Seeing in the Age of Dürer," in *Dürer and His Culture*, ed. Dagmar Eichberger and Charles Zika (Cambridge: Cambridge University Press, 1998), 109.
76. Edmund Colledge and James Walsh, ed., *A Book of Showings to the Anchoress Julian of Norwich*, 2 vols. (Toronto: Pontifical Institute of Mediaeval Studies, 1978), 2:447, quoted in Duffy, *Stripping of the Altars*, 161; on saints as friends and neighbors, see Duffy, *Stripping of the Altars*, 160–63.
77. Duffy, *Stripping of the Altars*, 180.
78. Eamon Duffy, "Devotion to the Crucifix and Related Images in England on the Eve of the Reformation," in *Bilder und Bildersturm im Spätmittelalter und in der frühen Neuzeit*, ed. Bob Scribner (Wiesbaden, Germany: Harrassowitz, 1990), 29.
79. Ibid., 26.
80. "A devoute, frutefull, and godly remembraunce of the passion of our Saviour Jesu Christ," in *Three Primers Put Forth in the Reign of Henry VIII*, ed. Edward Burton (Oxford, 1834), 198, quoted in Duffy, "Devotion," 31.
81. Duffy, "Devotion," 30–31.
82. *Records of Early English Drama: Oxford*, ed. John R. Elliott Jr. et al. (Toronto: University of Toronto Press, 2004), 1:387. On tragic affect and pity, see Marissa Greenberg, "The Tyranny of Tragedy: Catharsis in England and *The Roman Actor*," *Renaissance Drama* 39 (2011): 163–96.
83. Robert Tofte, *Alba The months minde of a melancholy louer, diuided into three parts* (London, 1598), G5r.
84. On treason, see Rebecca Lemon, *Treason by Words: Literature, Law, and Rebellion in Shakespeare's England* (Ithaca, NY: Cornell University Press, 2006); Peter Lake and Michael Questier, "Agency, Appropriation and Rhetoric Under the Gallows: Puritans, Romanists and the State in Early Modern England," *Past and Present* 153 (1996): 64–107; and John H. Langbein, *Torture and the Law of Proof: Europe and England in the Ancien Régime* (Chicago: University of Chicago Press, 1977).
85. The notion that the Clown and Jaquenetta are the only "true" folks in the play can also be seen in act 1, scene 1. Truth is associated with the lords' vows at the very beginning of the scene, when Berowne jokingly posits that "hauing sworne too hard a keeping oath," he will "[s]tudie to breake it, and not breake my troth" (TLN 70–71; 1.1.65–66). This wordplay returns at the end of the scene, when the Clown's breach of the recent proclamation is discovered. He declares, "I suffer for the truth sir: for true it is, I was taken with *Iaquenetta*, and *Iaquenetta* is a true girle" (TLN 306–7; 1.1.311–12).
86. Christopher Marsh, *Popular Religion in Sixteenth-Century England: Holding Their Peace* (New York: St. Martin's, 1998), 11. See also Diehl, *Staging Reform*, 96.
87. John Calvin, *Institutes of the Christian Religion*, trans. Ford Lewis Battles, ed. John T. McNeill, 2 vols. (Philadelphia: Westminster, 1960), 4.17.14, quoted in Diehl, *Staging Reform*, 106–7.
88. Diehl, *Staging Reform*, 102–9.
89. Calvin, *Institutes*, 4.17.10, quoted in Diehl, *Staging Reform*, 108.
90. On consubstantiation, see Anthony B. Dawson and Paul Yachnin, *The Culture of Playgoing in Shakespeare's England: A Collaborative Debate* (Cambridge: Cambridge University Press, 2001), 26.
91. "Mankind," in *Medieval Drama*, ed. David Bevington (Boston: Houghton Mifflin, 1975), 901–38. On speech acts producing discontinuous subjectivity in morality plays, see Catherine Belsey, *The Subject of Tragedy: Identity and Difference in Renaissance Drama* (London: Methuen, 1985), 18–32.
92. Duffy, *Stripping of the Altars*, 102.
93. "The Croxton Play of the Sacrament," in *Medieval Drama: An Anthology*, ed. Greg Walker (Oxford: Blackwell, 2000), 212–33.

94. Heribert Rosweyde, *Vitae Patrum* (Antwerp, 1615; repr., 1628), as quoted in Sinanoglou, "Christ Child," 491–92.
95. Dessen, *Recovering Shakespeare's Theatrical Vocabulary*, 49–55.
96. *OED Online*, 2nd ed., s.v. "aside, *adv., prep., adj.,* and *n.*" (def. D1), published online December 2011, http://www.oed.com/view/Entry/11484.
97. On the exposure of criminals by an omniscient God, see Alexandra Walsham, *Providence in Early Modern England* (Oxford: Oxford University Press, 1999).
98. See Dessen and Thomson, *Dictionary of Stage Directions*, 128. For discussion of theatrical conventions related to darkness and light, see also R. B. Graves, "*The Duchess of Malfi* at the Globe and Blackfriars," *Renaissance Drama* 9 (1978): 193–209; and R. B. Graves, *Lighting the Shakespearean Stage, 1567–1642* (Carbondale: Southern Illinois University Press, 1999).
99. Quoted in Dessen and Thomson, *Dictionary of Stage Directions*, 121. See also my chapter 4 on the term *vanish*.
100. Dessen, *Recovering Shakespeare's Theatrical Vocabulary*, 45–46.
101. Foakes, *Henslowe's Diary*, 325.
102. Barbara D. Palmer, "Staging Invisibility in English Early Modern Drama," *Early Theatre* 11, no. 2 (2008): 124.
103. Dessen and Thomson, *Dictionary of Stage Directions*, 149.
104. *OED Online*, 3rd ed. (2003), s.v. "net, *n.*1" (def. 2b), published online December 2011, http://www.oed.com/view/Entry/126280.
105. Philip Stubbes, *The anatomie of abuses contayning a discouerie, or briefe summarie of such notable vices and imperfections, as now raigne in many Christian countreyes of the worlde: but (especiallie) in a verie famous ilande called Ailgna...* (London, 1583), M5r.
106. John Hind, *Eliosto libidinoso described in two bookes: vvherein their imminent dangers are declared, who guiding the course of their life by the compasse of affection, either dash their ship against most dangerous shelues, or else attaine the hauen with extreame preiudice* (London, 1606), L1v.
107. Thomas Kyd, *The Spanish Tragedie Containing the lamentable end of Don Horatio, and Bel-imperia: with the pittifull death of olde Hieronimo* (London, 1592), K4v; Thomas Kyd, *The Spanish Tragedy*, ed. David Bevington (Manchester: Manchester University Press, 1996), 4.4.118.
108. John Heywood, *A play of loue a newe and a mery enterlude concernyng pleasure and payne in loue...* ([London], 1534), C1v.
109. Alan C. Dessen, *Elizabethan Stage Conventions and Modern Interpreters* (Cambridge: Cambridge University Press, 1984), 53.
110. Watt, *Cheap Print*, 138, 161.
111. Line 1520; quoted in Dessen, *Elizabethan Stage Conventions*, 141.
112. Ibid., 141–42.
113. Ibid., 142.
114. Ibid., 142–43.

3   Imaginary Forces: Allegory, Mimesis, and Audience Interpretation in *The Spanish Tragedy*

1. Quoted in Alan C. Dessen, *Elizabethan Stage Conventions and Modern Interpreters* (Cambridge: Cambridge University Press, 1984), 59.
2. R. A. Foakes, ed., *Henslowe's Diary*, 2nd ed. (Cambridge: Cambridge University Press, 2002), 317, 319.

3. I use *mimesis* to refer to dramatic representation that privileges verisimilitude—a limited and specific use of a term with a rich and diverse history. Other philosophical applications and meanings are summarized in Jonathan Holmes and Adrian Streete, eds., introduction to *Refiguring Mimesis: Representation in Early Modern Literature* (Hatfield, UK: University of Hertfordshire Press, 2005), 1–13. Modern usage is undeniably influenced by Erich Auerbach, *Mimesis: The Representation of Reality in Western Literature*, trans. Willard R. Trask (Princeton, NJ: Princeton University Press, 1953). See also Seth Lerer, ed., *Literary History and the Challenge of Philology: The Legacy of Erich Auerbach* (Stanford, CA: Stanford University Press, 1996).
4. Although thoroughly refuted in O. B. Hardison Jr., *Christian Rite and Christian Drama in the Middle Ages: Essays in the Origin and Early History of Modern Drama* (Baltimore: Johns Hopkins University Press, 1965), this teleological historical narrative is still widely influential.
5. Roslyn Lander Knutson, *The Repertory of Shakespeare's Company, 1594–1613* (Fayetteville: University of Arkansas Press, 1991), 42.
6. On allegory's continuing impact in later centuries, see Jane K. Brown, *The Persistence of Allegory: Drama and Neoclassicism from Shakespeare to Wagner* (Philadelphia: University of Pennsylvania Press, 2007).
7. Frederick Kiefer, *Shakespeare's Visual Theatre: Staging the Personified Characters* (Cambridge: Cambridge University Press, 2003), 43.
8. James L. Calderwood, *To Be and Not to Be: Negation and Metadrama in "Hamlet"* (New York: Columbia University Press, 1983), 30.
9. Bob Scribner, "Ways of Seeing in the Age of Dürer," in *Dürer and His Culture*, ed. Dagmar Eichberger and Charles Zika (Cambridge: Cambridge University Press, 1998), 99.
10. Eamon Duffy, "Devotion to the Crucifix and Related Images in England on the Eve of the Reformation," in *Bilder und Bildersturm im Spätmittelalter und in der frühen Neuzeit*, ed. Bob Scribner (Wiesbaden, Germany: Harrassowitz, 1990), 26.
11. On affective piety and visual devotion, see chapter 2; here I summarize only key points related to my current discussion. On the cult of images, see Hans Belting, *Likeness and Presence: A History of the Image before the Era of Art*, trans. Edmund Jephcott (Chicago: University of Chicago Press, 1994).
12. Scribner, "Ways of Seeing," 117.
13. Quoted in Eamon Duffy, *The Stripping of the Altars: Traditional Religion in England, c. 1400–c. 1580,* 2nd ed. (New Haven, CT: Yale University Press, 2005), 101–2.
14. Richard Brathwaite, *Essaies vpon the fiue senses with a pithie one vpon detraction. Continued vvith sundry Christian resolues...* (London, 1620), A8v.
15. Stephen Egerton, *The boring of the eare contayning a plaine and profitable discourse by way of dialogue: concerning 1. Our preparation before hearing, 2. Our demeanour in hearing, 3. Our exercise after we haue heard the Word of God* (London, 1623), A7r.
16. Brathwaite, *Essaies vpon the fiue senses*, A4r.
17. Gail Kern Paster, "Nervous Tension," in *The Body in Parts: Fantasies of Corporeality in Early Modern Europe,* ed. David Hillman and Carla Mazzio (New York: Routledge, 1997), 111; and Michael Schoenfeldt, *Bodies and Selves in Early Modern England: Physiology and Inwardness in Spenser, Shakespeare, Herbert, and Milton* (Cambridge: Cambridge University Press, 1999), 8.
18. Thomas Kyd, *The Spanish Tragedie Containing the lamentable end of Don Horatio, and Bel-imperia: with the pittifull death of olde Hieronimo* (London, 1592), A3r; Thomas Kyd, *The Spanish Tragedy*, ed. David Bevington (Manchester: Manchester University Press,

1996), 1.1.81–91. Bevington's text is based on Philip Edwards's 1959 scholarly Revels Plays edition. Perhaps because of the 1592 quarto's omitted "n" in "Horn," the 1599 edition refers to the gates of "Horror" (A3r), and this reading is reproduced in subsequent early editions. The compositor's emendation accords with the fact that the speaker is a ghost and thus associated with fear and dread in early modern popular discourse.

19. In Book 19 of George Chapman's translation of *The Odyssey*, for example, Penelope refers to the "two parts of Dreames" as

> Two two-leau'd gates; the one of Iuory;
> The other, Horne. Those dreames that *Fantasie*
> Takes from the polisht Iuory Port, delude
> The Dreamer euer, and no truth include:
> Those that the glittering Horn-gate, lets abrode,
> Do euermore, some certaine truth abode.

Edward Sherburne's translation of "The Rape of Hellen" likewise refers to

> Of Dreams the two Gates...: this of Horn,
> In which the Gods unerring Truths are born.
> T'other of Ivory: whence couzening Lies,
> And vain Delusions of false Dreams arise.

George Chapman, trans., *The whole works of Homer; prince of poetts in his Iliads, and Odysses* (London, 1616), Dd2r; and Edward Sherburne, trans., "The Rape of Hellen," in *Poems and translations amorous, lusory, morall, divine* (London, 1651), D5v.

20. William N. West, "'But this will be a mere confusion': Real and Represented Confusions on the Elizabethan Stage," *Theatre Journal* 60 (2008): 228–29. Of extensive work on revenge tragedy conventions, see especially Fredson Bowers, *Elizabethan Revenge Tragedy, 1587–1642* (Princeton, NJ: Princeton University Press, 1940); and the recent overview in Tanya Pollard, "Tragedy and Revenge," in *The Cambridge Companion to English Renaissance Tragedy*, ed. Emma Smith and Garrett A. Sullivan Jr. (New York: Cambridge University Press, 2010), 58–72.

21. Kiefer, *Shakespeare's Visual Theatre*, 47. The allegorical figure of Justice also falls asleep in the 1599 *A Warning for Fair Women* (240n62).

22. Intermissions between acts did not spread to the amphitheatres until after 1607. Andrew Gurr, *The Shakespearean Stage, 1574–1642*, 3rd ed. (Cambridge: Cambridge University Press, 1992), 177.

23. Thomas Hill, *A most briefe and pleasant treatise of the interpretation of sundrie dreames intituled to be Iosephs, and sundry other dreames out of the worke of the wise Salomon...* (London, 1601), B1r, B6r.

24. Daldianus Artemidorus, *The iudgement, or exposition of dreames, written by Artimodorus, an auntient and famous author, first in Greeke, then translated into Latin, after into French, and now into English* (London, 1606), E1r.

25. Angus Fletcher, *Allegory: The Theory of a Symbolic Mode* (Ithaca, NY: Cornell University Press, 1964), 7.

26. Ibid., 2–3. In *Allegory and Violence,* Gordon Teskey remarks that critical approaches to allegory may be divided into two camps, one analyzing it as a mode, another as a genre, with Fletcher as the primary example of the former and Maureen Quilligan of the latter. Those who treat allegory as a mode, he suggests, contend that allegory is "a means of encoding any discourse whatever" (10); those who consider it a genre argue that it is "an altogether separate category of discourse" through which "ideological structures, determined more or less in advance, are inserted into narratives by

adventitious encoding in such a way that those narratives become formally distinct from all others" (ibid.). Because my interests lie in theatrical signifiers and the cultural discourses that contributed to performance practices, my own methodology focuses on allegory as a mode and is thus aligned more closely with the view Teskey ascribes to Fletcher. However, I find persuasive Quilligan's emphasis on the way allegory as a genre responds to, constructs, and reproduces broader social formations. In this sense, her account of allegory squares with my own, since both are interested in the way literary form is constituted through the cultural discourses embedded within it. My work thus differs from Quilligan's not so much in our views of the connections between form and history but rather in the focus of our studies: I emphasize what Quilligan refers to as "allegorical modalities," whereas she centers her discussion on that "pure strain" of allegory "among all the multitudinous works displaying allegorical modalities... that is, a group of works which reveal the classic form of a distinct genre" (*Language of Allegory*, 14–15). Gordon Teskey, *Allegory and Violence* (Ithaca, NY: Cornell University Press, 1996); and Maureen Quilligan, *The Language of Allegory: Defining the Genre* (Ithaca, NY: Cornell University Press, 1979). See also Maureen Quilligan, *The Allegory of Female Authority: Christine de Pizan's "Cité des dames"* (Ithaca, NY: Cornell University Press, 1991); and Quilligan, "Freedom, Service, and the Trade in Slaves: The Problem of Labor in *Paradise Lost*," in *Subject and Object in Renaissance Culture*, ed. Margreta de Grazia, Maureen Quilligan, and Peter Stallybrass (Cambridge: Cambridge University Press, 1996), 213–34. For additional views, see Stephen Greenblatt, ed., *Allegory and Representation* (Baltimore: Johns Hopkins University Press, 1981).

27. Ben Jonson, *The alchemist* (London, 1612), E2r; Ben Jonson, *The Alchemist*, ed. Alvin B. Kernan (New Haven, CT: Yale University Press, 1974), 2.3.203–7.
28. Thomas Elyot, *The dictionary of syr Thomas Eliot knyght* (London, 1538), A6r.
29. Fletcher, *Allegory*, 2n1.
30. Artemidorus, *Exposition of dreames*, B4r.
31. Ibid., A7r–A7v.
32. Ibid., A7v.
33. Gonzalo, *The divine dreamer: or, a short treatise discovering the true effect and power of dreames...* ([London], 1641), C3v.
34. *Oxford English Dictionary (OED) Online*, 3rd ed. (2008), s.v. "bad, adj., n.2, and adv." (defs. AI1a, AII7, AII9, AIII10), published online December 2011, http://www.oed.com/view/Entry/14540.
35. *OED Online*, 2nd ed. (1989), s.v. "evil, adj. and n.1" (defs. AI1, AI4, AII7a, AII7b), published online December 2011, http://www.oed.com/view/Entry/65386.
36. On the interplay between the bodily and the religious, see also Steven F. Kruger, *Dreaming in the Middle Ages* (Cambridge: Cambridge University Press, 1992), who argues that even as Aristotelian and Arabic understandings of the physical origins of dreams circulated widely, traditional Christian beliefs could not be entirely displaced.
37. Hill, *Interpretation of sundrie dreames*, A5r–A5v.
38. Ibid., A4v.
39. Artemidorus, *Exposition of dreames*, B1r–B1v.
40. Carole Levin, *Dreaming the English Renaissance: Politics and Desire in Court and Culture* (New York: Palgrave Macmillan, 2008), 27–31.
41. Thomas Wright, *The passions of the minde* (London, 1601), 111 [H8r]. See also Karl H. Dannenfeldt, "Sleep: Theory and Practice in the Late Renaissance," *Journal of the History of Medicine and Allied Sciences* 41 (1986): 431–32.
42. Stuart Clark, *Vanities of the Eye: Vision in Early Modern European Culture* (Oxford: Oxford University Press, 2007), 304. See also Levin, *Dreaming the English Renaissance*,

72–86; Keith Thomas, *Religion and the Decline of Magic: Studies in Popular Beliefs in Sixteenth- and Seventeenth-Century England* (London: Weidenfeld & Nicolson, 1971; repr., London: Penguin, 1973), 151; and Michelle O'Callaghan, "Dreaming the Dead: Ghosts and History in the Early Seventeenth Century," in *Reading the Early Modern Dream: The Terrors of the Night,* ed. Katharine Hodgkin, Michelle O'Callaghan, and Susan Wiseman (New York: Routledge, 2008), 81–95.

43. Jackson I. Cope, *The Theater and the Dream: From Metaphor to Form in Renaissance Drama* (Baltimore: Johns Hopkins University Press, 1973), 8.
44. David Bevington, "Asleep Onstage," in *From Page to Performance: Essays in Early English Drama,* ed. John A. Alford (East Lansing: Michigan State University Press, 1995), 53.
45. Ibid., 68.
46. Lionel Abel, *Metatheatre: A New View of Dramatic Form* (New York: Hill and Wang, 1963), 79; emphasis in original.
47. For typical readings of metatheatricality, see, for example, Calderwood, *To Be and Not to Be*; François Laroque, ed., *The Show Within: Dramatic and Other Insets: English Renaissance Drama (1550–1642),* 2 vols. (Montpellier: Université Paul-Valéry, 1992); Howard Felperin, *Shakespearean Representation: Mimesis and Modernity in Elizabethan Tragedy* (Princeton, NJ: Princeton University Press, 1977); and Anne Righter [Barton], *Shakespeare and the Idea of the Play* (London: Chatto and Windus, 1962).
48. *OED Online,* 3rd ed. (2005), s.vv. "phantom, *n.* and *adj.,*" "phantasm, *n.* and *adj.,*" "fantasy | phantasy, *n.,*" published online December 2011, http://www.oed.com/view/Entry/142204, http://www.oed.com/view/Entry/142182, and http://www.oed.com/view/Entry/68119. "Fantasie" is precisely the term Chapman uses to refer to the gates of ivory in his translation of Homer, discussed earlier.
49. Francis Kinnaston, *Leoline and Sydanis a romance of the amorous adventures of princes: together with sundry affectionate addresses to his mistresse, under the name of Cynthia* (London, 1642), N4r [stanza 376].
50. Clark, *Vanities of the Eye,* 213–14, 248. See also Michael Cole, "The Demonic Arts and the Origin of the Medium," *Art Bulletin* 84 (2002): 621–40.
51. See Thomas, *Religion and the Decline of Magic,* 716–17, for examples extending to the late seventeenth century. On Purgatory, see Peter Marshall, *Beliefs and the Dead in Reformation England* (Oxford: Oxford University Press, 2002), 232–64; Thomas, *Religion and the Decline of Magic,* 701–24; and Clark, *Vanities of the Eye,* 206–35.
52. See Clark, *Vanities of the Eye;* and Clark, *Thinking with Demons: The Idea of Witchcraft in Early Modern Europe* (Oxford: Clarendon, 1997), 167–72.
53. John Deacon and John Walker, *Dialogicall discourses of spirits and divels declaring their proper essence, natures, dispositions, and operations...* (London, 1601), a4r (gathering between A8v and B1r).
54. Pierre le Loyer, *A treatise of specters or straunge sights, visions and apparitions appearing sensibly vnto men...,* trans. Zachary Jones (London, 1605), F4v–G1r.
55. Kristen Poole, "The Devil's in the Archive: *Doctor Faustus* and Ovidian Physics," *Renaissance Drama* 35 (2006): 192–96.
56. Thomas Nash, *The terrors of the night or, A discourse of apparitions* (London, 1594), B2v–B3r.
57. Jonas Barish, *The Antitheatrical Prejudice* (Berkeley: University of California Press, 1981), 96–106.
58. Marissa Greenberg, "The Tyranny of Tragedy: Catharsis in England and *The Roman Actor,*" *Renaissance Drama* 39 (2011): 163–96.

59. John D. Cox, *The Devil and the Sacred in English Drama, 1350–1642* (Cambridge: Cambridge University Press, 2000), 194.
60. Lukas Erne, *Beyond "The Spanish Tragedy": A Study of the Works of Thomas Kyd* (Manchester: Manchester University Press, 2001), 16–20.
61. Knutson, *Repertory*, 33; and Foakes, *Henslowe's Diary*, 16–20. Erne, accidentally omitting a showing on March 31, notes only three paired performances (*Beyond "The Spanish Tragedy,"* 14–15).
62. Knutson, *Repertory*, 33.
63. Erne agrees, arguing that the play was a serial but "understandable without the first part" (*Beyond "The Spanish Tragedy,"* 35).
64. Anne Lancashire, ed., *The Second Maiden's Tragedy* (Manchester: Manchester University Press, 1978), 5.2.152.s.d. On costuming ghosts, see also Alan C. Dessen and Leslie Thomson, *A Dictionary of Stage Directions in English Drama, 1580–1642* (Cambridge: Cambridge University Press, 1999), 100.
65. Ann Rosalind Jones and Peter Stallybrass, *Renaissance Clothing and the Materials of Memory* (Cambridge: Cambridge University Press, 2000), 245–56.
66. The phrase "portentous figure" appears only in Q2 (indeed, Barnardo's speech in which it appears is altogether omitted in the other editions), but the rest of the terms appear in all three editions: Q1 (1603), Q2 (1604), and F (1623).
67. Lines 110–11 appear in Q2 only.
68. For the last of these, F reads "euents wicked or charitable" for Q1 and Q2's "intents wicked or charitable."
69. On demonic manipulation of the bodily humors (and, thus, visual perception and the imagination), see Clark, *Vanities of the Eye*, 244, 318.
70. Erne, *Beyond "The Spanish Tragedy,"* 53.
71. Kiefer, *Shakespeare's Visual Theatre*, 46–47.
72. Ibid., 50.
73. R. B. Graves, *Lighting the Shakespearean Stage, 1567–1642* (Carbondale: Southern Illinois University Press, 1999), 19–20.
74. Le Loyer, *Treatise of specters*, E2v–E3r.
75. Kiefer, *Shakespeare's Visual Theatre*, 47.
76. On revenge and daggers, see Kiefer, *Shakespeare's Visual Theatre*, 50. On daggers and murder, see James I, *By the King, a proclamation against steelets, pocket daggers, pocket dagges and pistols* (London, 1616). On the Vice's dagger of lath as juxtaposed with God's sword of just vengeance, see Alan C. Dessen, *Elizabethan Drama and the Viewer's Eye* (Chapel Hill: University of North Carolina Press, 1977), 36–42.
77. On Kyd's Senecan influences, see Erne, *Beyond "The Spanish Tragedy,"* 79–84; and Carla Mazzio, *The Inarticulate Renaissance: Language Trouble in an Age of Eloquence* (Philadelphia: University of Pennsylvania Press, 2009), 126–36. On the integration of classical and morality traditions, see Bruce R. Smith, *Ancient Scripts & Modern Experience on the English Stage, 1500–1700* (Princeton, NJ: Princeton University Press, 1988), 199–248.
78. Smith, *Ancient Scripts*, 222–24.
79. Such blocking would be similar to that of the ghost in *Hamlet*. On Andrea's stage location, see Michael Hattaway, *Elizabethan Popular Theatre: Plays in Performance* (London: Routledge & Kegan Paul, 1982), 115. See also David Willbern, "Rape and Revenge in *Titus Andronicus*," *English Literary Renaissance* 8 (1978): 177, which cites Richard Hosley's suggestion that Tamora, disguised as Revenge, may have entered from the stage trap.
80. Kiefer, *Shakespeare's Visual Theatre*, 50.

81. Ibid., 237n20.
82. Mazzio, *Inarticulate Renaissance*, 110; Janette Dillon, *Language and Stage in Medieval and Renaissance England* (Cambridge: Cambridge University Press, 1998), 186–87; and West, "Real and Represented Confusions," 229–32.
83. On the complex publication history of Peirce's work, see Robert Burch, "Charles Sanders Peirce," in *The Stanford Encyclopedia of Philosophy*, ed. Edward N. Zalta, published online 2010, http://plato.stanford.edu/archives/fall2010/entries/peirce/. See also W. J. T. Mitchell, *Iconology: Image, Text, Ideology* (Chicago: University of Chicago Press, 1986), 25–31.
84. For a complementary analysis, see West, "Real and Represented Confusions," which argues that *The Spanish Tragedy* posits "a theory of theatre as correctable or accidental confusion, and then critiques that theory through its own practices, which set confusion at the center of theatre's performative effectiveness" (225). See also Mazzio, *Inarticulate Renaissance*, 136–39.
85. On the theological and political implications of Babel/Babylon in Kyd's play, see S. F. Johnson, "*The Spanish Tragedy*, or Babylon Revisited," in *Essays on Shakespeare and Elizabethan Drama in Honor of Hardin Craig*, ed. Richard Hosley (Columbia: University of Missouri Press, 1962), 23–36; and Frank Ardolino, "'Now Shall I See the Fall of Babylon': *The Spanish Tragedy* as Protestant Apocalypse," *Shakespeare Yearbook* 1 (1990): 93–115.
86. William Crashawe, *The sermon preached at the Crosse, Feb. xiiii. 1607... that the religion of Rome, as now it stands established, is still as bad as euer it was* (London, 1609), 169 [Z1r].
87. Brathwaite, *Essaies vpon the fiue senses*, B6r–B6v.
88. J[ohn] B[ulwer], *Chirologia, or, The naturall language of the hand composed of the speaking motions, and discoursing gestures thereof: whereunto is added Chironomia, or, The art of manuall rhetoricke ....* (London, 1644). On Bulwer and acting practices, see B. L. Joseph, *Elizabethan Acting*, 2nd ed. (London: Oxford University Press, 1964); and Joseph Roach, *The Player's Passion: Studies in the Science of Acting* (Ann Arbor: University of Michigan Press, 1993), 23–57.
89. See Jonathan Goldberg, *Writing Matter: From the Hands of the English Renaissance* (Stanford, CA: Stanford University Press, 1990), 173–229, for other examples of the kinds of dynamics found in Bulwer's text.
90. J[ohn] B[ulwer], *Philocophus: or, The deafe and dumbe mans friend. Exhibiting the philosophicall verity of that subtile art, which may inable one with an observant eie, to heare what any man speaks by the moving of his lips. Upon the same ground, with the advantage of an historicall exemplification, apparently proving, that a man borne deafe and dumbe, may be taught to heare the sound of words with his eie, & thence learne to speake with his tongue* (London, 1648), D1v.
91. Ibid., B8v.
92. David Browne, *The new invention, intituled, calligraphia: or, the arte of faire writing vvherein is comprehended the whole necessarie rules thereof...* (Saint Andrews, Scotland, 1622), ¶¶¶¶1v–¶¶¶¶2r.
93. Bulwer, *Philocophus*, H8v.
94. Ibid., H9r.
95. Ibid., H9v.
96. Ibid.
97. Bevington, *Spanish Tragedy*, 4.4.10.2–4n.
98. J. R. Mulryne, ed., *The Spanish Tragedy*, 2nd ed., The New Mermaids (London: A&C Black, 1989; repr., New York: Norton, 2000), 4.1.172n.

99. Dillon, *Language and Stage,* 185.
100. Mazzio, *Inarticulate Renaissance,* 102.
101. West, "Real and Represented Confusions," 228.
102. Short conglomerations of classical sayings in Latin appear at 1.3.15–17, 2.2.107, 3.11.102–3, 3.13.1, 3.13.6, and 3.13.35 in the 1592 edition and at line 47 in the fifth addition to the 1602 quarto. A few lines of Italian are included without translation at 2.1.41 and 3.15.168–69 and some apparently corrupt French at 3.2.94.
103. Modern editions, by contrast, often use italics for this episode. The King and the Viceroy's comments as onstage spectators are thus isolated visually in the printed text, and the representational frames are clearly distinguished from one another. The 1592 quarto also sets most stage directions in roman; speech prefixes and proper names in the dialogue are italicized.
104. Dillon, *Language and Stage,* 166–67; emphasis in original.
105. Mazzio, *Inarticulate Renaissance,* 102; and West, "Real and Represented Confusions," 228.
106. Thomas Wilson, *A Christian dictionarie Opening the signification of the chiefe words dispersed generally through Holy Scriptures*... (London, 1612), B4v.
107. Richard Mulcaster, *The First Part of the Elementarie* (London, 1582), quoted in Carla Mazzio, "Staging the Vernacular: Language and Nation in Thomas Kyd's *The Spanish Tragedy*," *Studies in English Literature, 1500–1900* 38 (1998): 208. Mazzio's article offers a useful discussion of tensions over linguistic hybridity in early modern England.
108. Ibid., 208.

4   Dancing and Other Delights: Spectacle and Participation in *Doctor Faustus* and *Macbeth*

1. *Malone Society Collections VI,* ed. David Cook and F. P. Wilson (Oxford: Oxford University Press, 1961 [1962]), 25, 27, quoted in Philip Butterworth, *Magic on the Early English Stage* (Cambridge: Cambridge University Press, 2005), 33.
2. Butterworth, *Magic on the Early English Stage,* 33.
3. Ibid., 26–30. *Oxford English Dictionary (OED) Online,* 3rd ed. (2010), s.v. "rope-dancing, n.," published online December 2011, http://www.oed.com/view/Entry/167413.
4. On references to the words *dance* and *fight* in stage directions, see Alan C. Dessen and Leslie Thomson, *A Dictionary of Stage Directions in English Drama, 1580–1642* (Cambridge: Cambridge University Press, 1999), 64, 91.
5. On the politics of spectacle, see Bertolt Brecht, *Brecht on Theatre: The Development of an Aesthetic,* ed. and trans. John Willett (New York: Hill and Wang, 1964); Walter Benjamin, "The Work of Art in an Era of Mechanical Reproduction," in *Illuminations,* ed. Hannah Arendt, trans. Harry Zohn (New York: Schocken, 1969), 217–51; and Walter Benjamin, *Understanding Brecht,* trans. Anna Bostock (London: NLB, 1973); Guy Debord, *The Society of the Spectacle* (1967; repr., New York: Zone Books, 1994). More recent discussions include Jonathan Crary, "Spectacle, Attention, Counter-Memory," *October* 50 (1989): 96–107; Susan Buck-Morss, "Aesthetics and Anaesthetics: Walter Benjamin's Artwork Essay Reconsidered," *October* 62 (1992): 3–41; Buck-Morss, *The Dialectics of Seeing: Walter Benjamin and the Arcades Project* (Cambridge, MA: MIT Press, 1989), 253–86; and Eugene Lunn, *Marxism and Modernism: An Historical Study*

of *Lukács, Brecht, Benjamin, and Adorno* (Berkeley: University of California Press, 1982), 33–71. I discuss Brecht's views on spectacle in more detail at the end of this chapter.
6. At performance events today, though spectators are indeed absolutely crucial to the show and in many cases the line between spectator and participant is blurred, viewers are discursively constructed as ontologically separate from the action they behold. On sanctioned forms of participatory spectatorship in the twentieth and twenty-first centuries, see Dennis Kennedy, *The Spectator and the Spectacle: Audiences in Modernity and Postmodernity* (Cambridge: Cambridge University Press, 2009), especially 153–88.
7. See, for example, Gail Kern Paster, Katherine Rowe, and Mary Floyd-Wilson, eds., introduction to *Reading the Early Modern Passions: Essays in the Cultural History of Emotion* (Philadelphia: University of Pennsylvania Press, 2004), 1–20.
8. On this phenomenological condition of theatre, see David Z. Saltz, "How to Do Things on Stage," *Journal of Aesthetics and Art Criticism* 49 (1991): 31–45.
9. Jean Alter, *A Sociosemiotic Theory of Theatre* (Philadelphia: University of Pennsylvania Press, 1990).
10. Stage combat did, however, overlap with dance in that both involved choreographed movement and both could function as festive observance. On festive combat, see Erika T. Lin, "Popular Festivity and the Early Modern Stage: The Case of *George a Greene*," *Theatre Journal* 61 (2009): 285–91. On the cultural valences of fighting, see Gregory M. Colón Semenza, *Sport, Politics, and Literature in the English Renaissance* (Newark: University of Delaware Press, 2003); Jennifer A. Low, *Manhood and the Duel: Masculinity in Early Modern Drama and Culture* (New York: Palgrave Macmillan, 2003); and Charles Edelman, *Brawl Ridiculous: Swordfighting in Shakespeare's Plays* (Manchester: Manchester University Press, 1992).
11. Alter, *Sociosemiotic Theory*, 52–60.
12. See Jonathan Gil Harris and Natasha Korda, eds., *Staged Properties in Early Modern English Drama* (Cambridge: Cambridge University Press, 2002), especially Jonathan Gil Harris, "Properties of Skill: Product Placement in Early English Artisanal Drama," 35–66, and Juana Green, "Properties of Marriage: Proprietary Conflict and the Calculus of Gender in *Epicoene*," 261–87; Ann Rosalind Jones and Peter Stallybrass, *Renaissance Clothing and the Materials of Memory* (Cambridge: Cambridge University Press, 2000); Elizabeth Williamson, *The Materiality of Religion in Early Modern English Drama* (Farnham, UK: Ashgate, 2009); and Anthony B. Dawson and Paul Yachnin, *The Culture of Playgoing in Shakespeare's England: A Collaborative Debate* (Cambridge: Cambridge University Press, 2001), 38–66, 111–30.
13. R[ichard] V[ennar], *An apology* (London, 1614), B6r, quoted in Andrew Gurr, *Playgoing in Shakespeare's London*, 3rd ed. (Cambridge: Cambridge University Press, 2004), 243.
14. John Florio, *Florio his firste fruites which yeelde familiar speech, merie prouerbes, wittie sentences, and golden sayings...* ([London], 1578), A1r. The "Bull" to which Florio refers is the Red Bull Theatre, a venue famous for jigs and spectacles.
15. William Kemp, *Kemps nine daies vvonder Performed in a daunce from London to Norwich...* (London, 1600). On the clown's dance, see John Forrest, *The History of Morris Dancing, 1458–1750* (Toronto: University of Toronto Press, 1999), 236–41; and Max W. Thomas, "*Kemps Nine Daies Wonder:* Dancing Carnival into Market," *PMLA* 107 (1992): 511–23. On differences between Kemp and Armin and their stage roles, see David Wiles, *Shakespeare's Clown: Actor and Text in the Elizabethan Playhouse* (Cambridge: Cambridge University Press, 1987), 136–63.
16. Matthew Steggle, *Laughing and Weeping in Early Modern Theatres* (Aldershot, UK: Ashgate, 2007), 69–80. On leaping and movement, see Joseph Hall, *Virgidemiarum*

sixe bookes. First three bookes, of tooth-lesse satyrs. 1. Poeticall. 2. Academicall. 3. Morall (London, 1597), B5v, discussed in a different context by Steggle, *Laughing and Weeping*, 70.
17. Steggle, *Laughing and Weeping*, 77.
18. Roslyn Lander Knutson, *The Repertory of Shakespeare's Company, 1594–1613* (Fayetteville: University of Arkansas Press, 1991), 41. Knutson observes, "Nearly half of the twenty-seven plays offered by Strange's men in 1592–93 were some kind of comedy (or seem to have been one from the title). Of the fifty-two new plays that the Admiral's men brought into production from June 1594 to July 1597, at least thirty-three were comedies (or seem to have been)" (41). Although she notes that "[t]he percentage of comedies appears to drop slightly in the repertories in the diary after 1597," they still composed the lion's share of the plays in production. "In 1599–1600, for example, the Admiral's men made payments on thirty-six projects. At least seventeen of these appear to have been comedies" (ibid.).
19. Stephen Gosson, *Playes confuted in fiue actions prouing that they are not to be suffred in a Christian common weale…* (London, 1582), F6r.
20. Gurr, *Playgoing*, 309n10.
21. Stephen Gosson, *The trumpet of vvarre A sermon preached at Paules Crosse the seuenth of Maie 1598* (London, 1598), C7v.
22. The Prologue to *Every Man in his Humour*, for example, states that theatregoers

>will be pleas'd to see
>One such, to day as other playes should be;
>Where neither *Chorus* wafts you ore the seas;
>Nor creaking throne comes downe, the boyes to please;
>Nor nimble squibbe is seene, to make afear'd
>The gentlewomen.

Ben Jonson, "Every Man in his Humour," in *The workes of Beniamin Ionson* (London, 1616), A3r. In describing what he does not want his play to be, Jonson ironically leaves us evidence of the descent machinery and firecrackers that spectators often sought.
23. W. B., commendatory verses to Philip Massinger, *The bond-man an antient storie. As it hath been often acted with good allowance, at the Cock-pit in Drury-lane: by the most excellent princesse, the Lady Elizabeth her Seruants* (London, 1624), A4r.
24. William Davenant, *The vnfortvnate lovers a tragedie: as it was lately acted with great applause at the private house in Black-Fryers by His Majesties servants* (London, 1643), A3r.
25. For further discussion of early modern divisions between seeing and hearing plays and the audience demographics they imply, see Andrew Gurr, "Hearers and Beholders in Shakespearean Drama," *Essays in Theatre* 3 (1984): 30–45.
26. Gabriel Egan, "Hearing or Seeing a Play? Evidence of Early Modern Theatrical Terminology," *Ben Jonson Journal* 8 (2001): 327–47.
27. William Lambarde, *A perambulation of Kent conteining the description, hystorie, and customes of that shyre…*, rev. ed. (London, 1596), 233 [Q2r].
28. William Davenant, "News from Plimouth," in *The works of Sr. William Davenant, Kt. consisting of those which were formerly printed and those which he design'd for the press…* (London, 1673), Aaaa1r.
29. James Shirley, *The doubtful heir. A tragi-comedie, as it was acted at the private house in Black-Friers* (London, 1652), A3r.
30. Ben Jonson, "The Staple of Newes," in *Bartholmew fayre: a comedie…; The diuell is an asse: a comedie…; The staple of newes: a comedie acted in the yeare, 1625, by His Maiesties seruants* (London, 1631), Aa3r.

31. John Lyly, *Euphues and his England Containing his voyage and his aduentures, myxed with sundry pretie discourses of honest loue, the discription of the countrey, the court, and the manners of that isle...* (London, 1580), S3r.
32. John Hind, *Eliosto libidinoso described in two bookes: vvherein their imminent dangers are declared, who guiding the course of their life by the compasse of affection, either dash their ship against most dangerous shelues, or else attaine the hauen with extreame preiudice* (London, 1606), C1r.
33. *Tarltons newes out of purgatorie Onely such a iest as his iigge, fit for gentlemen to laugh at an houre, &c. Published by an old companion of his, Robin Goodfellow* (London, 1590), B1r.
34. Jan Huygen van Linschoten, *Iohn Huighen van Linschoten. his discours of voyages into ye Easte & West Indies Deuided into foure bookes,* trans. William Phillip (London, 1598), 246 [Y1v].
35. Plutarch, *The philosophie, commonlie called, the morals vvritten by the learned philosopher Plutarch of Chaeronea... VVhereunto are annexed the summaries necessary to be read before every treatise,* trans. Philemon Holland (London, 1603), 161 [O3r].
36. José de Acosta, *The naturall and morall historie of the East and West Indies... together with the manners, ceremonies, lawes, governments, and warres of the Indians,* trans. Edward Grimeston (London, 1604), 493 [Ii8r]. This part of Acosta's account is also reprinted, more or less verbatim, in Samuel Purchas, *Purchas his pilgrimes In fiue bookes... The third, nauigations and voyages of English-men, alongst the coasts of Africa...,* 4 vols. (London, 1625), 3:1064–65 [Ssss6v–Ttttlr].
37. David Lindley, *Shakespeare and Music* (London: Thomson Learning, 2006), 13–49. On *disorder* in early modern music onstage, see Amanda Eubanks Winkler, *O Let Us Howle Some Heavy Note: Music for Witches, the Melancholic, and the Mad on the Seventeenth-Century English Stage* (Bloomington: Indiana University Press, 2006).
38. *OED Online,* 2nd ed. (1989), s.v. "behold, *v.,*" published online December 2011, http://www.oed.com/view/Entry/17232.
39. Ibid., def. 1. The quotation is from John Bourchier Berners, *The firste volum... of syr John Froissart, of the cronycles of Englande, Fraunce...* (1523–25; repr., 1812), II:lxiv [lxix], 222.
40. *OED Online,* 2nd ed., s.v. "behold, *v.*" (def. 6); *Middle English Dictionary* (*MED*), s.v. "biholden, *v.*" (defs. 2a, 2b), last updated February 2006, http://quod.lib.umich.edu/cgi/m/mec/med-idx?type=id&id=MED4526.
41. This sense of "beholding" as active, as something over which the viewer has both agency and responsibility, is foregrounded in the *OED*'s comment that "nearly all the early instances" of the term imply "active voluntary exercise of the faculty of vision." *OED Online,* 2nd ed., s.v. "behold, *v.*" (def. 7).
42. *OED Online,* 3rd ed. (2006), s.v. "pleasure, *n.*" (def. 1b), published online December 2011, http://www.oed.com/view/Entry/145578.
43. *MED,* s.v. "plesir(e, *n.*" (def. 2c), http://quod.lib.umich.edu/cgi/m/mec/med-idx?type=id&id=MED33717.
44. *MED,* s.v. "plesaunt(e, *adj.*" (defs. 1a, 3a), http://quod.lib.umich.edu/cgi/m/mec/med-idx?type=id&id=MED33711.
45. Adriano Banchieri, *The noblenesse of the Asse. A worke rare, learned, and excellent* (London, 1595), D1r.
46. Johannes Leo Africanus, *A geographical historie of Africa, written in Arabicke and Italian...,* trans. John Pory (London, 1600), 309 [Dd5r]; Leo Africanus, *The History and Description of Africa,* trans. John Pory, ed. Robert Brown, 3 vols. (London, 1896), 3:874. Given that this famous travel narrative circulated widely on the Continent,

presumably the reference in Banchieri is drawn from a European edition published prior to Pory's 1600 translation.

47. *OED Online*, 2nd ed., s.v. "delight, *v.*," published online December 2011, http://www.oed.com/view/Entry/49383.
48. *MED*, s.v. "delit(e, *n.*1" (defs. 1d, 2c), http://quod.lib.umich.edu/cgi/m/mec/med-idx?type=id&id=MED10979.
49. The *OED* notes that the current spelling "prevailed about 1575," although "the Bible of 1611 occasionally retained *delite*." *OED Online*, 2nd ed., s.v. "delight, *v.*"
50. Edmund Spenser, *The Faerie Queene*, ed. Thomas P. Roche Jr. (New York: Penguin, 1978), 3.1.31.9.
51. Thomas Nash, *Pierce Penilesse his supplication to the diuell* (London, 1592), F3r.
52. Richard Brathwaite, *Anniversaries upon his Panarete continued: With her contemplations, penned in the languishing time of her sicknesse. The second yeeres annivers* (London, 1635), A6r–A6v.
53. Catherine Wilson, *The Invisible World: Early Modern Philosophy and the Invention of the Microscope* (Princeton, NJ: Princeton University Press, 1995), 20; Katharine Park, "Impressed Images: Reproducing Wonders," in *Picturing Science, Producing Art*, ed. Caroline A. Jones and Peter Galison (New York: Routledge, 1998), 264. Theories about the emanation of particles later morphed into those about the multiplication of "species" (that is, nonparticle substances emitted by all objects that allowed them to be perceived), but both scientific explanations of intromission imagined vision as material penetration. On premodern and early modern theories of vision, see David C. Lindberg, *Theories of Vision from Al-Kindi to Kepler* (Chicago: University of Chicago Press, 1976). I discuss the theatrical implications of early modern visual paradigms further in chapter 2.
54. John Northbrooke, *Spiritus est vicarius Christi in terra. A treatise wherein dicing, dau[n]cing, vaine plaies or enterludes with other idle pastimes, &c. commonly vsed on the Sabboth day, are reprooued, by the authoritie of the worde of God and auncient vvriters* (London, 1579), S1r.
55. For a related argument about listening as a kind of aural penetration, see Gina Bloom, *Voice in Motion: Staging Gender, Shaping Sound in Early Modern England* (Philadelphia: University of Pennsylvania Press, 2007), 111–59. "Protestant sermons on hearing," she demonstrates, "characterize the ideal Christian as a womb that is both receptive to the implantation of God's Word and vulnerable to being pillaged by the devil" (113). As in Northbrooke's description of spectatorship, the hearer is gendered female. See also Winkler, *O Let Us Howle*, 7, on kinds of music thought to seduce the beholder.
56. John Lowin [I. L. Roscio, pseud.], *Brief conclusions of dancers and dancing Condemning the prophane vse thereof... also true physicall obseruations for the preseruation of the body in health, by the vse of the same exercise* (London, 1609), D2r.
57. Ibid., A4r.
58. Ibid., A4r, A4v.
59. Ibid., A4v.
60. Ibid.
61. Indeed, Orphinstrange's use of the word "heere" is analogous to its function in *The Spanish Tragedy*, discussed in chapter 3. In both instances, "heere" signals the convergence point of the subject matter being described (representation) and the medium through which that subject is communicated (presentation). What differs is that Orphinstrange's medium is printed text, and his subject is embodied movement, whereas for Kyd the medium itself is theatrical performance.

62. Leo Africanus, *Geographical historie of Africa*, 309 [Dd5r]; Leo Africanus, *History and Description of Africa*, 3:874.
63. Ibid.
64. Butterworth, *Magic on the Early English Stage*, 69.
65. John Dando and Harrie Runt [pseuds.], *Maroccus Extaticus. Or, Bankes bay horse in a Trance A Discourse set downe in a merry Dialogue, betweene Bankes and his beast...* ([London], 1595), B1v.
66. Ibid.
67. Acosta, *East and West Indies*, 494 [Ii8v].
68. John Playford, *The English dancing master: or, Plaine and easie rules for the dancing of country dances, with the tune to each dance* (London, 1651), epistle to the reader.
69. Acosta, *East and West Indies*, 491–92 [Ii7r–Ii7v].
70. Christiaan van Adrichem, *A briefe description of Hierusalem and of the suburbs therof, as it florished in the time of Christ...*, trans. Thomas Tymme (London, 1595), 17 [D1r].
71. John Banister, *The historie of man sucked from the sappe of the most approued anathomistes... for the vtilitie of all godly chirurgians, within this realme* (London, 1578), 103v [Ff3v].
72. Helkiah Crooke, *Mikrokosmographia: A Description of the Body of Man. Together vvith the controuersies thereto belonging...* (London, 1615), 547 [Aaa4r].
73. "3. *trans.* a. To refresh (a sense or sensory organ) by means of an agreeable object or impression; b. To refresh or enliven (the spirits or mind, a person) by means of a sensory or purely physical influence; to affect in this way." *OED Online*, 3rd ed. (2009), s.v. "recreate, *v.*1" (def. 3a, 3b), published online December 2011, http://www.oed.com/view/Entry/159950.
74. John Maplet, *A greene forest, or A naturall historie vvherein may bee seene first the most sufferaigne vertues in all the whole kinde of stones & mettals...* (London, 1567), 18v [D2v].
75. Robert Chester, *The anuals [sic] of great Brittaine. Or, A most excellent monument wherein may be seene all the antiquities of this kingdome...* (London, 1611), 106 [P1v].
76. George Puttenham, *The arte of English poesie Contriued into three bookes: the first of poets and poesie, the second of proportion, the third of ornament* (London, 1589), 3r (unlettered gathering between N4v and O1r). In a section on ancient poets, Puttenham also uses the term *recreate* as a verb to refer specifically to theatre: "There were also Poets that wrote onely for the stage, I mean playes and interludes, to rec[r]eate the people with matters of disporte, and to that intent did set forth in shewes pageants accompanied with speach the common behauiours and maner of life of priuate persons" (E2v).
77. *OED Online*, 3rd ed. (2009), s.v. "recreation, *n.*1" (def. 1), published online December 2011, http://www.oed.com/view/Entry/159954.
78. Simon Goulart, *Admirable and memorable histories containing the wonders of our time...*, trans. Edward Grimeston (London, 1607), 42–43 [D5v–D6r].
79. *OED Online*, 3rd ed. (2008), s.v. "ravished, *adj.*" (def. 2), published online December 2011, http://www.oed.com/view/Entry/158685.
80. *OED Online*, 2nd ed., s.v. "amaze, *v.,*" published online December 2011, http://www.oed.com/view/Entry/6066.
81. *OED Online*, 2nd ed., s.v. "amazed, *adj.*" (defs. 1, 3); the quotation is from Pierre de la Primaudaye, *The French academie wherin is discoursed the institution of maners*, trans. Thomas Bowes (London, 1586). On the word *rape*, and its cognate *rap*, as describing tragedy's ability to "strike" and "move" early modern viewers, see Marissa Greenberg,

"The Tyranny of Tragedy: Catharsis in England and *The Roman Actor*," *Renaissance Drama* 39 (2011): 172.

82. Christopher Marlowe, *The tragicall history of the life and death of Doctor Faustus* (London, 1616), B-text, B4r–B4v; David Bevington and Eric Rasmussen, eds., *Doctor Faustus A- and B-texts (1604, 1616): Christopher Marlowe and His Collaborator and Revisers*, The Revels Plays (Manchester: Manchester University Press, 1993), 2.1.74–89. Because many of the changes in the revised version appear to have catered to playgoer demands for spectacle, I quote from the B-text throughout, with cross-references to the A-text as needed.
83. On the circulation of aristocrats' clothes as theatrical costumes, see Jones and Stallybrass, *Renaissance Clothing*, 181–93.
84. I am grateful to Gina Bloom for drawing my attention to the tactile dimension of the "rich apparell" given to Faustus.
85. With the exception of this line and the fact that no separate entrance is marked for Mephistopheles (presumably he "Enter[s] with" the other devils), the A-text version of this scene is very similar to that found in the B-text. The A-text reads:

> *Fau. Consummatum est*, this Bill is ended,
> And Faustus hath bequeath'd his soule to *Lucifer*.
> But what is this inscription on mine arme?
> *Homo fuge*, whither should I flie?
> If vnto God, hee'le throwe thee downe to hell,
> My sences are deceiu'd, here's nothing writ,
> I see it plaine, here in this place is writ,
> *Homo fuge*, yet shall not *Faustus* flye.
>   *Me*. Ile fetch him somewhat to delight his minde.
>   *exit*.
> *Enter with diuels, giuing crownes and rich apparell to Faustus, and dance, and then depart.*
> *Fau*. Speake Mephastophilis, what meanes this shewe?
> *Me*. Nothing Faustus, but to delight thy minde withall,
> And to shewe thee what Magicke can performe.
> *Fau*. But may I raise vp spirits when I please?
> *Me*. I Faustus, and do greater things then these.
> *Fau*. Then theres inough for a thousand soules,
> Here Mephastophilis receiue this scrowle,
> A deede of gift of body and of soule.

Christopher Marlowe, *The tragicall history of D. Faustus As it hath bene acted by the right honorable the Earle of Nottingham his seruants* (London, 1604), A-text, C1r; 2.1.74–90.
86. John Davies, *Epigrammes and elegies* ([London?], 1599), B2v.
87. Thomas Middleton and Thomas Dekker, *The roaring girle. Or Moll Cut-Purse As it hath lately beene acted on the Fortune-stage by the Prince his Players* (London, 1611), B3r; Thomas Middleton and Thomas Dekker, *The Roaring Girl*, ed. Paul A. Mulholland, The Revels Plays (Manchester: Manchester University Press, 1987), 1.2.19. On whether this figure refers only to the standers in the yard or also to those in the galleries, see Gurr, *Playgoing*, 303n14.
88. Andrew Gurr, *The Shakespearean Stage, 1574–1642*, 3rd ed. (Cambridge: Cambridge University Press, 1992), 213; and Gurr, *Playgoing*, 24–25.
89. The word *note* also possessed connotations having to do with writing and inscribing, and it could include a sense of moral reprobation. The term's Latin root meant not only

"to put down in writing,... to make or put a mark on," but also "to mark with disgrace, to censure, stigmatize." *OED Online,* 3rd ed. (2003), s.v. "note, *v.*2," published online December 2011, http://www.oed.com/view/Entry/128550.

90. For a compelling reading of theatrical speech acts and/as conjuring, see Andrew Sofer, "How to Do Things with Demons: Conjuring Performatives in *Doctor Faustus*," *Theatre Journal* 61 (2009): 1–21. See also Marjorie Garber, "'Here's Nothing Writ': Scribe, Script, and Circumscription in Marlowe's Plays," *Theatre Journal* 36 (1984): 301–20.
91. Kristen Poole suggests that the scroll highlights its own material presence as text. In doing so, I would argue, the scene also foregrounds the semiotic disjunction between theatrical property scrolls and actual deeds with binding legal force, thus leading spectators to contemplate the materiality of performance as much as the materiality of text. Kristen Poole, "The Devil's in the Archive: *Doctor Faustus* and Ovidian Physics," *Renaissance Drama* 35 (2006): 203.
92. "Certaine Players at Exeter, acting upon the stage the tragical storie of Dr. Faustus the Conjurer; as a certaine number of Devels kept everie one his circle there, and as Faustus was busie in his magicall invocations, on a sudden they were all dasht, every one harkning other in the eare, for they were all perswaded, there was one devell too many amongst them; and so after a little pause desired the people to pardon them, they could go no further with this matter; the people also understanding the thing as it was, every man hastened to be first out of dores" (quoted in Sofer, "How to Do Things with Demons," 2n5).
93. See, for example, Philip Armstrong, *Shakespeare's Visual Regime: Tragedy, Psychoanalysis, and the Gaze* (Basingstoke, UK: Palgrave Macmillan, 2000), 167–203; Stuart Clark, *Vanities of the Eye: Vision in Early Modern European Culture* (Oxford: Oxford University Press, 2007), 236–65; Karen S. Coddon, "'Unreal Mockery': Unreason and the Problem of Spectacle in *Macbeth*," *ELH* 56 (1989): 485–501; Huston Diehl, "Horrid Image, Sorry Sight, Fatal Vision: The Visual Rhetoric of *Macbeth*," *Shakespeare Studies* 16 (1983): 191–204; and D. J. Palmer, "'A New Gorgon': Visual Effects in *Macbeth*," in *Focus on Macbeth,* ed. John Russell Brown (London: Routledge & Kegan Paul, 1982), 54–69.
94. Winkler, *O Let Us Howle,* 23. The "Musicke" that accompanies the witches' dance in *Macbeth* and its later revisions is discussed more extensively in Amanda Eubanks Winkler, ed., *Music for "Macbeth"* (Middleton, WI: A-R Editions, 2004). On disorderly music and early modern stage witches more generally, see Winkler, *O Let Us Howle,* 18–62.
95. The phrase, moreover, speaks to early modern notions of apparitions as constituted of air, an issue I touch on briefly in chapter 3.
96. If the play was performed at court, "King" may also have referred to the actual monarch, James I. However, as Nicholas Brooke argues, *Macbeth* is not a terribly flattering portrait of the Stuart ruler, and the oft-cited performance before James should not be taken as a given. Nicholas Brooke, ed., *Macbeth,* The Oxford Shakespeare (Oxford: Clarendon, 1990), 71–76. Certainly, the performance dynamics of this scene would support Brooke's view. It is worth noting, however, that James was known to enjoy music and dancing. In the pamphlet *Newes from Scotland,* a likely source text for *Macbeth,* the then-Scottish monarch actually called for one of the accused women to perform before him and experienced "delight." After hearing testimony that "*Geilles Duncane* did goe before them playing this reill or daunce vpon a small Trump, called a Iewes Trump," James "sent for ye said *Geillis Duncane,* who vpon the like Trump did playe the said daunce before the Kings Maiestie, who in respect of the strangenes of these matters, tooke great delight to bee present at their examinations." James

Carmichael, *Newes from Scotland, declaring the damnable life and death of Doctor Fian a notable sorcerer… With the true examination of the saide doctor and witches, as they vttered them in the presence of the Scottish king…* (London, 1592), B3v (mislabeled A3v in original).

97. D. J. Palmer proposes that the witches disappeared through a trapdoor. Glynne Wickham posits that Hecate may have used a flying machine but argues that the witches probably ran offstage. Frederick Kiefer opts for a flying machine as well. Iain Wright argues for elaborate special effects, including not only flying witches but also a magic lantern of prospective glass for the procession of kings. John Russell Brown agrees that the stage direction "provides no clue," but he insists that the witches require "a strong exit." D. J. Palmer, "'A New Gorgon,'" 63; Glynne Wickham, "To Fly or Not to Fly? The Problem of Hecate in Shakespeare's *Macbeth*," in *Essays on Drama and Theatre: Liber Amicorum Benjamin Hunningher* (Amsterdam: Baarn, 1973), 171–82; Frederick Kiefer, *Shakespeare's Visual Theatre: Staging the Personified Characters* (Cambridge: Cambridge University Press, 2003), 114; Iain Wright, "'Come like shadowes, so depart': The Ghostly Kings in *Macbeth*," *Shakespearean International Yearbook* 6 (2006): 215–29; and John Russell Brown, *Shakespeare's Plays in Performance* (New York: Applause, 1993), 179.

98. Dessen and Thomson, *Dictionary of Stage Directions*, 242. See also Alan C. Dessen, *Recovering Shakespeare's Theatrical Vocabulary* (Cambridge: Cambridge University Press, 1995), 196–215.

99. Dessen and Thomson, *Dictionary of Stage Directions*, 242.

100. Ibid.

101. John Orrell, "The Theaters," in *A New History of Early English Drama*, ed. John D. Cox and David Scott Kastan (New York: Columbia University Press, 1997), 109.

102. J. L. Styan, *Shakespeare's Stagecraft* (Cambridge: Cambridge University Press, 1967), 189–92.

103. Gurr, *Shakespearean Stage*, 178–79. On scenes that, unlike those in *Macbeth*, explicitly call for pauses, see Dessen and Thomson, *Dictionary of Stage Directions*, 160.

104. Bertolt Brecht, "A Short Organum for the Theatre," in *Brecht on Theatre*, 180–83. Brecht also addresses the issue of pleasure on pp. 35–36 of "The Modern Theatre Is the Epic Theatre," in *Brecht on Theatre*, 33–42.

105. Brecht, "Short Organum," 187.

106. Ibid. See also Brecht's critique of the "[w]itchcraft" of the dramatic theatre in "The Modern Theatre Is the Epic Theatre," 38.

107. See Anne Righter [Barton], *Shakespeare and the Idea of the Play* (London: Chatto and Windus, 1962), 23–31. Barton argues that the audience's role as *populus* in the Corpus Christi cycles and other biblical plays was transformed in the morality plays to generate a kind of double vision that led to the increasing divergence of play world and real world in early modern dramaturgy.

108. On devils and vices in morality drama as they pertain to Shakespeare and Marlowe, see, among others, David M. Bevington, *From Mankind to Marlowe: Growth of Structure in the Popular Drama of Tudor England* (Cambridge, MA: Harvard University Press, 1962); John D. Cox, *The Devil and the Sacred in English Drama, 1350–1642* (Cambridge: Cambridge University Press, 2000); Alan C. Dessen, *Shakespeare and the Late Moral Plays* (Lincoln: University of Nebraska Press, 1986); and Ruth Lunney, *Marlowe and the Popular Tradition: Innovation in the English Drama before 1595* (Manchester: Manchester University Press, 2002).

109. Translation in Gurr, *Shakespearean Stage*, 206.

110. Indeed, the two terms are etymologically linked: the adjective *beholden* was originally the past participle form of the verb *behold*. *OED*, 2nd ed., s.v. "beholden" (*adj.*).

5 Artful Sport: Violence, Dismemberment, and Games in *Titus Andronicus*, *Cymbeline*, and *Doctor Faustus*

1. *The Tragical Reign of Selimus, 1594*, ed. W[illy] Bang, Malone Society Reprints (London: Malone Society/Chiswick Press, 1909), F2v, F3r; lines 1415, 1431. Quotations from this facsimile of the 1594 quarto have been cross-checked against T. G., *The tragedy of Selimus Emperour of the Turkes* (London, 1638).
2. *Oxford English Dictionary (OED) Online*, 2nd ed. (1989), s.v. "bosom, *n.* and *adj.*" (defs. A3a, A3b), published online November 2010, http://www.oed.com/view/Entry/21761.
3. This interchangeability of body parts onstage was (probably unintentionally) heightened in a 2001 production of *Cymbeline* at the Philadelphia Shakespeare Theatre, then known as the Philadelphia Shakespeare Festival. The show used the same property head as had featured in a *Macbeth* performed that same year at the People's Light and Theatre Company in Malvern, Pennsylvania, a short drive outside the city. Audience members who attended both plays were startled to discover how much Cloten looked like the Scottish lord.
4. Christopher Marlowe, *The tragicall history of the life and death of Doctor Faustus* (London, 1616), B-text, G2v; David Bevington and Eric Rasmussen, eds., *Doctor Faustus A- and B-texts (1604, 1616): Christopher Marlowe and His Collaborator and Revisers*, The Revels Plays (Manchester: Manchester University Press, 1993), 4.6.125.
5. See Alan C. Dessen, *Titus Andronicus*, Shakespeare in Performance (Manchester: Manchester University Press, 1989); and G. Harold Metz, "Stage History of *Titus Andronicus*," *Shakespeare Quarterly* 28 (1977): 154–69.
6. See, for example, Stephen Greenblatt et al., eds., *The Norton Shakespeare* (New York: Norton, 1997), based on Stanley Wells and Gary Taylor's Oxford text. The earlier Oxford version edited by Eugene Waith changes "these things" to "this" but keeps "teeth." The *Riverside* and the Arden 3 editions cut the third line after "employed" but retain "teeth." Eugene M. Waith, ed., *Titus Andronicus*, The Oxford Shakespeare (Oxford: Clarendon, 1984); G. Blakemore Evans et al., eds., *The Riverside Shakespeare*, 2nd ed. (Boston: Houghton Mifflin, 1997); and Jonathan Bate, ed., *Titus Andronicus*, The Arden Shakespeare, 3rd series (London: Routledge, 1995). For other discussions of the hand-in-teeth moment, see Alan C. Dessen, *Recovering Shakespeare's Theatrical Vocabulary* (Cambridge: Cambridge University Press, 1995), 94–95, 242n5; and Heather James, *Shakespeare's Troy: Drama, Politics, and the Translation of Empire* (Cambridge: Cambridge University Press, 1997), 74–76.
7. Waith, *Titus Andronicus*, 141.
8. See, for example, Katherine Rowe, *Dead Hands: Fictions of Agency, Renaissance to Modern* (Stanford, CA: Stanford University Press, 1999), 52–85; Michael Neill, "'Amphitheatres in the Body': Playing with Hands on the Shakespearian Stage," *Shakespeare Survey* 48 (1995): 23–50; Heather James, "Cultural Disintegration in *Titus Andronicus:* Mutilating Titus, Vergil and Rome," in *Violence in Drama*, ed. James Redmond (Cambridge: Cambridge University Press, 1991), 123–40; and Gillian Murray Kendall, "'Lend Me Thy Hand': Metaphor and Mayhem in *Titus Andronicus*," *Shakespeare Quarterly* 40 (1989): 299–316.
9. Homer Swander, "No Exit for a Dead Body: What to Do with a Scripted Corpse?" *Journal of Dramatic Theory and Criticism* 5 (1991): 139. See also Mariko Ichikawa, "What to Do with a Corpse? Physical Reality and the Fictional World in the Shakespearean Theatre," *Theatre Research International* 29 (2004): 201–15. Early modern productions apparently had similar constraints. According to one writer, a pre-Interregnum performance

generated much laughter when one actor "brandisht his Sword & made his *Exit;* ne're minding to bring off his dead men; which they perceiving, crauld into the Tyreing house, at which *Fowler* grew angry, and told 'em, Dogs you should have laine there till you had been fetcht off; and so they crauld out again, which gave the People such an occasion of Laughter, they cry'd that again[,] that again, that again." John Tatham, *Knavery in all trades, or, The coffee-house a comedy: as it was acted in the Christmas holidays by several apprentices with great applause* (London, 1664), E1r.

10. Susan Dwyer Amussen, "Punishment, Discipline, and Power: The Social Meanings of Violence in Early Modern England," *Journal of British Studies* 34 (1995): 9.
11. Ibid., 9–10.
12. In this sense, this episode resonates with the one in *Selimus,* when Aga calls upon God and Bajazet's lords—and theatregoers—to "witnesse" his mutilation. On witnessing and this procession, see Marissa Greenberg's book in progress, *Metropolitan Tragedy.*
13. See J. H. Baker, "Criminal Courts and Procedure at Common Law 1550–1800," in *Crime in England, 1550–1800,* ed. J. S. Cockburn (Princeton, NJ: Princeton University Press, 1977), 15–48; and J. A. Sharpe, *Judicial Punishment in England* (London: Faber and Faber, 1990), 18–49.
14. Clare Williams, ed. and trans., *Thomas Platter's Travels in England, 1599* (London: Jonathan Cape, 1937), 155.
15. In *Cymbeline,* when Cloten fights Guidarius, the association of heads with treason is likewise present, though with more comic overtones. After Guidarius makes plain that he is unimpressed by his opponent's assertion "I am Sonne to'th'Queene" (TLN 2368; 4.2.93), Cloten boasts, "When I haue slaine thee with my proper hand, / Ile follow those that euen now fled hence: / And on the Gates of *Luds-Towne* set your heads" (TLN 2375–77; 4.2.97–99).
16. Peter Lake and Michael Questier, "Agency, Appropriation and Rhetoric under the Gallows: Puritans, Romanists and the State in Early Modern England," *Past and Present* 153 (1996): 77.
17. See ibid. for a list of relevant pamphlets and sources, including the examples cited here.
18. Quoted in ibid., 83.
19. On funeral practices, see Michael Neill, *Issues of Death: Mortality and Identity in English Renaissance Tragedy* (Oxford: Clarendon, 1997).
20. Similarly, at the end of *Doctor Faustus,* his limbs are "torne asunder" (B-text, H3r; 5.3.7). Dismemberment here reflects not only earthly but also eternal punishment: when "*Hell is discouered,*" Faustus sees "liue quarters broyling on the coles" (B-text, H2r; 5.2.120.s.d., 5.2.125).
21. Quoted in Amussen, "Punishment, Discipline, and Power," 7.
22. William Harrison, *The Description of England,* ed. Georges Edelen (London, 1587; Ithaca, NY: Cornell University Press, 1968), 187.
23. C. W., *The crying murther Contayning the cruell and most horrible bu[tchery] of Mr. Trat, curate of old Cleaue; who was first mu[rthered] as he trauailed vpon the high way, then was brought home to hi[s house] and there was quartered and imboweld: his quarters and bowels b[eing af]terwards perboyled and salted vp, in a most strange and fearefull manner...* (London, 1624), title page.
24. John H. Langbein, *Prosecuting Crime in the Renaissance: England, Germany, France* (Cambridge, MA: Harvard University Press, 1974), 47.
25. Malcolm Gaskill, *Crime and Mentalities in Early Modern England* (Cambridge: Cambridge University Press, 2000), 222.
26. *The horrible murther of a young boy of three yeres of age, whose sister had her tongue cut out and how it pleased God to reueale the offendors, by giuing speech to the tongueles childe…*

(London, 1606), B2r. Tongues are repeatedly linked with the revelation of murder, an association that extends to theatre, too, as we saw in *Titus Andronicus* and *The Spanish Tragedy*. On tongues, see Carla Mazzio, "Sins of the Tongue," in *The Body in Parts: Fantasies of Corporeality in Early Modern Europe*, ed. David Hillman and Carla Mazzio (New York: Routledge, 1997), 53–79.
27. Gaskill, *Crime and Mentalities*, 227.
28. *Three bloodie murders the first, committed by Francis Cartwright vpon William Storre… The second, committed by Elizabeth Iames, on the body of her mayde… The third, committed vpon a stranger…* (London, 1613), C3v.
29. Thomas Cooper, *The cry and reuenge of blood Expressing the nature and haynousnesse of wilfull murther…* (London, 1620), G1v.
30. On lay investigators, see Lorna Hutson, "Rethinking the 'Spectacle of the Scaffold': Juridical Epistemologies and English Revenge Tragedy," *Representations* 89 (2005): 30–58. On "searchers," see Gaskill, *Crime and Mentalities*, 254–61.
31. C. W., *Crying murther*, B4r.
32. Cooper, *Cry and reuenge of blood*, G2r.
33. Ibid.
34. *OED Online*, 2nd ed., s.v. "brawn, *n.*" (defs. 1a, 1b), published online June 2010, http://www.oed.com/view/Entry/22827.
35. Stephen Booth, *"King Lear," "Macbeth," Indefinition, and Tragedy* (New Haven, CT: Yale University Press, 1983), appendix 2 ("Speculations on Doubling in Shakespeare's Plays").
36. Translations in Peter Meredith and John E. Tailby, eds., *The Staging of Religious Drama in Europe in the Later Middle Ages: Texts and Documents in English Translation* (Kalamazoo, MI: Medieval Institute, 1983), 102–3, 105.
37. Véronique Plesch, "Notes for the Staging of a Late Medieval Passion Play," in *Material Culture and Medieval Drama*, ed. Clifford Davidson (Kalamazoo, MI: Medieval Institute, 1999), 80.
38. Translation in Meredith and Tailby, *Staging of Religious Drama*, 111.
39. Philip Massinger and Thomas Dekker, *The virgin martir a tragedie. As it hath bin diuers times publickely acted with great applause, by the seruants of his Maiesties Reuels* (London, 1622), K2v; John Fletcher and Philip Massinger, *Sir John Van Olden Barnavelt*, ed. T. H. Howard-Hill, Malone Society Reprints (1619; London: Malone Society, 1980), 94; and Gervase Markham and William Sampson, *The true tragedy of Herod and Antipater with the death of faire Marriam… publiquely acted (with great applause) at the Red Bull, by the Company of his Maiesties Reuels* (London, 1622), L4r. See also the beheading of Isabella in John Marston and William Barksted, *The insatiate countesse A tragedie: acted at VVhite-Fryers* (London, 1613), I2r.
40. Translations in Meredith and Tailby, *Staging of Religious Drama*, 110, 112.
41. John Spalding Gatton, "'There must be blood': Mutilation and Martyrdom on the Medieval Stage," in *Violence in Drama*, ed. James Redmond (Cambridge: Cambridge University Press, 1991), 86.
42. Quoted in Andrew Gurr, *The Shakespearean Stage, 1574–1642*, 3rd ed. (Cambridge: Cambridge University Press, 1992), 184.
43. Gretchen Schulz, "Sharing Shakespeare: An Academic's Adventures with the Atlanta Shakespeare Company" (talk presented at the Shakespeare in an Age of Visual Culture seminar, Folger Institute, Washington, DC, January 30, 1999).
44. "The Croxton Play of the Sacrament," in *Medieval Drama: An Anthology*, ed. Greg Walker (Oxford: Blackwell, 2000).
45. Eric Bentley, *The Life of Drama* (New York: Atheneum, 1964), 158.
46. Stephen Greenblatt, "Mutilation and Meaning," in Hillman and Mazzio, *Body in Parts*, 230.

47. Jonathan Sawday, *The Body Emblazoned: Dissection and the Human Body in Renaissance Culture* (New York: Routledge, 1995), 42.
48. *OED Online*, 2nd ed., s.v. "case, *n.*2" (defs. 3a, 4b), published online November 2010, http://www.oed.com/view/Entry/28394.
49. *OED Online*, 2nd ed., s.v. "case, *v.*2" (def. 1c), published online November 2010, http://www.oed.com/view/Entry/28398.
50. Frances Teague, *Shakespeare's Speaking Properties* (Lewisburg, PA: Bucknell University Press, 1991), 17–18. For further discussion of props, see Andrew Sofer's excellent study, *The Stage Life of Props* (Ann Arbor: University of Michigan Press, 2003).
51. On beggary and theatre, see William C. Carroll, *Fat King, Lean Beggar: Representations of Poverty in the Age of Shakespeare* (Ithaca, NY: Cornell University Press, 1996); and Paola Pugliatti, *Beggary and the Theatre in Early Modern England* (Aldershot, UK: Ashgate, 2003).
52. Jean-Christophe Agnew, *Worlds Apart: The Market and the Theater in Anglo-American Thought, 1550–1750* (Cambridge: Cambridge University Press, 1986).
53. A similar emphasis on deceit characterizes dismemberment in *Doctor Faustus*. In the scene with the horse-courser, the severed leg is associated overtly with cheating, and the question of exchange and false bargains is captured most notably in the doctor's summation that "*Faustus* hath his leg againe, and the Horse-courser a bundle of hay for his forty Dollors" (B-text, F3v; 4.4.43–45). I discuss this scene in further detail later in this chapter.
54. On laughter and tears in *Titus Andronicus,* see Matthew Steggle, *Laughing and Weeping in Early Modern Theatres* (Aldershot, UK: Ashgate, 2007), 128–31.
55. The phrase "to pull a person's leg"—meaning "to deceive a person humorously or playfully; to tease a person"—only came into currency in the late nineteenth century. *OED Online*, 3rd ed. (2007), s.v. "pull, *v.*" (def. P10), published online November 2010, http://www.oed.com/view/Entry/154317.
56. Because the B-text's action is, across the board, an expansion on that of the A-text, I would argue that the leg regenerated in the revised version is merely reattached in the earlier one. The evidence is, of course, ambiguous: certainly magical regeneration in the A-text would leave an extra leg for Faustus to carry offstage, which could perhaps be expanded as the B-text's more elaborate stage business.
57. The most relevant verb form may be found in the early modern phrase *to leg it,* meaning "to walk fast or run." *OED Online*, 2nd ed., s.v. "leg, *v.*" (def. 1), published online November 2010, http://www.oed.com/view/Entry/107004.
58. R. A. Foakes, ed., *Henslowe's Diary*, 2nd ed. (Cambridge: Cambridge University Press, 2002), 320.
59. To "make a leg" was an "obeisance made by drawing back one leg and bending the other." *OED Online*, 2nd ed., s.v. "leg, *n.*" (def. I4), published online November 2010, http://www.oed.com/view/Entry/107003. See also *OED Online*, 2nd ed., s.v. "leg, *v.*" (def. 2).
60. See Philip H. Highfill Jr., Kalman A. Burnim, and Edward A. Langhans, *A Biographical Dictionary of Actors, Actresses, Musicians, Dancers, Managers & Other Stage Personnel in London, 1660–1800* (Carbondale: Southern Illinois University Press, 1973–93), 14:433. The account from the *Universal Journal* is dated December 11, 1723, shortly after the show initially premiered on November 26.
61. Alan C. Dessen and Leslie Thomson, *A Dictionary of Stage Directions in English Drama, 1580–1642* (Cambridge: Cambridge University Press, 1999), 219. For an interesting exception, see Fletcher and Massinger, *Sir John Van Olden Barnavelt,* 94, where an onstage decapitation is marked only by a long dash.

62. The word *false* is not included in the *Dictionary of Stage Directions*, nor is it in Dessen and Thomson's online website of additions, http://www.sddictionary.com (accessed February 20, 2011).
63. See, for example, act 3, scene 2 of Shakespeare's *Comedy of Errors*, when Antipholus of Syracuse serves as straight man for Dromio of Syracuse's anatomizing of the body of the kitchen wench, Nell/Luce.
64. David Underdown, "Regional Cultures? Local Variation in Popular Culture during the Early Modern Period," in *Popular Culture in England, c. 1500–1850*, ed. Tim Harris (New York: St. Martin's, 1995), 37–39.
65. Ronald Hutton, *The Stations of the Sun: A History of the Ritual Year in Britain* (Oxford: Oxford University Press, 1996), 154.
66. Richard Carew, *The survey of Cornvvall* (London, 1602), V3r. On hurling and football, see Hutton, *Stations of the Sun*, 155. Philip Stubbes also condemns the sport and "such other deuilish pastimes." Early moderns often registered disapproval by condemning certain behaviors as demonic. Nevertheless, football's discursive associations with the devilish may well have reinforced associations between the sport and Faustus's head. Philip Stubbes, *The anatomie of abuses contayning a discouerie, or briefe summarie of such notable vices and imperfections, as now raigne in many Christian countreyes of the worlde: but (especiallie) in a verie famous ilande called Ailgna...* (London, 1583), L2v.
67. Arthur Freeman, "The 'Tapster Manuscript': An Analogue of Shakespeare's *Henry the Fourth Part One*," *English Manuscript Studies, 1100–1700* 6 (1997): 98; ellipses and brackets in Freeman's transcription.
68. Note, too, that the horse-courser's group is led by Robin the clown, as indicated in the original quarto's speech tags and stage directions. On the clown's adoption of the Vice's dramaturgical techniques, including his instigation of games, see David Wiles, *Shakespeare's Clown: Actor and Text in the Elizabethan Playhouse* (Cambridge: Cambridge University Press, 1987), 1–10.
69. Alfred Harbage, *Annals of English Drama, 975–1700*, 3rd ed., rev. S. Schoenbaum and Sylvia Stoler Wagonheim (New York: Routledge, 1989).
70. Indeed, the early eighteenth-century *Harlequin Doctor Faustus*, which I discussed earlier, involves further stage business with horns and asses' ears.
71. Thomas Meriton, *The wandring lover a tragy-comedie being acted severall times privately at sundry places by the author and his friends with great applause* (London, 1658), E1r.
72. Stubbes, *Anatomie of abuses*, P6v.
73. On the ineffectiveness of official prohibitions against football, see Hutton, *Stations of the Sun*, 154.
74. Stubbes, *Anatomie of abuses*, P6r.
75. Chester, for instance, sponsored a Shrovetide football match in the early sixteenth century and Carlisle in the early seventeenth; various cities and craft guilds in Scotland did the same (Hutton, *Stations of the Sun*, 152, 154).
76. Ibid., 153.
77. On baiting in relation to discourses of human and beast, see Erica Fudge, *Brutal Reasoning: Animals, Rationality, and Humanity in Early Modern England* (Ithaca, NY: Cornell University Press, 2006); Fudge, *Perceiving Animals: Humans and Beasts in Early Modern English Culture* (New York: St. Martin's, 2000); and Fudge, Ruth Gilbert, and S. J. Wiseman, eds., *At the Borders of the Human: Beasts, Bodies and Natural Philosophy in the Early Modern Period* (New York: St. Martin's, 1999).
78. Hutton, *Stations of the Sun*, 152. Carlisle hosted football matches as well; see *Records of Early English Drama: Cumberland, Westmorland, Gloucestershire*, ed. Audrey Douglas and Peter Greenfield (Toronto: University of Toronto Press, 1986), 25.
79. Carew, *Survey of Cornvvall*, V3v.

80. Sir Thomas Elyot, *The boke named the Gouernour* ([London], 1537), M4r.
81. For related arguments about the social functions of sport, see Gregory M. Colón Semenza, *Sport, Politics, and Literature in the English Renaissance* (Newark: University of Delaware Press, 2003).
82. See Martin Ingram, "Ridings, Rough Music and the 'Reform of Popular Culture' in Early Modern England," *Past and Present* 105 (1984): 79–113; and Sharpe, *Judicial Punishment in England*, 18–49.
83. Amussen, "Punishment, Discipline, and Power," 12. For other accounts of this incident, see Lake and Questier, "Agency, Appropriation and Rhetoric," 102; and David Underdown, *Fire from Heaven: Life in an English Town in the Seventeenth Century* (New Haven, CT: Yale University Press, 1992), 197–98.
84. Indeed, Elizabeth Willoughby, an early modern eyewitness at Green's execution, wrote that the football players "sported themselves" with the severed head (quoted in Underdown, *Fire from Heaven*, 198).
85. George Chapman, trans., *The Iliads of Homer prince of poets... With a co[m]ment vppon some of his chiefe places* (London, 1611), O1r.
86. Homer, *The Iliad*, trans. Robert Fagles with introduction and notes by Bernard Knox (New York: Viking Penguin, 1990), 11.166–70.
87. Richard Pike, *Three to one being, an English-Spanish combat, performed by a westerne gentleman, of Tauystoke in Deuon shire with an English quarter-staffe, against three Spanish rapiers and poniards, at Sherries in Spaine, the fifteene day of Nouember, 1625. In the presence of dukes, condes, marquesses, and other great dons of Spaine, being the counsell of warre...* (London, 1626), B3r–B3v.
88. *OED Online*, 2nd ed., s.v. "spurn, *v*.1," published online November 2010, http://www.oed.com/view/Entry/187998.
89. John Webster, *The white diuel, or, The tragedy of Paulo Giordano Vrsini, Duke of Brachiano with the life and death of Vittoria Corombona the famous Venetian curtizan. Acted by the Queenes Maiesties Seruants* (London, 1612), G2v; John Webster, *The White Devil*, ed. Christina Luckyj, The New Mermaids (London: A&C Black; New York: Norton, 1996), 4.2.136–37.
90. Richard Brathwaite, *The captive-captain, or, The restrain'd cavalier drawn to his full bodie in these characters...* (London, 1665), H6v. For the continued relevance of the proverbial phrase, see an anonymous pamphlet that states, "You and the inhumane Irish hold concurrency in this: you cannot be secure from fear, till you can play at football with the Head of your foe." *The maze: contrived, digested, and couched in these distinct subjects: representatives for these present times to admire...* (n.p., 1659), H3v. *Early English Books Online* misdates this text to 1699, apparently because of a stray mark on the title page.
91. Patricia Palmer, "'An headlesse Ladie' and 'a horses loade of heades': Writing the Beheading," *Renaissance Quarterly* 60 (2007): 25–57.
92. Ibid., 31–32.
93. For more on prizefighting, see my article, "Popular Festivity and the Early Modern Stage: The Case of *George a Greene*," *Theatre Journal* 61 (2009): 284–91.
94. Francis Beaumont and John Fletcher, *Comedies and tragedies* (London, 1647), Ppp3r.
95. Ibid.
96. See Giles E. Dawson, "London's Bull-Baiting and Bear-Baiting Arena in 1562," *Shakespeare Quarterly* 15 (1964): 98–99. For an overview of baiting, see Oscar Brownstein, "The Popularity of Baiting in England before 1600: A Study in Social and Theatrical History," *Educational Theatre Journal* 21 (1969): 237–50. On baiting and playing, see Brownstein, "Why Didn't Burbage Lease the Beargarden? A Conjecture in Comparative Architecture," in *The First Public Playhouse: The Theatre in Shoreditch,*

1576–1598, ed. Herbert Berry (Montreal: McGill-Queen's University Press, 1979), 81–96.
97. Brownstein, "Popularity of Baiting," 240–44; S. P. Cerasano, "The Master of the Bears in Art and Enterprise," *Medieval and Renaissance Drama in England* 5 (1991): 195–209; and Andrew Gurr, "Bears and Players: Philip Henslowe's Double Acts," *Shakespeare Bulletin* 22, no. 4 (2004): 31–41.
98. See, for instance, Stephen Dickey, "Shakespeare's Mastiff Comedy," *Shakespeare Quarterly* 42 (1991): 255–75; Jason Scott-Warren, "When Theaters Were Bear-Gardens; or, What's at Stake in the Comedy of Humors," *Shakespeare Quarterly* 54 (2003): 63–82; Rebecca Ann Bach, "Bearbaiting, Dominion, and Colonialism," in *Race, Ethnicity, and Power in the Renaissance,* ed. Joyce Green MacDonald (Madison, NJ: Fairleigh Dickinson University Press, 1997), 19–35; and Tobias Hug, "'You should go to *Hockley in the Hole,* and to *Marybone,* child, to learn valour': On the Social Logic of Animal Baiting in Early Modern London," *Renaissance Journal* 2, no. 1 (2004): 17–26. Andreas Höfele, *Stage, Stake, and Scaffold: Humans and Animals in Shakespeare's Theatre* (Oxford: Oxford University Press, 2011), unfortunately appeared too late to be taken into account here.
99. One important exception, however, is William N. West, "*Non Plus,* or a Peculiar and Proper Kind of Fight" (work in progress), which explores baiting's overlaps with fencing and verbal sparring. West argues that playing in theatre, as in these other arenas, was structured around contest and imagined as a series of "agonistic" encounters.
100. Oscar Brownstein, "Stake and Stage: The Baiting Ring and the Public Playhouse in Elizabethan England" (PhD diss., University of Iowa, 1963), appendix A, offers a quite extensive compilation of primary documents related to baiting. Unless otherwise noted, accounts of bearbaiting cited in this chapter can be found there, organized by date.
101. From a 1575 letter by Robert Laneham, quoted in Brownstein, "Stake and Stage," 277.
102. From an early modern advertisement for a baiting, reprinted in W. W. Greg, ed., *Henslowe Papers: Being Documents Supplementary to Henslowe's Diary* (London: A. H. Bullen, 1907), 106.
103. See, for instance, the 1575 letter by Robert Laneham, quoted in Brownstein, "Stake and Stage," 277.
104. John Davies, *Epigrammes and elegies* ([London?], 1599), D2r–D2v.
105. Richard Brome, *The antipodes a comedie. Acted in the yeare 1638. by the Queenes Majesties Servants, at Salisbury Court in Fleet-street* (London, 1640), H1v.
106. Lin, "Popular Festivity," 284–91.
107. Quoted in Bevington and Rasmussen, *Doctor Faustus,* 51.
108. Ibid.
109. John Webster, *The tragedy of the Dutchesse of Malfy As it was presented priuatly, at the Black-Friers; and publiquely at the Globe, by the Kings Maiesties Seruants...* (London, 1623), I2v; John Webster, *The Duchess of Malfi,* 2nd ed., ed. John Russell Brown, The Revels Plays (Manchester: Manchester University Press, 2009), 4.1.111–15.

Bibliography

Abel, Lionel. *Metatheatre: A New View of Dramatic Form.* New York: Hill and Wang, 1963.
Acosta, José de. *The naturall and morall historie of the East and West Indies... together with the manners, ceremonies, lawes, governments, and warres of the Indians.* Translated by Edward Grimeston. London, 1604.
Adrichem, Christiaan van. *A briefe description of Hierusalem and of the suburbs therof, as it florished in the time of Christ....* Translated by Thomas Tymme. London, 1595.
Agnew, Jean-Christophe. *Worlds Apart: The Market and the Theater in Anglo-American Thought, 1550–1750.* Cambridge: Cambridge University Press, 1986.
Alpers, Svetlana. *The Art of Describing: Dutch Art in the Seventeenth Century.* Chicago: University of Chicago Press, 1983.
Alter, Jean. *A Sociosemiotic Theory of Theatre.* Philadelphia: University of Pennsylvania Press, 1990.
Amussen, Susan Dwyer. "Punishment, Discipline, and Power: The Social Meanings of Violence in Early Modern England." *Journal of British Studies* 34 (1995): 1–34.
Anderson, Christy. *Inigo Jones and the Classical Tradition.* Cambridge: Cambridge University Press, 2007.
Ardolino, Frank. "'Now Shall I See the Fall of Babylon': *The Spanish Tragedy* as Protestant Apocalypse." *Shakespeare Yearbook* 1 (1990): 93–115.
Armstrong, Philip. *Shakespeare's Visual Regime: Tragedy, Psychoanalysis, and the Gaze.* Basingstoke, UK: Palgrave Macmillan, 2000.
Artemidorus, Daldianus. *The iudgement, or exposition of dreames, written by Artimodorus, an auntient and famous author, first in Greeke, then translated into Latin, after into French, and now into English.* London, 1606.
Astington, John H. *Actors and Acting in Shakespeare's Time: The Art of Stage Playing.* New York: Cambridge University Press, 2010.
Aston, Elaine. *Feminist Theatre Practice: A Handbook.* London: Routledge, 1999.
Auerbach, Erich. *Mimesis: The Representation of Reality in Western Literature.* Translated by Willard R. Trask. Princeton, NJ: Princeton University Press, 1953.
Bach, Rebecca Ann. "Bearbaiting, Dominion, and Colonialism." In *Race, Ethnicity, and Power in the Renaissance,* edited by Joyce Green MacDonald, 19–35. Madison, NJ: Fairleigh Dickinson University Press, 1997.
Baker, J. H. "Criminal Courts and Procedure at Common Law 1550–1800." In *Crime in England, 1550–1800,* edited by J. S. Cockburn, 15–48. Princeton, NJ: Princeton University Press, 1977.
Banchieri, Adriano. *The noblenesse of the Asse. A worke rare, learned, and excellent.* London, 1595.
Banister, John. *The historie of man sucked from the sappe of the most approued anathomistes... for the vtilitie of all godly chirurgians, within this realme.* London, 1578.

Barish, Jonas. *The Antitheatrical Prejudice.* Berkeley: University of California Press, 1981.
Bartels, Emily C. "Breaking the Illusion of Being: Shakespeare and the Performance of Self." *Theatre Journal* 46 (1994): 171–85.
Bartolovich, Crystal. "Oh, Dear, What Can the Matter Be? A Response to Peter Stallybrass's 'The Value of Culture and the Disavowal of Things.'" *Early Modern Culture* 1, no. 1 (2000). http://emc.eserver.org/1-1/bartolovich.html.
Baskervill, Charles Read. *The Elizabethan Jig and Related Song Drama.* Chicago: University of Chicago Press, 1929.
Bate, Jonathan, ed. *Titus Andronicus.* The Arden Shakespeare. 3rd series. London: Routledge, 1995.
Beaumont, Francis, and John Fletcher. *Comedies and tragedies.* London, 1647.
Beckerman, Bernard. *Shakespeare at the Globe, 1599–1609.* New York: Macmillan, 1962.
Belsey, Catherine. *The Subject of Tragedy: Identity and Difference in Renaissance Drama.* London: Methuen, 1985.
Belting, Hans. *Likeness and Presence: A History of the Image before the Era of Art.* Translated by Edmund Jephcott. Chicago: University of Chicago Press, 1994.
Benjamin, Walter. *Illuminations.* Edited by Hannah Arendt. Translated by Harry Zohn. New York: Schocken, 1969.
———. *Understanding Brecht.* Translated by Anna Bostock. London: NLB, 1973.
Bentley, Eric. *The Life of the Drama.* New York: Atheneum, 1964.
Bethell, S. L. *Shakespeare and the Popular Dramatic Tradition.* Durham, NC: Duke University Press, 1944.
Bevington, David. *Action Is Eloquence: Shakespeare's Language of Gesture.* Cambridge, MA: Harvard University Press, 1984.
———. "Asleep Onstage." In *From Page to Performance: Essays in Early English Drama,* edited by John A. Alford, 51–83. East Lansing: Michigan State University Press, 1995.
———. *From Mankind to Marlowe: Growth of Structure in the Popular Drama of Tudor England.* Cambridge, MA: Harvard University Press, 1962.
———, ed. *Medieval Drama.* Boston: Houghton Mifflin, 1975.
Bevington, David, and Eric Rasmussen, eds. *Doctor Faustus A- and B-texts (1604, 1616): Christopher Marlowe and His Collaborator and Revisers.* The Revels Plays. Manchester: Manchester University Press, 1993.
Black, James. "*King Lear*: Art Upside-Down." *Shakespeare Survey* 33 (1980): 35–42.
Blayney, Peter W. M. "The Publication of Playbooks." In Cox and Kastan, *New History,* 383–422.
Bloom, Gina. *Voice in Motion: Staging Gender, Shaping Sound in Early Modern England.* Philadelphia: University of Pennsylvania Press, 2007.
Booth, Stephen. "Doubling in Shakespeare's Plays." In McGuire and Samuelson, *Shakespeare, the Theatrical Dimension,* 103–31.
———. *"King Lear," "Macbeth," Indefinition, and Tragedy.* New Haven, CT: Yale University Press, 1983.
Bowers, Fredson. *Elizabethan Revenge Tragedy, 1587–1642.* Princeton, NJ: Princeton University Press, 1940.
Bradshaw, Graham, Tom Bishop, and David Schalkwyk, eds. "The Achievement of Robert Weimann." Special issue, *Shakespearean International Yearbook* 10 (2010).
Branagh, Kenneth. *Love's Labour's Lost.* Shepperton, UK: Pathé Pictures et al., 2000. 35 mm film.
Brathwaite, Richard. *Anniversaries upon his Panarete continued: With her contemplations, penned in the languishing time of her sicknesse. The second yeeres annivers.* London, 1635.

———. *The captive-captain, or, The restrain'd cavalier drawn to his full bodie in these characters*.... London, 1665.

———. *Essaies vpon the fiue senses with a pithie one vpon detraction. Continued vvith sundry Christian resolues*.... London, 1620.

Brecht, Bertolt. *Brecht on Theatre: The Development of an Aesthetic*. Edited and translated by John Willett. New York: Hill and Wang, 1964.

Brissenden, Alan. *Shakespeare and the Dance*. London: Macmillan, 1981.

Brome, Richard. *The antipodes a comedie. Acted in the yeare 1638. by the Queenes Majesties Servants, at Salisbury Court in Fleet-street*. London, 1640.

Brooke, Nicholas, ed. *Macbeth*. The Oxford Shakespeare. Oxford: Clarendon, 1990.

Brooks, Douglas A. *From Playhouse to Printing House: Drama and Authorship in Early Modern England*. New York: Cambridge University Press, 2000.

Brown, Jane K. *The Persistence of Allegory: Drama and Neoclassicism from Shakespeare to Wagner*. Philadelphia: University of Pennsylvania Press, 2007.

Brown, John Russell. *Shakespeare's Plays in Performance*. New York: Applause, 1993.

Browne, David. *The new invention, intituled, calligraphia: or, the arte of faire writing vvherein is comprehended the whole necessarie rules thereof*.... Saint Andrews, Scotland, 1622.

Brownstein, Oscar. "The Popularity of Baiting in England before 1600: A Study in Social and Theatrical History." *Educational Theatre Journal* 21 (1969): 237–50.

———. "Stake and Stage: The Baiting Ring and the Public Playhouse in Elizabethan England." PhD diss., University of Iowa, 1963.

———. "Why Didn't Burbage Lease the Beargarden? A Conjecture in Comparative Architecture." In *The First Public Playhouse: The Theatre in Shoreditch, 1576–1598*, edited by Herbert Berry, 81–96. Montreal: McGill-Queen's University Press, 1979.

Bruster, Douglas. *Shakespeare and the Question of Culture: Early Modern Literature and the Cultural Turn*. New York: Palgrave Macmillan, 2003.

Bruster, Douglas, and Robert Weimann. *Prologues to Shakespeare's Theatre: Performance and Liminality in Early Modern Drama*. London: Routledge, 2004.

Buck-Morss, Susan. "Aesthetics and Anaesthetics: Walter Benjamin's Artwork Essay Reconsidered." *October* 62 (1992): 3–41.

———. *The Dialectics of Seeing: Walter Benjamin and the Arcades Project*. Cambridge, MA: MIT Press, 1989.

Bulman, James C., ed. *Shakespeare, Theory, and Performance*. London: Routledge, 1996.

B[ulwer], J[ohn]. *Chirologia, or, The naturall language of the hand composed of the speaking motions, and discoursing gestures thereof: whereunto is added Chironomia, or, The art of manuall rhetoricke*.... London, 1644.

———. *Philocophus: or, The deafe and dumbe mans friend. Exhibiting the philosophicall verity of that subtile art, which may inable one with an observant eie, to heare what any man speaks by the moving of his lips. Upon the same ground, with the advantage of an historicall exemplification, apparently proving, that a man borne deafe and dumbe, may be taught to heare the sound of words with his eie, & thence learne to speake with his tongue*. London, 1648.

Burch, Robert. "Charles Sanders Peirce." In *The Stanford Encyclopedia of Philosophy*, edited by Edward N. Zalta. Published online 2010. http://plato.stanford.edu/archives/fall2010/entries/peirce/.

Burke, Peter. *Popular Culture in Early Modern Europe*. Rev. ed. Aldershot, UK: Ashgate, 1988.

Butler, Judith. *Bodies That Matter: On the Discursive Limits of "Sex."* New York: Routledge, 1993.

———. *Gender Trouble: Feminism and the Subversion of Identity*. New York: Routledge, 1990.

Butterworth, Philip. *Magic on the Early English Stage.* Cambridge: Cambridge University Press, 2005.

C. W. *The crying murther Contayning the cruell and most horrible bu[tchery] of Mr. Trat, curate of old Cleaue; who was first mu[rthered] as he trauailed vpon the high way, then was brought home to hi[s house] and there was quartered and imboweld: his quarters and bowels b[eing af]terwards perboyled and salted vp, in a most strange and fearefull manner....* London, 1624.

Calderwood, James L. *To Be and Not to Be: Negation and Metadrama in "Hamlet."* New York: Columbia University Press, 1983.

Campbell, Thomas P. "Liturgy and Drama: Recent Approaches to Medieval Theatre." *Theatre Journal* 33 (1981): 289–301.

Carew, Richard. *The survey of Cornvvall.* London, 1602.

Carlson, Marvin A. *Theatre Semiotics: Signs of Life.* Bloomington: Indiana University Press, 1990.

Carmichael, James. *Newes from Scotland, declaring the damnable life and death of Doctor Fian a notable sorcerer... With the true examination of the saide doctor and witches, as they vttered them in the presence of the Scottish king....* London, 1592.

Carroll, William C. *Fat King, Lean Beggar: Representations of Poverty in the Age of Shakespeare.* Ithaca, NY: Cornell University Press, 1996.

Cartwright, Kent. *Shakespearean Tragedy and Its Double: The Rhythms of Audience Response.* University Park: Pennsylvania State University Press, 1991.

Cerasano, S. P. "The Master of the Bears in Art and Enterprise." *Medieval and Renaissance Drama in England* 5 (1991): 195–209.

Chambers, E. K. *The Elizabethan Stage.* 4 vols. Oxford: Clarendon, 1923.

———. *The Mediaeval Stage.* 2 vols. Oxford: Oxford University Press, 1903.

Chapman, George, trans. *The Iliads of Homer prince of poets... With a co[m]ment vppon some of his chiefe places.* London, 1611.

———, trans. *The whole works of Homer; prince of poetts in his Iliads, and Odysses.* London, 1616.

Chester, Robert. *The anuals [sic] of great Brittaine. Or, A most excellent monument wherein may be seene all the antiquities of this kingdome....* London, 1611.

Clark, Stuart. *Thinking with Demons: The Idea of Witchcraft in Early Modern Europe.* Oxford: Clarendon, 1997.

———. *Vanities of the Eye: Vision in Early Modern European Culture.* Oxford: Oxford University Press, 2007.

Coddon, Karen S. "'Unreal Mockery': Unreason and the Problem of Spectacle in *Macbeth.*" *ELH* 56 (1989): 485–501.

Cohen, Stephen, ed. *Shakespeare and Historical Formalism.* Aldershot, UK: Ashgate, 2007.

Cole, Michael. "The Demonic Arts and the Origin of the Medium." *Art Bulletin* 84 (2002): 621–40.

Comenius, Johann Amos. *Orbis sensualium pictus... Joh. Amos Come[nius's] Visible world. Or, a picture and nomenclature of all the chief things that are in the world; and of mens employments therein....* Translated by Charles Hoole. London, 1685.

Cooper, Thomas. *The cry and reuenge of blood Expressing the nature and haynousnesse of wilfull murther....* London, 1620.

Cope, Jackson I. *The Theater and the Dream: From Metaphor to Form in Renaissance Drama.* Baltimore: Johns Hopkins University Press, 1973.

Corbin, Peter, and Douglas Sedge, eds. *Three Jacobean Witchcraft Plays.* Manchester: Manchester University Press, 1986.

Counsell, Colin. *Signs of Performance: An Introduction to Twentieth-Century Theatre*. London: Routledge, 1996.
Cox, John D. *The Devil and the Sacred in English Drama, 1350–1642*. Cambridge: Cambridge University Press, 2000.
Cox, John D., and David Scott Kastan, eds. *A New History of Early English Drama*. New York: Columbia University Press, 1997.
Crane, Mary Thomas. "What Was Performance?" *Criticism* 43, no. 2 (2001): 169–87.
Crary, Jonathan. "Spectacle, Attention, Counter-Memory." *October* 50 (1989): 96–107.
Crashawe, William. *The sermon preached at the Crosse, Feb. xiiii. 1607... that the religion of Rome, as now it stands established, is still as bad as euer it was*. London, 1609.
Cremona, Vicki Ann, Peter Eversmann, Hans van Maanen, Willmar Sauter, and John Tulloch, eds. *Theatrical Events: Borders, Dynamics, Frames*. Amsterdam: Rodopi, 2004.
Crooke, Helkiah. *Mikrokosmographia: A Description of the Body of Man. Together vvith the controuersies thereto belonging....* London, 1615.
Cunningham, Vanessa. *Shakespeare and Garrick*. Cambridge: Cambridge University Press, 2008.
Dando, John, and Harrie Runt [pseuds.]. *Maroccus Extaticus. Or, Bankes bay horse in a Trance A Discourse set downe in a merry Dialogue, betweene Bankes and his beast ....* [London], 1595.
Dane, Joseph A. *Abstractions of Evidence in the Study of Manuscripts and Early Printed Books*. Farnham, UK: Ashgate, 2009.
Dannenfeldt, Karl H. "Sleep: Theory and Practice in the Late Renaissance." *Journal of the History of Medicine and Allied Sciences* 41 (1986): 415–41.
Davenant, William. *The vnfortvnate lovers a tragedie: as it was lately acted with great applause at the private house in Black-Fryers by His Majesties servants*. London, 1643.
———. *The works of Sr. William Davenant, Kt. consisting of those which were formerly printed and those which he design'd for the press....* London, 1673.
Davidson, Clifford. *Festivals and Plays in Late Medieval Britain*. Aldershot, UK: Ashgate, 2007.
Davies, John. *Epigrammes and elegies*. [London?], 1599.
———. *Humours heau'n on earth with the ciuile warres of death and fortune ....* London, 1609.
Dawson, Anthony B., and Paul Yachnin. *The Culture of Playgoing in Shakespeare's England: A Collaborative Debate*. Cambridge: Cambridge University Press, 2001.
Dawson, Giles E. "London's Bull-Baiting and Bear-Baiting Arena in 1562." *Shakespeare Quarterly* 15 (1964): 97–101.
Deacon, John, and John Walker. *Dialogicall discourses of spirits and divels declaring their proper essence, natures, dispositions, and operations ....* London, 1601.
Debord, Guy. *The Society of the Spectacle*. 1967. Reprint, New York: Zone Books, 1994.
de Grazia, Margreta. "World Pictures, Modern Periods, and the Early Stage." In Cox and Kastan, *New History*, 7–21.
de Grazia, Margreta, Maureen Quilligan, and Peter Stallybrass, eds. *Subject and Object in Renaissance Culture*. Cambridge: Cambridge University Press, 1996.
Dekker, Thomas. *A strange horse-race at the end of which, comes in the catch-poles masque ....* London, 1613.
Dessen, Alan C. *Elizabethan Drama and the Viewer's Eye*. Chapel Hill: University of North Carolina Press, 1977.
———. *Elizabethan Stage Conventions and Modern Interpreters*. Cambridge: Cambridge University Press, 1984.

Dessen, Alan C. *Recovering Shakespeare's Theatrical Vocabulary.* Cambridge: Cambridge University Press, 1995.
———. *Rescripting Shakespeare: The Text, the Director, and Modern Productions.* Cambridge: Cambridge University Press, 2002.
———. *Shakespeare and the Late Moral Plays.* Lincoln: University of Nebraska Press, 1986.
———. *Titus Andronicus.* Shakespeare in Performance. Manchester: Manchester University Press, 1989.
———. "Two Falls and a Trap: Shakespeare and Spectacles of Realism." *English Literary Renaissance* 5 (1975): 291–307.
Dessen, Alan C., and Leslie Thomson. *A Dictionary of Stage Directions in English Drama, 1580–1642.* Cambridge: Cambridge University Press, 1999.
Dickey, Stephen. "Shakespeare's Mastiff Comedy." *Shakespeare Quarterly* 42 (1991): 255–75.
Diehl, Huston. "Horrid Image, Sorry Sight, Fatal Vision: The Visual Rhetoric of *Macbeth.*" *Shakespeare Studies* 16 (1983): 191–204.
———. *Staging Reform, Reforming the Stage: Protestantism and Popular Theatre in Early Modern England.* Ithaca, NY: Cornell University Press, 1997.
Dillon, Janette. *Language and Stage in Medieval and Renaissance England.* Cambridge: Cambridge University Press, 1998.
Donaldson, Peter S. *Shakespearean Films/Shakespearean Directors.* Boston: Unwin Hyman, 1990.
Douglas, Audrey, and Sally-Beth MacLean, eds. *REED in Review: Essays in Celebration of the First Twenty-Five Years.* Toronto: University of Toronto Press, 2006.
Dowd, Michelle M., and Natasha Korda, eds. *Working Subjects in Early Modern English Drama.* Farnham, UK: Ashgate, 2011.
Duffy, Eamon. "Devotion to the Crucifix and Related Images in England on the Eve of the Reformation." In *Bilder und Bildersturm im Spätmittelalter und in der frühen Neuzeit,* edited by Bob Scribner, 21–36. Wiesbaden, Germany: Harrassowitz, 1990.
———. *The Stripping of the Altars: Traditional Religion in England, c. 1400–c. 1580.* 2nd ed. New Haven, CT: Yale University Press, 2005.
Dugan, Holly. *The Ephemeral History of Perfume: Scent and Sense in Early Modern England.* Baltimore: Johns Hopkins University Press, 2011.
Dürer, Albrecht. *Vnderweysuug* [sic] *der Messung: mit dem Zirckel vnd richtscheyt, in Linien Ebnen vn[d] gantzen Corporen.* Nuremberg, 1538.
Eck, Caroline van, ed. *British Architectural Theory, 1540–1750: An Anthology of Texts.* Aldershot, UK: Ashgate, 2003.
Edelman, Charles. *Brawl Ridiculous: Swordfighting in Shakespeare's Plays.* Manchester: Manchester University Press, 1992.
Egan, Gabriel. "Hearing or Seeing a Play? Evidence of Early Modern Theatrical Terminology." *Ben Jonson Journal* 8 (2001): 327–47.
Egerton, Stephen. *The boring of the eare contayning a plaine and profitable discourse by way of dialogue: concerning 1. Our preparation before hearing, 2. Our demeanour in hearing, 3. Our exercise after we haue heard the Word of God.* London, 1623.
Elam, Keir. *The Semiotics of Theatre and Drama.* 2nd ed. London: Routledge, 2002.
Elliott, John R. Jr. "Early Staging in Oxford." In Cox and Kastan, *New History,* 68–76.
Elyot, Thomas. *The boke named the Gouernour.* [London], 1537.
———. *The dictionary of syr Thomas Eliot knyght.* London, 1538.
Emeljanow, Victor. "Editorial." *Popular Entertainment Studies* 1, no. 1 (2010): 1–5.
Enders, Jody. *Death by Drama and Other Medieval Urban Legends.* Chicago: University of Chicago Press, 2002.

Erne, Lukas. *Beyond "The Spanish Tragedy": A Study of the Works of Thomas Kyd.* Manchester: Manchester University Press, 2001.
———. "The Popularity of Shakespeare in Print." *Shakespeare Survey* 62 (2009): 12–29.
———. *Shakespeare as Literary Dramatist.* Cambridge: Cambridge University Press, 2003.
Evans, G. Blakemore, et al., eds. *The Riverside Shakespeare.* 2nd ed. Boston: Houghton Mifflin, 1997.
Evans, M. Blakemore. *The Passion Play of Lucerne: An Historical and Critical Introduction.* New York: Modern Language Association of America, 1943.
———. "The Staging of the Donaueschingen Passion Play." Parts 1 and 2. *Modern Language Review* 15 (1920): 65–76 and 279–97.
Felperin, Howard. *Shakespearean Representation: Mimesis and Modernity in Elizabethan Tragedy.* Princeton, NJ: Princeton University Press, 1977.
Fischer-Lichte, Erika. *The Semiotics of Theater.* Translated by Jeremy Gaines and Doris L. Jones. Bloomington: Indiana University Press, 1992.
Fleming, Juliet. *Graffiti and the Writing Arts of Early Modern England.* Philadelphia: University of Pennsylvania Press, 2001.
Fletcher, Angus. *Allegory: The Theory of a Symbolic Mode.* Ithaca, NY: Cornell University Press, 1964.
Fletcher, John, and Philip Massinger. *Sir John Van Olden Barnavelt.* 1619. Edited by T. H. Howard-Hill. Malone Society Reprints. London: Malone Society, 1980.
Fletcher, John, and William Shakespeare. *The two noble kinsmen presented at the Blackfriers by the Kings Maiesties servants, with great applause.* London, 1634.
Florio, John. *Florio his firste fruites which yeelde familiar speech, merie prouerbes, wittie sentences, and golden sayings....* [London], 1578.
Foakes, R. A., ed. *Henslowe's Diary.* 2nd ed. Cambridge: Cambridge University Press, 2002.
Foister, Susan. "Sixteenth-Century English Portraiture and the Idea of the Classical." In Gent, *Albion's Classicism*, 163–80.
Folkerth, Wes. *The Sound of Shakespeare.* London: Routledge, 2002.
Forman, Valerie. *Tragicomic Redemptions: Global Economics and the Early Modern English Stage.* Philadelphia: University of Pennsylvania Press, 2008.
Forrest, John. *The History of Morris Dancing, 1458–1750.* Toronto: University of Toronto Press, 1999.
Fortier, Mark. *Theory/Theatre: An Introduction.* 2nd ed. London: Routledge, 2002.
Foucault, Michel. *The Archaeology of Knowledge; and, The Discourse on Language.* Translated by A. M. Sheridan Smith. New York: Pantheon, 1972.
Fox, Adam. *Oral and Literate Culture in England, 1500–1700.* Oxford: Clarendon, 2000.
Fredell, Joel. "The Three Clerks and St. Nicholas in Medieval England." *Studies in Philology* 92 (1995): 181–202.
Freeman, Arthur. "The 'Tapster Manuscript': An Analogue of Shakespeare's *Henry the Fourth Part One*." *English Manuscript Studies, 1100–1700* 6 (1997): 93–105.
Fudge, Erica. *Brutal Reasoning: Animals, Rationality, and Humanity in Early Modern England.* Ithaca, NY: Cornell University Press, 2006.
———. *Perceiving Animals: Humans and Beasts in Early Modern English Culture.* New York: St. Martin's, 2000.
Fudge, Erica, Ruth Gilbert, and S. J. Wiseman, eds. *At the Borders of the Human: Beasts, Bodies and Natural Philosophy in the Early Modern Period.* New York: St. Martin's, 1999.
Fumerton, Patricia, and Simon Hunt, eds. *Renaissance Culture and the Everyday.* Philadelphia: University of Pennsylvania Press, 1999.

Garber, Marjorie. "'Here's Nothing Writ': Scribe, Script, and Circumscription in Marlowe's Plays." *Theatre Journal* 36 (1984): 301–20.
Gaskill, Malcolm. *Crime and Mentalities in Early Modern England*. Cambridge: Cambridge University Press, 2000.
Gatton, John Spalding. "'There must be blood': Mutilation and Martyrdom on the Medieval Stage." In Redmond, *Violence in Drama*, 79–91.
Gay, Penny. "*Twelfth Night*: 'The Babbling Gossip of the Air.'" In *A Companion to Shakespeare's Works*, edited by Richard Dutton and Jean E. Howard, 3:429–46. Malden, MA: Blackwell, 2003.
Gayton, Edmund. *Pleasant notes upon Don Quixot*. London, 1654.
Gent, Lucy, ed. *Albion's Classicism: The Visual Arts in Britain, 1550–1660*. New Haven, CT: Yale University Press, 1995.
———. "'The Rash Gazer': Economies of Vision in Britain, 1550–1660." In Gent, *Albion's Classicism*, 377–93.
Gilbert, Miriam. "The Disappearance and Return of *Love's Labor's Lost*." In *Shakespeare's Sweet Thunder: Essays on the Early Comedies*, edited by Michael J. Collins, 155–75. Newark: University of Delaware Press, 1997.
———. *Love's Labour's Lost*. Shakespeare in Performance. Manchester: Manchester University Press, 1993.
Gildon, Charles. "Critical Remarks on His Plays." In *The Works of Mr. William Shakespear* [sic], edited by Nicholas Rowe. 7 vols. 1709–10. Reprint, New York: AMS, 1967.
Gillies, John. "Place and Space in Three Late Plays." In *A Companion to Shakespeare's Works*, edited by Richard Dutton and Jean E. Howard, 4:175–93. Malden, MA: Blackwell, 2003.
Goldberg, Jonathan. *Writing Matter: From the Hands of the English Renaissance*. Stanford, CA: Stanford University Press, 1990.
Goldman, Michael. *Shakespeare and the Energies of Drama*. Princeton, NJ: Princeton University Press, 1972.
Gonzalo. *The divine dreamer: or, a short treatise discovering the true effect and power of dreames....* [London], 1641.
Gosson, Stephen. *Plays confuted in fiue actions prouing that they are not to be suffred in a Christian common weale....* London, 1582.
———. *The trumpet of vvarre A sermon preached at Paules Crosse the seuenth of Maie 1598*. London, 1598.
Goulart, Simon. *Admirable and memorable histories containing the wonders of our time....* Translated by Edward Grimeston. London, 1607.
Grady, Hugh. *Shakespeare's Universal Wolf: Studies in Early Modern Reification*. Oxford: Clarendon, 1996.
Graves, R. B. "*The Duchess of Malfi* at the Globe and Blackfriars." *Renaissance Drama* 9 (1978): 193–209.
———. *Lighting the Shakespearean Stage, 1567–1642*. Carbondale: Southern Illinois University Press, 1999.
Green, Juana. "Properties of Marriage: Proprietary Conflict and the Calculus of Gender in *Epicoene*." In Harris and Korda, *Staged Properties*, 261–87.
Greenberg, Marissa. "The Tyranny of Tragedy: Catharsis in England and *The Roman Actor*." *Renaissance Drama* 39 (2011): 163–96.
Greenblatt, Stephen, ed. *Allegory and Representation*. Baltimore: Johns Hopkins University Press, 1981.
———. "Mutilation and Meaning." In Hillman and Mazzio, *Body in Parts*, 220–41.
Greenblatt, Stephen, Walter Cohen, Jean E. Howard, and Katharine Eisaman Maus, eds. *The Norton Shakespeare*. New York: Norton, 1997.

Greg, W. W., ed. *Henslowe Papers: Being Documents Supplementary to Henslowe's Diary.* London: A. H. Bullen, 1907.
Gurr, Andrew. "Bears and Players: Philip Henslowe's Double Acts." *Shakespeare Bulletin* 22, no. 4 (2004): 31–41.
——. "Hearers and Beholders in Shakespearean Drama." *Essays in Theatre* 3 (1984): 30–45.
——. *Playgoing in Shakespeare's London.* 3rd ed. Cambridge: Cambridge University Press, 2004.
——. *The Shakespeare Company, 1594–1642.* Cambridge: Cambridge University Press, 2004.
——. *The Shakespearean Stage, 1574–1642.* 3rd ed. Cambridge: Cambridge University Press, 1992.
Habicht, Werner. "Tree Properties and Tree Scenes in Elizabethan Theater." *Renaissance Drama* 4 (1971): 69–92.
Hall, Joseph. *Virgidemiarum sixe bookes. First three bookes, of tooth-lesse satyrs. 1. Poeticall. 2. Academicall. 3. Morall.* London, 1597.
Harbage, Alfred. *Annals of English Drama, 975–1700.* 3rd ed. Revised by S. Schoenbaum and Sylvia Stoler Wagonheim. New York: Routledge, 1989.
Hardison, O. B. Jr. *Christian Rite and Christian Drama in the Middle Ages: Essays in the Origin and Early History of Modern Drama.* Baltimore: Johns Hopkins University Press, 1965.
Harris, Jonathan Gil. "Properties of Skill: Product Placement in Early English Artisanal Drama." In Harris and Korda, *Staged Properties,* 35–66.
Harris, Jonathan Gil, and Natasha Korda, eds. *Staged Properties in Early Modern English Drama.* Cambridge: Cambridge University Press, 2002.
Harris, Tim, ed. *Popular Culture in England, c. 1500–1850.* New York: St. Martin's, 1995.
Harrison, William. *The Description of England.* 1587. Edited by Georges Edelen. Ithaca, NY: Cornell University Press, 1968.
Harvey, Elizabeth D., ed. *Sensible Flesh: On Touch in Early Modern Culture.* Philadelphia: University of Pennsylvania Press, 2003.
Hattaway, Michael. *Elizabethan Popular Theatre: Plays in Performance.* London: Routledge & Kegan Paul, 1982.
Hauptfleisch, Temple, Shulamith Lev-Aladgem, Jacqueline Martin, Willmar Sauter, and Henri Schoenmakers, eds. *Festivalising! Theatrical Events, Politics and Culture.* Amsterdam: Rodopi, 2007.
Hazlitt, William. *Characters of Shakespear's Plays.* London, 1817.
Helgerson, Richard. *Forms of Nationhood: The Elizabethan Writing of England.* Chicago: University of Chicago Press, 1992.
Helms, Lorraine. "Acts of Resistance: The Feminist Player." In *The Weyward Sisters: Shakespeare and Feminist Politics,* edited by Dympna C. Callaghan, Lorraine Helms, and Jyotsna Singh, 102–56. Cambridge, MA: Blackwell, 1994.
Heywood, John. *A play of loue a newe and a mery enterlude concernyng pleasure and payne in loue....* [London], 1534.
Hibbard, G. R., ed. *Love's Labour's Lost.* The Oxford Shakespeare. Oxford: Oxford University Press, 1990.
Highfill, Philip H. Jr., Kalman A. Burnim, and Edward A. Langhans. *A Biographical Dictionary of Actors, Actresses, Musicians, Dancers, Managers & Other Stage Personnel in London, 1660–1800.* 16 vols. Carbondale: Southern Illinois University Press, 1973–93.

Hill, Thomas. *A most briefe and pleasant treatise of the interpretation of sundrie dreames intituled to be Iosephs, and sundry other dreames out of the worke of the wise Salomon* .... London, 1601.

Hillman, David, and Carla Mazzio, eds. *The Body in Parts: Fantasies of Corporeality in Early Modern Europe*. New York: Routledge, 1997.

Hind, John. *Eliosto libidinoso described in two bookes: vvherein their imminent dangers are declared, who guiding the course of their life by the compasse of affection, either dash their ship against most dangerous shelues, or else attaine the hauen with extreame preiudice*. London, 1606.

Hinman, Charlton, ed. *The First Folio of Shakespeare*. New York: Norton, 1968.

Hodgdon, Barbara. "Rehearsal Process as Critical Practice: John Barton's 1978 *Love's Labour's Lost*." *Theatre History Studies* 8 (1988): 11–34.

Höfele, Andreas. *Stage, Stake, and Scaffold: Humans and Animals in Shakespeare's Theatre*. Oxford: Oxford University Press, 2011.

Holland, Peter. "Theatre without Drama: Reading REED." In *From Script to Stage in Early Modern England*, edited by Peter Holland and Stephen Orgel, 43–67. Basingstoke, UK: Palgrave Macmillan, 2004.

Holmes, Jonathan, and Adrian Streete, eds. *Refiguring Mimesis: Representation in Early Modern Literature*. Hatfield, UK: University of Hertfordshire Press, 2005.

Homer. *The Iliad*. Translated by Robert Fagles with introduction and notes by Bernard Knox. New York: Viking Penguin, 1990.

Hopkins, D. J. *City/Stage/Globe: Performance and Space in Shakespeare's London*. New York: Routledge, 2008.

The horrible murther of a young boy of three yeres of age, whose sister had her tongue cut out and how it pleased God to reueale the offendors, by giuing speech to the tongueles childe .... London, 1606.

Hortmann, Wilhelm. *Shakespeare on the German Stage: The Twentieth Century*. Cambridge: Cambridge University Press, 1998.

Hosley, Richard, ed. *Essays on Shakespeare and Elizabethan Drama in Honor of Hardin Craig*. Columbia: University of Missouri Press, 1962.

Howard, Jean E. *The Stage and Social Struggle in Early Modern England*. London: Routledge, 1994.

——— . *Theater of a City: The Places of London Comedy, 1598–1642*. Philadelphia: University of Pennsylvania Press, 2007.

Howard, Jean E., and Phyllis Rackin. *Engendering a Nation: A Feminist Account of Shakespeare's English Histories*. London: Routledge, 1997.

Howard, Skiles. *The Politics of Courtly Dancing in Early Modern England*. Amherst: University of Massachusetts Press, 1998.

Hug, Tobias. "'You should go to *Hockley in the Hole*, and to *Marybone*, child, to learn valour': On the Social Logic of Animal Baiting in Early Modern London." *Renaissance Journal* 2, no. 1 (2004): 17–26.

Hutson, Lorna. "Rethinking the 'Spectacle of the Scaffold': Juridical Epistemologies and English Revenge Tragedy." *Representations* 89 (2005): 30–58.

Hutton, Ronald. *The Stations of the Sun: A History of the Ritual Year in Britain*. Oxford: Oxford University Press, 1996.

Ichikawa, Mariko. "What to Do with a Corpse? Physical Reality and the Fictional World in the Shakespearean Theatre." *Theatre Research International* 29 (2004): 201–15.

Ingram, Martin. "Ridings, Rough Music and the 'Reform of Popular Culture' in Early Modern England." *Past and Present* 105 (1984): 79–113.

James, Heather. "Cultural Disintegration in *Titus Andronicus*: Mutilating Titus, Vergil and Rome." In Redmond, *Violence in Drama*, 123–40.

———. *Shakespeare's Troy: Drama, Politics, and the Translation of Empire.* Cambridge: Cambridge University Press, 1997.
James I. *By the King, a proclamation against steelets, pocket daggers, pocket dagges and pistols.* London, 1616.
Jensen, Phebe. *Religion and Revelry in Shakespeare's Festive World.* Cambridge: Cambridge University Press, 2008.
Johnson, Nora. *The Actor as Playwright in Early Modern Drama.* Cambridge: Cambridge University Press, 2003.
Johnson, S. F. "*The Spanish Tragedy,* or Babylon Revisited." In Hosley, *Hardin Craig,* 23–36.
Jones, Ann Rosalind, and Peter Stallybrass. *Renaissance Clothing and the Materials of Memory.* Cambridge: Cambridge University Press, 2000.
Jonson, Ben. *The Alchemist.* Edited by Alvin B. Kernan. New Haven, CT: Yale University Press, 1974.
———. *The alchemist.* London, 1612.
———. *Bartholmew fayre: a comedie...; The diuell is an asse: a comedie...; The staple of newes: a comedie acted in the yeare, 1625, by His Maiesties seruants.* London, 1631.
———. *The workes of Beniamin Ionson.* London, 1616.
Joseph, B. L. *Elizabethan Acting.* 2nd ed. London: Oxford University Press, 1964.
Kastan, David Scott, and Peter Stallybrass, eds. *Staging the Renaissance: Reinterpretations of Elizabethan and Jacobean Drama.* New York: Routledge, 1991.
Kemp, William. *Kemps nine daies vvonder Performed in a daunce from London to Norwich....* London, 1600.
Kendall, Gillian Murray. "'Lend Me Thy Hand': Metaphor and Mayhem in *Titus Andronicus.*" *Shakespeare Quarterly* 40 (1989): 299–316.
Kennedy, Dennis. "Shakespeare without His Language." In *Shakespeare, Theory, and Performance,* edited by James C. Bulman, 133–48. London: Routledge, 1996.
———. *The Spectator and the Spectacle: Audiences in Modernity and Postmodernity.* Cambridge: Cambridge University Press, 2009.
Kernan, Alvin B. "Formalism and Realism in Elizabethan Drama: The Miracles in *King Lear.*" *Renaissance Drama* 9 (1966): 59–66.
Kernodle, George R. *From Art to Theatre: Form and Convention in the Renaissance.* Chicago: University of Chicago Press, 1944.
Kerrigan, John, ed. *Love's Labour's Lost.* The New Penguin Shakespeare. Harmondsworth, UK: Penguin, 1982.
Kidnie, Margaret Jane, ed. *Philip Stubbes, The Anatomie of Abuses.* Tempe: Arizona Center for Medieval and Renaissance Studies, 2002.
Kiefer, Frederick. *Shakespeare's Visual Theatre: Staging the Personified Characters.* Cambridge: Cambridge University Press, 2003.
Kiernan, Pauline. *Staging Shakespeare at the New Globe.* New York: St. Martin's, 1999.
Kinnaston, Francis. *Leoline and Sydanis a romance of the amorous adventures of princes: together with sundry affectionate addresses to his mistresse, under the name of Cynthia.* London, 1642.
Kinney, Arthur F. *Shakespeare by Stages: An Historical Introduction.* Malden, MA: Blackwell, 2003.
Knowles, Ric. *Reading the Material Theatre.* Cambridge: Cambridge University Press, 2004.
Knutson, Roslyn Lander. *Playing Companies and Commerce in Shakespeare's Time.* Cambridge: Cambridge University Press, 2001.
———. *The Repertory of Shakespeare's Company, 1594–1613.* Fayetteville: University of Arkansas Press, 1991.
Ko, Yu Jin. "A Little Touch of Harry in the Light: *Henry V* at the New Globe." *Shakespeare Survey* 52 (1999): 107–19.

Kruger, Loren. *Post-Imperial Brecht: Politics and Performance, East and South.* Cambridge: Cambridge University Press, 2004.

Kruger, Steven F. *Dreaming in the Middle Ages.* Cambridge: Cambridge University Press, 1992.

Kyd, Thomas. *The Spanish Tragedie Containing the lamentable end of Don Horatio, and Belimperia: with the pittifull death of olde Hieronimo.* London, 1592.

———. *The Spanish Tragedie: or, Hieronimo is mad againe. Containing the lamentable end of Don Horatio, and Belimperia; with the pittifull death of Hieronimo* .... Rev. ed. London, 1615.

———. *The Spanish Tragedy.* Edited by David Bevington. Manchester: Manchester University Press, 1996.

Lake, Peter, and Michael Questier. "Agency, Appropriation and Rhetoric under the Gallows: Puritans, Romanists and the State in Early Modern England." *Past and Present* 153 (1996): 64–107.

Lambarde, William. *A perambulation of Kent conteining the description, hystorie, and customes of that shyre* .... Rev. ed. London, 1596.

Lancashire, Anne, ed. *The Second Maiden's Tragedy.* Manchester: Manchester University Press, 1978.

Langbein, John H. *Prosecuting Crime in the Renaissance: England, Germany, France.* Cambridge, MA: Harvard University Press, 1974.

———. *Torture and the Law of Proof: Europe and England in the Ancien Régime.* Chicago: University of Chicago Press, 1977.

Langhans, Edward A. "The Post-1660 Theatres as Performance Spaces." In *A Companion to Restoration Drama,* edited by Susan J. Owen, 3–18. Oxford: Blackwell, 2001.

Laroque, François, ed. *The Show Within: Dramatic and Other Insets: English Renaissance Drama (1550–1642).* 2 vols. Montpellier: Université Paul-Valéry, 1992.

Lehmann, Hans-Thies. *Postdramatic Theatre.* Translated by Karen Jürs-Munby. London: Routledge, 2006.

Leibing, Franz. *Die Inscenirung des zweitägigen Luzerner Osterspieles vom Jahre 1583 durch Renwart Cysat.* Elberfeld, 1869.

Lemon, Rebecca. *Treason by Words: Literature, Law, and Rebellion in Shakespeare's England.* Ithaca, NY: Cornell University Press, 2006.

Lenton, Francis. *Characterismi: or, Lentons leasures Expressed in essayes and characters* .... London, 1631.

Leo Africanus, Johannes. *A geographical historie of Africa, written in Arabicke and Italian* .... Translated by John Pory. London, 1600.

———. *The History and Description of Africa.* Translated by John Pory. Edited by Robert Brown. 3 vols. London, 1896.

Lerer, Seth, ed. *Literary History and the Challenge of Philology: The Legacy of Erich Auerbach.* Stanford, CA: Stanford University Press, 1996.

Lesser, Zachary. *Renaissance Drama and the Politics of Publication: Readings in the English Book Trade.* Cambridge: Cambridge University Press, 2004.

Lesser, Zachary, Peter Stallybrass, and G. K. Hunter. "The First Literary *Hamlet* and the Commonplacing of Professional Plays." *Shakespeare Quarterly* 59 (2008): 371–420.

Levin, Carole. *Dreaming the English Renaissance: Politics and Desire in Court and Culture.* New York: Palgrave Macmillan, 2008.

Levin, Harry. *Shakespeare and the Revolution of the Times: Perspectives and Commentaries.* New York: Oxford University Press, 1976.

———. "Sitting in the Sky (*Love's Labor's Lost,* 4.3)." In *Shakespeare's "Rough Magic": Renaissance Essays in Honor of C. L. Barber,* edited by Peter Erickson and Coppélia Kahn, 113–130. Newark: University of Delaware Press, 1985.

Levinson, Marjorie. "What Is New Formalism?" *PMLA* 122 (2007): 558–69.
Lin, Erika T. "'Lord of thy presence': Bodies, Performance, and Audience Interpretation in Shakespeare's *King John*." In Low and Myhill, *Imagining the Audience*, 113–33.
———. "Popular Festivity and the Early Modern Stage: The Case of *George a Greene*." *Theatre Journal* 61 (2009): 271–97.
Lindberg, David C. *Theories of Vision from Al-Kindi to Kepler*. Chicago: University of Chicago Press, 1976.
Lindley, David. *Shakespeare and Music*. London: Thomson Learning, 2006.
Linschoten, Jan Huygen van. *Iohn Huighen van Linschoten. his discours of voyages into ye Easte & West Indies Deuided into foure bookes*. Translated by William Phillip. London, 1598.
Londré, Felicia Hardison. "From a Theatregoer's Notebook: The RSC's *Love's Labour's Lost*." In Londré, *"Love's Labour's Lost": Critical Essays*, 411–14.
———, ed. *"Love's Labour's Lost": Critical Essays*. New York: Garland, 1997.
Lopez, Jeremy. *Theatrical Convention and Audience Response in Early Modern Drama*. Cambridge: Cambridge University Press, 2003.
Low, Jennifer A. *Manhood and the Duel: Masculinity in Early Modern Drama and Culture*. New York: Palgrave Macmillan, 2003.
Low, Jennifer A., and Nova Myhill, eds. *Imagining the Audience in Early Modern Drama, 1558–1642*. New York: Palgrave Macmillan, 2011.
Lowin, John [I. L. Roscio, pseud.]. *Brief conclusions of dancers and dancing Condemning the prophane vse thereof... also true physicall obseruations for the preseruation of the body in health, by the vse of the same exercise*. London, 1609.
Loyer, Pierre le. *A treatise of specters or straunge sights, visions and apparitions appearing sensibly vnto men....* Translated by Zachary Jones. London, 1605.
Lunn, Eugene. *Marxism and Modernism: An Historical Study of Lukács, Brecht, Benjamin, and Adorno*. Berkeley: University of California Press, 1982.
Lunney, Ruth. *Marlowe and the Popular Tradition: Innovation in the English Drama before 1595*. Manchester: Manchester University Press, 2002.
Lyly, John. *Euphues and his England Containing his voyage and his aduentures, myxed with sundry pretie discourses of honest loue, the discription of the countrey, the court, and the manners of that isle....* London, 1580.
MacIntyre, Jean, and Garrett P. J. Epp. "'Cloathes worth all the rest': Costumes and Properties." In Cox and Kastan, *New History*, 269–85.
Mack, Maynard. "Engagement and Detachment in Shakespeare's Plays." In Hosley, *Hardin Craig*, 275–96.
Maplet, John. *A greene forest, or A naturall historie vvherein may bee seene first the most sufferaigne vertues in all the whole kinde of stones & mettals....* London, 1567.
Markham, Gervase, and William Sampson. *The true tragedy of Herod and Antipater with the death of faire Marriam... publiquely acted (with great applause) at the Red Bull, by the Company of his Maiesties Reuels*. London, 1622.
Marlowe, Christopher. *The tragicall history of D. Faustus As it hath bene acted by the right honorable the Earle of Nottingham his seruants*. London, 1604.
———. *The tragicall history of the life and death of Doctor Faustus*. London, 1616.
Marolles, Michel de. *Tableaux du temple des muses: tirez du cabinet de feu Mr. Faverau, conseiller du roy en sa cour des Aydes & grauez en tailles-douces par les meilleurs maistres de son temps pour representer les vertus & les vices sur les plus illustres fables de l'antiquité*. Paris, 1655.
Marsh, Christopher. *Popular Religion in Sixteenth-Century England: Holding Their Peace*. New York: St. Martin's, 1998.
Marshall, Peter. *Beliefs and the Dead in Reformation England*. Oxford: Oxford University Press, 2002.

Marston, John, and William Barksted. *The insatiate countesse A tragedie: acted at VVhite-Fryers*. London, 1613.

Massinger, Philip. *The bond-man an antient storie. As it hath been often acted with good allowance, at the Cock-pit in Drury-lane: by the most excellent princesse, the Lady Elizabeth her Seruants*. London, 1624.

Massinger, Philip, and Thomas Dekker. *The virgin martir a tragedie. As it hath bin diuers times publickely acted with great applause, by the seruants of his Maiesties Reuels*. London, 1622.

The maze: contrived, digested, and couched in these distinct subjects: representatives for these present times to admire . . . . N.p., 1659.

Mazzio, Carla. *The Inarticulate Renaissance: Language Trouble in an Age of Eloquence*. Philadelphia: University of Pennsylvania Press, 2009.

———. "Sins of the Tongue." In Hillman and Mazzio, *Body in Parts*, 53–79.

———. "Staging the Vernacular: Language and Nation in Thomas Kyd's *The Spanish Tragedy*." *Studies in English Literature, 1500–1900* 38 (1998): 207–32.

McAuley, Gay. *Space in Performance: Making Meaning in the Theatre*. Ann Arbor: University of Michigan Press, 1999.

McGuire, Philip C., and David A. Samuelson, eds. *Shakespeare, the Theatrical Dimension*. New York: AMS, 1979.

Mercer, Eric. *English Art, 1553–1625*. Oxford: Clarendon, 1962.

Meredith, Peter, and John E. Tailby, eds. *The Staging of Religious Drama in Europe in the Later Middle Ages: Texts and Documents in English Translation*. Kalamazoo, MI: Medieval Institute, 1983.

Meriton, Thomas. *The wandring lover a tragy-comedie being acted severall times privately at sundry places by the author and his friends with great applause*. London, 1658.

Metz, G. Harold. "Stage History of *Titus Andronicus*." *Shakespeare Quarterly* 28 (1977): 154–69.

Middleton, Thomas, and Thomas Dekker. *The Roaring Girl*. Edited by Paul A. Mulholland. The Revels Plays. Manchester: Manchester University Press, 1987.

———. *The roaring girle. Or Moll Cut-Purse As it hath lately beene acted on the Fortune-stage by the Prince his Players*. London, 1611.

Mitchell, W. J. T. *Iconology: Image, Text, Ideology*. Chicago: University of Chicago Press, 1986.

Montrose, Louis. *The Purpose of Playing: Shakespeare and the Cultural Politics of the Elizabethan Theatre*. Chicago: University of Chicago Press, 1996.

Mooney, Michael E. "'Edgar I Nothing Am': 'Figurenposition' in *King Lear*." *Shakespeare Survey* 38 (1985): 153–66.

———. *Shakespeare's Dramatic Transactions*. Durham, NC: Duke University Press, 1990.

Mullaney, Steven. *The Place of the Stage: License, Play, and Power in Renaissance England*. Chicago: University of Chicago Press, 1988.

Mulryne, J. R., ed. *The Spanish Tragedy*. 2nd ed. The New Mermaids. London: A&C Black, 1989. Reprint, New York: Norton, 2000.

Musaeus, Grammaticus. *The divine poem of Musaeus. First of all bookes*. Translated by George Chapman. London, 1616.

Nagler, A. M. *The Medieval Religious Stage: Shapes and Phantoms*. Translated by George C. Schoolfield. New Haven, CT: Yale University Press, 1976.

Nash, Thomas. *Pierce Penilesse his supplication to the diuell*. London, 1592.

———. *The terrors of the night or, A discourse of apparitions*. London, 1594.

Neill, Michael. "'Amphitheatres in the Body': Playing with Hands on the Shakespearian Stage." *Shakespeare Survey* 48 (1995): 23–50.

———. *Issues of Death: Mortality and Identity in English Renaissance Tragedy.* Oxford: Clarendon, 1997.
Nelson, Robert S. "Descartes' Cow and Other Domestications of the Visual." In Nelson, *Visuality,* 1–21.
———, ed. *Visuality Before and Beyond the Renaissance: Seeing as Others Saw.* Cambridge: Cambridge University Press, 2000.
Northbrooke, John. *Spiritus est vicarius Christi in terra. A treatise wherein dicing, dau[n]cing, vaine plaies or enterludes with other idle pastimes, &c. commonly vsed on the Sabboth day, are prerooued, by the authoritie of the worde of God and auncient vvriters.* London, 1579.
O'Callaghan, Michelle. "Dreaming the Dead: Ghosts and History in the Early Seventeenth Century." In *Reading the Early Modern Dream: The Terrors of the Night,* edited by Katharine Hodgkin, Michelle O'Callaghan, and Susan Wiseman, 81–95. New York: Routledge, 2008.
O'Connell, Michael. *The Idolatrous Eye: Iconoclasm and Theater in Early-Modern England.* New York: Oxford University Press, 2000.
Old Meg of Hereford-shire, for a Mayd-Marian: and Hereford towne for a Morris-daunce. Or Twelue Morris-dancers in Hereford-shire, of twelue hundred yeares old. London, 1609.
Orgel, Stephen. *The Illusion of Power: Political Theater in the English Renaissance.* Berkeley: University of California Press, 1975.
———. *Impersonations: The Performance of Gender in Shakespeare's England.* Cambridge: Cambridge University Press, 1996.
Orlin, Lena Cowen, ed. *Material London, ca. 1600.* Philadelphia: University of Pennsylvania Press, 2000.
Orme, Nicholas. "The Culture of Children in Medieval England." *Past and Present* 148 (1995): 48–88.
Orrell, John. *The Human Stage: English Theatre Design, 1567–1640.* Cambridge: Cambridge University Press, 1988.
———. *The Quest for Shakespeare's Globe.* Cambridge: Cambridge University Press, 1983.
———. "The Theaters." In Cox and Kastan, *New History,* 93–112.
Overbury, Thomas. *Sir Thomas Ouerburie his wife with new elegies vpon his (now knowne) vntimely death: whereunto are annexed, new newes and characters.* London, 1616.
Palmer, Barbara D. "Staging Invisibility in English Early Modern Drama." *Early Theatre* 11, no. 2 (2008): 113–28.
Palmer, D. J. "'A New Gorgon': Visual Effects in *Macbeth.*" In *Focus on Macbeth,* edited by John Russell Brown, 54–69. London: Routledge & Kegan Paul, 1982.
Palmer, Patricia. "'An headlesse Ladie' and 'a horses loade of heades': Writing the Beheading." *Renaissance Quarterly* 60 (2007): 25–57.
Panofsky, Erwin. *The Life and Art of Albrecht Dürer.* 4th ed. Princeton, NJ: Princeton University Press, 1971.
Park, Katharine. "Impressed Images: Reproducing Wonders." In *Picturing Science, Producing Art,* edited by Caroline A. Jones and Peter Galison, 254–71. New York: Routledge, 1998.
Parker, Andrew, and Eve Kosofsky Sedgwick, eds. *Performativity and Performance.* New York: Routledge, 1995.
Paster, Gail Kern. "Nervous Tension." In Hillman and Mazzio, *Body in Parts,* 106–25.
Paster, Gail Kern, Katherine Rowe, and Mary Floyd-Wilson, eds. *Reading the Early Modern Passions: Essays in the Cultural History of Emotion.* Philadelphia: University of Pennsylvania Press, 2004.
Pavis, Patrice. *Languages of the Stage: Essays in the Semiology of the Theatre.* New York: Performing Arts Journal Publications, 1982.

Peat, Derek. "'And that's true too': *King Lear* and the Tension of Uncertainty." *Shakespeare Survey* 33 (1980): 43–53.

———. "Looking Back to Front: The View from the Lords' Room." In Thompson and Thompson, *Shakespeare and the Sense of Performance*, 180–94.

Phelan, Peggy. *Unmarked: The Politics of Performance*. London: Routledge, 1993.

Pike, Richard. *Three to one being, an English-Spanish combat, performed by a westerne gentleman, of Tauystoke in Deuon shire with an English quarter-staffe, against three Spanish rapiers and poniards, at Sherries in Spaine, the fifteene day of Nouember, 1625. In the presence of dukes, condes, marquesses, and other great dons of Spaine, being the counsell of warre....* London, 1626.

Playford, John. *The English dancing master: or, Plaine and easie rules for the dancing of country dances, with the tune to each dance*. London, 1651.

A pleasant commodie, called Looke about you. As it was lately played by the right honourable the Lord High Admirall his seruaunts. London, 1600.

Plesch, Véronique. "Notes for the Staging of a Late Medieval Passion Play." In *Material Culture and Medieval Drama*, edited by Clifford Davidson, 75–102. Kalamazoo, MI: Medieval Institute, 1999.

Plutarch. *The philosophie, commonlie called, the morals vvritten by the learned philosopher Plutarch of Chaeronea... VVhereunto are annexed the summaries necessary to be read before every treatise*. Translated by Philemon Holland. London, 1603.

Pollard, Tanya. "Tragedy and Revenge." In *The Cambridge Companion to English Renaissance Tragedy*, edited by Emma Smith and Garrett A. Sullivan Jr., 58–72. New York: Cambridge University Press, 2010.

Poole, Kristen. "The Devil's in the Archive: *Doctor Faustus* and Ovidian Physics." *Renaissance Drama* 35 (2006): 191–219.

Pugliatti, Paola. *Beggary and Theatre in Early Modern England*. Aldershot, UK: Ashgate, 2003.

Purchas, Samuel. *Purchas his pilgrimes In fiue bookes... The third, nauigations and voyages of English-men, alongst the coasts of Africa....* 4 vols. London, 1625.

Puttenham, George. *The arte of English poesie Contriued into three bookes: the first of poets and poesie, the second of proportion, the third of ornament*. London, 1589.

Quilligan, Maureen. *The Allegory of Female Authority: Christine de Pizan's "Cité des Dames."* Ithaca, NY: Cornell University Press, 1991.

———. "Freedom, Service, and the Trade in Slaves: The Problem of Labor in *Paradise Lost*." In de Grazia, Quilligan, and Stallybrass, *Subject and Object*, 213–34.

———. *The Language of Allegory: Defining the Genre*. Ithaca, NY: Cornell University Press, 1979.

Rainolds, John. *Th'overthrow of stage-playes... Wherein is manifestly proved, that it is not onely vnlawfull to bee an actor, but a beholder of those vanities....* London, 1599.

Rasmussen, Mark David, ed. *Renaissance Literature and Its Formal Engagements*. New York: Palgrave Macmillan, 2002.

Records of Early English Drama: Cumberland, Westmorland, Gloucestershire. Edited by Audrey Douglas and Peter Greenfield. Toronto: University of Toronto Press, 1986.

Records of Early English Drama: Herefordshire, Worcestershire. Edited by David N. Klausner. Toronto: University of Toronto Press, 1990.

Records of Early English Drama: Oxford. 2 vols. Edited by John R. Elliott Jr., Alan H. Nelson, Alexandra F. Johnston, and Diana Wyatt. Toronto: University of Toronto Press, 2004.

Records of Early English Drama: Somerset. 2 vols. Edited by James Stokes. Toronto: University of Toronto Press, 1996.

Redmond, James, ed. *Violence in Drama*. Cambridge: Cambridge University Press, 1991.

Reynolds, Bryan, and William N. West, eds. *Rematerializing Shakespeare: Authority and Representation on the Early Modern English Stage.* New York: Palgrave Macmillan, 2005.
Ridout, Nicholas. *Stage Fright, Animals, and Other Theatrical Problems.* Cambridge: Cambridge University Press, 2006.
Righter [Barton], Anne. *Shakespeare and the Idea of the Play.* London: Chatto and Windus, 1962.
Roach, Joseph. *The Player's Passion: Studies in the Science of Acting.* Ann Arbor: University of Michigan Press, 1993.
Rochester, Joanne. *Staging Spectatorship in the Plays of Philip Massinger.* Burlington, VT: Ashgate, 2010.
Rowe, Katherine. *Dead Hands: Fictions of Agency, Renaissance to Modern.* Stanford, CA: Stanford University Press, 1999.
Rubin, Miri. *Corpus Christi: The Eucharist in Late Medieval Culture.* Cambridge: Cambridge University Press, 1991.
Saltz, David Z. "How to Do Things on Stage." *Journal of Aesthetics and Art Criticism* 49 (1991): 31–45.
Sauter, Willmar. *The Theatrical Event: Dynamics of Performance and Perception.* Iowa City: University of Iowa Press, 2000.
Sawday, Jonathan. *The Body Emblazoned: Dissection and the Human Body in Renaissance Culture.* London: Routledge, 1995.
Schalkwyk, David. *Speech and Performance in Shakespeare's Sonnets and Plays.* Cambridge: Cambridge University Press, 2002.
Schneider, Rebecca. *Performing Remains: Art and War in Times of Theatrical Reenactment.* London: Routledge, 2011.
Schoenfeldt, Michael C. *Bodies and Selves in Early Modern England: Physiology and Inwardness in Spenser, Shakespeare, Herbert, and Milton.* Cambridge: Cambridge University Press, 1999.
Schulz, Gretchen. "Sharing Shakespeare: An Academic's Adventures with the Atlanta Shakespeare Company." Talk presented at the Shakespeare in an Age of Visual Culture seminar, Folger Institute, Washington, DC, January 30, 1999.
Scott-Warren, Jason. "When Theaters Were Bear-Gardens; or, What's at Stake in the Comedy of Humors." *Shakespeare Quarterly* 54 (2003): 63–82.
Scribner, Bob. "Ways of Seeing in the Age of Dürer." In *Dürer and His Culture,* edited by Dagmar Eichberger and Charles Zika, 93–117. Cambridge: Cambridge University Press, 1998.
Semenza, Gregory M. Colón. *Sport, Politics, and Literature in the English Renaissance.* Newark: University of Delaware Press, 2003.
Sharpe, J. A. *Judicial Punishment in England.* London: Faber and Faber, 1990.
Shaw, Bernard. *Shaw on Shakespeare: An Anthology of Bernard Shaw's Writings on the Plays and Production of Shakespeare.* Edited by Edwin Wilson. London: Dutton, 1961. Reprint, New York: Applause, 1989.
Sherburne, Edward. *Poems and translations amorous, lusory, morall, divine.* London, 1651.
Sherman, William H. *Used Books: Marking Readers in Renaissance England.* Philadelphia: University of Pennsylvania Press, 2008.
Shirley, James. *Changes: or, Love in a maze A comedie, as it was presented at the Private House in Salisbury Court, by the Company of His Majesties Revels.* London, 1632.
———. *The doubtful heir. A tragi-comedie, as it was acted at the private house in Black-Friers.* London, 1652.
Shurgot, Michael W. *Stages of Play: Shakespeare's Theatrical Energies in Elizabethan Performance.* Newark: University of Delaware Press, 1998.

Sinanoglou, Leah. "The Christ Child as Sacrifice: A Medieval Tradition and the Corpus Christi Plays." *Speculum* 48 (1973): 491–509.
Smith, Bruce R. *The Acoustic World of Early Modern England: Attending to the O-Factor.* Chicago: University of Chicago Press, 1999.
———. *Ancient Scripts & Modern Experience on the English Stage, 1500–1700.* Princeton, NJ: Princeton University Press, 1988.
———. *Phenomenal Shakespeare.* Chichester, UK: Wiley-Blackwell, 2010.
———. "Premodern Sexualities." *PMLA* 115 (2000): 318–29.
Sofer, Andrew. "How to Do Things with Demons: Conjuring Performatives in *Doctor Faustus.*" *Theatre Journal* 61 (2009): 1–21.
———. *The Stage Life of Props.* Ann Arbor: University of Michigan Press, 2003.
Spenser, Edmund. *The Faerie Queene.* Edited by Thomas P. Roche Jr. New York: Penguin, 1978.
Sprigg, Douglas C. "Shakespeare's Visual Stagecraft: The Seduction of Cressida." In McGuire and Samuelson, *Shakespeare, the Theatrical Dimension,* 149–63.
Stallybrass, Peter, Roger Chartier, John Franklin Mowery, and Heather Wolfe. "Hamlet's Tables and the Technologies of Writing in Renaissance England." *Shakespeare Quarterly* 55 (2004): 379–419.
Steggle, Matthew. *Laughing and Weeping in Early Modern Theatres.* Aldershot, UK: Ashgate, 2007.
Stern, Tiffany. "'On each Wall and Corner Poast': Playbills, Title-pages, and Advertising in Early Modern London." *English Literary Renaissance* 36 (2006): 57–89.
Streitberger, W. R. "Personnel and Professionalization." In Cox and Kastan, *New History,* 337–55.
Strong, Roy C. *Art and Power: Renaissance Festivals, 1450–1650.* Berkeley: University of California Press, 1984.
Stubbes, Philip. *The anatomie of abuses contayning a discouerie, or briefe summarie of such notable vices and imperfections, as now raigne in many Christian countreyes of the worlde: but (especiallie) in a verie famous ilande called Ailgna....* London, 1583.
Styan, J. L. *Shakespeare's Stagecraft.* Cambridge: Cambridge University Press, 1967.
Summit, Jennifer, and David Wallace, eds. "Medieval/Renaissance: After Periodization." Special issue, *Journal of Medieval and Early Modern Studies* 37, no. 3 (2007).
Swander, Homer. "No Exit for a Dead Body: What to Do with a Scripted Corpse?" *Journal of Dramatic Theory and Criticism* 5 (1991): 139–52.
Tailby, John E. "Die Luzerner Passionsspielaufführung des Jahres 1583: zur Deutung der Bühnenpläne Renward Cysats." In *The Theatre in the Middle Ages,* edited by Herman Braet, Johan Nowé, and Gilbert Tournoy, 352–61. Leuven, Belgium: Leuven University Press, 1985.
Tarltons newes out of purgatorie Onely such a iest as his iigge, fit for gentlemen to laugh at an houre, &c. Published by an old companion of his, Robin Goodfellow. London, 1590.
Tatham, John. *Knavery in all trades, or, The coffee-house a comedy: as it was acted in the Christmas holidays by several apprentices with great applause.* London, 1664.
Teague, Frances. *Shakespeare's Speaking Properties.* Lewisburg, PA: Bucknell University Press, 1991.
Tennenhouse, Leonard. "Strategies of State and Political Plays: *A Midsummer Night's Dream, Henry IV, Henry V, Henry VIII.*" In *Political Shakespeare: Essays in Cultural Materialism,* 2nd ed., edited by Jonathan Dollimore and Alan Sinfield, 109–28. Ithaca, NY: Cornell University Press, 1994.
Teskey, Gordon. *Allegory and Violence.* Ithaca, NY: Cornell University Press, 1996.
T. G. *The tragedy of Selimus Emperour of the Turkes.* London, 1638.

Thomas, Keith. *Religion and the Decline of Magic: Studies in Popular Beliefs in Sixteenth- and Seventeenth-Century England.* London: Weidenfeld & Nicolson, 1971. Reprint, London: Penguin, 1973.

Thomas, Max W. "*Kemps Nine Daies Wonder:* Dancing Carnival into Market." *PMLA* 107 (1992): 511–23.

Thompson, Marvin, and Ruth Thompson, eds. *Shakespeare and the Sense of Performance: Essays in the Tradition of Performance Criticism in Honor of Bernard Beckerman.* Newark: University of Delaware Press, 1989.

Thomson, Peter. *Shakespeare's Theatre.* 2nd ed. London: Routledge, 1992.

Three bloodie murders the first, committed by Francis Cartwright vpon William Storre... The second, committed by Elizabeth Iames, on the body of her mayde... The third, committed vpon a stranger.... London, 1613.

Tofte, Robert. *Alba The months minde of a melancholy louer, diuided into three parts.* London, 1598.

The Tragical Reign of Selimus, 1594. Edited by W[illy] Bang. Malone Society Reprints. London: Malone Society/Chiswick Press, 1909.

Tribble, Evelyn B. *Cognition in the Globe: Attention and Memory in Shakespeare's Theatre.* New York: Palgrave Macmillan, 2011.

Turner, Henry S. *The English Renaissance Stage: Geometry, Poetics, and the Practical Spatial Arts, 1580–1630.* Oxford: Oxford University Press, 2006.

Ubersfeld, Anne. *Reading Theatre.* Translated by Frank Collins. Toronto: University of Toronto Press, 1999.

Underdown, David. *Fire from Heaven: Life in an English Town in the Seventeenth Century.* New Haven, CT: Yale University Press, 1992.

———. "Regional Cultures? Local Variation in Popular Culture during the Early Modern Period." In Harris, *Popular Culture,* 28–47.

Waith, Eugene M., ed. *Titus Andronicus.* The Oxford Shakespeare. Oxford: Clarendon, 1984.

Walker, Greg, ed. *Medieval Drama: An Anthology.* Oxford: Blackwell, 2000.

Walls, Peter. "Common Sixteenth-Century Dance Forms: Some Further Notes." *Early Music* 2 (1974): 164–65.

Walsham, Alexandra. *Providence in Early Modern England.* Oxford: Oxford University Press, 1999.

Watt, Tessa. *Cheap Print and Popular Piety, 1550–1640.* Cambridge: Cambridge University Press, 1991.

Webster, John. *The Duchess of Malfi.* 2nd ed. Edited by John Russell Brown. The Revels Plays. Manchester: Manchester University Press, 2009.

———. *The tragedy of the Dutchesse of Malfy As it was presented priuatly, at the Black-Friers; and publiquely at the Globe, by the Kings Maiesties Seruants....* London, 1623.

———. *The white diuel, or, The tragedy of Paulo Giordano Vrsini, Duke of Brachiano with the life and death of Vittoria Corombona the famous Venetian curtizan. Acted by the Queenes Maiesties Seruants.* London, 1612.

———. *The White Devil.* Edited by Christina Luckyj. The New Mermaids. London: A&C Black; New York: Norton, 1996.

Weimann, Robert. *Authority and Representation in Early Modern Discourse.* Edited by David Hillman. Baltimore: Johns Hopkins University Press, 1996.

———. *Author's Pen and Actor's Voice: Playing and Writing in Shakespeare's Theatre.* Edited by Helen Higbee and William West. Cambridge: Cambridge University Press, 2000.

———. "Bifold Authority in Shakespeare's Theatre." *Shakespeare Quarterly* 39 (1988): 401–17.

Weimann, Robert. *Shakespeare and the Popular Tradition in the Theater: Studies in the Social Dimension of Dramatic Form and Function.* Edited by Robert Schwartz. Baltimore: Johns Hopkins University Press, 1978.

Weimann, Robert, and Douglas Bruster. *Shakespeare and the Power of Performance: Stage and Page in the Elizabethan Theatre.* Cambridge: Cambridge University Press, 2008.

West, William N. "'But this will be a mere confusion': Real and Represented Confusions on the Elizabethan Stage." *Theatre Journal* 60 (2008): 217–33.

———. "When Is the Jig Up—and What Is It Up To?" In *Locating the Queen's Men, 1583–1603: Material Practices and Conditions of Playing,* edited by Helen Ostovich, Holger Schott Syme, and Andrew Griffin, 201–15. Farnham, UK: Ashgate, 2009.

White, Paul Whitfield. *Drama and Religion in English Provincial Society, 1485–1660.* Cambridge: Cambridge University Press, 2008.

Whitney, Charles. *Early Responses to Renaissance Drama.* Cambridge: Cambridge University Press, 2006.

Wickham, Glynne. "To Fly or Not to Fly? The Problem of Hecate in Shakespeare's *Macbeth.*" In *Essays on Drama and Theatre: Liber Amicorum Benjamin Hunningher,* 171–82. Amsterdam: Baarn, 1973.

Wiles, David. *Shakespeare's Clown: Actor and Text in the Elizabethan Playhouse.* Cambridge: Cambridge University Press, 1987.

———. *A Short History of Western Performance Space.* Cambridge: Cambridge University Press, 2003.

Willbern, David. "Rape and Revenge in *Titus Andronicus.*" *English Literary Renaissance* 8 (1978): 159–82.

Williams, Clare, ed. and trans. *Thomas Platter's Travels in England, 1599.* London: Jonathan Cape, 1937.

Williamson, Elizabeth. *The Materiality of Religion in Early Modern English Drama.* Farnham, UK: Ashgate, 2009.

Wilson, Catherine. *The Invisible World: Early Modern Philosophy and the Invention of the Microscope.* Princeton, NJ: Princeton University Press, 1995.

Wilson, Thomas. *A Christian dictionarie Opening the signification of the chiefe words dispersed generally through Holy Scriptures . . . .* London, 1612.

Winkler, Amanda Eubanks, ed. *Music for "Macbeth."* Middleton, WI: A-R Editions, 2004.

———. *O Let Us Howle Some Heavy Note: Music for Witches, the Melancholic, and the Mad on the Seventeenth-Century English Stage.* Bloomington: Indiana University Press, 2006.

Worthen, W. B. "Drama, Performativity, and Performance." *PMLA* 113 (1998): 1093–107.

———. *Shakespeare and the Authority of Performance.* Cambridge: Cambridge University Press, 1997.

———. *Shakespeare and the Force of Modern Performance.* Cambridge: Cambridge University Press, 2003.

Wright, Iain. "'Come like shadowes, so depart': The Ghostly Kings in *Macbeth.*" *Shakespearean International Yearbook* 6 (2006): 215–29.

Wright, Thomas. *The passions of the minde.* London, 1601.

Index

Abel, Lionel, 83
absence. *See* nothing
Acosta, José de, 114, 119
acting companies, 12–13
   See also Admiral's Men; Atlanta Shakespeare Company; Chamberlain's Men; King's Men; People's Light and Theatre Company; Philadelphia Shakespeare Theatre; Royal Shakespeare Company; Strange's Men
actors
  audience as, 21
  bodies of, 36, 89, 116, 136–49, 161, 164
  and characters, 64, 88–90
  as devils, 85
  doubling of parts, 144–45, 148
  gender of, 7
  as Machiavels, 85
  as signifiers, 36, 136, 149
Acts of the Apostles plays, 3, 144–45
Admiral's Men, 107, 111, 192n18
Adrichem, Christiaan van, 119
Aeneid, 76, 88
affective experience, 11, 88, 108–10, 121, 132, 130, 151–53
  religious, 57, 59, 74
agency, 6, 11, 130, 135, 138, 193n41
Agnew, Jean-Christophe, 150
Alberti, Leon Battista, 52, 55
Alchemist, The (Jonson), 15, 81
alcohol, 82, 115, 157
alehouses, 157
alienation effect (Brechtian), 11, 68, 136, 165
All's Well That Ends Well (Shakespeare), 30–31, 32, 33

allegory, 21, 62, 67–69, 80–81, 90–93, 120, 185n26
  characters as, 62, 72–73
  and mimesis, 71–104
Alleyn, Edward, 161
Alter, Jean, 109–10, 123, 148
amaze(ment), 120–21, 126–27
ambassador, 135–36
Amussen, Susan Dwyer, 139, 159
anatomy and physiology, 4, 43, 46–47, 54–57, 81–82, 119, 148, 177n50
animal baiting, 22, 112, 150, 152, 159, 161–63
  See also cockfighting
animals, 117–19, 159
  See also animal baiting; cockfighting
Antichrist plays, 3, 145
Antipodes, The (Brome), 162–63
antitheatricalism, 14, 19, 58, 66, 85, 111–12, 115–17
architecture, 43, 53–54, 174n22
  See also playhouses: architecture of
argument, 100, 124
Armin, Robert, 111
art, 43, 52–54
  theatre as, 10, 44, 73, 83, 164–65
Artemidorus, 80–83
As You Like It (Shakespeare), 7, 60, 62
asides, 21, 30, 32, 41–42, 60, 65, 132
  definition, 64
assumptions. *See* audience: conventions assumed by; conventions
atheism, 85
Atlanta Shakespeare Company, 146
Attewell, George, 107

audience
  and actors, 57–61, 116, 167n4
  as actors or characters, 21, 139
  bodies of, 57, 116
  and class, 24, 28, 121, 172n8
  as community, 11, 21, 24, 109, 131–33, 141, 163
  conventions assumed by, 5, 7–8, 14–22, 36, 42, 44, 51, 90–93, 109, 128, 146, 148, 165 (*See also* conventions: acquisition of; literacy: theatrical)
  description of performances by members of, 15–16, 18–19, 59, 111, 131–32, 162
  disapproval displayed by throwing things, 18
  effect of theatre on, 103
  at executions, 141, 159
  and gender, 116
  and hierarchy, 52
  interpretation by, 71–104
  laughter, 111, 199n9
  numbers of, 12–13, 123–24
  physical contact among, 57
  and vision, 32, 52, 57
  See also spectatorship
authority (theatrical), 12, 34–37
  definition, 172n8
  See also *locus* and *platea*

Babel and Babylon, 95–96, 98, 101–3
baiting. *See* animal baiting
Banchieri, Adriano, 115
Banister, John, 119
Barish, Jonas, 85
Barton, Anne Righter, 198n107
Baskervill, Charles Read, 15
bearbaiting. *See* animal baiting
Becon, Thomas, 56
beholding, 59, 74, 79, 112, 113–15, 119, 130–32, 153
Benjamin, Walter, 21, 109
  See also vision
Bentley, Eric, 148
Bethell, S. L., 27
Bevington, David, 83, 95, 99, 157
Blackfriars, 13–14, 112
Blayney, Peter, 12, 13

blindness, 3–5, 30–32, 34, 64, 68, 74, 135–36, 162
  See also vision
blocking (theatrical), 21, 41–42, 44, 54, 57, 64, 174n24, 188n79
  See also *locus* and *platea*; upstage vs. downstage
Bloom, Gina, 178n7, 194n55, 196n84
Bluett, Henry, 18–19
body
  and spirit, 82, 84, 89
  See also anatomy; body parts
body parts, 21–22, 133–65
  See also under props *and specific body parts*
Bond-man, The (Massinger), 112
books. *See* print
Booth, Stephen, 144
bosom, 135
Branagh, Kenneth, 177n3
Brathwaite, Richard, 75, 95, 115, 160
Brazen Age, The, 158
Brecht, Bertolt, 11, 21, 68, 109, 130–31, 136, 165, 174n30
Brissenden, Alan, 17
Brome, Richard, 162–63
Brooke, Nicholas, 197n96
Brown, John Russell, 17, 198n97
Browne, David, 98
Brownstein, Oscar, 204n96, 205n100
Brunelleschi, Filippo, 52
Bruster, Douglas, 27
Buckingham, Duke of, 131–32
Bulwer, John, 96–99
Burke, Peter, 11
Busino, Orazio, 131
Butler, Judith, 7, 8
Butterworth, Philip, 107

Calvin, John, 62
Carew, Richard, 156, 159
Castle of Perseverance, The, 24
catharsis, 85, 158
Catholicism. See *under* religion
center and periphery, 28
Chamberlain's Men, 111
Chambers, E. K., 46, 179n31
Changes (Shirley), 16

Chapman, George, 52, 159, 185n19, 187n48
characters (theatrical)
  and class, 24
  distinguished from actors, 64
  and vision, 32
Chester, Robert, 119
chorus, 80, 92–93
citation, 7
Clark, Stuart, 83
class
  and audience, 24, 28, 121, 172n8
  and characters, 24
  and genre, 11
  inversion, 19–20, 83
  and print, 14, 26
  and spectacle, 112
  and the verbal, 26
  See also elite vs. popular
clothing, 33, 123–24, 135, 149, 162
  See also costume; sumptuary laws
clowns and fools, 15, 24–25, 47, 60–61, 111, 113, 135–36, 154, 157, 177n51, 203n68
cockfighting, 158
Coke, Edward, 141
Collier, John Payne, 45
combat, 158–59, 163
  festive, 158–59, 163
  stage, 23, 36, 107, 109, 112, 164, 200n15, 205n99
Comedy of Errors, The (Shakespeare), 149–50, 160, 203n63
commerce. *See* economic exchange; theatre: as commerce
communal practices, 11, 21
  See also audience: as community
community
  audience as (*See under* audience)
  and festive combat, 163
  and hierarchy, 47
conventions
  acquisition of, 44, 61–62, 72, 78
  artistic and architectural, 43
  religious, 61–62
  theatrical (*See* audience: conventions assumed by)
Cope, Jackson, 83

Corpus Christi cycle plays, 10, 198n107
costume (theatrical), 35–36, 65, 72, 86–87, 89–90, 93, 110, 143, 145, 149
  See also clothing; disguise
Courageous Turk, The (Goffe), 86
Crane, Mary Thomas, 14
Crashawe, William, 95
crime
  at playhouses, 16
  See also law: and punishment
Crooke, Helkiah, 4, 119
Croxton *Play of the Sacrament,* 63, 146–47
cruentation, 143
cultural materialism, 168n8
Cymbeline (Shakespeare), 21, 85–86, 135–36, 141–45, 153, 164, 199n3, 200n15
Cysat, Renward, 47–49

dance, 14–18, 21, 46, 66, 148, 107–33, 151, 155
  devils', 21, 109, 122–24
  and hierarchy, 19–20
  as holy, 116–17
  as recreation, 118–19
  witches', 17, 21, 122, 126–28
  See also jig
Davenant, William, 17, 112
Davies, John, 123, 162, 179n18
Deacon, John, 85
deafness, 96
  See also hearing
death (onstage), 59, 77, 86–87
  by drowning, 72
  feigned, 36–37
  See also execution; ghosts; murder
decapitation, 136, 141, 144–45, 155–56
  See also execution; heads
deception, 83, 84–85, 88–89, 148, 150–53, 157, 164–65
  and hearing, 33–34, 35, 74, 128–29
  and vision, 63, 64, 74, 128
  See also disguise; identity: mistaken
de Grazia, Margreta, 176n43, 181n58
Dekker, Thomas, 16, 100, 123, 145
delight, 109–13, 115, 119, 121, 123–25, 127, 131
demons. *See* devils

Dessen, Alan, 18, 45, 64, 65, 66, 67–68, 128, 157
devils (onstage), 84–90, 92, 125, 131, 157, 164
    dances, 21, 109, 122–24
devils (spirits). *See under* religion
Devil's Charter, The, 128
Dillon, Janette, 99, 101
disguise, 19–20, 35–36, 84
    See also deception
dismemberment. *See* body parts; mutilation
Doctor Faustus (Marlowe), 127, 130, 137, 145, 153–58, 163–64, 200n20, 202n53
    devils' dance in, 21, 109, 121–26
    homo fuge episode, 124–25
    as morality play, 131
    seven deadly sins in, 73
documents (props), 125, 197n91
Doubtful Heir, The (Shirley), 112
downstage. *See under* upstage
dramatis personae, 86
dreams. *See* sleep
drowning (onstage), 72
Duchess of Malfi, The (Webster), 164–65
Duffy, Eamon, 59, 63
dumb show, 79–80, 90–93
dummies, 144–45, 164
Dürer, Albrecht, 55–56

ears, 74, 75, 95, 97
    See also hearing
eavesdropping, 31–34, 41, 45, 59–60, 64–65, 152–53
Eck, Caroline van, 54
economic exchange, 149–50, 153
    See also commerce; theatre: as commerce
Egan, Gabriel, 112
Egerton, Stephen, 75
Eliosto Libidinoso (Hind), 66, 113
elite vs. popular, 11, 14, 24, 26, 43, 54
Elizabeth I, Queen, 52, 53, 107
Elliott, John, 52
Elyot, Thomas, 81, 159
emotion. *See* affective experience
entertainment
    animal baiting as, 161–63
    theatre as, 10, 14–16, 109–13, 127, 137, 148, 153, 157, 163, 165

epistemology, 7, 10, 22, 63, 69, 78–80, 83, 85–90, 93, 94, 103–4
Epp, Garrett, 35
Erne, Lukas, 13, 88, 188n61, 188n63
Eucharist. *See under* religion
Euphues and His England (Lyly), 113
Europe, continental, 3, 85, 15, 47–48, 52–54, 117, 144–45, 174n22, 193n46
    holiday entertainments in, 46
    modern theatre in, 25
    See also language: foreign
Every Man in his Humour (Jonson), 192n22
execution, 22, 61, 75, 137–41, 159
eyes, 3–5, 56–57, 74–75, 97, 116, 119, 126, 135, 164
    See also vision

Faerie Queene, The (Spenser), 115
feast days. *See* holidays
feats of activity, 21, 107–8, 109, 120, 130, 132, 148
    See also spectacle
Fletcher, Angus, 80, 185n26
Fletcher, John, 18–20, 145, 160–61, 202n61
Florio, John, 111
Foister, Susan, 55
food, 82, 151–52, 163
fools. *See* clowns and fools
football, 22, 61, 149, 156–61
foreground, definition, 172n8
Forrest, John, 18
Fortier, Mark, 25
Fortune Theatre, 16, 28, 123, 164
Foucault, Michel, 8, 22
fourth wall, 11, 27, 104, 165
Foxe, John, 141
Frazer, James, 19
Furies, 90–92

games, 137, 149–56
    "all hid," 46
    cards, 152
    See also sport
Garrick, David, 170n53
Gaskill, Malcolm, 142

Gatton, John Spalding, 145
Gayton, Edmund, 18
gaze (the), 32–33, 37, 51, 56–57, 64, 111, 117
   sacramental, 57, 59, 74
   See also vision
gender, 12, 25, 58, 90, 95
   and cross-dressing, 7, 89, 108
   and hearing, 194n55
   and vision, 56, 115
genre, 10–11, 77, 111, 185n26
   and class, 11
Gent, Lucy, 53, 56
gesture, theatrical, 42, 64, 65–66, 97, 100, 111, 138, 139, 156
ghosts, 65, 79–90, 93, 128
   See also under *Hamlet*
Gilbert, Miriam, 43, 45
Gildon, Charles, 43
Globe Theatre, 28, 111, 112, 128, 139, 161
   burning (1613), 18–19
   modern, 25, 28, 53
gods
   Christian (*See under* religion)
   theatrical characters, 24, 45–47
Goffe, Thomas, 86
Gonzalo (author of *Divine Dreamer*), 82
Gosson, Stephen, 58, 111–12
Goulart, Simon, 120–21
Gower, George, 53
Green, Hugh, 159
Greenberg, Marissa, 85, 182n82, 195n81, 200n12
Greenblatt, Stephen, 148
Gunpowder Plot, 83
Gurr, Andrew, 13, 28, 111

Hamlet (Shakespeare), 17, 164
   gesture in, 66
   ghost in, 65, 87, 164, 188n79
   graveyard scene, 87, 177n51
   "Oh what a rogue" speech, 87–88
   play-within-play in, 84, 85, 87–88
hands, 97, 135–136, 137–39, 141, 145–47, 150–52, 160–61, 164
Hanse, Everard, 140

Harbage, Alfred, 157
Harlequin Doctor Faustus (Thurmond), 155, 203n70
Harrison, William, 141
Hart, William, 140–41
Hazlitt, William, 43
heads
   displayed on pikes, 139–40
   onstage, 21–22, 136, 137, 138, 151–53, 155–56
   used as footballs, 156–57, 159–61
   See also decapitation
hearing, 33–34, 35, 53, 112–14, 180n34
   as deceptive/unreliable, 74, 128
   spiritual and moral implications of, 63, 74
   See also deafness; ears; eavesdropping
Helgerson, Richard, 25
hell. *See under* religion
Henry IV, Part 1 (Shakespeare), 36–37, 108, 157
Henry IV, Part 2 (Shakespeare), 73
Henry V (Shakespeare)
   French-language scene, 100
   Prologue, 71, 89–90, 103, 112
Henry VIII (Shakespeare and Fletcher), 18–20, 177n51
Henry of Langenstein [Henry of Hesse], 57
Henslowe, Philip, and his diary, 45, 65, 72–73, 86, 111, 154, 161, 171n64
   See also props
Herod and Antipater (Markham and Sampson), 145
Heywood, John, 66
hierarchy
   and audience, 52–53
   and clothing, 33
   and community, 47
   and dance, 19–20
   and gaze, 32–33
   moral, 47
   and spectacle, 32–33
   and stage space, 44–49
   and verisimilitude, 48
Hill, Thomas, 80, 82
Hind, John, 66, 113
historical formalism, 11
historical phenomenology, 11

holidays, 12, 18–20
    carnival inversion during (*See* Lord of Misrule; *See also under* class)
    Corpus Christi, 10, 198n107
    entertainments on, 46
    Holy Innocents, 46
    Shrove Tuesday, 158–59, 161
Holinshed's *Chronicles*, 19
Holles, John, 52
Homer, 76, 159
Hopkins, D. J., 175n35
Horestes (Pikering), 92
horns (on head), 157–58
Hortmann, Wilhelm, 25
Hosley, Richard, 188n79
Howard, Jean, 25, 169n17, 175n35
Howard, Skiles, 20
humors (medical theory), 81, 88
hurling (sport), 156, 159
Hutton, Ronald, 156, 158

iconography, 65, 72, 90–91, 92, 93
identity
    and body, 142–43
    and costume, 35, 87, 89, 144
    mistaken, 33–36, 164
    and voice, 35, 176n47
idolatry. *See under* religion
Iliad, 159
intermission, 17–18, 185n22
invisibility, 41–42, 65–66, 124–25, 12–29
    robe for, 65
    See also vision
Ionicus [Joshua Armitage], 51
Irving, Henry, 170n53
Island Princess, The (Fletcher), 160–61

James I of England, King, 52–53, 131–32, 197n96
Jews. *See under* religion
jig, 15–17, 112, 191n14
Johnson, S. F., 99
Johnson, Samuel, 45
Jones, Ann Rosalind, 87, 196n83
Jones, Inigo, 52, 171n72, 180n45
Jonson, Ben, 15, 17, 81, 112–13, 171n72, 192n22
Joseph, Stephen, 51

Julian of Norwich, 59
justice, 95, 138–39, 142, 185n21

Kastan, David Scott, 25
Kemp, Will, 111
Kiefer, Frederick, 73, 90, 93, 198n97
King John (Shakespeare), 177n50, 177n51
King Lear (Shakespeare), 12, 25, 55, 158, 164, 177n51
    blinding-of-Gloucester scene, 3–5, 164
    cliffs-of-Dover scene, 30–36
kings and queens
    mock, 19
    real, 32–33, 52, 197n96
    theatrical characters, 24, 63–64, 126, 197n96
King's Men, 17, 116, 128
Kinnaston, Francis, 84
Klausner, David, 46
Knutson, Roslyn Lander, 18, 19, 73, 86, 111
Kyd, Thomas, 21, 66, 71–104, 194n61, 200n26
Kyle, Barry, 177n3

Lake, Peter, 140
Lambarde, William, 112
Lancaster [Onsager], Sarah, 146
Langbein, John, 142
language, 94–103
    dialects, 33
    foreign, 33, 98–103
    gestural, 97–98, 138
    inadequacy of, 94, 101–4, 107–8
    oral, 5, 33, 35–36, 94, 97–99 (*See also* speech acts)
    translation, 33, 100–101
    written, 53, 54, 94, 97–98, 124, 125, 139 (*See also* print)
lanterns (props), 65, 90–91
    See also lighting
law
    and the body, 143, 148
    and justice, 95, 138–39, 142
    legal documents, 125, 142, 161
    and punishment, 137–43, 159–60 (*See also* execution; mutilation; punishment, corporal)
    See also treason

legs, 153–55, 157, 160–61, 202n53
Leibing, Franz, 48–49
Lenton, Francis, 14–15
Leo Africanus, 115, 117
Leoline and Sydanis (Kinnaston), 84
Lesser, Zachary, 13
lighting, 5, 17, 42
  See also lanterns
Lilburne, John, 139
Lindberg, David, 57
Linschoten, Jan Huygen van, 113
literacy, 12
  theatrical, 6, 44, 72 (*See also* conventions: acquisition of)
locus and *platea*, 20, 23–37, 45–46
  definitions, 24, 27, 37
Look About You, 36
Looking Glass for London and England, A, 73
Lord of Misrule, 19, 46
Love's Labor's Lost (Shakespeare), 21, 32, 41–69, 176n44
Lowin, John, 116–17
Loyer, Pierre le, 85, 92
Luther, Martin, 62
Lyly, John, 113

Macbeth (Davenant), 17
Macbeth (Shakespeare), 130–32, 177n51, 199n3
  witches' dance, 17, 21, 109, 122, 126–30
  procession of kings, 109, 126–30
Machiavelli/Machiavels, 85
MacIntyre, Jean, 35
Mankind, 62–63, 66
Maplet, John, 119
Markham, Gervase, 145
Marlowe, Christopher, 21, 73, 121–27, 130, 137, 145, 153–58, 163–64, 200n20, 202n53
Marolles, Michel de, 76–77
Marsh, Christopher, 61
Martini, Martin, 48–49
martyrs. *See under* religion
Marx, Karl, 8
Marxist scholarship, 7–8, 168n8
Masque of Queens (Jonson), 17
masques, 17, 19–20, 73, 131–32, 171n72

mass. *See* religion: Eucharist
Massinger, Philip, 112, 145, 202n61
materiality
  definition, 6–9
  of performance, 6–9, 104, 197n91
  of texts, 6, 197n91
material text studies, 6, 11–14
  See also print: history of
Mazzio, Carla, 99, 190n107
McGuire, Philip, 174n21
medium
  of performance, 6, 9, 14, 20–22, 23, 101, 148–49
  of text, 6, 9, 11, 14, 100, 101
Merchant of Venice, The (Shakespeare), 175n38
Meriton, Thomas, 158
Merry Wives of Windsor, The (Shakespeare), 64
metatheatricality, 21, 73, 76–84, 88, 93–104, 123, 125
  See also plays-within-plays
methodology, 9–14, 24–29, 172n8, 185n26
Middleton, Thomas, 17, 123
Midsummer Night's Dream, A (Shakespeare), 84, 177n51
mimesis, 6, 8
  and allegory, 21, 71–104
  definition, 184n3
  necessity of, 42–43, 60
  and plays-within-plays, 76, 83–85
  unreliability of, 84
  See also representation; verisimilitude
miracles, 141–43, 147
  See also visions, miraculous
moderation, 114, 121
modernity
  and Shakespeare, 11, 72–73
Montrose, Louis, 25–26
Mooney, Michael, 27, 176n47
morality plays, 10, 24, 73, 92–93, 131, 198n107
  See also Vice figure; *and titles of individual plays*
Much Ado About Nothing (Shakespeare), 32, 34
Mulcaster, Richard, 102
Mulryne, J. R., 99

murder, 77, 90–91, 92, 127, 137–49, 160
murder pamphlets, 64, 142–44, 148
music, 15, 17–18, 75, 108, 111, 114, 127, 151
mutilation, 3–5, 63, 75, 133–65
  See also body parts

Nagler, A. M., 179n31
Najera, Duke of, 162
Nash, Thomas, 85, 115
Nelson, Robert, 179n27
nets (props), 66, 68–69
New Historicism, 6, 26
new materialism, 6–7
News from Plymouth (Davenant), 112
Northbrooke, John, 58, 116–17
Northumberland, Ninth Earl of, 52
note (the term), 196n89
nothing/absence, 124–25, 136, 142, 144, 145–48, 154–55

objects. See new materialism; subject and object
Odyssey, 76
Old Meg of Herefordshire, 46
Onsager [Lancaster], Sarah, 146
ontology, theatrical, 147–48, 153, 164–65
Orphinstrange, John, 116–17
Othello (Shakespeare), 59
Ottewell [Attewell], George, 107
Overbury, Thomas, 53
Oxford, 52, 53, 86, 148

paganism. See under religion
Palmer, Barbara, 65
Palmer, D. J., 198n97
Palmer, Patricia, 160
Panofsky, Erwin, 53
pantomime, 155
Paris Gardens, 161
Passion plays, 47–49, 145, 179n31
pauses, 80, 128–29
Peat, Derek, 50
Peirce, Charles Sanders, 94, 99
People's Light and Theatre Company, 199n3
Pepys, Samuel, 17

performance
  definitions of, 14–20
  materiality of (*See under* materiality)
  as medium, 6, 9, 14, 20–22, 23, 101, 148–49
performativity, 61–67, 75, 94–103, 141
  definition, 7–9
  of Eucharist, 62–64
  See also speech acts
Pericles (Shakespeare), 64
periodization, 10–11, 72–73
perspective (in art), 52–53, 55–56, 174n22
Philadelphia Shakespeare Theatre/Festival, 199n3
physiology. See anatomy and physiology
Pike, Richard, 159
Pikering, John, 92
platea. See *locus* and *platea*
Platter, Thomas, 15–16, 139–40
playbooks. See print: and drama
Playford, John, 118
playhouses, 10–12
  architecture/geography of, 24, 27–29, 44–49, 128, 188n79, 198n97 (See also *locus* and *platea*; sightlines; trapdoors)
  crime at, 16
  See also Blackfriars; Fortune Theatre; Globe Theatre; Paris Gardens; Red Bull Theatre; Rose Theatre; Theatre, the (Shoreditch)
Play of Love (Heywood), 66
plays-within-plays, 17, 21, 73, 76–80, 83–84, 87–88, 94–103
  See also metatheatricality
pleasure, 14, 95, 104, 108–19, 121, 123–24, 130
Plutarch, 114
Poole, Kristen, 85, 197n91
popular vs. elite. See under elite
presentation, 9, 20, 42, 54, 109, 132, 163
pride, 64–65, 95–96, 98
Pride of Life, The, 24, 45
print
  and class, 14
  and drama, 11–14, 100–101, 107
  history of, 6–7, 11–14
privilege
  definition, 172n8

prizefighting, 159–60
props
  body parts, 21–22, 136–65 (*See also* specific body parts)
  documents, 125, 197n91
  dummies, 144–45, 164
  horns (on head), 157–58
  invisibility robe, 65
  lanterns/torches, 65, 90–91
  nets, 66, 68–69
  as signifiers, 65, 72, 110, 136, 143, 145, 150
  as spectacle, 110, 123
  trees, 41–42, 43, 44–45
  Tritons'/Neptune's attributes, 72
  See also Henslowe, Philip
proscenium arch theatres, 28, 44, 50–51, 54
  See also upstage vs. downstage
Prynne, William, 139
punishment, corporal, 75, 148
  See also law: and punishment
Purgatory. *See under* religion
Puttenham, George, 120

Questier, Michael, 140
Quilligan, Maureen, 185n26

Rackin, Phyllis, 25
Rainolds, John, 14
rape/rap (the terms), 195n81
Rasmussen, Eric, 157
ravishment, 121, 130
Rebellion of Naples, The, 145
Records of Early English Drama (REED), 19, 107, 167n3
recreation/"recreate," 118–20, 124, 132, 158
Red Bull Theatre, 72, 191n14
Reformation. *See under* religion
religion
  atheism, 85
  Catholicism, 11, 46, 56, 58, 59, 61–63, 74, 84, 140–41, 159
  devils, 83–90, 203n66 (*See also* devils [onstage])
  Eucharist, 56, 61–63, 74, 104, 146–47
  feast days (*See* holidays)
  hell, 47–48, 76, 86–88, 91–93, 104, 200n20
  idolatry, 57–61, 67, 119
  Jews, 56, 63, 146–47
  martyrs, 139–41, 143, 148
  paganism, 19, 58, 88
  Protestant Reformation, 19, 46, 47, 56–59, 61–63, 67–68, 74–75, 84, 88–89, 140–1, 148
  Purgatory, 84, 88–89
  relics, 140–1
  ritual efficacy, 62–63
  saints, 58–59, 74
  and spiritual and moral implications of vision and hearing, 56–59, 67–68, 74–75
Renaissance (the term), 11, 168n13
repetition, 7, 53–54, 60, 102, 104, 127, 139
representation, 9, 11, 20, 42, 51, 54, 109, 132, 136–37, 148, 163, 165
revenge, 73, 76–80, 84, 90–93, 95
revenge tragedy, 77, 142
Richard III (Shakespeare), 25, 28, 82, 85–86, 143, 177n51
Righter [Barton], Anne. *See* Barton, Anne Righter
ritual efficacy. *See under* religion; speech acts
Roaring Girl, The (Middleton and Dekker), 123
Robin Hood, 19
Romeo and Juliet (Shakespeare), 177n51
rope-dancing, 107–8, 120
Rose Theatre, 28, 139
Royal Shakespeare Company, 42, 44
Rubin, Miri, 56

saints. *See under* religion
saints plays, 145
Sampson, William, 145
Schalkwyk, David, 172n8
science, 54, 56–57, 116
  See also anatomy and physiology
Scot, Reginald, 85
Scribner, Bob, 58, 74
Second Maiden's Tragedy, The, 86–87
secularization, 11, 72–73, 81, 140, 148
self-referentiality, 20
  See also metatheatricality

Selimus, The Tragical Reign of, 135–36, 200n12
semiotics
  of Eucharist, 62
  iconic vs. indexical vs. symbolic, 47, 67, 72, 73, 75, 90, 94, 99, 102
  and material, 7–9, 94–103, 104
  of violence, 135–65
Serlio, Sebastiano, 52
sets (theatrical), 44–45
sexuality, 58, 114–16, 152
Shakespeare, William
  as "modern," 11, 72–73
  See also titles of individual plays
Shaw, Bernard, 41–42, 63
shepherds
  in holiday festivities, 18–20
Sherburne, Edward, 185n19
Shirley, James, 16, 112
Shoemaker's Holiday, The (Dekker), 100
show (the term), 112, 126
sight. *See* blindness; invisibility; vision
sightlines, 28, 50–53, 55
signifiers
  actors as, 36, 136
  costume as, 36, 110
  Eucharist as, 62
  gesture as, 65–66, 97
  props as, 65, 72, 110, 150
  theatrical, 21, 34, 43, 94–104, 128
  See also semiotics
Sir John Van Olden Barnavelt (Fletcher and Massinger), 145, 202n61
sleep, 76–86, 87–89, 91, 93, 94, 120, 130, 153
Smith, Bruce, 15, 55, 169n16, 180n34
Sofer, Andrew, 125
soliloquies, 23, 24–25, 28, 30, 36, 50, 88, 93
sound, 32–34, 42, 53, 55, 97–99, 127, 129, 180n34
  See also deafness; hearing; language: oral; music
Spanish Tragedy, The (Kyd), 21, 66, 71–104, 194n61, 200n26
spectacle, 8, 17, 18, 21, 107–33, 136–37, 163, 165
  and class, 112
  as dangerous, 124
  functions of, 122–23
  and hierarchy, 32–33
  props as, 110, 123
  and verisimilitude, 65
spectatorship, 167n4
  active and passive, 32–33, 57, 109, 114, 121, 130, 132, 174n30
  onstage and offstage, 58, 59–60, 64–65, 95, 100, 121, 124, 123, 128–29, 163–64, 190n103
  See also audience
speech acts, 7, 9, 62–64, 76, 103–4, 124–25
  and Eucharist, 62–63
  See also performativity
Spenser, Edmund, 115
spirit
  and body, 82, 84, 89
  See also under religion
sport, 22, 109–10, 113, 137, 151–53, 157–58, 163
  See also animal baiting; football; games; hurling; prizefighting
spying. *See* eavesdropping
stage directions, 18, 36, 45, 64, 65, 66, 67–68, 86, 107–8, 128, 155
stage space. See *locus* and *platea*; playhouses: architecture/geography of
Stallybrass, Peter, 25, 87, 169n18, 169n31, 196n83
Staple of News, The (Jonson), 112–13
Steggle, Matthew, 111
Strange's Men, 73, 107, 192n18
Streitberger, W. R., 12
Strong, Sampson, 53
Stubbes, Philip, 19, 66, 158, 203n66
Styan, J. L., 128, 180n33
subject and object, 32, 117, 135–36, 149, 154, 156, 161, 164
substance and accident, 62
  See also religion: Eucharist
sumptuary laws, 150
  See also clothing
surface and depth, 53–55, 78
Sutton, Robert, 141
Swander, Homer, 138
synesthesia, 55–56, 97

tapestries, 53–54
Tapster Manuscript, 156–57
Tarlton, Richard, 111, 113
Tatham, John, 199n9
taverns. *See* alehouses
Teague, Frances, 150
Teskey, Gordon, 185n26
text(s)
   materiality of (*See under* materiality)
   as medium, 6, 9, 11, 14, 100, 101
   See also print
theatre, 73, 83, 164–65
   as art, 10, 44
   as commerce, 6, 13, 28, 107, 148, 171n72
   as entertainment, 10, 14–16, 109–13, 127, 137, 148, 153, 157, 163, 165
   medieval, 24, 45–46, 72–73, 131, 177n51
   referential and performant functions of, 109–10, 123, 125, 148, 164
   as verbal, 26
Theatre, the (Shoreditch), 112
theatres (the buildings). *See* playhouses
theatre-in-the-round, 50–51
Thirkill, Richard, 141
Thomson, Leslie, 18, 45, 128, 157
Thomson, Peter, 25
Three Lords and Three Ladies of London (Wilson), 101
thrust stage, 28, 50
Thurmond, John, 155, 203n70
ticket prices, 14, 28, 51
Tide Tarrieth No Man, The, 67–68
Titus Andronicus (Shakespeare), 21, 137–53, 158, 164, 177n51, 188n79
Tofte, Robert, 59
tongue, 94, 137, 139, 142–43, 145–6, 151
torches (props). *See* lanterns
transubstantiation and consubstantiation, 62, 63–64
   See also religion: Eucharist
trapdoors, 87, 93, 128
travel narratives, 26, 108, 113–14, 115, 117–19
treason, 61, 83, 139–40
trees (props), 41–42, 63
Troilus and Cressida (Shakespeare), 31–32
tumbling, 107

Turner, Henry, 169n17, 175n35
Twelfth Night (Shakespeare), 15, 32, 36, 89, 176n44
Two Merry Milkmaids, The, 18
Two Noble Kinsmen, The (Shakespeare and Fletcher), 18, 37
Two Noble Ladies, The, 65, 72

Underdown, David, 156
Unfortunate Lovers, The (Davenant), 112
upstage vs. downstage, 28–29, 30–31, 50, 174n24
   See also *locus* and *platea*

Vennar, Richard, 111
verbal, the
   and class, 26
   as impetus for action, 4–5
   theatre as, 26
   See also speech acts
verisimilitude, 16, 21, 42–44, 46, 48, 54, 65, 184n3
   See also mimesis
Vice figure, 66, 92–93, 131, 151, 203n68
   See also morality plays
violence (stage), 3–5, 21–22, 36–37, 94, 102, 122, 133–65
   See also combat: stage
Virgil, 76, 88
Virgin Martyr, The (Massinger and Dekker), 145
vision, 21, 41–69
   as allegory, 67
   audience's, 32, 52, 57
   characters', 32
   as deceptive/unreliable, 63, 64, 66, 74, 124, 128, 143
   intromission and extramission theories of, 56–57, 116, 194n53
   as ocular proof, 63
   philosophy of, 43, 115–16
   physiology of, 43, 46–47, 54–56
   as recreation, 119–20
   spiritual and moral implications of, 56–61, 74
   See also blindness; invisibility; sightlines
visions, miraculous, 56, 63, 126
voice. *See* language: oral

Waith, Eugene, 138
Walker, John, 85
Wandering Lover, The (Meriton), 158
Watt, Tessa, 54, 67
Webster, John, 160, 164–65
Weimann, Robert, 20, 23–37, 45–46
West, William, 15, 99, 189n84, 205n99
White Devil, The (Webster), 160
Wickham, Glynne, 198n97
Wiles, David, 51, 203n68
Wilson, Robert, 101
Wilson, Thomas, 101–2
Winkler, Amanda Eubanks, 17, 127
Winstanley, William, 164
Winter's Tale, The (Shakespeare), 73, 108, 177n51
Witch, The (Middleton), 17
witchcraft pamphlets, 142
witches (stage), 126, 129
 dances, 17, 21, 122, 126–28
wordplay, 111, 139, 149, 151, 152, 182n85
words. *See* verbal, the
Worthen, W. B., 26, 168n9, 168n13
Wright, Iain, 198n97
Wright, Thomas, 83
Wright, W. A., 138
writing. *See* language: written
Wycliff, John, 62

GPSR Compliance
The European Union's (EU) General Product Safety Regulation (GPSR) is a set of rules that requires consumer products to be safe and our obligations to ensure this.

If you have any concerns about our products, you can contact us on

ProductSafety@springernature.com

In case Publisher is established outside the EU, the EU authorized representative is:

Springer Nature Customer Service Center GmbH
Europaplatz 3
69115 Heidelberg, Germany

www.ingramcontent.com/pod-product-compliance
Lightning Source LLC
LaVergne TN
LVHW021947060526
838200LV00043B/1948